P9-DDI-306

The Translator

SEAMUS HEANEY (1939–2013) was the author of many volumes of poetry, criticism, and translation. An Irish poet of international stature, he was awarded the Nobel Prize in Literature in 1995 and the Whitbread Prize in 2000 for his translation of *Beowulf.*

The Editor

DANIEL DONOGHUE is the John P. Marquand Professor of English at Harvard University. He is the author of *How the Anglo-Saxons Read Their Poems, Lady Godiva: A History of a Legend*, and many articles on Old and Middle English literature.

NORTON CRITICAL EDITIONS
Ancient, Classical, and Medieval Eras

For a complete list of Norton Critical Editions, visit
wwnorton.com/nortoncriticals

A NORTON CRITICAL EDITION

BEOWULF
A Verse Translation

AUTHORITATIVE TEXT
CONTEXTS
CRITICISM

SECOND EDITION

Translated by

SEAMUS HEANEY
LATE OF HARVARD UNIVERSITY

Edited by

DANIEL DONOGHUE
HARVARD UNIVERSITY

W · W · NORTON & COMPANY · *New York* · *London*

W. W. Norton & Company has been independent since its founding in 1923, when William Warder Norton and Mary D. Herter Norton first published lectures delivered at the People's Institute, the adult education division of New York City's Cooper Union. The firm soon expanded its program beyond the Institute, publishing books by celebrated academics from America and abroad. By midcentury, the two major pillars of Norton's publishing program—trade books and college texts—were firmly established. In the 1950s, the Norton family transferred control of the company to its employees, and today—with a staff of four hundred and a comparable number of trade, college, and professional titles published each year—W. W. Norton & Company stands as the largest and oldest publishing house owned wholly by its employees.

Library of Congress Cataloging-in-Publication Data

Names: Heaney, Seamus, 1939–2013, translator. | Donoghue, Daniel,
    1956– editor.
Title: Beowulf : a verse translation : authoritative text, contexts, criticism /
    translated by Seamus Heaney ; edited by Daniel Donoghue.
Other titles: Beowulf. English.
Description: Second edition. | New York : W. W. Norton & Company, [2019] |
    Series: A Norton critical edition | Includes bibliographical references.
Identifiers: LCCN 2018033807 | ISBN 9780393938371 (pbk.)
Subjects: LCSH: Epic poetry, English (Old) | Epic poetry, English
    (Old) —History and criticism. | Scandinavia—Poetry. | Monsters—Poetry. |
    Dragons—Poetry. | Beowulf.
Classification: LCC PR1583 .H43 2019 | DDC 829/.3—dc23 LC record
    available at https://lccn.loc.gov/2018033807

ISBN: 978-0-393-93837-1 (pbk.)

W. W. Norton & Company, Inc., 500 Fifth Avenue, New York, NY 10110
            wwnorton.com
W. W. Norton & Company Ltd., 15 Carlisle Street, London W1D 3BS

3   4   5   6   7   8   9   0

Contents

Illustrations

Preface

This Norton Critical Edition differs from others because the literary text at its center carries a double identity. The Old English *Beowulf* is a verse narrative that survives in a manuscript transcribed around the year 1000, but the version printed here is Seamus Heaney's poetic translation from the cusp of the year 2000. Both deserve to be read as literary texts, but the fact that one translates the other sets up an intriguing dynamic involving interpretation, poetic invention, and fidelity to the source text.

Over eighty translations of *Beowulf* have appeared since the early nineteenth century, but none has caught the reading public's attention as much as Heaney's. Given its popular reception, it is remarkable how little his translation concedes to the contemporary reader. A moment's thought will reveal extensive differences between the poem's medieval and current audience, yet Heaney does not provide a new or updated version of an old story but the old story itself. Obscure allusions, abrupt transitions, and words lost because of damage to the manuscript remain as problematic as they ever were. No episodes or characters are added or dropped. Even when Heaney's verse line adopts a different rhythm (lines 1070–1159), the correspondence with the Old English remains close. Both the old poem and the new poem end on line 3182.

What sets Heaney's apart from other translations, however, is the language. His Translator's Introduction explains how, when he was searching for the "enabling note" to give the right voice to his project, he made the surprising turn to the speech of some older relatives in Ulster. It was a bold choice, but finding a language that was "speakable" by one of his "Scullion" relatives enabled him to make a clean break with the scholarly glossaries, which have a way of insinuating their formal, literary, and slightly archaic language into most *Beowulf* translations. Turning his translator's ear to a rural Ulster dialect carries ideological and political consequences that will be discussed elsewhere. Of more immediate concern is the odd fact that the translation requires footnotes to gloss its language, even for the intended audience. Most of the words in question are Hibernicisms, that is, usages characteristic of the English spoken in Ireland—or more specifically the English Heaney recalls from his Ulster relatives. There are about a dozen such words, like "bothy," "tarn," and "thole," not all of which are Irish in origin; some go back to Scandinavian languages and others to Old English. Perhaps the overriding lesson to be learned from the idiolect that Heaney fashions is that all dialects including the one he learned as a child have an equal claim on the remote origins of English because they all have a parallel history. The voice of the Scullions is as adequate to the task as any variety of English. On a more practical level the simple task of looking at the footnote explaining "kesh" may trigger a parallel reminder that an older *Beowulf* stands behind Heaney's poem.

Beowulf is a poem of many dimensions. Over the years it has been assigned to the genres epic, heroic narrative, and folk-tale, and it incorporates a variety of other poetic forms such as creation hymn, elegy, heroic boast, and nuggets of traditional wisdom known as gnomic verse. While it is clear that the *Beowulf* poet was drawing from traditional sources, it is equally clear that those sources were oral and thus hard to recover today. The great exception is the Bible, which supplies the stories of Cain and Abel and Noah's flood from the book of Genesis. So the material in the Contexts section, immediately after the poem, includes explanatory material (such as genealogies of the various royal families) and analogues (such as an episode from a fourteenth-century Icelandic saga).

This revised Norton Critical Edition capitalizes on recent developments in the fields of *Beowulf* studies and early medieval England more broadly. For example, a proliferation of new finds such as the spectacular Staffordshire Hoard in 2009 has transformed the field of archaeology, which Leslie Webster captures in her extensive revisions to "*Beowulf* and Archaeology," undertaken especially for this volume. In addition, a new critical edition of the poem, *Klaeber's Beowulf* (2008), incorporating the fruits of almost six decades of scholarship since the previous edition, has informed and updated the broader critical discussion in the following pages. The online *Electronic Beowulf* (2015) now makes high-quality images of each folio of the *Beowulf* manuscript freely available along with an electronic edition and other aids to scholarship. These resources and others are listed in the Selected Bibliography, which has been updated to include recent work.

The Translator's Introduction and my essay, "The Philologer Poet," address the process of translation and situate Heaney's *Beowulf* within the trajectory of his career as a poet. While the other critical essays were written with the Old English poem in mind, they have been chosen in part because they work well with Heaney's translation. Most *Beowulf* criticism over the years pays close attention to the language of the poem, but because the users of this volume are not expected to read Old English, the essays selected do not rely on sustained close readings and instead address broad topics. A literal translation accompanies each Old English quotation, which can provide an interesting point of comparison with Heaney's, because every translation (no matter how literal) is also an interpretation.

The opening sentence of the Translator's Introduction indicates a period of about 350 years for the composition of *Beowulf*, "some time between the middle of the seventh and the end of the tenth century of the first millennium." The interval is so extensive that, if accepted at face value, it would frustrate any attempt to historicize the poem, because Anglo-Saxon England was anything but a static society from the years 650 to 1000—an interval equivalent to that from John Milton to the present day. The range reflects the lack of consensus among *Beowulf* scholars and signals that (for the purposes of his translation) Heaney prefers to remain noncommittal about the issue. Since about 1980, the time and place of *Beowulf's* composition has attracted considerable scholarly attention without arriving at a resolution, but the evidence favoring one position over another has come into sharper focus. The uncertainty is reflected within the critical essays collected in this volume: some sidestep the question of date altogether, one finds a tenth-century context more likely, and others accept evidence that *Beowulf* is an eighth-century poem.

J. R. R. Tolkien's "*Beowulf*, the Monsters and the Critics" has been the most influential reading of the poem since it was published over eighty years ago. Arguing against a clumsy historicism in earlier *Beowulf* criticism, Tolkien makes a spirited case for the artistic merits of the poem. Today even those who take issue with Tolkien or who feel that the field has moved on have to reckon with the essay's influence. Marijane Osborn's "The Great Feud" responds to Tolkien's exhortation to consider the artistry of the poem by throwing light on its narrative control in distinguishing between two registers of knowledge, that of the pagan characters and the poem's intended, Christian audience. Jane Chance's "Structural Unity of *Beowulf*" offers a foil to Tolkien, both in its attention to Grendel's mother (ignored by Tolkien) and in its gendered reading of Beowulf's struggle with her. What it shares with Tolkien is an admiration for the poem's artistic accomplishment.

Beowulf is often seen as a fictional character who inhabits a world of myth and legend, but Roberta Frank's essay reminds us that the poem develops a sophisticated historical vision that avoids anachronism and even extends a sense of the past to its characters. A different historical context motivates Fred C. Robinson's essay, which argues against a simplistic pagan vs. Christian dichotomy. Instead,

Robinson finds a sensitive balance between the poem's admiration for a noble pagan past and a Christian perspective capacious enough to accommodate that admiration. While the other essays focus on the poem in its original Old English, my essay suggests that Heaney's turn to *Beowulf* is in many ways a return to the language that has always informed his poetry. His translation self-consciously reverses the movement of colonization by invoking an Irish dialect to appropriate a foundational text of English literary history, but over and above the linguistic politics it is also a gesture of deep respect from one master poet to another across the expanse of a millennium.

Three critical essays have been added to this revised edition, including Marijane Osborn's, discussed above. Michael Lapidge's "*Beowulf* and Perception" and Andrew Scheil's "'Beowulf' and the Emergent Occasion" complement one another in bringing to light the poem's sophisticated manipulation of narrative time. For Lapidge the discontinuities in *Beowulf*'s narrative progression create a philosophical perspective on human perception; for Scheil the poem dramatizes the capacity of human response when confronted with moments of unprecedented change. As with the other essays, each also has the virtue of speaking both to specialists who read Old English and to readers who encounter the poem through Heaney's translation.

Besides minor updates and corrections throughout, this revision also adds a summary of the legends surrounding the dragon-slaying hero Sigemund, to whom Beowulf is favorably compared after defeating Grendel. As a new feature, two excerpts of the original Old English have been printed in a facing-page layout for the opening and closing pages of the poem. The passages have been edited especially for this volume to align their sentences with Heaney's translation, so a reader—whether a novice or an expert—can compare the words side-by-side.

Daniel Donoghue
2018

Acknowledgments

I wish to thank Carol Bemis and the superb staff at W. W. Norton for their ongoing and unflagging support. Thanks also go to my students in Harvard College and the Harvard Extension School, whose classroom responses have helped with the overall shape of changes in this revision. Special thanks to Rafael Pascual for his assistance in surveying articles on *Beowulf* scholarship. Finally, with great sadness, I must mention a profound change since the first publication of this edition, which is the death of Seamus Heaney in 2013,

> a carrier of tales,
> a traditional singer deeply schooled
> in the lore of the past.

He gave so much poetic brilliance and human warmth to his verse translation of *Beowulf*, as he did to everything he touched.

Old English Language and Poetics

Many students are surprised to learn that English poetry is older than prose—older by many centuries. We are accustomed to think of prose as naturally prior because of our personal experience: being simpler, prose is something we learn to write in the early days of our schooling. Poetry seems more challenging to read, and most of us never learn to compose it. We are also accustomed to think of prose as little more than a transcription of speech. But it is not. Written prose has its own conventions, which did not emerge in English until well after the Anglo-Saxons converted to christianity around 700 C.E. and the subsequent introduction of the Latin system of writing. For centuries before that time, Germanic tribes all over Europe had fashioned a sophisticated practice of poetry, which was learned and passed on by memory. Several passages in *Beowulf* describe how an Anglo-Saxon *scop* (pronounced "shop") either improvised a poem or recounted a traditional story in verse, and the presence of an official *scop* in Hrothgar's court gives an idea of how highly valued they were in society. By the time Latin letters were introduced to England, the Anglo-Saxons were already in possession of a vigorous tradition of oral poetry. The familiarity of the conventions helps explain why, when clerics began to write down poems, they felt little need to indicate where clauses or verse lines ended. Any reader, it seems, would bring that knowledge to the task. To our eyes, the poems are lineated as if they were prose.

The words not only look foreign in the manuscript (written in a script called Anglo-Saxon square minuscule), they also sound strange to the ear. The reason is not simply that the sounds of individual words are different: *Þæt wæs god cyning* is recognizable as "That was a good king." And the reason is not found in the use of alliteration or compound words, which are still everyday features of English. The pronunciation, spelling, and word endings of Old English take some time to understand, but even at that stage the syntax and rhythm of *Beowulf* can resist comprehension. Many people find this residue of strangeness intriguing, as if a parallel poetic world opens up that forces them to reconsider the received wisdom. Generations of admirers (like Longfellow, Tennyson, Auden, and Heaney) have been attracted to *Beowulf*'s faintly disorienting strangeness within an otherwise familiar English tradition.

Since about the thirteenth century, the dominant verse pattern in English has been built on the iambic foot, a sequence in which an unstressed syllable (x) is followed by a stressed syllable (/). The pattern is immediately recognizable from just a brief example, such as these lines from a Wordsworth poem:

x   /   x / x / x   /
I wandered lonely as a cloud
  x   /   x   /   x   /   x   /
  that floats on high o'er vales and hills.

The syllables are drawn into the iambic rhythm to the extent that even the humble "as" gets carried along by a stress that it would rarely have in normal speech, and "o'er" is reduced to one syllable to keep the count right. The iambic regularity sets up a "prosodic contract" with the reader, so that even if another kind of foot is substituted, the rhythm plays off the underlying expectation of regularly alternating syllables. To those who have become habituated to the iambic rhythm, it can come to seem natural, but it is a highly conventionalized artifice, against which free verse and other metrical innovations of modernism and postmodernism have defined themselves.

The Old English prosodic contract works from equally arbitrary but entirely different principles. It is almost as though the Germanic innovators of this prosody (some time before the fifth century) selected a limited number of phrasings from their ordinary speech and formalized those rhythms as the basic units of the poetic line. Other rhythms were excluded. So rather than elevate a regularly repeating pattern (like the iamb), they pieced together phrasal units from already-familiar rhythms. Two such phrases, called halflines, combine to form an Old English verse line. In pairing them together a premium is placed on variety, so that the same rhythm is rarely repeated in both halves of the line (thus ruling out an iambic line), and two successive lines are rarely alike. The paired half-lines are linked by alliteration on the stressd syllables, as in the *g*-sounds of

1   2   3   4
Grendel gongan,   Godes yrre bær.

In translating this line Heaney preserves the alliterating pattern in

1   2   3   4
God-cursed Grendel came greedily loping.

Page from the *Beowulf* manuscript: Cotton Vitellius A. xv, folio 191r. By permission of the British Library / Granger. All rights reserved. Note the hole in the top half, which was likely caused by a blemish in the animal's skin from which the vellum was made. Letters from the next folio can be seen through it. The folio's ragged, distorted edge is the result of damage from a fire in 1731.

Each half-line typically has two primary stresses that qualify for alliteration, which add up to four per line, as numbered in the example. The conventions say that in the first half of the line either 1 and 2 alliterate (as in this line), or just 1 by itself; in the latter half 3 always alliterates and 4 never does. One final source of variety: the alliterating sound is rarely repeated from one line to the next. Thus if one line alliterates on [b], the next line will alliterate on any sound but [b]. Other features that cannot be discussed here, such as syllable length, also come into play. Taken together, the metrical constraints favor an economy of expression within the half-lines so that each syllable is carefully weighed. For example, not only do compound words create vivid juxtapositions but their conciseness as a single word (as opposed to a phrase) offers a metrically compact element that is useful in constructing half-lines: "earthdragon" is shorter than "dragon of the earth," but it has the same number of stressed syllables.

The following passage from *Beowulf* shows the intricate interplay of these features.[1] It is based on a transcription from the folio reproduced here, beginning with the large Ð (a letter known to the Anglo-Saxons as "eth"). For reasons that will become clear later, the gloss given above the lines makes little concession to Modern English syntax:

> Then it came about to the man un-aged
> **Ða wæs gegongen   gumun unfrodum**
>
> with difficulty that he on earth saw
> **earfoðlice   þæt he on eorðan geseah**
>
> the most beloved of life at end
> **þone leofestan   lifes æt ende**   2823
>
> wretchedly faring. Killer likewise lay
> **bleate gebæran.   Bona swylce læg**
>
> terrible earthdragon of life bereft
> **egeslic eorð-draca   ealdre bereafod**
>
> by aggression afflicted. Ring-hoards longer
> **bealwe gebæded.   Beah-hordum leng**   2826
>
> dragon coiled to possess was not allowed,
> **wyrm woh-bogen   wealdan ne moste,**

---

1. This passage is given a thematic and rhetorical interpretation in Donoghue, "The Philologer Poet," pp. 230–41 in this Norton Critical Edition.

but him of iron the edges took
ac him irenna   ecga fornamon

hard battle-sharp of hammers remnant
hearde heaðo-scear[p]e   homera lafe,   2829

so that the wide-flier because of wounds quiet
x   x /   \ x   / x /   x
þæt se wid-floga   wundum stille

fell to earth the hoard-cave near.
/   x   / x   / \ x   /
hreas on hrusan   hord-ærne neah.   2831

No pair of half-lines duplicates the rhythm, yet each conforms to
one of the established patterns found throughout the poem. Simi-
larly, the alliterating sounds of each line are not repeated in its
neighbors. By way of illustration, the last two lines are scanned using
the conventional notations for an unstressed syllable [x], full stress
[/], and the kind of secondary stress [\] found in the latter half of
compounds like *wid-floga*. Taken together, these conventions give
each line of Old English verse a precisely modulated but endlessly
variable rhythmic and alliterating contour. The very features that
the Anglo-Saxons found aesthetically pleasing can make the poetry
seem foreign today. Where the iambic line sets up the expectation
of regularity, the Old English line insists on rhythmic variety.
Where end-rhyme puts the most prominent aural feature at the end
of the verse, alliteration creates a dynamic across the middle of the
line.

The syntax can seem baffling. The order of words is sometimes
called "free," but "free" must not be understood as a kind of linguistic
liberty where words can be scattered around without constraint.
For the phrase *lifes æt ende* (line 2823) another idiomatic word order
might be *æt lifes ende*, which snaps into focus as "at life's end," but
as such it would be unmetrical. The line reads *lifes æt ende* not
because of some syntactic whim but because the meter requires *lifes*,
which takes the alliteration, to precede the unstressed syllable of *æt*.
Other half-lines, such as *wealdan ne moste*, are poetic formulas that
had a practical usefulness as prefabricated elements in the construc-
tion of verse.

Another syntactic feature, called "variation" or "apposition," is also
a pervasive rhetorical device. In the sentence beginning on line
2824, for example, two separate nouns refer to the dragon, and they
in turn are modified by two separate phrases. By way of illustration,
they can be reconfigured to align the parallel elements:

Bona
egeslic eorð-draca ⎫ swylce læg ⎧ ealdre bereafod
bealwe gebæded

A literal translation:

the killer
terrible earthdragon ⎫ likewise lay ⎧ bereft of life
afflicted by aggression

It is a construction in which separate words have the same referent and the same syntactic function within a clause, but they are placed as parallel elements without any formal linking—not even a conjunction like "and."[2] At times the effect of apposition is simply cumulative, so that the additional information supplied by successive words fills out the first reference, such as "the killer, the terrible earthdragon." On other occasions, however, there can be more subtle rhetorical effects. The dead dragon, for example, is "bereft of life, afflicted by aggression," where the Old English word *bealwe*, means "aggression," but it also carries connotations of "evil." One way to read this apposed element, then, is to be alert to the clue that the dragon's death was justified because its violence was evil. This meaning is not explicit, but rather an interpretive possibility available to readers attentive to the connotations of *bealwe*.

One of the rhetorical advantages of apposition is its openendedness: the aggression in this case can be both Beowulf's (with less emphasis on evil) or the dragon's. The same passage has another set of parallel epithets in "edges of iron" and "the hard, battle-sharp remnants of hammers," both of which are descriptive phrases for "sword." In fact, the half-line *homera lafe* ("remnants of hammers") is an instance of a highly compressed and enigmatic figure of speech known as a kenning. Kennings are especially characteristic of Old English (and Old Norse), and their spare allusiveness lends itself to the economy of the alliterative line. If one were to expand *homera lafe* into a more prosaic expression, it might be "what remains after the blacksmith's hammers have finished their work"—that is, "a sword."

The principle of apposition can be extended in two directions. In the lexicon, the effort to give multiple perspectives and the requirements of alliteration lead to a proliferation of synonyms. Common concepts like "horse," "hall," and "man" may have over a dozen variants, a number that does not include the many possible compounds. Some of these words, like *guma* ("man," in the first line of

---

2. For a lucid account of apposition, see Fred C. Robinson, *Beowulf and the Appositive Style* (Knoxville: U of Tennessee P, 1985).

the passage), are found only in poetry and were part of a specialized lexicon that would also include poetic compounds and kennings. In any language, however, true synonyms are very rare, and the Old English synonyms for a word like "man" had connotations which in many (perhaps most) cases are lost to us.

The absence of conjunctions that characterize apposition leads to the second direction: the syntax of sentences. Old English poetry is sparing in its use of subordinating conjunctions like "although," "while," "because," and "if." The sentences in the passage under discussion are typical: the most adventurous conjunctions are "so that" and "but." But in the same way that apposed elements within a sentence can suggest nuances, the sparing use of conjunctions can induce the reader to make interpretive connections between clauses.

This brief survey has identified a number of areas where the language of *Beowulf* seems to diverge from contemporary English. The most pronounced case might be apposition. Today the repetition of words and phrases with the same referent, even the kind of "elegant variation" once favored by some Victorian writers, is actively discouraged. A student paper that included passages like "the killer, the terrible earth-dragon, deprived of life, afflicted by evil aggression" would be savaged in red ink. In the case of *homera lafe* and the other variations on sword, Heaney restructures the syntax into an epithet followed by descriptive adjectives, "Hard-edged blades, hammered out / and keenly filed," where "hammered out" is itself a kind of remnant (*laf*) of the original kenning. But he does not always rephrase apposition out of existence. By preserving it on occasion, Heaney's translation reminds the reader that another tradition lies behind his text. In addition, there are other areas where the old conventions resist an easy assimilation. Old English favors metrical variety over iambic regularity; alliteration within the line to rhyme at the end; a specialized vocabulary that includes compounds and kennings; and a sparing use of subordinating conjunctions. Within each half-line there is a strict economy of syllables and word order. In units larger than the half-line, however, the clauses have an elasticity that allows them to grow very long. Much of the "feel" of Old English verse results from the tension between the constraint of one and the expansiveness of the other. Just how Seamus Heaney finds the right pitch between the two is described in his Translator's Introduction.

Because the Anglo-Saxons left no *ars poetica*, the principles outlined here are a scholarly reconstruction from some thirty-two thousand lines of Old English verse that survive in written form. Even though there is much still to learn, it is clear that Old English verse was complex. And conversely, Anglo-Saxon audiences were

sophisticated in their ability to understand how poets manipulated
the conventions.[3] It is wrong to assume that because the material
conditions of Anglo-Saxon society were primitive by today's stan-
dards, everything else about it was underdeveloped as well. Such an
assumption flies in the face of what we know about many oral cul-
tures, some of which are still active today. Even without an Anglo-
Saxon *ars poetica* we know that oral poetry was a primary art form
in their culture. After the introduction of writing some poets were
able to fuse the oral and literary traditions into profoundly power-
ful compositions like *Beowulf.*

3. See Daniel Donoghue, *How the Anglo-Saxons Read Their Poems* (Philadelphia: University
of Pennsylvania Press, 2018).

Translator's Introduction[†]

And now this is 'an inheritance'—
Upright, rudimentary, unshiftably planked
In the long ago, yet willable forward

Again and again and again.

1. *Beowulf*: The Poem

The poem called *Beowulf* was composed some time between the middle of the seventh and the end of the tenth century of the first millennium, in the language that is today called Anglo-Saxon or Old English. It is a heroic narrative, more than three thousand lines long, concerning the deeds of a Scandinavian prince, also called Beowulf, and it stands as one of the foundation works of poetry in English. The fact that the English language has changed so much in the last thousand years means, however, that the poem is now generally read in translation and mostly in English courses at schools and universities. This has contributed to the impression that it was written (as Osip Mandelstam said of *The Divine Comedy*) "on official paper," which is unfortunate, since what we are dealing with is a work of the greatest imaginative vitality, a masterpiece where the structuring of the tale is as elaborate as the beautiful contrivances of its language. Its narrative elements may belong to a previous age but as a work of art it lives in its own continuous present, equal to our knowledge of reality in the present time.

The poem was written in England but the events it describes are set in Scandinavia, in a "once upon a time" that is partly historical. Its hero, Beowulf, is the biggest presence among the warriors in the land of the Geats, a territory situated in what is now southern Sweden, and early in the poem Beowulf crosses the sea to the land of the Danes in order to rid their country of a man-eating monster called Grendel. From this expedition (which involves him in a second contest with Grendel's mother) he returns in triumph and eventually rules for fifty years as king of his homeland. Then a dragon

† From Seamus Heaney, *Beowulf: A New Verse Translation* (New York: Norton, 2001).

begins to terrorize the countryside and Beowulf must confront it. In a final climactic encounter, he does manage to slay the dragon, but he also meets his own death and enters the legends of his people as a warrior of high renown.

We know about the poem more or less by chance, because it exists in one manuscript only. This unique copy (now in the British Library) barely survived a fire in the eighteenth century and was then transcribed and titled, retranscribed and edited, translated and adapted, interpreted and taught, until it has become an acknowledged classic. For decades it has been a set book on English syllabuses at university level all over the world. The fact that many English departments require it to be studied in the original continues to generate resistance, most notably at Oxford University, where the pros and cons of the inclusion of part of it as a compulsory element in the English course have been debated regularly in recent years.

For generations of undergraduates, academic study of the poem was often just a matter of construing the meaning, getting a grip on the grammar and vocabulary of Anglo-Saxon, and being able to recognize, translate, and comment upon random extracts that were presented in the examinations. For generations of scholars too the interest had been textual and philological; then there developed a body of research into analogues and sources, a quest for stories and episodes in the folklore and legends of the Nordic peoples that would parallel or foreshadow episodes in *Beowulf*. Scholars were also preoccupied with fixing the exact time and place of the poem's composition, paying minute attention to linguistic, stylistic, and scribal details. More generally, they tried to establish the history and genealogy of the dynasties of Swedes, Geats, and Danes to which the poet makes constant allusion; and they devoted themselves to a consideration of the world-view behind the poem, asking to what extent (if at all) the newly established Christian religion, which was fundamental to the poet's intellectual formation, displaced him from his imaginative at-homeness in the world of his poem—a pagan Germanic society governed by a heroic code of honor, one where the attainment of a name for warrior-prowess among the living overwhelms any concern about the soul's destiny in the afterlife.

However, when it comes to considering *Beowulf* as a work of literature, one publication stands out. In 1936, Oxford scholar and teacher J. R. R. Tolkien published an epoch-making paper entitled "*Beowulf*: The Monsters and the Critics," which took for granted the poem's integrity and distinction as a work of art and proceeded to show in what this integrity and distinction inhered. Tolkien assumed that the poet had felt his way through the inherited material—the fabulous elements and the traditional accounts of an heroic past—and by a combination of creative intuition and conscious structuring had arrived at a unity of effect and a balanced order. He assumed, in other words, that the *Beowulf* poet was an imaginative writer rather than some kind of back-formation derived from nineteenth-century folklore and philology. Tolkien's brilliant literary treatment changed the way the poem was valued and initiated a new era—and new terms—of appreciation.

It is impossible to attain a full understanding and estimate of *Beowulf* without recourse to this immense body of commentary and elucidation. Nevertheless, readers coming to the poem for the first time are likely to experience something other than mere discomfiture when faced with the strangeness of the names and the immediate lack of known reference points. An English-speaker new to *The Iliad* or *The Odyssey* or *The Aeneid* will probably at least have heard of Troy and Helen, or of Penelope and the Cyclops, or of Dido and the Golden Bough. These epics may be in Greek and Latin, yet the classical heritage has entered the cultural memory enshrined in English so thoroughly that their worlds are more familiar than that of the first native epic, even though it was composed centuries after them. Achilles rings a bell, but not *Scyld Scēfing*. Ithaca leads the mind in a certain direction, but not *Heorot*. The Sibyl of Cumae will stir certain associations, but not bad Queen Modthryth. * * *

Still, in spite of the sensation of being caught between a "shield-wall" of opaque references and a "word-hoard" that is old and strange, such readers are also bound to feel a certain "shock of the new." This is because the poem possesses a mythic potency. Like Shield Sheafson (as *Scyld Scēfing* is known in this translation), it arrives from somewhere beyond the known bourne of our experience, and having fulfilled its purpose (again like Shield) it passes once more into the beyond. In the intervening time, the poet conjures up a work as remote as Shield's funeral boat borne toward the horizon, as commanding as the horn-pronged gables of King Hrothgar's hall, as solid and dazzling as Beowulf's funeral pyre that is set ablaze at the end. These opening and closing scenes retain a haunting presence in the mind; they are set pieces but they have the life-marking power of certain dreams. They are like the pillars of the gate of horn, through which the wise dreams of true art can still be said to pass.

What happens in between is what W. B. Yeats would have called a phantasmagoria. Three agons—three struggles in which the preternatural force-for-evil of the hero's enemies comes springing at him in demonic shapes; three encounters with what the critical literature and the textbook glossaries call "the monsters"—in three archetypal sites of fear: the barricaded night-house, the infested underwater current and the reptile-haunted rocks of a wilderness. If we think of the poem in this way, its place in world art becomes clearer and more secure. We can conceive of it represented and transformed in performance in a *bunraku* theater in Japan, where the puppetry and the poetry are mutually supportive, a mixture of technicolor spectacle and ritual chant. Or we can equally envisage it as an animated cartoon (and there has been at least one shot at this already), full of mutating graphics and minatory stereophonics. We can avoid, at any rate, the slightly cardboard effect that the word "monster" tends to introduce, and give the poem a fresh chance to sweep "in off the moors, down through the mist-bands" of Anglo-Saxon England, forward into the global village of the third millennium.

Nevertheless, the dream element and overall power to haunt come at a certain readerly price. The poem abounds in passages that will leave an unprepared audience bewildered. Just when the narrative seems ready to take another step ahead, it sidesteps. For a moment it is as if we have been channel-surfed into another poem, and at two points in this translation I indicate that we are in fact participating in a poem-within-our-poem not only by the use of italics but by a slight quickening of pace and shortening of metrical rein. The passages comprise lines 883–914 and 1070–158,[1] and on each occasion a minstrel has begun to chant a poem as part of the celebration of Beowulf's achievements. In the former case, the minstrel expresses his praise by telling the story of Sigemund's victory over a dragon, which both parallels Beowulf's triumph over Grendel and prefigures his fatal encounter with the *wyrm* in his old age. In the latter—the most famous of what were once called the "digressions" in the poem, the one dealing with a fight between Danes and Frisians at the stronghold of Finn, the Frisian king—the song the minstrel sings has a less obvious bearing on the immediate situation of the hero, but its import is nevertheless central to both the historical and imaginative worlds of the poem.

The "Finnsburg episode" immerses us in a society that is at once honor bound and blood stained, presided over by the laws of the blood feud, where the kin of a person slain are bound to exact a price for the death, either by slaying the killer or by receiving satisfaction in the form of *wergild* (the "man-price"), a legally fixed compensation. The claustrophobic and doomladen atmosphere of this interlude gives the reader an intense intimation of what *wyrd*, or fate, meant not only to the characters in the Finn story but to those participating in the main action of *Beowulf* itself. All conceive of themselves as hooped within the great wheel of necessity, in thrall to a code of loyalty and bravery, bound to seek glory in the eye of the warrior world. The little nations are grouped around their lord; the

---

1. Line numbers given in the Translator's Introduction refer to this translation, not to the Old English text [*Editor*].

greater nations spoil for war and menace the little ones; a lord dies, defenselessness ensues; the enemy strikes; vengeance for the dead becomes an ethic for the living, bloodshed begets further bloodshed; the wheel turns, the generations tread and tread and tread—which is what I meant above when I said that the import of the Finnsburg passage is central to the historical and imaginative worlds of the poem as a whole.

One way of reading *Beowulf* is to think of it as three agons in the hero's life, but another way would be to regard it as a poem that contemplates the destinies of three peoples by tracing their interweaving histories in the story of the central character. First we meet the Danes—variously known as the Shieldings (after Shield Sheafson, the founder of their line), the Ingwins, the Spear-Danes, the Bright-Danes, the West-Danes, and so on—a people in the full summer of their power, symbolized by the high hall built by King Hrothgar, one "meant to be a wonder of the world." The threat to this superb people comes from within their own borders, from marshes beyond the pale, from the bottom of the haunted mere where "Cain's clan," in the shape of Grendel and his troll-dam, trawl and scavenge and bide their time. But it also comes from without, from the Heatho bards, for example, whom the Danes have defeated in battle and from whom they can therefore expect retaliatory war (see lines 2020–69).

Beowulf actually predicts this turn of events when he goes back to his own country after saving the Danes (for the time being, at any rate) by staving off the two "reavers from hell." In the hall of his "ring-giver," Hygelac, lord of the Geats, the hero discourses about his adventures in a securely fortified cliff-top enclosure. But this security is only temporary, for it is the destiny of the Geat people to be left lordless in the end. Hygelac's alliances eventually involve him in deadly war with the Swedish king, Ongentheow, and even though he does not personally deliver the fatal stroke (two of his thanes are responsible for this—see lines 2484–89 and then the lengthier reprise of this incident at lines 2922–3003), he is known in the poem as "Ongentheow's killer." Hence it comes to pass that after the death of Beowulf, who eventually succeeds Hygelac, the Geats experience a great foreboding and the poem closes in a mood of somber expectation. A world is passing away, the Swedes and others are massing on the borders to attack, and there is no lord or hero to rally the defence.

The Swedes, therefore, are the third nation whose history and destiny are woven into the narrative, and even though no part of the main action is set in their territory, they and their kings constantly stalk the horizon of dread within which the main protagonists pursue their conflicts and allegiances. The Swedish dimension

gradually becomes an important element in the poem's emotional
and imaginative geography, a geography that entails, it should be
said, no very clear map-sense of the world, more an apprehension
of menaced borders, of danger gathering beyond the mere and the
marshes, of *mearc-stapas* "prowling the moors, huge marauders /
from some other world."

Within these phantasmal boundaries, each lord's hall is an actual
and a symbolic refuge. Here are heat and light, rank and ceremony,
human solidarity and culture; the *duguþ* share the mead-benches
with the *geogoþ*, the veterans with their tales of warrior-kings and
hero-saviors from the past rub shoulders with young braves—*þegnas,
eorlas,* thanes, retainers—keen to win such renown in the future.
The prospect of gaining a glorious name in the *wæl-ræs* (the rush of
battle-slaughter), the pride of defending one's lord and bearing heroic
witness to the integrity of the bond between him and his hall-
companions—a bond sealed in the *glēo* and *gidd* of peace-time
feasting and ring-giving—this is what gave drive and sanction to the
Germanic warrior-culture enshrined in *Beowulf.*

Heorot and Hygelac's hall are the hubs of this value system upon
which the poem's action turns. But there is another, outer rim of
value, a circumference of understanding within which the heroic
world is occasionally viewed as from a distance and recognized for
what it is, an earlier state of consciousness and culture, one that has
not been altogether shed but that has now been comprehended as
part of another pattern. And this circumference and pattern arise,
of course, from the poet's Christianity and from his perspective as
an Englishman looking back at places and legends that his ances-
tors knew before they made their migration from continental Europe
to their new home on the island of the Britons. As a consequence of
his doctrinal certitude, which is as composed as it is ardent, the
poet can view the story-time of his poem with a certain historical
detachment and even censure the ways of those who lived *in illo
tempore*:

> Sometimes at pagan shrines they vowed
> offerings to idols, swore oaths
> that the killer of souls might come to their aid
> and save the people. That was their way,
> their heathenish hope; deep in their hearts
> they remembered hell.   (175–80)

At the same time, as a result of his inherited vernacular culture
and the imaginative sympathy that distinguishes him as an artist,
the poet can lend the full weight of his rhetorical power to
Beowulf as he utters the first principles of the northern warrior's
honor-code:

> It is always better
> to avenge dear ones than to indulge in mourning.
> For every one of us, living in this world
> means waiting for our end. Let whoever can
> win glory before death. When a warrior is gone,
> that will be his best and only bulwark.   (1384–89)

In an age when "the instability of the human subject" is constantly argued for if not presumed, there should be no problem with a poem that is woven from two such different psychic fabrics. In fact, *Beowulf* perfectly answers the early modern conception of a work of creative imagination as one in which conflicting realities find accommodation within a new order; and this reconciliation occurs, it seems to me, most poignantly and most profoundly in the poem's third section, once the dragon enters the picture and the hero in old age must gather his powers for the final climactic ordeal. From the moment Beowulf advances under the crags, into the comfortless arena bounded by the rock wall, the reader knows he is one of those "marked by fate." The poetry is imbued with a strong intuition of *wyrd* hovering close, "unknowable but certain," and yet, because it is imagined within a consciousness that has learned to expect that the soul will find an ultimate home "among the steadfast ones," this primal human emotion has been transmuted into something less "zero at the bone," more metaphysically tempered.

A similar transposition from a plane of regard that is, as it were, helmeted and hall bound to one that sees things in a slightly more heavenly light is discernible in the different ways the poet imagines gold. Gold is a constant element, gleaming solidly in underground vaults, on the breasts of queens or the arms and regalia of warriors on the mead benches. It is loaded into boats as spoil, handed out in bent bars as hall gifts, buried in the earth as treasure, persisting underground as an affirmation of a people's glorious past and an elegy for it. It pervades the ethos of the poem and adds luster to its diction. And yet the bullion with which Waels's son Sigemund weighs down the hold after an earlier dragon-slaying triumph (in the old days, long before Beowulf's time) is a more trustworthy substance than that which is secured behind the walls of Beowulf's barrow. By the end of the poem, gold has suffered a radiation from the Christian vision. It is not that it yet equals riches in the medieval sense of worldly corruption, just that its status as the ore of all value has been put in doubt. It is *læne*, transitory, passing from hand to hand, and its changed status is registered as a symptom of the changed world. Once the dragon is disturbed, the melancholy and sense of displacement that pervade the last movement of the poem enter the hoard as a disabling and ominous light. And the dragon himself, as a genius of the older order, is bathed in this light, so that even as he begins to stir, the reader has a premonition that the days of his empery are numbered.

Nevertheless, the dragon has a wonderful inevitability about him and a unique glamor. It is not that the other monsters are lacking in presence and aura; it is more that they remain, for all their power to terrorize, creatures of the physical world. Grendel comes alive in the reader's imagination as a kind of dog breath in the dark, a fear of collision with some hard-boned and immensely strong android frame, a mixture of Caliban and hoplite. And while his mother too has a definite brute bearing about her, a creature of slouch and lunge on land if seal-swift in the water, she nevertheless retains a certain nonstrangeness. As antagonists of a hero being tested, Grendel and his mother possess an appropriate head-on strength. The poet may need them as figures who do the devil's work, but the poem needs them more as figures who call up and show off Beowulf's physical strength and his superb gifts as a warrior. They are the right enemies for a young glory hunter, instigators of the formal boast, worthy trophies to be carried back from the grim testing ground—Grendel's hand is ripped off and nailed up, his head severed and paraded in Heorot. It is all consonant with the surge of youth and the compulsion to win fame "as wide as the wind's home, / as the sea around cliffs," utterly a manifestation of the Germanic heroic code.

Enter then, fifty years later, the dragon—from his dry-stone vault, from a nest where he is heaped in coils around the body-heated gold. Once he is wakened, there is something glorious in the way he manifests himself, a Fourth of July effulgence fireworking its path across the night sky; and yet, because of the centuries he has spent dormant in the tumulus, there is a foundedness as well as a lambency about him. He is at once a stratum of the earth and a streamer in the air, no painted dragon but a figure of real oneiric power, one that can easily survive the prejudice that arises at the very mention of the word "dragon." Whether in medieval art or modern Disney cartoons, the dragon can strike us as far less horrific than he is meant to be, but in the final movement of *Beowulf* he lodges himself in the imagination as *wyrd* rather than *wyrm*, more a destiny than a set of reptilian vertebrae.

Grendel and his mother enter Beowulf's life from the outside, accidentally, challenges which in other circumstances he might not have taken up, enemies from whom he might have been distracted or deflected. The dragon, on the other hand, is a given of his home ground, abiding in his under-earth as in his understanding, waiting for the meeting, the watcher at the ford, the questioner who sits so sly, the "lion-limb," as Gerard Manley Hopkins might have called him, against whom Beowulf's body and soul must measure themselves. Dragon equals shadow line, the psalmist's valley of the shadow of death, the embodiment of a knowledge deeply ingrained in the species—the knowledge, that is, of the price to be paid for physical and spiritual survival.

It has often been observed that all the scriptural references in *Beowulf* are to the Old Testament. The poet is more in sympathy with the tragic, waiting, unredeemed phase of things than with any transcendental promise. Beowulf's mood as he gets ready to fight the dragon—who could be read as a projection of Beowulf's own chthonic wisdom refined in the crucible of experience—recalls the mood of other tragic heroes: Oedipus at Colonus, Lear at his "ripeness is all" extremity, Hamlet in the last illuminations of his "prophetic soul":

>   no easy bargain
> would be made in that place by any man.
> The veteran king sat down on the cliff-top.
> He wished good luck to the Geats who had shared
> his hearth and his gold. He was sad at heart,
> unsettled yet ready, sensing his death.
> His fate hovered near, unknowable but certain.
>   (2415–21)

Here the poet attains a level of insight that approaches the visionary. The subjective and the inevitable are in perfect balance, what is solidly established is bathed in an element that is completely sixth-sensed, and indeed the whole, slow-motion, constantly self-deferring approach to the hero's death and funeral continues to be like this. Beowulf's soul may not yet have fled "to its destined place among the steadfast ones," but there is already a beyond-the-grave aspect to him, a revenant quality about his resoluteness. This is not just metrical narrative full of anthropological interest and typical heroic-age motifs; it is poetry of a high order, in which passages of great lyric intensity—such as the "Lay of the Last Survivor" (lines 2247–66) and, even more remarkably, the so-called Father's Lament (2444–62)—rise like emanations from some fissure in the bedrock of the human capacity to endure:

> It was like the misery endured by an old man
> who has lived to see his son's body
> swing on the gallows. He begins to keen
> and weep for his boy, watching the raven
> gloat where he hangs; he can be of no help.
> The wisdom of age is worthless to him.
> Morning after morning, he wakes to remember

> that his child is gone; he has no interest
> in living on until another heir
> is born in the hall . . .
> Alone with his longing, he lies down on his bed
> and sings a lament; everything seems too large,
> the steadings and the fields.   (2444–53, 2460–62)

Such passages mark an ultimate stage in poetic attainment; they are
the imaginative equivalent of Beowulf's spiritual state at the end,
when he tells his men that "doom of battle will bear [their] lord
away," in the same way that the sea-journeys so vividly described in
lines 210–28 and lines 1903–24 are the equivalent of his exultant
prime.

At these moments of lyric intensity, the keel of the poetry is deeply
set in the element of sensation while the mind's lookout sways met-
rically and far-sightedly in the element of pure comprehension—
which is to say that the elevation of *Beowulf* is always, paradoxically,
buoyantly down-to-earth. And nowhere is this more obviously and
memorably the case than in the account of the hero's funeral with
which the poem ends. Here the inexorable and the elegiac combine
in a description of the funeral pyre being got ready, the body being
burnt and the barrow being constructed—a scene at once immemo-
rial and oddly contemporary. The Geat woman who cries out in
dread as the flames consume the body of her dead lord could come
straight from a late-twentieth-century news report, from Rwanda or
Kosovo; her keen is a nightmare glimpse into the minds of people
who have survived traumatic, even monstrous events and who are
now being exposed to a comfortless future. We immediately recog-
nize her predicament and the pitch of her grief and find ourselves
the better for having them expressed with such adequacy, dignity
and unforgiving truth:

> On a height they kindled the hugest of all
> funeral fires; fumes of woodsmoke
> billowed darkly up, the blaze roared
> and drowned out their weeping, wind died down
> and flames wrought havoc in the hot bone-house,
> burning it to the core. They were disconsolate
> and wailed aloud for their lord's decease.
> A Geat woman too sang out in grief;
> with hair bound up, she unburdened herself
> of her worst fears, a wild litany
> of nightmare and lament: her nation invaded,
> enemies on the rampage, bodies in piles,
> slavery and abasement. Heaven swallowed the smoke.
>   (3143–55)

2. About This Translation

When I was an undergraduate at Queen's University, Belfast, I studied *Beowulf* and other Anglo-Saxon poems and developed not only a feel for the language, but a fondness for the melancholy and fortitude that characterized the poetry. Consequently, when an invitation to translate the poem arrived from the editors of *The Norton Anthology of English Literature*, I was tempted to try my hand. While I had no great expertise in Old English, I had a strong desire to get back to the first stratum of the language and to "assay the hoard" (line 2509). This was during the middle years of the 1980s, when I had begun a regular teaching job at Harvard and was opening my ear to the unmoored speech of some contemporary American poetry. Saying yes to the *Beowulf* commission would be (I argued with myself) a kind of aural antidote, a way of ensuring that my linguistic anchor would stay lodged on the Anglo-Saxon sea-floor. So I undertook to do it.

Very soon, however, I hesitated. It was labor-intensive work, scriptorium slow. I proceeded dutifully like a sixth-former at homework. I would set myself twenty lines a day, write out my glossary of hard words in longhand, try to pick a way through the syntax, get the run of the meaning established in my head and then hope that the lines could be turned into metrical shape and raised to the power of verse. Often, however, the whole attempt to turn it into modern English seemed to me like trying to bring down a megalith with a toy hammer. What had been so attractive in the first place, the hand-built, rock-sure feel of the thing, began to defeat me. I turned to other work, the commissioning editors did not pursue me, and the project went into abeyance.

Even so, I had an instinct that it should not be let go. An understanding I had worked out for myself concerning my own linguistic and literary origins made me reluctant to abandon the task. I had noticed, for example, that without any conscious intent on my part certain lines in the first poem in my first book conformed to the requirements of Anglo-Saxon metrics. These lines were made up of two balancing halves, each half containing two stressed syllables— "The spade sinks into gravelly ground: / My father digging. I look down . . ."—and in the case of the second line there was alliteration linking "digging" and "down" across the caesura. Part of me, in other words, had been writing Anglo-Saxon from the start.

This was not surprising, given that the poet who had first formed my ear was Gerard Manley Hopkins. Hopkins was a chip off the Old English block, and the earliest lines I published when I was a student were as much pastiche Anglo-Saxon as they were pastiche

Hopkins: "Starling thatch-watches and sudden swallow / Straight breaks to mud-nest, home-rest rafter," and so on. I have written about all this elsewhere and about the relation of my Hopkins ventriloquism to the speech patterns of Ulster—especially as these were caricatured by the poet W. R. Rodgers. Ulster people, according to Rodgers, are "an abrupt people / who like the spiky consonants of speech / and think the soft ones cissy," and get a kick out of "anything that gives or takes attack / like Micks, Teagues, tinkers' gets, Vatican."

Joseph Brodsky once said that poets' biographies are present in the sounds they make, and I suppose all I am saying is that I consider *Beowulf* to be part of my voice-right. And yet to persuade myself that I was born into its language and that its language was born into me took a while: for somebody who grew up in the political and cultural conditions of Lord Brookeborough's Northern Ireland, it could hardly have been otherwise.

Sprung from an Irish nationalist background and educated at a Northern Irish Catholic school, I had learned the Irish language and lived within a cultural and ideological frame that regarded it as the language that I should by rights have been speaking but I had been robbed of. I have also written, for example, about the thrill I experienced when I stumbled upon the word *lachtar* in my Irish-English dictionary and found that this word, which my aunt had always used when speaking of a flock of chicks, was in fact an Irish language word and, more than that, an Irish word associated in particular with County Derry. Yet here it was, surviving in my aunt's English speech generations after her forebears and mine had ceased to speak Irish. For a long time, therefore, the little word was—to borrow a simile from Joyce—like a rapier point of consciousness pricking me with an awareness of language-loss and cultural dispossession, and tempting me into binary thinking about language. I tended to conceive of English and Irish as adversarial tongues, as either/or conditions rather than both/and, and this was an attitude that for a long time hampered the development of a more confident and creative way of dealing with the whole vexed question—the question, that is, of the relationship between nationality, language, history, and literary tradition in Ireland.

Luckily, I glimpsed the possibility of release from this kind of cultural determination early on, in my first arts year at Queen's University, Belfast, when we were lectured on the history of the English Language by Professor John Braidwood. Braidwood could not help informing us, for example, that the word "whiskey" is the same word as the Irish and Scots Gaelic word *uisce*, meaning water, and that the River Usk in Britain is therefore to some extent the River Uisce (or Whiskey); and so in my mind the stream was suddenly turned into a kind of linguistic river of rivers issuing from a pristine Celto-British Land of Cockaigne, a riverrun of Finnegans Wakespeak pouring out of the cleft rock of some prepolitical, prelapsarian, ur-philological Big Rock Candy Mountain—and all of this had a wonderfully sweetening effect upon me. The Irish/English duality, the Celtic/Saxon antithesis were momentarily collapsed and in the resulting etymological eddy a gleam of recognition flashed through the synapses and I glimpsed an elsewhere of potential that seemed at the same time to be a somewhere being remembered. The place on the language map where the Usk and the *uisce* and the whiskey coincided was definitely a place where the spirit might find a loop-hole, an escape route from what John Montague has called "the partitioned intellect," away into some unpartitioned linguistic country, a region where one's language would not be simply a badge of ethnicity or a matter of cultural preference or an official imposi-tion, but an entry into further language. And I eventually came upon one of these loopholes in *Beowulf* itself.

What happened was that I found in the glossary to C. L. Wrenn's edition of the poem the Old English word meaning "to suffer," the word *þolian*; and although at first it looked completely strange with its *thorn* symbol instead of the familiar *th*, I gradually realized that it was not strange at all, for it was the word that older and less edu-cated people would have used in the country where I grew up. "They'll just have to learn to thole," my aunt would say about some family who had suffered an unforeseen bereavement. And now sud-denly here was "thole" in the official textual world, mediated through the apparatus of a scholarly edition, a little bleeper to remind me that my aunt's language was not just a self-enclosed family posses-sion but an historical heritage, one that involved the journey *þolian* had made north into Scotland and then across into Ulster with the planters, and then across from the planters to the locals who had originally spoken Irish, and then farther across again when the Scots Irish emigrated to the American South in the eighteenth century. When I read in John Crowe Ransom the line, "Sweet ladies, long may ye bloom, and toughly I hope ye may thole," my heart lifted again, the world widened, something was furthered. The far-flungness of the word, the phenomenological pleasure of finding it variously transformed by Ransom's modernity and *Beowulf*'s venerability made me feel vaguely something for which again I only found the words years later. What I was experiencing as I kept meeting up with *thole* on its multicultural odyssey was the feeling that Osip Mandelstam once defined as a "nostalgia for world culture." And this was a nostalgia I didn't even know I suffered until I experienced its fulfilment in this little epiphany. It was as if, on the analogy of baptism by desire, I had undergone something like illumination by philology. And even though I did not know it at the time, I had by then reached the point where I was ready to translate *Beowulf*. Þolian had opened my right of way.

So, in a sense, the decision to accept Norton's invitation was taken thirty-five years before the invitation was actually issued. But between one's sense of readiness to take on a subject and the actual inscription of the first lines, there is always a problematical hiatus. To put it another way: from the point of view of the writer, words in a poem need what the Polish poet Anna Swir once called "the equivalent of a biological right to life." The erotics of composition are essential to the process, some prereflective excitation and orientation, some sense that your own little verse craft can dock safe and sound at the big quay of the language. And this is as true for translators as it is for poets attempting original work.

It is one thing to find lexical meanings for the words and to have some feel for how the meter might go, but it is quite another thing to find the tuning fork that will give you the note and pitch for the overall music of the work. Without some melody sensed or promised, it is simply impossible for a poet to establish the translator's right of way into and through a text. I was therefore lucky to hear this enabling note almost straight away, a familiar local voice, one that had belonged to relatives of my father, people whom I had once described (punning on their surname) as "big-voiced scullions."

I called them "big-voiced" because when the men of the family spoke, the words they uttered came across with a weighty distinctness, phonetic units as separate and defined as delph platters displayed on a dresser shelf. A simple sentence such as "We cut the corn today" took on immense dignity when one of the Scullions spoke it. They had a kind of Native American solemnity of utterance, as if they were announcing verdicts rather than making small talk. And when I came to ask myself how I wanted *Beowulf* to sound in my version, I realized I wanted it to be speakable by one of those relatives. I therefore tried to frame the famous opening lines in cadences that would have suited their voices, but that still echoed with the sound and sense of the Anglo-Saxon:

> Hwæt. Wē Gār-Dena   in geār-dagum
> þēod-cyninga   þrym gefrūnon,
> hū ðā æþelingas   ellen fremedon.[2]

Conventional renderings of *hwæt*, the first word of the poem, tend toward the archaic literary, with "lo," "hark," "behold," "attend"

---

2. These lines are quoted from the opening passage of the Old English text printed herein, p. 2 [*Editor*].

and—more colloquially—"listen" being some of the solutions offered previously. But in Hiberno-English Scullion-speak, the particle "so" came naturally to the rescue, because in that idiom "so" operates as an expression that obliterates all previous discourse and narrative, and at the same time functions as an exclamation calling for immediate attention. So, "so" it was:

> So. The Spear-Danes in days gone by
> and the kings who ruled them had courage and greatness.
> We have heard of those princes' heroic campaigns.

I came to the task of translating *Beowulf* with a prejudice in favor of forthright delivery. I remembered the voice of the poem as being attractively direct, even though the diction was ornate and the narrative method at times oblique. What I had always loved was a kind of foursquareness about the utterance, a feeling of living inside a constantly indicative mood, in the presence of an understanding that assumes you share an awareness of the perilous nature of life and are yet capable of seeing it steadily and, when necessary, sternly. There is an undeluded quality about the *Beowulf* poet's sense of the world that gives his lines immense emotional credibility and allows him to make general observations about life that are far too grounded in experience and reticence to be called "moralizing." These so-called "gnomic" parts of the poem have the cadence and force of earned wisdom, and their combination of cogency and verity was again something that I could remember from the speech I heard as a youngster in the Scullion kitchen. When I translate lines 24–25 as "Behavior that's admired / is the path to power among people everywhere," I am attending as much to the grain of my original vernacular as to the content of the Anglo-Saxon lines. But then the evidence suggests that this middle ground between oral tradition and the demands of written practice was also the ground occupied by the *Beowulf* poet. The style of the poem is hospitable to the kind of formulaic phrases that are the stock-in-trade of oral bards, and yet it is marked too by the self-consciousness of an artist convinced that "we must labor to be beautiful."

In one area, my own labors have been less than thorough-going. I have not followed the strict metrical rules that bound the Anglo-Saxon *scop*. I have been guided by the fundamental pattern of four stresses to the line, but I allow myself several transgressions. For example, I don't always employ alliteration, and sometimes I alliterate only in one half of the line. When these breaches occur, it is because I prefer to let the natural "sound of sense" prevail over the demands of the convention: I have been reluctant to force an artificial shape or an unusual word choice just for the sake of correctness.

In general, the alliteration varies from the shadowy to the sub-stantial, from the properly to the improperly distributed. Substan-tial and proper are such lines as

> The *f*órtunes of wár   *f*ávored Hróthgar (line 64)
> the híghest in the *l*ánd,   would *l*énd advíce (line 172)
> and *f*índ *f*ríendship   in the *F*áther's embráce (line 188)

Here the caesura is definite, there are two stresses in each half of the line, and the first stressed syllable of the second half alliterates with the first or the second or both of the stressed syllables in the first half. The main deviation from this is one that other translators have allowed themselves—the freedom, that is, to alliterate on the fourth stressed syllable, a practice that breaks the rule but that nev-ertheless does bind the line together:

> We have héard of those *p*rínces'   heroic cam*p*áigns (line 3)
> and he *c*róssed óver   into the Lórd's *k*éeping (line 27)

In the course of the translation, such deviations, distortions, synco-pations, and extensions do occur; what I was after first and foremost was a narrative line that sounded as if it meant business and I was prepared to sacrifice other things in pursuit of this directness of utterance.

The appositional nature of the Old English syntax, for example, is somewhat slighted here, as is the *Beowulf* poet's resourcefulness with synonyms and (to a lesser extent) his genius for compound-making, kennings, and all sorts of variation. Usually—as at line 1209, where I render *ȳða ful* as "frothing wave-vat." and at line 1523, where *beado-lēoma* becomes "battle-torch"—I try to match the poet's analogy-seeking habit at its most original; and I use all the common coinages for the lord of the nation, variously referred to as "ring-giver," "treasure-giver," "his people's shield" or "shepherd" or "hel-met." I have been less faithful, however, to the way the poet rings the changes when it comes to compounds meaning a sword or a spear, or a battle or any bloody encounter with foes. Old English abounds in vigorous, evocative and specifically poetic words for these things, but I have tended to follow modern usage and in the main have called a sword a sword.

There was one area, however, where a certain strangeness in the diction came naturally. In those instances where a local Ulster word seemed either poetically or historically right, I felt free to use it. For example, at lines 324 and 2988 I use the word "graith" for "harness," and at 3026 "hoked" for "rooted about," because the local term seemed in each case to have special body and force. Then, for rea-sons of historical suggestiveness, I have in several instances used the word "bawn" to refer to Hrothgar's hall. In Elizabethan English, "bawn" (from the Irish *bó-dhún*, a fort for cattle) referred specifically to the fortified dwellings that the English planters built in Ireland to keep the dispossessed natives at bay, so it seemed the proper term to apply to the embattled keep where Hrothgar waits and watches. Indeed, every time I read the lovely interlude that tells of the minstrel singing in Heorot just before the first attacks of Grendel, I cannot help thinking of Edmund Spenser in Kilcolman Castle, reading the early cantos of *The Faerie Queene* to Sir Walter Raleigh, just before the Irish would burn the castle and drive Spenser out of Munster back to the Elizabethan court. Putting a bawn into *Beowulf* seems one way for an Irish poet to come to terms with that complex history of conquest and colony, absorption and resistance, integrity and antagonism, a history that has to be clearly acknowledged by all concerned in order to render it ever more "willable forward / again and again and again."

SEAMUS HEANEY

The Text of
BEOWULF
A Verse Translation

Hwæt. Wē Gār-Dena   in geār-dagum
þēod-cyninga   þrym gefrūnon,
hū ðā æþelingas   ellen fremedon.
    Oft Scyld Scēfing   sceaþena þrēatum
monegum mǣgþum   meodo-setla oftēah,   5
egsode eorlas.   Syððan ǣrest wearð
fēa-sceaft funden,   hē þæs frōfre gebād,
wēox under wolcnum,   weorð-myndum þāh.
Oð þæt him ǣghwylc   ymb-sittendra
ofer hron-rāde   hȳran scolde,   10
gomban gyldan.   Þæt wæs gōd cyning.
    Ðǣm eafera wæs   æfter cenned
geong in geardum,   þone God sende
folce tō frōfre.   Fyren-ðearfe ongeat,
þæt hīe ǣr drugon   aldorlēase   15
lange hwīle;   him þæs Līf-Frēa
wuldres Wealdend   worold-āre forgeaf.
Bēow wæs brēme   —blǣd wīde sprang—
Scyldes eafera   Scede-landum in.
Swā sceal geong guma   gōde gewyrcean   20
fromum feoh-giftum   on fæder bearme,
þæt hine on ylde   eft gewunigen
wil-gesīþas   þonne wīg cume
lēode gelǣsten.   Lof-dǣdum sceal
in mǣgþa gehwǣre   man geþēon.*   25

---

* The text of the original Old English for the first twenty-five lines has been provided to enable comparison with Heaney's translation. A similar *en face* passage of Old English accompanies the concluding lines of the poem.

Beowulf

[Prologue: The Rise of the Danes]

So. The Spear-Danes[1] in days gone by
and the kings who ruled them had courage and greatness.
We have heard of those princes' heroic campaigns.
    There was Shield Sheafson,[2] scourge of many tribes,
a wrecker of mead-benches, rampaging among foes.   5
This terror of the hall-troops had come far.
A foundling to start with, he would flourish later on
as his powers waxed and his worth was proved.
In the end each clan on the outlying coasts
beyond the whale-road[3] had to yield to him   10
and begin to pay tribute. That was one good king.
    Afterward a boy-child was born to Shield,
a cub in the yard, a comfort sent
by God to that nation. He knew what they had tholed,[4]
the long times and troubles they'd come through   15
without a leader; so the Lord of Life,
the glorious Almighty, made this man renowned.
Shield had fathered a famous son:
Beow's name was known through the north.
And a young prince must be prudent like that,   20
giving freely while his father lives
so that afterward in age when fighting starts
steadfast companions will stand by him
and hold the line. Behavior that's admired
is the path to power among people everywhere.   25

---

1. The Danes are identified by a variety of names, all referring to the same tribe: Spear-Danes, East-Danes, Victory-Shieldings, etc. See "The Kingdoms and Tribes of *Beowulf*," p. 105.
2. The poem up to line 52 recounts the story of Shield, who arrived as a "foundling to start with," but as an adult established the Danish royal family. For the pronunciation of Old English names, see the glossary, p. 287; for the legend of Shield, see p. 101.
3. A literal translation of the Old English *hron-rad*, an example of a compressed figure of speech known as a kenning. Other kennings for "ocean" are "swan's road" (line 200) and "gannet's bath" (line 1861).
4. Suffered, endured [*Translator's note*]. Heaney takes advantage of the fact that the Old English *þolian*, while long obsolete in Standard English, survived in the Ulster dialect of his parents. See the Translator's Introduction, pp. xxxv–xxxvi.

Shield was still thriving when his time came
and he crossed over into the Lord's keeping.
His warrior band did what he bade them
when he laid down the law among the Danes:
they shouldered him out to the sea's flood,   30
the chief they revered who had long ruled them.
A ring-whorled prow rode in the harbor,
ice-clad, outbound, a craft for a prince.
They stretched their beloved lord in his boat,
laid out by the mast, amidships,   35
the great ring-giver. Far-fetched treasures
were piled upon him, and precious gear.
I never heard before of a ship so well furbished
with battle-tackle, bladed weapons
and coats of mail. The massed treasure   40
was loaded on top of him: it would travel far
on out into the ocean's sway.
They decked his body no less bountifully
with offerings than those first ones did
who cast him away when he was a child   45
and launched him alone out over the waves.
And they set a gold standard up
high above his head and let him drift
to wind and tide, bewailing him
and mourning their loss. No man can tell,   50
no wise man in hall or weathered veteran
knows for certain who salvaged that load.
    Then it fell to Beow to keep the forts.
He was well regarded and ruled the Danes
for a long time after his father took leave   55
of his life on earth. And then his heir,
the great Halfdane,[5] held sway
for as long as he lived, their elder and warlord.
He was four times a father, this fighter prince:
one by one they entered the world,   60
Heorogar, Hrothgar, the good Halga,
and a daughter, I have heard, who was Onela's queen,
a balm in bed to the battle-scarred Swede.
    The fortunes of war favored Hrothgar.
Friends and kinsmen flocked to his ranks,   65
young followers, a force that grew

5. According to an early source, Halfdane's mother was Swedish.

to be a mighty army. So his mind turned
to hall-building: he handed down orders
for men to work on a great mead-hall
meant to be a wonder of the world forever; 70
it would be his throne-room and there he would dispense
his God-given goods to young and old—
but not the common land or people's lives.[6]
Far and wide through the world, I have heard,
orders for work to adorn that wallstead 75
were sent to many peoples. And soon it stood there
finished and ready, in full view,
the hall of halls. Heorot[7] was the name
he had settled on it, whose utterance was law.
Nor did he renege, but doled out rings 80
and torques at the table. The hall towered,
its gables wide and high and awaiting
a barbarous burning.[8] That doom abided,
but in time it would come: the killer instinct
unleashed among in-laws, the blood-lust rampant. 85

[Heorot Is Attacked]

Then a powerful demon, a prowler through the dark,
nursed a hard grievance. It harrowed him
to hear the din of the loud banquet
every day in the hall, the harp being struck
and the clear song of a skilled poet 90
telling with mastery of man's beginnings,
how the Almighty had made the earth
a gleaming plain girdled with waters;
in His splendor He set the sun and the moon
to be earth's lamplight, lanterns for men, 95
and filled the broad lap of the world
with branches and leaves; and quickened life
in every other thing that moved.
So times were pleasant for the people there
until finally one, a fiend out of hell, 100

6. Even a powerful king could not dispose of land or unlawfully kill his subjects without
consulting his advisers.
7. "Hart" or "stag," a symbol of royalty.
8. An allusion to the future destruction of the hall as a result of a feud between the Danes
and the Heatho-Bards. Upon his arrival back among the Geats, Beowulf brings the news
that Hrothgar plans to give his daughter Freawaru in marriage to Ingeld, the Heatho-
Bard king, to settle the feud (lines 2020–69). He predicts, however, that hostilities will
flare up again, leading (by implication) to the burning of Heorot.

began to work his evil in the world.
Grendel was the name of this grim demon
haunting the marches, marauding round the heath
and the desolate fens; he had dwelt for a time
in misery among the banished monsters,   105
Cain's clan, whom the Creator had outlawed
and condemned as outcasts.[9] For the killing of Abel
the Eternal Lord had exacted a price:
Cain got no good from committing that murder
because the Almighty made him anathema,   110
and out of the curse of his exile there sprang
ogres and elves and evil phantoms
and the giants too who strove with God
time and again until He gave them their reward.

   So, after nightfall, Grendel set out   115
for the lofty house, to see how the Ring-Danes
were settling into it after their drink,
and there he came upon them, a company of the best
asleep from their feasting, insensible to pain
and human sorrow. Suddenly then   120
the God-cursed brute was creating havoc:
greedy and grim, he grabbed thirty men
from their resting places and rushed to his lair,
flushed up and inflamed from the raid,
blundering back with the butchered corpses.   125

   Then as dawn brightened and the day broke,
Grendel's powers of destruction were plain:
their wassail was over, they wept to heaven
and mourned under morning. Their mighty prince,
the storied leader, sat stricken and helpless,   130
humiliated by the loss of his guard,
bewildered and stunned, staring aghast
at the demon's trail, in deep distress.
He was numb with grief, but got no respite
for one night later merciless Grendel   135
struck again with more gruesome murders.
Malignant by nature, he never showed remorse.
It was easy then to meet with a man
shifting himself to a safer distance
to bed in the bothies,[1] for who could be blind   140
to the evidence of his eyes, the obviousness

---

9. See Genesis 4.1–16, pp. 90–91 in this Norton Critical Edition.
1. The Irish word *bothóg* means "hut" or "shanty," often for unmarried workers on a farm. Grendel occupies Heorot, the seat of Danish culture, and ignores the outlying buildings.

of the hall-watcher's hate? Whoever escaped
kept a weather-eye open and moved away.
  So Grendel ruled in defiance of right,
one against all, until the greatest house   145
in the world stood empty, a deserted wallstead.
For twelve winters, seasons of woe,
the lord of the Shieldings suffered under
his load of sorrow; and so, before long,
the news was known over the whole world.   150
Sad lays were sung about the beset king,
the vicious raids and ravages of Grendel,
his long and unrelenting feud,
nothing but war; how he would never
parley or make peace with any Dane   155
nor stop his death-dealing nor pay the death-price.[2]
No counselor could ever expect
fair reparation from those rabid hands.
All were endangered; young and old
were hunted down by that dark death-shadow   160
who lurked and swooped in the long nights
on the misty moors; nobody knows
where these reavers from hell roam on their errands.
  So Grendel waged his lonely war,
inflicting constant cruelties on the people,   165
atrocious hurt. He took over Heorot,
haunted the glittering hall after dark,
but the throne itself, the treasure-seat,
he was kept from approaching; he was the Lord's outcast.
  These were hard times, heartbreaking   170
for the prince of the Shieldings; powerful counselors,
the highest in the land, would lend advice,
plotting how best the bold defenders
might resist and beat off sudden attacks.
Sometimes at pagan shrines they vowed   175
offerings to idols, swore oaths
that the killer of souls[3] might come to their aid
and save the people. That was their way,
their heathenish hope; deep in their hearts
they remembered hell. The Almighty Judge   180
of good deeds and bad, the Lord God,

2. According to Anglo-Saxon law, a murder or any unlawful killing could be resolved by
   the payment of a substantial fine to the family of the victim. It was the society's means
   of preventing the cycles of feuds from beginning.
3. I.e., the devil. Christians identified the old pagan gods with devils.

Heavens and High King of the World,
ᵕ   n to them. Oh, cursed is he
         of trouble has to thrust his soul
         embrace, forfeiting help;   185
         here to turn. But blessed is he
who after death can approach the Lord
and find friendship in the Father's embrace.

[The Hero Comes to Heorot]

So that troubled time continued, woe
that never stopped, steady affliction   190
for Halfdane's son, too hard an ordeal.
There was panic after dark, people endured
raids in the night, riven by the terror.
When he heard about Grendel, Hygelac's thane[4]
was on home ground, over in Geatland.   195
There was no one else like him alive.
In his day, he was the mightiest man on earth,
highborn and powerful. He ordered a boat
that would ply the waves. He announced his plan:
to sail the swan's road and seek out that king,   200
the famous prince who needed defenders.
Nobody tried to keep him from going,
no elder denied him, dear as he was to them.
Instead, they inspected omens and spurred
his ambition to go, while he moved about   205
like the leader he was, enlisting men,
the best he could find; with fourteen others
the warrior boarded the boat as captain,
a canny pilot along coast and currents.
Time went by, the boat was on water,   210
in close under the cliffs.
Men climbed eagerly up the gangplank,
sand churned in surf, warriors loaded
a cargo of weapons, shining war-gear
in the vessel's hold, then heaved out,   215
away with a will in their wood-wreathed ship.

---

4. I.e., Beowulf. His name is withheld until he reveals it in dialogue in line 343. In Old
English poetry "thane" means "warrior, follower of the king," though in Anglo-Saxon
society it designated a specific, relatively high rank.

Over the waves, with the wind behind her
and foam at her neck, she flew like a bird
until her curved prow had covered the distance,
and on the following day, at the due hour,   220
those seafarers sighted land,
sunlit cliffs, sheer crags
and looming headlands, the landfall they sought.[5]
It was the end of their voyage and the Geats vaulted
over the side, out on to the sand,   225
and moored their ship. There was a clash of mail
and a thresh of gear. They thanked God
for that easy crossing on a calm sea.
    When the watchman on the wall, the Shieldings' lookout
whose job it was to guard the sea-cliffs,   230
saw shields glittering on the gangplank
and battle-equipment being unloaded
he had to find out who and what
the arrivals were. So he rode to the shore,
this horseman of Hrothgar's, and challenged them   235
in formal terms, flourishing his spear:
"What kind of men are you who arrive
rigged out for combat in your coats of mail,
sailing here over the sea-lanes
in your steep-hulled boat? I have been stationed   240
as lookout on this coast for a long time.
My job is to watch the waves for raiders,
any danger to the Danish shore.
Never before has a force under arms
disembarked so openly—not bothering to ask   245
if the sentries allowed them safe passage
or the clan had consented. Nor have I seen
a mightier man-at-arms on this earth
than the one standing here: unless I am mistaken,
he is truly noble. This is no mere   250
hanger-on in a hero's armor.
So now, before you fare inland
as interlopers, I have to be informed
about who you are and where you hail from.
Outsiders from across the water,   255
I say it again: the sooner you tell
where you come from and why, the better."

---

5. They journey from the south coast of what is now Sweden to the Danish island of Zea-
land (Sjælland), where Heorot was located.

The leader of the troop unlocked his word-hoard;
the distinguished one delivered this answer:
"We belong by birth to the Geat people   260
and owe allegiance to Lord Hygelac.
In his day, my father was a famous man,
a noble warrior-lord named Ecgtheow.
He outlasted many a long winter
and went on his way. All over the world   265
men wise in counsel continue to remember him.
We come in good faith to find your lord
and nation's shield, the son of Halfdane.
Give us the right advice and direction.
We have arrived here on a great errand   270
to the lord of the Danes, and I believe therefore
there should be nothing hidden or withheld between us.
So tell us if what we have heard is true
about this threat, whatever it is,
this danger abroad in the dark nights,   275
this corpse-maker mongering death
in the Shieldings' country. I come to proffer
my wholehearted help and counsel.
I can show the wise Hrothgar a way
to defeat his enemy and find respite—   280
if any respite is to reach him, ever.
I can calm the turmoil and terror in his mind.
Otherwise, he must endure woes
and live with grief for as long as his hall
stands at the horizon on its high ground."   285
    Undaunted, sitting astride his horse,
the coast-guard answered: "Anyone with gumption
and a sharp mind will take the measure
of two things: what's said and what's done.
I believe what you have told me, that you are a troop   290
loyal to our king. So come ahead
with your arms and your gear, and I will guide you.
What's more, I'll order my own comrades
on their word of honor to watch your boat
down there on the strand—keep her safe   295
in her fresh tar, until the time comes
for her curved prow to preen on the waves
and bear this hero back to Geatland.
May one so valiant and venturesome
come unharmed through the clash of battle."   300
    So they went on their way. The ship rode the water,
broad-beamed, bound by its hawser

and anchored fast. Boar-shapes[6] flashed
above their cheek-guards, the brightly forged
work of goldsmiths, watching over   305
those stern-faced men. They marched in step,
hurrying on till the timbered hall
rose before them, radiant with gold.
Nobody on earth knew of another
building like it. Majesty lodged there,   310
its light shone over many lands.
So their gallant escort guided them
to that dazzling stronghold and indicated
the shortest way to it; then the noble warrior
wheeled on his horse and spoke these words: 315
"It is time for me to go. May the Almighty
Father keep you and in His kindness
watch over your exploits. I'm away to the sea,
back on alert against enemy raiders."

It was a paved track, a path that kept them   320
in marching order. Their mail-shirts glinted,
hard and hand-linked; the high-gloss iron
of their armor rang. So they duly arrived
in their grim war-graith[7] and gear at the hall,
and, weary from the sea, stacked wide shields   325
of the toughest hardwood against the wall,
then collapsed on the benches; battle-dress
and weapons clashed. They collected their spears
in a seafarers' stook, a stand of grayish
tapering ash. And the troops themselves   330
were as good as their weapons.
                              Then a proud warrior
questioned the men concerning their origins:
"Where do you come from, carrying these
decorated shields and shirts of mail,
these cheek-hinged helmets and javelins?   335
I am Hrothgar's herald and officer.
I have never seen so impressive or large
an assembly of strangers. Stoutness of heart,
bravery not banishment, must have brought you to Hrothgar."
The man whose name was known for courage,   340
the Geat leader, resolute in his helmet,

---

6. Helmets decorated with images of boars have been found at a number of archaeological
   sites. It is thought that boars were valued for their aggressiveness and possibly for religious
   reasons. For armor and its decoration, see pp. 210–26.
7. *Graith* is a dialectal word for "harness" or "gear." See the Translator's Introduction,
   p. xxxviii.

answered in return: "We are retainers
from Hygelac's band. Beowulf is my name.
If your lord and master, the most renowned
son of Halfdane, will hear me out   345
and graciously allow me to greet him in person,
I am ready and willing to report my errand."
    Wulfgar replied, a Wendel chief
renowned as a warrior, well known for his wisdom
and the temper of his mind: "I will take this message,   350
in accordance with your wish, to our noble king,
our dear lord, friend of the Danes,
the giver of rings. I will go and ask him
about your coming here, then hurry back
with whatever reply it pleases him to give."   355
    With that he turned to where Hrothgar sat,
an old man among retainers;
the valiant follower stood foursquare
in front of his king: he knew the courtesies.
Wulfgar addressed his dear lord: 360
"People from Geatland have put ashore.
They have sailed far over the wide sea.
They call the chief in charge of their band
by the name of Beowulf. They beg, my lord,
an audience with you, exchange of words   365
and formal greeting. Most gracious Hrothgar,
do not refuse them, but grant them a reply.
From their arms and appointment, they appear well born
and worthy of respect, especially the one
who has led them this far: he is formidable indeed."   370
    Hrothgar, protector of Shieldings, replied:
"I used to know him when he was a young boy.
His father before him was called Ecgtheow.
Hrethel the Geat[8] gave Ecgtheow
his daughter in marriage. This man is their son,   375
here to follow up an old friendship.
A crew of seamen who sailed for me once
with a gift-cargo across to Geatland
returned with marvelous tales about him:
a thane, they declared, with the strength of thirty   380
in the grip of each hand. Now Holy God
has, in His goodness, guided him here
to the West-Danes, to defend us from Grendel.
This is my hope; and for his heroism

---

8. Hygelac's father and Beowulf's grandfather.

I will recompense him with a rich treasure.   385
Go immediately, bid him and the Geats
he has in attendance to assemble and enter.
Say, moreover, when you speak to them,
they are welcome to Denmark."
                    At the door of the hall,
Wulfgar duly delivered the message: 390
"My lord, the conquering king of the Danes,
bids me announce that he knows your ancestry;
also that he welcomes you here to Heorot
and salutes your arrival from across the sea.
You are free now to move forward   395
to meet Hrothgar in helmets and armor,
but shields must stay here and spears be stacked
until the outcome of the audience is clear."
    The hero arose, surrounded closely
by his powerful thanes. A party remained   400
under orders to keep watch on the arms;
the rest proceeded, led by their prince
under Heorot's roof. And standing on the hearth
in webbed links that the smith had woven,
the fine-forged mesh of his gleaming mail-shirt,   405
resolute in his helmet, Beowulf spoke:
"Greetings to Hrothgar. I am Hygelac's kinsman,
one of his hall-troop. When I was younger,
I had great triumphs. Then news of Grendel,
hard to ignore, reached me at home: 410
sailors brought stories of the plight you suffer
in this legendary hall, how it lies deserted,
empty and useless once the evening light
hides itself under heaven's dome.
So every elder and experienced councilman   415
among my people supported my resolve
to come here to you, King Hrothgar,
because all knew of my awesome strength.
They had seen me boltered° in the blood of enemies
when I battled and bound five beasts,   420
raided a troll-nest and in the night-sea
slaughtered sea-brutes. I have suffered extremes
and avenged the Geats (their enemies brought it
upon themselves; I devastated them).
Now I mean to be a match for Grendel,   425

9. The *Oxford English Dictionary* defines "blood-boltered" as "clotted or clogged with blood, *esp.* having the hair matted with blood."

settle the outcome in single combat.
And so, my request, O king of Bright-Danes,
dear prince of the Shieldings, friend of the people
and their ring of defense, my one request
is that you won't refuse me, who have come this far,   430
the privilege of purifying Heorot,
with my own men to help me, and nobody else.
I have heard moreover that the monster scorns
in his reckless way to use weapons;
therefore, to heighten Hygelac's fame   435
and gladden his heart, I hereby renounce
sword and the shelter of the broad shield,
the heavy war-board: hand-to-hand
is how it will be, a life-and-death
fight with the fiend. Whichever one death fells   440
must deem it a just judgment by God.
If Grendel wins, it will be a gruesome day;
he will glut himself on the Geats in the war-hall,
swoop without fear on that flower of manhood
as on others before. Then my face won't be there   445
to be covered in death: he will carry me away
as he goes to ground, gorged and bloodied;
he will run gloating with my raw corpse
and feed on it alone, in a cruel frenzy
fouling his moor-nest. No need then   450
to lament for long or lay out my body:[1]
if the battle takes me, send back
this breast-webbing that Weland[2] fashioned
and Hrethel gave me, to Lord Hygelac.
Fate goes ever as fate must."[3]   455
    Hrothgar, the helmet of Shieldings, spoke:
"Beowulf, my friend, you have traveled here
to favor us with help and to fight for us.
There was a feud one time, begun by your father.
With his own hands he had killed Heatholaf   460
who was a Wulfing; so war was looming
and his people, in fear of it, forced him to leave.
He came away then over rolling waves
to the South-Danes here, the sons of honor.
I was then in the first flush of kingship,   465
establishing my sway over the rich strongholds

1. There can be no funeral because no corpse will be left behind.
2. The mythical Germanic blacksmith; thus a chain-mail shirt of superior workmanship.
3. One of many gnomic or proverbial expressions.

of this heroic land. Heorogar,
my older brother and the better man,
also a son of Halfdane's, had died.
Finally I healed the feud by paying: 470
I shipped a treasure-trove to the Wulfings,
and Ecgtheow acknowledged me with oaths of allegiance.

    "It bothers me to have to burden anyone
with all the grief that Grendel has caused
and the havoc he has wreaked upon us in Heorot,   475
our humiliations. My household guard
are on the wane, fate sweeps them away
into Grendel's clutches—but God can easily
halt these raids and harrowing attacks!

    "Time and again, when the goblets passed   480
and seasoned fighters got flushed with beer
they would pledge themselves to protect Heorot[4]
and wait for Grendel with their whetted swords.
But when dawn broke and day crept in
over each empty, blood-spattered bench,   485
the floor of the mead-hall where they had feasted
would be slick with slaughter. And so they died,
faithful retainers, and my following dwindled.
Now take your place at the table, relish
the triumph of heroes to your heart's content."   490

[Feast at Heorot]

    Then a bench was cleared in that banquet hall
so the Geats could have room to be together
and the party sat, proud in their bearing,
strong and stalwart. An attendant stood by
with a decorated pitcher, pouring bright   495
helpings of mead. And the minstrel sang,
filling Heorot with his head-clearing voice,
gladdening that great rally of Geats and Danes.

    From where he crouched at the king's feet,
Unferth, a son of Ecglaf's, spoke   500
contrary words. Beowulf's coming,
his sea-braving, made him sick with envy:
he could not brook or abide the fact
that anyone else alive under heaven

4. Hrothgar refers to a formal speech-act made by a warrior in front of his peers, sealed by
   ceremonial drinking, which pledges him to a course of action.

might enjoy greater regard than he did: 505
"Are you the Beowulf who took on Breca
in a swimming match on the open sea,
risking the water just to prove that you could win?
It was sheer vanity made you venture out
on the main deep. And no matter who tried,   510
friend or foe, to deflect the pair of you,
neither would back down: the sea-test obsessed you.
You waded in, embracing water,
taking its measure, mastering currents,
riding on the swell. The ocean swayed,   515
winter went wild in the waves, but you vied
for seven nights; and then he outswam you,
came ashore the stronger contender.
He was cast up safe and sound one morning
among the Heatho-Reams, then made his way   520
to where he belonged in Bronding country,
home again, sure of his ground
in strongroom and bawn.[5] So Breca made good
his boast upon you and was proved right.
No matter, therefore, how you may have fared   525
in every bout and battle until now,
this time you'll be worsted; no one has ever
outlasted an entire night against Grendel."
     Beowulf, Ecgtheow's son, replied:
"Well, friend Unferth, you have had your say   530
about Breca and me. But it was mostly beer
that was doing the talking. The truth is this:
when the going was heavy in those high waves,
I was the strongest swimmer of all.
We'd been children together and we grew up   535
daring ourselves to outdo each other,
boasting and urging each other to risk
our lives on the sea. And so it turned out.
Each of us swam holding a sword,
a naked, hard-proofed blade for protection   540
against the whale-beasts. But Breca could never
move out farther or faster from me
than I could manage to move from him.
Shoulder to shoulder, we struggled on
for five nights, until the long flow   545

---

5. Fortified outwork of a court or castle. The word was used by English planters in Ulster
to describe fortified dwellings they erected on lands confiscated from the Irish [*Transla-tor's note*]. See also pp. xxxviii–xxxix.

and pitch of the waves, the perishing cold,
night falling and winds from the north
drove us apart. The deep boiled up
and its wallowing sent the sea-brutes wild.
My armor helped me to hold out;   550
my hard-ringed chain-mail, hand-forged and linked,
a fine, close-fitting filigree of gold,
kept me safe when some ocean creature
pulled me to the bottom. Pinioned fast
and swathed in its grip, I was granted one   555
final chance: my sword plunged
and the ordeal was over. Through my own hands,
the fury of battle had finished off the sea-beast.
   "Time and again, foul things attacked me,
lurking and stalking, but I lashed out,   560
gave as good as I got with my sword.
My flesh was not for feasting on,
there would be no monsters gnawing and gloating
over their banquet at the bottom of the sea.
Instead, in the morning, mangled and sleeping   565
the sleep of the sword, they slopped and floated
like the ocean's leavings. From now on
sailors would be safe, the deep-sea raids
were over for good. Light came from the east,
bright guarantee of God, and the waves   570
went quiet; I could see headlands
and buffeted cliffs. Often, for undaunted courage,
fate spares the man it has not already marked.
However it occurred, my sword had killed
nine sea-monsters. Such night dangers   575
and hard ordeals I have never heard of
nor of a man more desolate in surging waves.
But worn out as I was, I survived,
came through with my life. The ocean lifted
and laid me ashore, I landed safe   580
on the coast of Finland.
                   Now I cannot recall
any fight you entered, Unferth,
that bears comparison. I don't boast when I say
that neither you nor Breca were ever much
celebrated for swordsmanship   585
or for facing danger on the field of battle.
You killed your own kith and kin,
so for all your cleverness and quick tongue,
you will suffer damnation in the depths of hell.

The fact is, Unferth, if you were truly   590
as keen or courageous as you claim to be
Grendel would never have got away with
such unchecked atrocity, attacks on your king,
havoc in Heorot and horrors everywhere.
But he knows he need never be in dread   595
of your blade making a mizzle of his blood
or of a vengeance arriving ever from this quarter—
from the Victory-Shieldings, the shoulderers of the spear.
He knows he can trample down you Danes
to his heart's content, humiliate and murder   600
without fear of reprisal. But he will find me different.
I will show him how Geats shape to kill
in the heat of battle. Then whoever wants to
may go bravely to mead, when the morning light,
scarfed in sun-dazzle, shines forth from the south   605
and brings another daybreak to the world."
    Then the gray-haired treasure-giver was glad;
far-famed in battle, the prince of Bright-Danes
and keeper of his people counted on Beowulf,
on the warrior's steadfastness and his word.   610
So the laughter started, the din got louder
and the crowd was happy. Wealhtheow came in,
Hrothgar's queen, observing the courtesies.
Adorned in her gold, she graciously saluted
the men in the hall, then handed the cup   615
first to Hrothgar, their homeland's guardian,
urging him to drink deep and enjoy it
because he was dear to them. And he drank it down
like the warlord he was, with festive cheer.
So the Helming woman went on her rounds,   620
queenly and dignified, decked out in rings,
offering the goblet to all ranks,
treating the household and the assembled troop,
until it was Beowulf's turn to take it from her hand.
With measured words she welcomed the Geat   625
and thanked God for granting her wish
that a deliverer she could believe in would arrive
to ease their afflictions. He accepted the cup,
a daunting man, dangerous in action
and eager for it always. He addressed Wealhtheow;   630
Beowulf, son of Ecgtheow, said:
"I had a fixed purpose when I put to sea.
As I sat in the boat with my band of men,
I meant to perform to the uttermost

what your people wanted or perish in the attempt,   635
in the fiend's clutches. And I shall fulfill that purpose,
prove myself with a proud deed
or meet my death here in the mead-hall."
This formal boast by Beowulf the Geat
pleased the lady well and she went to sit   640
by Hrothgar, regal and arrayed with gold.
    Then it was like old times in the echoing hall,
proud talk and the people happy,
loud and excited; until soon enough
Halfdane's heir had to be away   645
to his night's rest. He realized
that the demon was going to descend on the hall,
that he had plotted all day, from dawn light
until darkness gathered again over the world
and stealthy night-shapes came stealing forth   650
under the cloud murk. The company stood
as the two leaders took leave of each other:
Hrothgar wished Beowulf health and good luck,
named him hall-warden and announced as follows:
"Never, since my hand could hold a shield   655
have I entrusted or given control
of the Danes' hall to anyone but you.
Ward and guard it, for it is the greatest of houses.
Be on your mettle now, keep in mind your fame,
beware of the enemy. There's nothing you wish for   660
that won't be yours if you win through alive."

[The Fight with Grendel]

    Hrothgar departed then with his house-guard.
The lord of the Shieldings, their shelter in war,
left the mead-hall to lie with Wealhtheow,
his queen and bedmate. The King of Glory   665
(as people learned) had posted a lookout
who was a match for Grendel, a guard against monsters,
special protection to the Danish prince.
And the Geat placed complete trust
in his strength of limb and the Lord's favor.   670
    He began to remove his iron breast-mail,
took off the helmet and handed his attendant
the patterned sword, a smith's masterpiece,
ordering him to keep the equipment guarded.
And before he bedded down, Beowulf,   675

that prince of goodness, proudly asserted:
"When it comes to fighting, I count myself
as dangerous any day as Grendel.
So it won't be a cutting edge I'll wield
to mow him down, easily as I might.   680
He has no idea of the arts of war,
of shield or sword-play, although he does possess
a wild strength. No weapons, therefore,
for either this night: unarmed he shall face me
if face me he dares. And may the Divine Lord   685
in His wisdom grant the glory of victory
to whichever side He sees fit."
        Then down the brave man lay with his bolster
under his head and his whole company
of sea-rovers at rest beside him.   690
None of them expected he would ever see
his homeland again or get back
to his native place and the people who reared him.
They knew too well the way it was before,
how often the Danes had fallen prey   695
to death in the mead-hall. But the Lord was weaving
a victory on His war-loom for the Weather-Geats.
Through the strength of one they all prevailed;
they would crush their enemy and come through
in triumph and gladness. The truth is clear: 700
Almighty God rules over mankind
and always has.
                Then out of the night
came the shadow-stalker, stealthy and swift.
The hall-guards were slack, asleep at their posts,
all except one; it was widely understood   705
that as long as God disallowed it,
the fiend could not bear them to his shadow-bourne.
One man, however, was in fighting mood,
awake and on edge, spoiling for action.
    In off the moors, down through the mist-bands   710
God-cursed Grendel came greedily loping.
The bane of the race of men roamed forth,
hunting for a prey in the high hall.
Under the cloud-murk he moved toward it
until it shone above him, a sheer keep   715
of fortified gold. Nor was that the first time
he had scouted the grounds of Hrothgar's dwelling—
although never in his life, before or since,

did he find harder fortune or hall-defenders.
Spurned and joyless, he journeyed on ahead   720
and arrived at the bawn. The iron-braced door
turned on its hinge when his hands touched it.
Then his rage boiled over, he ripped open
the mouth of the building, maddening for blood,
pacing the length of the patterned floor   725
with his loathsome tread, while a baleful light,
flame more than light, flared from his eyes.
He saw many men in the mansion, sleeping,
a ranked company of kinsmen and warriors
quartered together. And his glee was demonic,   730
picturing the mayhem: before morning
he would rip life from limb and devour them,
feed on their flesh; but his fate that night
was due to change, his days of ravening
had come to an end.
                          Mighty and canny,   735
Hygelac's kinsman was keenly watching
for the first move the monster would make.
Nor did the creature keep him waiting
but struck suddenly and started in;
he grabbed and mauled a man on his bench,   740
bit into his bone-lappings, bolted down his blood
and gorged on him in lumps, leaving the body
utterly lifeless, eaten up
hand and foot. Venturing closer,
his talon was raised to attack Beowulf   745
where he lay on the bed, he was bearing in
with open claw when the alert hero's
comeback and armlock forestalled him utterly.
The captain of evil discovered himself
in a handgrip harder than anything   750
he had ever encountered in any man
on the face of the earth. Every bone in his body
quailed and recoiled, but he could not escape.
He was desperate to flee to his den and hide
with the devil's litter, for in all his days   755
he had never been clamped or cornered like this.
Then Hygelac's trusty retainer recalled
his bedtime speech, sprang to his feet
and got a firm hold. Fingers were bursting,
the monster back-tracking, the man overpowering.   760
The dread of the land was desperate to escape,

to take a roundabout road and flee
to his lair in the fens. The latching power
in his fingers weakened; it was the worst trip
the terror-monger had taken to Heorot.   765
And now the timbers trembled and sang,
a hall-session⁶ that harrowed every Dane
inside the stockade: stumbling in fury,
the two contenders crashed through the building.
The hall clattered and hammered, but somehow   770
survived the onslaught and kept standing:
it was handsomely structured, a sturdy frame
braced with the best of blacksmith's work
inside and out. The story goes
that as the pair struggled, mead-benches were smashed   775
and sprung off the floor, gold fittings and all.
Before then, no Shielding elder would believe
there was any power or person upon earth
capable of wrecking their horn-rigged hall
unless the burning embrace of a fire   780
engulf it in flame. Then an extraordinary
wail arose, and bewildering fear
came over the Danes. Everyone felt it
who heard that cry as it echoed off the wall,
a God-cursed scream and strain of catastrophe,   785
the howl of the loser, the lament of the hell-serf
keening his wound. He was overwhelmed,
manacled tight by the man who of all men
was foremost and strongest in the days of this life.

    But the earl-troop's leader was not inclined   790
to allow his caller to depart alive:
he did not consider that life of much account
to anyone anywhere. Time and again,
Beowulf's warriors worked to defend
their lord's life, laying about them   795
as best they could, with their ancestral blades.
Stalwart in action, they kept striking out
on every side, seeking to cut
straight to the soul. When they joined the struggle
there was something they could not have known at the time,   800
that no blade on earth, no blacksmith's art
could ever damage their demon opponent.
He had conjured the harm from the cutting edge

---

6. In Hiberno-English the word "session" (*seissiún* in Irish) can mean a gathering where
   musicians and singers perform for their own enjoyment [*Translator's note*].

of every weapon.[7] But his going away
out of this world and the days of his life   805
would be agony to him, and his alien spirit
would travel far into fiends' keeping.
    Then he who had harrowed the hearts of men
with pain and affliction in former times
and had given offense also to God   810
found that his bodily powers failed him.
Hygelac's kinsman kept him helplessly
locked in a handgrip. As long as either lived,
he was hateful to the other. The monster's whole
body was in pain; a tremendous wound   815
appeared on his shoulder. Sinews split
and the bone-lappings burst. Beowulf was granted
the glory of winning; Grendel was driven
under the fen-banks, fatally hurt,
to his desolate lair. His days were numbered,   820
the end of his life was coming over him,
he knew it for certain; and one bloody clash
had fulfilled the dearest wishes of the Danes.
The man who had lately landed among them,
proud and sure, had purged the hall,   825
kept it from harm; he was happy with his nightwork
and the courage he had shown. The Geat captain
had boldly fulfilled his boast to the Danes:
he had healed and relieved a huge distress,
unremitting humiliations,   830
the hard fate they'd been forced to undergo,
no small affliction. Clear proof of this
could be seen in the hand the hero displayed
high up near the roof: the whole of Grendel's
shoulder and arm, his awesome grasp.   835

[Celebration at Heorot]

    Then morning came and many a warrior
gathered, as I've heard, around the gift-hall,
clan-chiefs flocking from far and near
down wide-ranging roads, wondering greatly
at the monster's footprints. His fatal departure   840
was regretted by no one who witnessed his trail,

---

7. By some unknown sorcery, Grendel (unlike his mother) has been rendered impervious
   to human weapons.

the ignominious marks of his flight
where he'd skulked away, exhausted in spirit
and beaten in battle, bloodying the path,
hauling his doom to the demons' mere.[8]   845
The bloodshot water wallowed and surged,
there were loathsome upthrows and overturnings
of waves and gore and wound-slurry.
With his death upon him, he had dived deep
into his marsh-den, drowned out his life   850
and his heathen soul: hell claimed him there.

      Then away they rode, the old retainers
with many a young man following after,
a troop on horseback, in high spirits
on their bay steeds. Beowulf's doings   855
were praised over and over again.
Nowhere, they said, north or south
between the two seas or under the tall sky
on the broad earth was there anyone better
to raise a shield or to rule a kingdom.   860
Yet there was no laying of blame on their lord,
the noble Hrothgar; he was a good king.

      At times the war-band broke into a gallop,
letting their chestnut horses race
wherever they found the going good   865
on those well-known tracks. Meanwhile, a thane
of the king's household, a carrier of tales,
a traditional singer deeply schooled
in the lore of the past, linked a new theme
to a strict meter. The man started   870
to recite with skill, rehearsing Beowulf's
triumphs and feats in well-fashioned lines,
entwining his words.

                        He told what he'd heard
repeated in songs about Sigemund's exploits,[9]
all of those many feats and marvels,   875
the struggles and wanderings of Waels's son,
things unknown to anyone
except to Fitela, feuds and foul doings

8. A lake or pond. Grendel and his mother live in a cave that can be reached only through
   the water.
9. Legends concerning Sigemund circulated throughout the Germanic-speaking regions
   of medieval Europe. They are most fully recorded in the Icelandic *Volsung's Saga* from
   the thirteenth century, although Sigemund's fight with the dragon is found only in
   Beowulf. Fitela is Sigemund's son and nephew; Waels is Sigemund's father. The Danish
   poet's comparison between Beowulf and Sigemund is a compliment of the highest order.
   For a summary of the Sigemund legend, see pp. 95–96.

confided by uncle to nephew when he felt
the urge to speak of them: always they had been   880
partners in the fight, friends in need.
They killed giants, their conquering swords
had brought them down.
                         After his death
Sigemund's glory   grew and grew
because of his courage   when he killed the dragon,   885
the guardian of the hoard.   Under gray stone
he had dared to enter   all by himself
to face the worst   without Fitela.
But it came to pass   that his sword plunged
right through   those radiant scales   890
and drove into the wall.   The dragon died of it.
His daring had given him   total possession
of the treasure-hoard   his to dispose of
however he liked.   He loaded a boat:
Waels's son   weighted her hold   895
with dazzling spoils.   The hot dragon melted.
   Sigemund's name   was known everywhere.
He was utterly valiant   and venturesome,
a fence round his fighters,   and flourished therefore
after King Heremod's[1]   prowess declined   900
and his campaigns slowed down.   The king was betrayed,
ambushed in Jutland   overpowered
and done away with.   The waves of his grief
had beaten him down,   made him a burden,
a source of anxiety   to his own nobles: 905
that expedition   was often condemned
in those earlier times   by experienced men,
men who relied   on his lordship for redress,
who presumed that the part   of a prince was to thrive
on his father's throne   and defend the nation,   910
the Shielding land   where they lived and belonged,
its holdings and strongholds.   Such was Beowulf
in the affection of his friends   and of everyone alive.
But evil entered   into Heremod.
   They kept racing each other, urging their mounts   915
down sandy lanes. The light of day
broke and kept brightening. Bands of retainers
galloped in excitement to the gabled hall
to see the marvel; and the king himself,

---

1. Heremod started off as an admirable Danish hero but became, over the years, a vicious,
   miserly king who alienated his own people. See also lines 1709–22.

guardian of the ring-hoard, goodness in person,   920
walked in majesty from the women's quarters
with a numerous train, attended by his queen
and her crowd of maidens, across to the mead-hall.
    When Hrothgar arrived at the hall, he spoke,
standing on the steps, under the steep eaves,   925
gazing toward the roofwork and Grendel's talon:
"First and foremost, let the Almighty Father
be thanked for this sight. I suffered a long
harrowing by Grendel. But the Heavenly Shepherd
can work His wonders always and everywhere.   930
Not long since, it seemed I would never
be granted the slightest solace or relief
from any of my burdens: the best of houses
glittered and reeked and ran with blood.
This one worry outweighed all others—   935
a constant distress to counselors entrusted
with defending the people's forts from assault
by monsters and demons. But now a man,
with the Lord's assistance, has accomplished something
none of us could manage before now   940
for all our efforts. Whoever she was
who brought forth this flower of manhood,
if she is still alive, that woman can say
that in her labor the Lord of Ages
bestowed a grace on her. So now, Beowulf,   945
I adopt you in my heart as a dear son.
Nourish and maintain this new connection,
you noblest of men; there'll be nothing you'll want for,
no worldly goods that won't be yours.
I have often honored smaller achievements,   950
recognized warriors not nearly as worthy,
lavished rewards on the less deserving.
But you have made yourself immortal
by your glorious action. May the God of Ages
continue to keep and requite you well."   955
    Beowulf, son of Ecgtheow, spoke:
"We have gone through with a glorious endeavor
and been much favored in this fight we dared
against the unknown. Nevertheless,
if you could have seen the monster himself   960
where he lay beaten, I would have been better pleased.
My plan was to pounce, pin him down
in a tight grip and grapple him to death—
have him panting for life, powerless and clasped

in my bare hands, his body in thrall.   965
But I couldn't stop him from slipping my hold.
The Lord allowed it, my lock on him
wasn't strong enough; he struggled fiercely
and broke and ran. Yet he bought his freedom
at a high price, for he left his hand   970
and arm and shoulder to show he had been here,
a cold comfort for having come among us.
And now he won't be long for this world.
He has done his worst but the wound will end him.
He is hasped and hooped and hirpling[2] with pain,   975
limping and looped in it. Like a man outlawed
for wickedness, he must await
the mighty judgment of God in majesty."
      There was less tampering and big talk then
from Unferth the boaster, less of his blather   980
as the hall-thanes eyed the awful proof
of the hero's prowess, the splayed hand
up under the eaves. Every nail,
claw-scale and spur, every spike
and welt on the hand of that heathen brute   985
was like barbed steel. Everybody said
there was no honed iron hard enough
to pierce him through, no time-proofed blade
that could cut his brutal, blood-caked claw.
      Then the order was given for all hands   990
to help to refurbish Heorot immediately:
men and women thronging the wine-hall,
getting it ready. Gold thread shone
in the wall-hangings, woven scenes
that attracted and held the eye's attention.[3]   995
But iron-braced as the inside of it had been,
that bright room lay in ruins now.
The very doors had been dragged from their hinges.
Only the roof remained unscathed
by the time the guilt-fouled fiend turned tail   1000
in despair of his life. But death is not easily
escaped from by anyone:
all of us with souls, earth-dwellers
and children of men, must make our way
to a destination already ordained   1005

2. Limping or hobbling.
3. The Anglo-Saxon nobility decorated their halls with tapestries. From what little has sur-
   vived the centuries, it is clear that some were made with exquisite skill.

where the body, after the banqueting,
sleeps on its deathbed.
                          Then the due time arrived
for Halfdane's son to proceed to the hall.
The king himself would sit down to feast.
No group ever gathered in greater numbers   1010
or better order around their ring-giver.
The benches filled with famous men
who fell to with relish; round upon round
of mead was passed; those powerful kinsmen
Hrothgar and Hrothulf, were in high spirits   1015
in the raftered hall. Inside Heorot
there was nothing but friendship. The Shielding nation
was not yet familiar with feud and betrayal.[4]
    Then Halfdane's son presented Beowulf
with a gold standard as a victory gift,   1020
an embroidered banner; also breast-mail
and a helmet; and a sword carried high,
that was both precious object and token of honor.
So Beowulf drank his drink, at ease;
it was hardly a shame to be showered with such gifts   1025
in front of the hall-troops. There haven't been many
moments, I am sure, when men exchanged
four such treasures at so friendly a sitting.
An embossed ridge, a band lapped with wire
arched over the helmet: head-protection   1030
to keep the keen-ground cutting edge
from damaging it when danger threatened
and the man was battling behind his shield.
Next the king ordered eight horses
with gold bridles to be brought through the yard   1035
into the hall. The harness of one
included a saddle of sumptuous design,
the battle-seat where the son of Halfdane
rode when he wished to join the sword-play:
wherever the killing and carnage were the worst,   1040
he would be to the fore, fighting hard.
Then the Danish prince, descendant of Ing,
handed over both the arms and the horses,
urging Beowulf to use them well.
And so their leader, the lord and guard   1045

---

4. By contrasting the present comity with future "feud and betrayal," these lines seem to
   intimate that Hrothulf, King Hrothgar's nephew, will later betray Hrothgar's sons and
   usurp the throne. See also lines 1163–64, 1179–86, 1228.

of coffer and strongroom, with customary grace
bestowed upon Beowulf both sets of gifts.
A fair witness can see how well each one behaved.
   The chieftain went on to reward the others:
each man on the bench who had sailed with Beowulf   1050
and risked the voyage received a bounty,
some treasured possession. And compensation,
a price in gold, was settled for the Geat
Grendel had cruelly killed earlier—
as he would have killed more, had not mindful God   1055
and one man's daring prevented that doom.
Past and present, God's will prevails.
Hence, understanding is always best
and a prudent mind. Whoever remains
for long here in this earthly life   1060
will enjoy and endure more than enough.
   They sang then and played to please the hero,
words and music for their warrior prince,
harp tunes and tales of adventure:
there were high times on the hall benches,   1065
and the king's poet performed his part
with the saga of Finn and his sons, unfolding
the tale of the fierce attack in Friesland
where Hnaef, king of the Danes, met death.[5]

Hildeburh
      had little cause   1070
to credit the Jutes:
      son and brother,
she lost them both
      on the battlefield.
She, bereft
    and blameless, they
foredoomed, cut down
      and spear-gored. She,
the woman in shock,
      waylaid by grief,   1075
Hoc's daughter—
    how could she not
lament her fate
     when morning came

5. The "saga of Finn," recounted by the court poet, is summarized from the point of view of Hildeburh, who lost her son, her brother, and her husband in the tragedy. The passage achieves its poignancy in part by being allusive and sparing in details. For a reconstruction of the events and a fragment from another poem on the subject, see pp. 96–98.

and the light broke
                on her murdered dears?
And so farewell
            delight on earth,
war carried away
                Finn's troop of thanes   1080
all but a few.
                How then could Finn
hold the line
            or fight on
to the end with Hengest,
                    how save
the rump of his force
                from that enemy chief?
So a truce was offered
                as follows:[6] first   1085
separate quarters
                to be cleared for the Danes,
hall and throne
                to be shared with the Frisians.
Then, second:
            every day
at the dole-out of gifts
                Finn, son of Folcwald,
should honor the Danes,
                bestow with an even   1090
hand to Hengest
                and Hengest's men
the wrought-gold rings,
                bounty to match
the measure he gave
                his own Frisians—
to keep morale
            in the beer-hall high.
Both sides then
            sealed their agreement.   1095
With oaths to Hengest
                Finn swore
openly, solemnly,
                that the battle survivors

6. The Frisian king Finn offers terms to the Danes, who are now led by Hengest after
Hnaef's death.

would be guaranteed
                    honor and status.
No infringement
                    by word or deed,
no provocation
                    would be permitted.   1100
Their own ring-giver
                    after all
was dead and gone,
                    they were leaderless,
in forced allegiance
                    to his murderer.
So if any Frisian
                    stirred up bad blood
with insinuations
                    or taunts about this,   1105
the blade of the sword
                    would arbitrate it.
A funeral pyre
                    was then prepared,
effulgent gold
                    brought out from the hoard.
The pride and prince
                    of the Shieldings lay
awaiting the flame.
                    Everywhere   1110
there were blood-plastered
                    coats of mail.
The pyre was heaped
                    with boar-shaped helmets
forged in gold,
                    with the gashed corpses
of wellborn Danes—
                    many had fallen.
Then Hildeburh
                    ordered her own   1115
son's body
            be burnt with Hnaef's,
the flesh on his bones
                    to sputter and blaze
beside his uncle's.
                    The woman wailed
and sang keens,
            the warrior went up.

Carcass flame
              swirled and fumed,   1120
they stood round the burial
                  mound and howled
as heads melted,
              crusted gashes
spattered and ran
              bloody matter.
The glutton element
              flamed and consumed
the dead of both sides.
                  Their great days were gone.   1125
Warriors scattered
              to homes and forts
all over Friesland,
              fewer now, feeling
loss of friends.
              Hengest stayed,
lived out that whole
              resentful, blood-sullen
winter with Finn,
              homesick and helpless.   1130
No ring-whorled prow
              could up then
and away on the sea.
              Wind and water
raged with storms,
              wave and shingle
were shackled in ice
              until another year
appeared in the yard
              as it does to this day,   1135
the seasons constant,
              the wonder of light
coming over us.
              Then winter was gone,
earth's lap grew lovely,
              longing woke
in the cooped-up exile
              for a voyage home—
but more for vengeance,
              some way of bringing   1140
things to a head:
              his sword arm hankered

to greet the Jutes.
                      So he did not balk
once Hunlafing
                      placed on his lap
Dazzle-the-Duel,
                      the best sword of all,[7]
whose edges Jutes
                      knew only too well.   1145
Thus blood was spilled,
                      the gallant Finn
slain in his home
                      after Guthlaf and Oslaf[8]
back from their voyage
                      made old accusation:
the brutal ambush,
                      the fate they had suffered,
all blamed on Finn.
                      The wildness in them   1150
had to brim over.
                      The hall ran red
with blood of enemies.
                      Finn was cut down,
the queen brought away
                      and everything
the Shieldings could find
                      inside Finn's walls—
the Frisian king's
                      gold collars and gemstones—   1155
swept off to the ship.
                      Over sea-lanes then
back to Daneland
                      the warrior troop
bore that lady home.

                      The poem was over,
the poet had performed, a pleasant murmur
started on the benches, stewards did the rounds   1160
with wine in splendid jugs, and Wealhtheow came to sit
in her gold crown between two good men,

7. The identity of Hunlafing is unknown, but the ceremonial presentation of a famous
   sword to Hengest seems to be a symbolic gesture prompting revenge. It is unclear
   whether this action takes place back in Denmark or whether the Danes never left Frisia
   (Friesland) before renewing the fighting. Famous swords were sometimes given names,
   such as Beowulf's Naegling and Unferth's Hrunting.
8. This pair may be the same Ordlaf and Guthlaf mentioned in the Finnsburg Fragment,
   but aside from their Danish affiliation, nothing is known about them.

uncle and nephew, each one of whom
still trusted the other;[9] and the forthright Unferth,
admired by all for his mind and courage   1165
although under a cloud for killing his brothers,
reclined near the king.
              The queen spoke:
"Enjoy this drink, my most generous lord;
raise up your goblet, entertain the Geats
duly and gently, discourse with them,   1170
be open-handed, happy and fond.
Relish their company, but recollect as well
all of the boons that have been bestowed on you.
The bright court of Heorot has been cleansed
and now the word is that you want to adopt   1175
this warrior as a son. So, while you may,
bask in your fortune, and then bequeath
kingdom and nation to your kith and kin,
before your decease. I am certain of Hrothulf.
He is noble and will use the young ones well.   1180
He will not let you down. Should you die before him,
he will treat our children truly and fairly.
He will honor, I am sure, our two sons,
repay them in kind, when he recollects
all the good things we gave him once,   1185
the favor and respect he found in his childhood."
She turned then to the bench where her boys sat,
Hrethric and Hrothmund, with other nobles' sons,
all the youth together; and that good man,
Beowulf the Geat, sat between the brothers.   1190
   The cup was carried to him, kind words
spoken in welcome and a wealth of wrought gold
graciously bestowed: two arm bangles,
a mail-shirt and rings, and the most resplendent
torque of gold I ever heard tell of   1195
anywhere on earth or under heaven.
There was no hoard like it since Hama snatched
the Brosings' neck-chain and bore it away
with its gems and settings to his shining fort,
away from Eormenric's wiles and hatred,[1]   1200
and thereby ensured his eternal reward.
Hygelac the Geat, grandson of Swerting,

---

9. Hrothgar and Hrothulf; see line 1018, p. 28, n. 4.
1. The treasures presented to Beowulf are compared to a legendary necklace once worn
   by the goddess Freyja in Germanic legend, which later came into the possession of Eor-
   menric, whom legends portray as a treacherous tyrant.

wore this neck-ring on his last raid;[2]
at bay under his banner, he defended the booty,
treasure he had won. Fate swept him away   1205
because of his proud need to provoke
a feud with the Frisians. He fell beneath his shield,
in the same gem-crusted, kingly gear
he had worn when he crossed the frothing wave-vat.
So the dead king fell into Frankish hands.   1210
They took his breast-mail, also his neck-torque,
and punier warriors plundered the slain
when the carnage ended; Geat corpses
covered the field.
                    Applause filled the hall.
Then Wealhtheow pronounced in the presence of the company:
"Take delight in this torque, dear Beowulf,
wear it for luck and wear also this mail
from our people's armory: may you prosper in them!
Be acclaimed for strength, for kindly guidance
to these two boys, and your bounty will be sure.   1220
You have won renown: you are known to all men
far and near, now and forever.
Your sway is wide as the wind's home,
as the sea around cliffs. And so, my prince,
I wish you a lifetime's luck and blessings   1225
to enjoy this treasure. Treat my sons
with tender care, be strong and kind.
Here each comrade is true to the other,
loyal to lord, loving in spirit.
The thanes have one purpose, the people are ready: 1230
having drunk and pledged, the ranks do as I bid."
    She moved then to her place. Men were drinking wine
at that rare feast; how could they know fate,
the grim shape of things to come,
the threat looming over many thanes   1235
as night approached and King Hrothgar prepared
to retire to his quarters? Retainers in great numbers
were posted on guard as so often in the past.
Benches were pushed back, bedding gear and bolsters
spread across the floor, and one man   1240
lay down to his rest, already marked for death.
At their heads they placed their polished timber

2. Beowulf later gives the necklace to Hygd, Hygelac's queen. Hygelac was to wear it dur-
   ing the ill-fated raid on Frankish territories near the mouth of the Rhine, where he lost
   his life and the necklace. The raid, which can be dated to c. 520 C.E., is alluded to sev-
   eral times in the poem.

battle-shields; and on the bench above them,
each man's kit was kept to hand:
a towering war-helmet, webbed mail-shirt   1245
and great-shafted spear. It was their habit
always and everywhere to be ready for action,
at home or in the camp, in whatever case
and at whatever time the need arose
to rally round their lord. They were a right people.   1250

[Another Attack]

They went to sleep. And one paid dearly
for his night's ease, as had happened to them often,
ever since Grendel occupied the gold-hall,
committing evil until the end came,
death after his crimes. Then it became clear,   1255
obvious to everyone once the fight was over,
that an avenger lurked and was still alive,
grimly biding time. Grendel's mother,
monstrous hell-bride, brooded on her wrongs.
She had been forced down into fearful waters,   1260
the cold depths, after Cain had killed
his father's son, felled his own
brother with a sword. Branded an outlaw,
marked by having murdered, he moved into the wilds,
shunned company and joy. And from Cain there sprang   1265
misbegotten spirits, among them Grendel,
the banished and accursed, due to come to grips
with that watcher in Heorot waiting to do battle.
The monster wrenched and wrestled with him,
but Beowulf was mindful of his mighty strength,   1270
the wondrous gifts God had showered on him:
he relied for help on the Lord of All,
on His care and favor. So he overcame the foe,
brought down the hell-brute. Broken and bowed,
outcast from all sweetness, the enemy of mankind   1275
made for his death-den. But now his mother
had sallied forth on a savage journey,
grief-racked and ravenous, desperate for revenge.
She came to Heorot. There, inside the hall,
Danes lay asleep, earls who would soon endure   1280
a great reversal, once Grendel's mother
attacked and entered. Her onslaught was less

only by as much as an amazon warrior's
strength is less than an armed man's
when the hefted sword, its hammered edge   1285
and gleaming blade slathered in blood,
razes the sturdy boar-ridge off a helmet.
Then in the hall, hard-honed swords
were grabbed from the bench, many a broad shield
lifted and braced; there was little thought of helmets   1290
or woven mail when they woke in terror.

    The hell-dam[3] was in panic, desperate to get out,
in mortal terror the moment she was found.
She had pounced and taken one of the retainers
in a tight hold, then headed for the fen.   1295
To Hrothgar, this man was the most beloved
of the friends he trusted between the two seas.
She had done away with a great warrior,
ambushed him at rest.
                     Beowulf was elsewhere.
Earlier, after the award of the treasure,   1300
the Geat had been given another lodging.

    There was uproar in Heorot. She had snatched their trophy,
Grendel's bloodied hand. It was a fresh blow
to the afflicted bawn. The bargain was hard,
both parties having to pay   1305
with the lives of friends. And the old lord,
the gray-haired warrior, was heartsore and weary
when he heard the news: his highest-placed adviser,
his dearest companion, was dead and gone.

    Beowulf was quickly brought to the chamber: 1310
the winner of fights, the arch-warrior,
came first-footing in with his fellow troops
to where the king in his wisdom waited,
still wondering whether Almighty God
would ever turn the tide of his misfortunes.   1315
So Beowulf entered with his band in attendance
and the wooden floorboards banged and rang
as he advanced, hurrying to address
the prince of the Ingwins, asking if he'd rested
since the urgent summons had come as a surprise.   1320

    Then Hrothgar, the Shieldings' helmet, spoke:
"Rest? What is rest? Sorrow has returned.
Alas for the Danes! Aeschere is dead.

---

3. Dam is a variant of dame ("lady") used contemptuously; cf. the expression "the devil
and his dam."

He was Yrmenlaf's elder brother
and a soul-mate to me, a true mentor,   1325
my right-hand man when the ranks clashed
and our boar-crests had to take a battering
in the line of action. Aeschere was everything
the world admires in a wise man and a friend.
Then this roaming killer came in a fury   1330
and slaughtered him in Heorot. Where she is hiding,
glutting on the corpse and glorying in her escape,
I cannot tell; she has taken up the feud
because of last night, when you killed Grendel,
wrestled and racked him in ruinous combat   1335
since for too long he had terrorized us
with his depredations. He died in battle,
paid with his life; and now this powerful
other one arrives, this force for evil
driven to avenge her kinsman's death.   1340
Or so it seems to thanes in their grief,
in the anguish every thane endures
at the loss of a ring-giver, now that the hand
that bestowed so richly has been stilled in death.
   "I have heard it said by my people in hall,   1345
counselors who live in the upland country,
that they have seen two such creatures
prowling the moors, huge marauders
from some other world. One of these things,
as far as anyone ever can discern,   1350
looks like a woman; the other, warped
in the shape of a man, moves beyond the pale
bigger than any man, an unnatural birth
called Grendel by the country people
in former days. They are fatherless creatures,   1355
and their whole ancestry is hidden in a past
of demons and ghosts. They dwell apart
among wolves on the hills, on windswept crags
and treacherous keshes,[4] where cold streams
pour down the mountain and disappear   1360
under mist and moorland.
                     A few miles from here
a frost-stiffened wood waits and keeps watch
above a mere; the overhanging bank
is a maze of tree-roots mirrored in its surface.
At night there, something uncanny happens: 1365

---

4. A causeway or bridge across a bog.

the water burns. And the mere bottom
has never been sounded by the sons of men.
On its bank, the heather-stepper halts:
the hart in flight from pursuing hounds
will turn to face them with firm-set horns   1370
and die in the wood rather than dive
beneath its surface. That is no good place.
When wind blows up and stormy weather
makes clouds scud and the skies weep,
out of its depths a dirty surge   1375
is pitched toward the heavens. Now help depends
again on you and on you alone.
The gap of danger where the demon waits
is still unknown to you. Seek it if you dare.
I will compensate you for settling the feud   1380
as I did the last time with lavish wealth,
coffers of coiled gold, if you come back."

[Beowulf Fights Grendel's Mother]

Beowulf, son of Ecgtheow, spoke:
"Wise sir, do not grieve. It is always better
to avenge dear ones than to indulge in mourning.   1385
For every one of us, living in this world
means waiting for our end. Let whoever can
win glory before death. When a warrior is gone,
that will be his best and only bulwark.
So arise, my lord, and let us immediately   1390
set forth on the trail of this troll-dam.
I guarantee you: she will not get away,
not to dens under ground nor upland groves
nor the ocean floor. She'll have nowhere to flee to.
Endure your troubles today. Bear up   1395
and be the man I expect you to be."
    With that the old lord sprang to his feet
and praised God for Beowulf's pledge.
Then a bit and halter were brought for his horse
with the plaited mane. The wise king mounted   1400
the royal saddle and rode out in style
with a force of shield-bearers. The forest paths
were marked all over with the monster's tracks,
her trail on the ground wherever she had gone
across the dark moors, dragging away   1405
the body of that thane, Hrothgar's best

counselor and overseer of the country.
So the noble prince proceeded undismayed
up fells and screes,[5] along narrow footpaths
and ways where they were forced into single file,   1410
ledges on cliffs above lairs of water-monsters.
He went in front with a few men,
good judges of the lie of the land,
and suddenly discovered the dismal wood,
mountain trees growing out at an angle   1415
above gray stones: the bloodshot water
surged underneath. It was a sore blow
to all of the Danes, friends of the Shieldings,
a hurt to each and every one
of that noble company when they came upon   1420
Aeschere's head at the foot of the cliff.
      Everybody gazed as the hot gore
kept wallowing up and an urgent war-horn
repeated its notes: the whole party
sat down to watch. The water was infested   1425
with all kinds of reptiles. There were writhing sea-dragons
and monsters slouching on slopes by the cliff,
serpents and wild things such as those that often
surface at dawn to roam the sail-road
and doom the voyage. Down they plunged,   1430
lashing in anger at the loud call
of the battle-bugle. An arrow from the bow
of the Geat chief got one of them
as he surged to the surface: the seasoned shaft
stuck deep in his flank and his freedom in the water   1435
got less and less. It was his last swim.
He was swiftly overwhelmed in the shallows,
prodded by barbed boar-spears,
cornered, beaten, pulled up on the bank,
a strange lake-birth, a loathsome catch   1440
men gazed at in awe.
                        Beowulf got ready,
donned his war-gear, indifferent to death;
his mighty, hand-forged, fine-webbed mail
would soon meet with the menace underwater.
It would keep the bone-cage of his body safe: 1445
no enemy's clasp could crush him in it,
no vicious armlock choke his life out.
To guard his head he had a glittering helmet

---

5. Mountain slopes of loose rock.

that was due to be muddied on the mere bottom
and blurred in the upswirl. It was of beaten gold,
princely headgear hooped and hasped
by a weapon-smith who had worked wonders
in days gone by and adorned it with boar-shapes;
since then it had resisted every sword.
And another item lent by Unferth   1455
at that moment of need was of no small importance:
the brehon[6] handed him a hilted weapon,
a rare and ancient sword named Hrunting.
The iron blade with its ill-boding patterns
had been tempered in blood. It had never failed   1460
the hand of anyone who hefted it in battle,
anyone who had fought and faced the worst
in the gap of danger. This was not the first time
it had been called to perform heroic feats.

    When he lent that blade to the better swordsman,   1465
Unferth, the strong-built son of Ecglaf,
could hardly have remembered the ranting speech
he had made in his cups. He was not man enough
to face the turmoil of a fight under water
and the risk to his life. So there he lost   1470
fame and repute. It was different for the other
rigged out in his gear, ready to do battle.

    Beowulf, son of Ecgtheow, spoke:
"Wisest of kings, now that I have come
to the point of action, I ask you to recall   1475
what we said earlier: that you, son of Halfdane
and gold-friend to retainers, that you, if I should fall
and suffer death while serving your cause,
would act like a father to me afterward.
If this combat kills me, take care   1480
of my young company, my comrades in arms.
And be sure also, my beloved Hrothgar,
to send Hygelac the treasures I received.
Let the lord of the Geats gaze on that gold,
let Hrethel's son take note of it and see   1485
that I found a ring-giver of rare magnificence
and enjoyed the good of his generosity.
And Unferth is to have what I inherited:
to that far-famed man I bequeath my own
sharp-honed, wave-sheened wonder-blade.   1490
With Hrunting I shall gain glory or die."

6. One of an ancient class of lawyers in Ireland [Translator's note].

s, the prince of the Weather-Geats
away and plunged suddenly:
e dived into the heaving
t was the best part of a day   1495
the solid bottom.
ho haunted those waters,
⁀⁀⁀⁀ and gone her gluttonous rounds
for a hundred seasons, sensed a human
observing her outlandish lair from above.   1500
So she lunged and clutched and managed to catch him
in her brutal grip; but his body, for all that,
remained unscathed: the mesh of the chain-mail
saved him on the outside. Her savage talons
failed to rip the web of his war-shirt.   1505
Then once she touched bottom, that wolfish swimmer
carried the ring-mailed prince to her court
so that for all his courage he could never use
the weapons he carried; and a bewildering horde
came at him from the depths, droves of sea-beasts   1510
who attacked with tusks and tore at his chain-mail
in a ghastly onslaught. The gallant man
could see he had entered some hellish turn-hole
and yet the water there did not work against him
because the hall-roofing held off   1515
the force of the current; then he saw firelight,
a gleam and flare-up, a glimmer of brightness.
    The hero observed that swamp-thing from hell,
the tarn-hag[7] in all her terrible strength,
then heaved his war-sword and swung his arm: 1520
the decorated blade came down ringing
and singing on her head. But he soon found
his battle-torch extinguished; the shining blade
refused to bite. It spared her and failed
the man in his need. It had gone through many   1525
hand-to-hand fights, had hewed the armor
and helmets of the doomed, but here at last
the fabulous powers of that heirloom failed.
//   Hygelac's kinsman kept thinking about
his name and fame: he never lost heart.   1530
Then, in a fury, he flung his sword away.
The keen, inlaid, worm-loop-patterned steel
was hurled to the ground: he would have to rely
on the might of his arm. So must a man do

7. *Tarn*: a small mountain lake.

who intends to gain enduring glory
in a combat. Life doesn't cost him a thought.
Then the prince of War-Geats, warming to this fight
with Grendel's mother, gripped her shoulder
and laid about him in a battle frenzy:
he pitched his killer opponent to the floor   1540
but she rose quickly and retaliated,
grappled him tightly in her grim embrace.
The sure-footed fighter felt daunted,
the strongest of warriors stumbled and fell.//
So she pounced upon him and pulled out   1545
a broad, whetted knife: now she would avenge
her only child. But the mesh of chain-mail
on Beowulf's shoulder shielded his life,
turned the edge and tip of the blade.
The son of Ecgtheow would have surely perished   1550
and the Geats lost their warrior under the wide earth
had the strong links and locks of his war-gear
not helped to save him: holy God
decided the victory. It was easy for the Lord,
the Ruler of Heaven, to redress the balance   1555
once Beowulf got back up on his feet.   //
    Then he saw a blade that boded well,
a sword in her armory, an ancient heirloom
from the days of the giants, an ideal weapon,
one that any warrior would envy,   1560
but so huge and heavy of itself
only Beowulf could wield it in a battle.
So the Shieldings' hero hard-pressed and enraged,
took a firm hold of the hilt and swung
the blade in an arc, a resolute blow   1565
that bit deep into her neck-bone
and severed it entirely, toppling the doomed
house of her flesh; she fell to the floor.
The sword dripped blood, the swordsman was elated.
    A light appeared and the place brightened   1570
the way the sky does when heaven's candle
is shining clearly. He inspected the vault:
with sword held high, its hilt raised
to guard and threaten, Hygelac's thane
scouted by the wall in Grendel's wake.   1575
Now the weapon was to prove its worth.
The warrior determined to take revenge
for every gross act Grendel had committed—
and not only for that one occasion

to slaughter the sleeping troops,   1580
ar's house-guards
r benches and ruthlessly devoured,
n carried away,
Beowulf in his fury
core: he saw the monster   1585
in his resting place, war-weary and wrecked,
a lifeless corpse, a casualty
of the battle in Heorot. The body gaped
at the stroke dealt to it after death:
Beowulf cut the corpse's head off.   1590
    Immediately the counselors keeping a lookout
with Hrothgar, watching the lake water,
saw a heave-up and surge of waves
and blood in the backwash. They bowed gray heads,
spoke in their sage, experienced way   1595
about the good warrior, how they never again
expected to see that prince returning
in triumph to their king. It was clear to many
that the wolf of the deep had destroyed him forever.
    The ninth hour of the day arrived.   1600
The brave Shieldings abandoned the cliff-top
and the king went home; but sick at heart,
staring at the mere, the strangers held on.
They wished, without hope, to behold their lord,
Beowulf himself.
            Meanwhile, the sword   1605
began to wilt into gory icicles
to slather and thaw. It was a wonderful thing,
the way it all melted as ice melts
when the Father eases the fetters off the frost
and unravels the water-ropes, He who wields power   1610
over time and tide: He is the true Lord.
    The Geat captain saw treasure in abundance
but carried no spoils from those quarters
except for the head and the inlaid hilt
embossed with jewels; its blade had melted   1615
and the scrollwork on it burned, so scalding was the blood
of the poisonous fiend who had perished there.
Then away he swam, the one who had survived
the fall of his enemies, flailing to the surface.
The wide water, the waves and pools,   1620
were no longer infested once the wandering fiend
let go of her life and this unreliable world.
    The seafarers' leader made for land,

resolutely swimming, delighted with his prize,
the mighty load he was lugging to the surface.   1625
His thanes advanced in a troop to meet him,
thanking God and taking great delight
in seeing their prince back safe and sound.
Quickly the hero's helmet and mail-shirt
were loosed and unlaced. The lake settled,   1630
clouds darkened above the bloodshot depths.
    With high hearts they headed away
along footpaths and trails through the fields,
roads that they knew, each of them wrestling
with the head they were carrying from the lakeside cliff,   1635
men kingly in their courage and capable
of difficult work. It was a task for four
to hoist Grendel's head on a spear
and bear it under strain to the bright hall.
But soon enough they neared the place,   1640
fourteen Geats in fine fettle,
striding across the outlying ground
in a delighted throng around their leader.
    In he came then, the thanes' commander,
the arch-warrior, to address Hrothgar: 1645
his courage was proven, his glory was secure.
Grendel's head was hauled by the hair,
dragged across the floor where the people were drinking,
a horror for both queen and company to behold.
They stared in awe. It was an astonishing sight.   1650

[Another Celebration at Heorot]

    Beowulf, son of Ecgtheow, spoke:
"So, son of Halfdane, prince of the Shieldings,
we are glad to bring this booty from the lake.
It is a token of triumph and we tender it to you.
I barely survived the battle under water.   1655
It was hard-fought, a desperate affair
that could have gone badly; if God had not helped me
the outcome would have been quick and fatal.
Although Hrunting is hard-edged,
I could never bring it to bear in battle.   1660
But the Lord of Men allowed me to behold—
for He often helps the unbefriended—
an ancient sword shining on the wall,
a weapon made for giants, there for the wielding.

Then my moment came in the combat and I struck   1665
the dwellers in that den. Next thing the damascened
sword blade melted; it bloated and it burned
in their rushing blood. I have wrested the hilt
from the enemies' hand, avenged the evil
done to the Danes; it is what was due.   1670
And this I pledge, O prince of the Shieldings:
you can sleep secure with your company of troops
in Heorot Hall. Never need you fear
for a single thane of your sept[8] or nation,
young warriors or old, that laying waste of life   1675
that you and your people endured of yore."
    Then the gold hilt was handed over
to the old lord, a relic from long ago
for the venerable ruler. That rare smithwork
was passed on to the prince of the Danes   1680
when those devils perished; once death removed
that murdering, guilt-steeped, God-cursed fiend,
eliminating his unholy life
and his mother's as well, it was willed to that king
who of all the lavish gift-lords of the north   1685
was the best regarded between the two seas.
    Hrothgar spoke; he examined the hilt,
that relic of old times. It was engraved all over
and showed how war first came into the world
and the flood destroyed the tribe of giants.   1690
They suffered a terrible severance from the Lord;
the Almighty made the waters rise,
drowned them in the deluge for retribution.[9]
In pure gold inlay on the sword-guards
there were rune-markings[1] correctly incised,   1695
stating and recording for whom the sword
had been first made and ornamented
with its scrollworked hilt. Then everyone hushed
as the son of Halfdane spoke this wisdom:
"A protector of his people, pledged to uphold   1700
truth and justice and to respect tradition,
is entitled to affirm that this man

8. A clan or subgroup of a tribe, especially in Ireland.
9. Near the beginning of the story of Noah, Genesis 6.4 in the Douay-Rheims Bible reads, "Now giants were upon the earth in those days, for after the sons of God went in to the daughters of men and they brought forth children, these are the mighty men of old, men of renown."
1. The rune-markings (Old English *run-stafas*) were a system of writing developed by early Germanic tribes before the introduction of Latin letters following the tribes' conversion to Christianity. In some contexts runes also had associations with mystery, counsel, and magic.

was born to distinction. Beowulf, my friend,
your fame has gone far and wide,
you are known everywhere. In all things you are
                              even-tempered,   1705
prudent and resolute. So I stand firm by the promise of
                                    friendship
we exchanged before. Forever you will be
your people's mainstay and your own warriors'
helping hand.
            Heremod was different,
the way he behaved to Ecgwela's sons.   1710
His rise in the world brought little joy
to the Danish people, only death and destruction.
He vented his rage on men he caroused with,
killed his own comrades, a pariah king,
who cut himself off from his own kind,   1715
even though Almighty God had made him
eminent and powerful and marked him from the start
for a happy life. But a change happened,
he grew bloodthirsty, gave no more rings
to honor the Danes. He suffered in the end   1720
for having plagued his people for so long:
his life lost happiness.
                    So learn from this
and understand true values. I who tell you
have wintered into wisdom.
                            It is a great wonder
how Almighty God in His magnificence   1725
favors our race with rank and scope
and the gift of wisdom; His sway is wide.
Sometimes He allows the mind of a man
of distinguished birth to follow its bent,
grants him fulfillment and felicity on earth   1730
and forts to command in his own country.
He permits him to lord it in many lands
until the man in his unthinkingness
forgets that it will ever end for him.
He indulges his desires; illness and old age   1735
mean nothing to him; his mind is untroubled
by envy or malice or the thought of enemies
with their hate-honed swords. The whole world
conforms to his will, he is kept from the worst
until an element of overweening   1740
enters him and takes hold
while the soul's guard, its sentry, drowses,

grown too distracted. A killer stalks him,
an archer who draws a deadly bow.
And then the man is hit in the heart,   1745
the arrow flies beneath his defenses,
the devious promptings of the demon start.
His old possessions seem paltry to him now.
He covets and resents; dishonors custom
and bestows no gold; and because of good things   1750
that the Heavenly Powers gave him in the past
he ignores the shape of things to come.
Then finally the end arrives
when the body he was lent collapses and falls
prey to its death; ancestral possessions   1755
and the goods he hoarded are inherited by another
who lets them go with a liberal hand.
    "O flower of warriors, beware of that trap.
Choose, dear Beowulf, the better part,
eternal rewards. Do not give way to pride.   1760
For a brief while your strength is in bloom
but it fades quickly; and soon there will follow
illness or the sword to lay you low,
or a sudden fire or surge of water
or jabbing blade or javelin from the air   1765
or repellent age. Your piercing eye
will dim and darken; and death will arrive,
dear warrior, to sweep you away.
    "Just so I ruled the Ring-Danes' country
for fifty years, defended them in wartime   1770
with spear and sword against constant assaults
by many tribes: I came to believe
my enemies had faded from the face of the earth.
Still, what happened was a hard reversal
from bliss to grief. Grendel struck   1775
after lying in wait. He laid waste to the land
and from that moment my mind was in dread
of his depredations. So I praise God
in His heavenly glory that I lived to behold
this head dripping blood and that after such harrowing   1780
I can look upon it in triumph at last.
Take your place, then, with pride and pleasure,
and move to the feast. Tomorrow morning
our treasure will be shared and showered upon you."
    The Geat was elated and gladly obeyed   1785
the old man's bidding; he sat on the bench.
And soon all was restored, the same as before.

Happiness came back, the hall was thronged,
and a banquet set forth; black night fell
and covered them in darkness.
                        Then the company rose   1790
for the old campaigner: the gray-haired prince
was ready for bed. And a need for rest
came over the brave shield-bearing Geat.
He was a weary seafarer, far from home,
so immediately a house-guard guided him out,   1795
one whose office entailed looking after
whatever a thane on the road in those days
might need or require. It was noble courtesy.

[Beowulf Returns Home]

That great heart rested. The hall towered,
gold-shingled and gabled, and the guest slept in it   1800
until the black raven with raucous glee
announced heaven's joy, and a hurry of brightness
overran the shadows. Warriors rose quickly,
impatient to be off: their own country
was beckoning the nobles; and the bold voyager   1805
longed to be aboard his distant boat.
Then that stalwart fighter ordered Hrunting
to be brought to Unferth, and bade Unferth
take the sword and thanked him for lending it.
He said he had found it a friend in battle   1810
and a powerful help; he put no blame
on the blade's cutting edge. He was a considerate man.
    And there the warriors stood in their war-gear,
eager to go, while their honored lord
approached the platform where the other sat.   1815
The undaunted hero addressed Hrothgar.
Beowulf, son of Ecgtheow, spoke:
"Now we who crossed the wide sea
have to inform you that we feel a desire
to return to Hygelac. Here we have been welcomed   1820
and thoroughly entertained. You have treated us well.
If there is any favor on earth I can perform
beyond deeds of arms I have done already,
anything that would merit your affections more,
I shall act, my lord, with alacrity.   1825
If ever I hear from across the ocean
that people on your borders are threatening battle

as attackers have done from time to time,
I shall land with a thousand thanes at my back
to help your cause. Hygelac may be young   1830
to rule a nation, but this much I know
about the king of the Geats: he will come to my aid
and want to support me by word and action
in your hour of need, when honor dictates
that I raise a hedge of spears around you.   1835
Then if Hrethric should think about traveling
as a king's son to the court of the Geats,
he will find many friends. Foreign places
yield more to one who is himself worth meeting."
    Hrothgar spoke and answered him: 1840
"The Lord in his wisdom sent you those words
and they came from the heart. I have never heard
so young a man make truer observations.
You are strong in body and mature in mind,
impressive in speech. If it should come to pass   1845
that Hrethel's descendant² dies beneath a spear,
if deadly battle or the sword blade or disease
fells the prince who guards your people
and you are still alive, then I firmly believe
the seafaring Geats won't find a man   1850
worthier of acclaim as their king and defender
than you, if only you would undertake
the lordship of your homeland. My liking for you
deepens with time, dear Beowulf.
What you have done is to draw two peoples,   1855
the Geat nation and us neighboring Danes,
into shared peace and a pact of friendship
in spite of hatreds we have harbored in the past.
For as long as I rule this far-flung land
treasures will change hands and each side will treat   1860
the other with gifts; across the gannet's bath,
over the broad sea, whorled prows will bring
presents and tokens. I know your people
are beyond reproach in every respect,
steadfast in the old way with friend or foe."   1865
    Then the earls' defender furnished the hero
with twelve treasures and told him to set out,
sail with those gifts safely home
to the people he loved, but to return promptly.
And so the good and gray-haired Dane,   1870

---

2. I.e., Hygelac.

that highborn king, kissed Beowulf
and embraced his neck, then broke down
in sudden tears. Two forebodings
disturbed him in his wisdom, but one was stronger:
nevermore would they meet each other   1875
face to face. And such was his affection
that he could not help being overcome:
his fondness for the man was so deep-founded,
it warmed his heart and wound the heartstrings
tight in his breast.
             The embrace ended   1880
and Beowulf, glorious in his gold regalia,
stepped the green earth. Straining at anchor
and ready for boarding, his boat awaited him.
So they went on their journey, and Hrothgar's generosity
was praised repeatedly. He was a peerless king   1885
until old age sapped his strength and did him
mortal harm, as it has done so many.
   Down to the waves then, dressed in the web
of their chain-mail and war-shirts the young men marched
in high spirits. The coast-guard spied them,   1890
thanes setting forth, the same as before.
His salute this time from the top of the cliff
was far from unmannerly; he galloped to meet them
and as they took ship in their shining gear,
he said how welcome they would be in Geatland.   1895
Then the broad hull was beached on the sand
to be cargoed with treasure, horses and war-gear.
The curved prow motioned; the mast stood high
above Hrothgar's riches in the loaded hold.
   The guard who had watched the boat was given   1900
a sword with gold fittings, and in future days
that present would make him a respected man
at his place on the mead-bench.
             Then the keel plunged
and shook in the sea; and they sailed from Denmark.
   Right away the mast was rigged with its sea-shawl;   1905
sail-ropes were tightened, timbers drummed
and stiff winds kept the wave-crosser
skimming ahead; as she heaved forward,
her foamy neck was fleet and buoyant,
a lapped prow loping over currents,   1910
until finally the Geats caught sight of coastline
and familiar cliffs. The keel reared up,
wind lifted it home, it hit on the land.

The harbor guard came hurrying out
to the rolling water: he had watched the offing   1915
long and hard, on the lookout for those friends.
With the anchor cables, he moored their craft
right where it had beached, in case a backwash
might catch the hull and carry it away.
Then he ordered the prince's treasure-trove   1920
to be carried ashore. It was a short step
from there to where Hrethel's son and heir,
Hygelac the gold-giver, makes his home
on a secure cliff, in the company of retainers.

The building was magnificent, the king majestic,   1925
ensconced in his hall; and although Hygd, his queen,
was young, a few short years at court,
her mind was thoughtful and her manners sure.
Haereth's daughter behaved generously
and stinted nothing when she distributed   1930
bounty to the Geats.

              Great Queen Modthryth
perpetrated terrible wrongs.[3]
If any retainer ever made bold
to look her in the face, if an eye not her lord's[4]
stared at her directly during daylight,   1935
the outcome was sealed: he was kept bound,
in hand-tightened shackles, racked, tortured
until doom was pronounced—death by the sword,
slash of blade, blood-gush, and death-qualms
in an evil display. Even a queen   1940
outstanding in beauty must not overstep like that.
A queen should weave peace, not punish the innocent
with loss of life for imagined insults.
But Hemming's kinsman[5] put a halt to her ways
and drinkers round the table had another tale: 1945
she was less of a bane to people's lives,
less cruel-minded, after she was married
to the brave Offa, a bride arrayed
in her gold finery, given away

---

3. Modthryth's excessive cruelty suggests a negative exemplum to Hygd's virtues, and the
   abruptness of the transition finds parallels elsewhere in the poem. The origins of the
   story are obscure, but they seem to combine historical legend with folk-tale motifs. By
   the end of the passage the story shifts focus to Modthryth's husband, King Offa (of the
   continental Angles), who changed her ways. It may be an oblique compliment to a later,
   Anglo-Saxon Offa, who was king of Mercia in the eighth century. Mercian genealogies
   traced their kings' lineage back to the continental Offa.
4. Either her father before her marriage or Offa afterward.
5. I.e., Offa.

by a caring father, ferried to her young prince   1950
over dim seas. In days to come
she would grace the throne and grow famous
for her good deeds and conduct of life,
her high devotion to the hero king
who was the best king, it has been said,   1955
between the two seas or anywhere else
on the face of the earth. Offa was honored
far and wide for his generous ways,
his fighting spirit and his farseeing
defense of his homeland; from him there sprang Eomer,   1960
Garmund's grandson, kinsman of Hemming,
his warriors' mainstay and master of the field.
   Heroic Beowulf and his band of men
crossed the wide strand, striding along
the sandy foreshore; the sun shone,   1965
the world's candle warmed them from the south
as they hastened to where, as they had heard,
the young king, Ongentheow's killer
and his people's protector,[6] was dispensing rings
inside his bawn. Beowulf's return   1970
was reported to Hygelac as soon as possible,
news that the captain was now in the enclosure,
his battle-brother back from the fray
alive and well, walking to the hall.
Room was quickly made, on the king's orders,   1975
and the troops filed across the cleared floor.
   After Hygelac had offered greetings
to his loyal thane in a lofty speech,
he and his kinsman, that hale survivor,
sat face to face. Haereth's daughter   1980
moved about with the mead-jug in her hand,
taking care of the company, filling the cups
that warriors held out. Then Hygelac began
to put courteous questions to his old comrade
in the high hall. He hankered to know   1985
every tale the Sea-Geats had to tell:
"How did you fare on your foreign voyage,
dear Beowulf, when you abruptly decided
to sail away across the salt water
and fight at Heorot? Did you help Hrothgar   1990

---

6. I.e., Hygelac. Ongentheow was king of the Swedish people, with whom the Geats had a long running feud. The poem circles back on a number of occasions to their battles, and one episode reveals that it was Eofor, one of Hygelac's warriors, who actually killed Ongentheow.

much in the end? Could you ease the prince
of his well-known troubles? Your undertaking
cast my spirits down, I dreaded the outcome
of your expedition and pleaded with you
long and hard to leave the killer be,[7]   1995
let the South-Danes settle their own
blood-feud with Grendel. So God be thanked
I am granted this sight of you, safe and sound."
    Beowulf, son of Ecgtheow, spoke:
"What happened, Lord Hygelac, is hardly a secret   2000
any more among men in this world—
myself and Grendel coming to grips
on the very spot where he visited destruction
on the Victory-Shieldings and violated
life and limb, losses I avenged   2005
so no earthly offspring of Grendel's
need ever boast of that bout before dawn,
no matter how long the last of his evil
family survives.
             When I first landed
I hastened to the ring-hall and saluted Hrothgar.   2010
Once he discovered why I had come,
the son of Halfdane sent me immediately
to sit with his own sons on the bench.
It was a happy gathering. In my whole life
I have never seen mead enjoyed more   2015
in any hall on earth. Sometimes the queen
herself appeared, peace-pledge between nations,
to hearten the young ones and hand out
a torque to a warrior, then take her place.
Sometimes Hrothgar's daughter distributed   2020
ale to older ranks, in order on the benches:
I heard the company call her Freawaru
as she made her rounds, presenting men
with the gem-studded bowl, young bride-to-be
to the gracious Ingeld,[8] in her gold-trimmed attire.   2025
The friend of the Shieldings favors her betrothal:
the guardian of the kingdom sees good in it
and hopes this woman will heal old wounds

7. Note the discrepancy between what Hygelac recalls here and what Beowulf tells Hroth-
   gar at lines 415–18.
8. King of a rival tribe called the Heatho-Bards. Ingeld's father, Froda, was killed by the
   Danes. Beowulf's speculative account here amounts to a prophecy that Freawaru's mar-
   riage to Ingeld will never resolve the deep-seated animosity between the two tribes. See
   p. 5, n. 8.

and grievous feuds.
             But generally the spear
is prompt to retaliate when a prince is killed,   2030
no matter how admirable the bride may be.
    "Think how the Heatho-Bards are bound to feel,
their lord, Ingeld, and his loyal thanes,
when he walks in with that woman to the feast:
Danes are at the table, being entertained,   2035
honored guests in glittering regalia,
burnished ring-mail that was their hosts' birthright,
looted when the Heatho-Bards could no longer wield
their weapons in the shield-clash, when they went down
with their beloved comrades and forfeited their lives.   2040
Then an old spearman will speak while they are drinking,
having glimpsed some heirloom that brings alive
memories of the massacre; his mood will darken
and heart-stricken, in the stress of his emotion,
he will begin to test a young man's temper   2045
and stir up trouble, starting like this:
'Now, my friend, don't you recognize
your father's sword, his favorite weapon,
the one he wore when he went out in his war-mask
to face the Danes on that final day?   2050
After Withergeld[9] died and his men were doomed,
the Shieldings quickly claimed the field;
and now here's a son of one or other
of those same killers coming through our hall
overbearing us, mouthing boasts,   2055
and rigged in armor that by right is yours.'
And so he keeps on, recalling and accusing,
working things up with bitter words
until one of the lady's retainers lies
spattered in blood, split open   2060
on his father's account.[1] The killer knows
the lie of the land and escapes with his life.
Then on both sides the oath-bound lords
will break the peace, a passionate hate
will build up in Ingeld, and love for his bride   2065
will falter in him as the feud rankles.
I therefore suspect the good faith of the Heatho-Bards,
the truth of their friendship and the trustworthiness

---

9. A Heatho-Bard leader in the battle against the Danes
1. The young Heatho-Bard, goaded by the veteran, kills the Dane who is now wearing his
   dead father's armor and sword.

of their alliance with the Danes.

But now, my lord,
I shall carry on with my account of Grendel,   2070
the whole story of everything that happened
in the hand-to-hand fight.

After heaven's gem
had gone mildly to earth, that maddened spirit,
the terror of those twilights, came to attack us
where we stood guard, still safe inside the hall.   2075
There deadly violence came down on Hondscio
and he fell as fate ordained, the first to perish,
rigged out for the combat. A comrade from our ranks
had come to grief in Grendel's maw:
he ate up the entire body.   2080
There was blood on his teeth, he was bloated and furious,
all roused up, yet still unready
to leave the hall empty-handed;
renowned for his might, he matched himself against me,
wildly reaching. He had this roomy pouch,[2]   2085
a strange accoutrement, intricately strung
and hung at the ready, a rare patchwork
of devilishly fitted dragon-skins.
I had done him no wrong, yet the raging demon
wanted to cram me and many another   2090
into this bag—but it was not to be
once I got to my feet in a blind fury.
It would take too long to tell how I repaid
the terror of the land for every life he took
and so won credit for you, my king,   2095
and for all your people. And although he got away
to enjoy life's sweetness for a while longer,
his right hand stayed behind him in Heorot,
evidence of his miserable overthrow
as he dived into murk on the mere bottom.   2100
    "I got lavish rewards from the lord of the Danes
for my part in the battle, beaten gold
and much else, once morning came
and we took our places at the banquet table.
There was singing and excitement: an old reciter,   2105
a carrier of stories, recalled the early days.
At times some hero made the timbered harp
tremble with sweetness, or related true

---

2. This is the only mention of Grendel's "pouch" (Old English *glof*). Its significance is
unknown, although it has associations with trolls in Germanic mythology.

and tragic happenings; at times the king
gave the proper turn to some fantastic tale,   2110
or a battle-scarred veteran, bowed with age,
would begin to remember the martial deeds
of his youth and prime and be overcome
as the past welled up in his wintry heart.
　　"We were happy there the whole day long   2115
and enjoyed our time until another night
descended upon us. Then suddenly
the vehement mother avenged her son
and wreaked destruction. Death had robbed her,
Geats had slain Grendel, so his ghastly dam   2120
struck back and with bare-faced defiance
laid a man low. Thus life departed
from the sage Aeschere, an elder wise in counsel.
But afterward, on the morning following,
the Danes could not burn the dead body   2125
nor lay the remains of the man they loved
on his funeral pyre. She had fled with the corpse
and taken refuge beneath torrents on the mountain.
It was a hard blow for Hrothgar to bear,
harder than any he had undergone before.   2130
And so the heartsore king beseeched me
in your royal name to take my chances
underwater, to win glory
and prove my worth. He promised me rewards.
Hence, as is well known, I went to my encounter   2135
with the terror-monger at the bottom of the tarn.
For a while it was hand-to-hand between us,
then blood went curling along the currents
and I beheaded Grendel's mother in the hall
with a mighty sword. I barely managed   2140
to escape with my life; my time had not yet come.
But Halfdane's heir, the shelter of those earls,
again endowed me with gifts in abundance.
　　"Thus the king acted with due custom.
I was paid and recompensed completely,   2145
given full measure and the freedom to choose
from Hrothgar's treasures by Hrothgar himself.
These, King Hygelac, I am happy to present
to you as gifts. It is still upon your grace
that all favor depends. I have few kinsmen   2150
who are close, my king, except for your kind self."
Then he ordered the boar-framed standard to be brought,
the battle-topping helmet, the mail-shirt gray as hoar-frost,

and the precious war-sword; and proceeded with his speech:
"When Hrothgar presented this war-gear to me   2155
he instructed me, my lord, to give you some account
of why it signifies his special favor.
He said it had belonged to his older brother,
King Heorogar, who had long kept it,
but that Heorogar had never bequeathed it   2160
to his son Heoroward, that worthy scion,
loyal as he was.
                    Enjoy it well."
   I heard four horses were handed over next.
Beowulf bestowed four bay steeds
to go with the armor, swift gallopers,   2165
all alike. So ought a kinsman act,
instead of plotting and planning in secret
to bring people to grief, or conspiring to arrange
the death of comrades. The warrior king
was uncle to Beowulf and honored by his nephew: 2170
each was concerned for the other's good.
   I heard he presented Hygd with a gorget,
the priceless torque that the prince's daughter,
Wealhtheow, had given him; and three horses,
supple creatures brilliantly saddled.   2175
The bright necklace would be luminous on Hygd's breast.
   Thus Beowulf bore himself with valor;
he was formidable in battle yet behaved with honor
and took no advantage; never cut down
a comrade who was drunk, kept his temper   2180
and, warrior that he was, watched and controlled
his God-sent strength and his outstanding
natural powers. He had been poorly regarded
for a long time, was taken by the Geats
for less than he was worth:[3] and their lord too   2185
had never much esteemed him in the mead-hall.
They firmly believed that he lacked force,
that the prince was a weakling; but presently
every affront to his deserving was reversed.
   The battle-famed king, bulwark of his earls,   2190
ordered a gold-chased heirloom of Hrethel's[4]
to be brought in; it was the best example
of a gem-studded sword in the Geat treasury.

---

3. No other mention is made of Beowulf's unpromising youth, which is a folk motif. It is
   inconsistent with his own account of the swimming match with Breca.
4. Hygelac's father; Beowulf's grandfather.

This he laid on Beowulf's lap
and then rewarded him with land as well,   2195
seven thousand hides; and a hall and a throne.
Both owned land by birth in that country,
ancestral grounds; but the greater right
and sway were inherited by the higher born.

[The Dragon Wakes]

A lot was to happen in later days   2200
in the fury of battle. Hygelac fell
and the shelter of Heardred's shield proved useless
against the fierce aggression of the Shylfings:[5]
ruthless swordsmen, seasoned campaigners,
they came against him and his conquering nation,   2205
and with cruel force cut him down
so that afterwards
                    the wide kingdom
reverted to Beowulf. He ruled it well
for fifty winters, grew old and wise
as warden of the land
                    until one began   2210
to dominate the dark, a dragon on the prowl
from the steep vaults of a stone-roofed barrow
where he guarded a hoard; there was a hidden passage,
unknown to men, but someone managed
to enter by it and interfere   2215
with the heathen trove. He had handled and removed
a gem-studded goblet; it gained him nothing,
though with a thief's wiles he had outwitted
the sleeping dragon. That drove him into rage,
as the people of that country would soon discover.   2220
    The intruder who broached the dragon's treasure
and moved him to wrath had never meant to.[6]
It was desperation on the part of a slave
fleeing the heavy hand of some master,
guilt-ridden and on the run,   2225

---

5. After Hygelac was killed in the raid on Frisia, his son Heardred became king of the
   Geats. The Swedish (or Shylfing) king Onela later invades and kills Heardred, after
   which Beowulf becomes king. Note the abrupt transitions in events (Beowulf becomes
   king) and time (fifty years pass). For a summary of the wars between the Swedes and
   Geats, see p. 102.
6. The manuscript folio for this passage shows extensive damage, perhaps from rainwater,
   which leaves some words completely illegible, while others have been reconstructed by
   editorial conjecture.

going to ground. But he soon began
to shake with terror; . . . . . . in shock
the wretch . . . .
. . . . panicked and ran
away with the precious   2230
metalwork. There were many other
heirlooms heaped inside the earth-house,
because long ago, with deliberate care,
some forgotten person had deposited the whole
rich inheritance of a highborn race   2235
in this ancient cache. Death had come
and taken them all in times gone by
and the only one left to tell their tale,
the last of their line, could look forward to nothing
but the same fate for himself: he foresaw that his joy   2240
in the treasure would be brief.

                    A newly constructed
barrow stood waiting, on a wide headland
close to the waves, its entryway secured.
Into it the keeper of the hoard had carried
all the goods and golden ware   2245
worth preserving. His words were few:
"Now, earth, hold what earls once held
and heroes can no more; it was mined from you first
by honorable men. My own people
have been ruined in war; one by one   2250
they went down to death, looked their last
on sweet life in the hall. I am left with nobody
to bear a sword or to burnish plated goblets,
put a sheen on the cup. The companies have departed.
The hard helmet, hasped with gold,   2255
will be stripped of its hoops; and the helmet-shiner
who should polish the metal of the war-mask sleeps;
the coat of mail that came through all fights,
through shield-collapse and cut of sword,
decays with the warrior. Nor may webbed mail   2260
range far and wide on the warlord's back
beside his mustered troops. No trembling harp,
no tuned timber, no tumbling hawk
swerving through the hall, no swift horse
pawing the courtyard. Pillage and slaughter   2265
have emptied the earth of entire peoples."
And so he mourned as he moved about the world,
deserted and alone, lamenting his unhappiness
day and night, until death's flood

brimmed up in his heart.
                              Then an old harrower of the dark   2270
happened to find the hoard open,
the burning one who hunts out barrows,
the slick-skinned dragon, threatening the night sky
with streamers of fire. People on the farms
are in dread of him. He is driven to hunt out   2275
hoards under ground, to guard heathen gold
through age-long vigils, though to little avail.
For three centuries, this scourge of the people
had stood guard on that stoutly protected
underground treasury, until the intruder   2280
unleashed its fury; he hurried to his lord
with the gold-plated cup and made his plea
to be reinstated. Then the vault was rifled,
the ring-hoard robbed, and the wretched man
had his request granted. His master gazed   2285
on that find from the past for the first time.
    When the dragon awoke, trouble flared again.
He rippled down the rock, writhing with anger
when he saw the footprints of the prowler who had stolen
too close to his dreaming head.   2290
So may a man not marked by fate
easily escape exile and woe
by the grace of God.
                              The hoard-guardian
scorched the ground as he scoured and hunted
for the trespasser who had troubled his sleep.   2295
Hot and savage, he kept circling and circling
the outside of the mound. No man appeared
in that desert waste, but he worked himself up
by imagining battle; then back in he'd go
in search of the cup, only to discover   2300
signs that someone had stumbled upon
the golden treasures. So the guardian of the mound,
the hoard-watcher, waited for the gloaming
with fierce impatience; his pent-up fury
at the loss of the vessel made him long to hit back   2305
and lash out in flames. Then, to his delight,
the day waned and he could wait no longer
behind the wall, but hurtled forth
in a fiery blaze. The first to suffer
were the people on the land, but before long   2310
it was their treasure-giver who would come to grief.
    The dragon began to belch out flames

and burn bright homesteads; there was a hot glow
that scared everyone, for the vile sky-winger
would leave nothing alive in his wake.   2315
Everywhere the havoc he wrought was in evidence.
Far and near, the Geat nation
bore the brunt of his brutal assaults
and virulent hate. Then back to the hoard
he would dart before daybreak, to hide in his den.   2320
He had swinged the land, swathed it in flame,
in fire and burning, and now he felt secure
in the vaults of his barrow; but his trust was unavailing.
    Then Beowulf was given bad news,
the hard truth: his own home,   2325
the best of buildings, had been burned to a cinder,
the throne-room of the Geats. It threw the hero
into deep anguish and darkened his mood:
the wise man thought he must have thwarted
ancient ordinance of the eternal Lord,   2330
broken His commandment. His mind was in turmoil,
unaccustomed anxiety and gloom
confused his brain; the fire-dragon
had razed the coastal region and reduced
forts and earthworks to dust and ashes,   2335
so the war-king planned and plotted his revenge.
The warriors' protector, prince of the hall-troop,
ordered a marvelous all-iron shield
from his smithy works. He well knew
that linden boards would let him down   2340
and timber burn. After many trials,
he was destined to face the end of his days,
in this mortal world, as was the dragon,
for all his long leasehold on the treasure.
    Yet the prince of the rings was too proud   2345
to line up with a large army
against the sky-plague. He had scant regard
for the dragon as a threat, no dread at all
of its courage or strength, for he had kept going
often in the past, through perils and ordeals   2350
of every sort, after he had purged
Hrothgar's hall, triumphed in Heorot
and beaten Grendel. He outgrappled the monster
and his evil kin.
                        One of his cruelest
hand-to-hand encounters had happened   2355
when Hygelac, king of the Geats, was killed

in Friesland: the people's friend and lord,
Hrethel's son, slaked a swordblade's
thirst for blood. But Beowulf's prodigious
gifts as a swimmer guaranteed his safety: 2360
he arrived at the shore, shouldering thirty
battle-dresses, the booty he had won.
There was little for the Hetware[7] to be happy about
as they shielded their faces and fighting on the ground
began in earnest. With Beowulf against them,   2365
few could hope to return home.
     Across the wide sea, desolate and alone,
the son of Ecgtheow swam back to his people.
There Hygd offered him throne and authority
as lord of the ring-hoard: with Hygelac dead,   2370
she had no belief in her son's ability
to defend their homeland against foreign invaders.
Yet there was no way the weakened nation
could get Beowulf to give in and agree
to be elevated over Heardred as his lord   2375
or to undertake the office of kingship.
But he did provide support for the prince,
honored and minded him until he matured
as the ruler of Geatland.
                              Then over sea-roads
exiles arrived, sons of Ohthere.[8]   2380
They had rebelled against the best of all
the sea-kings in Sweden, the one who held sway
in the Shylfing nation, their renowned prince,
lord of the mead-hall. That marked the end
for Hygelac's son: his hospitality   2385
was mortally rewarded with wounds from a sword
Heardred lay slaughtered and Onela returned
to the land of Sweden, leaving Beowulf
to ascend the throne, to sit in majesty
and rule over the Geats. He was a good king.   2390
     In days to come, he contrived to avenge
the fall of his prince; he befriended Eadgils
when Eadgils was friendless, aiding his cause
with weapons and warriors over the wide sea,
sending him men. The feud was settled   2395
on a comfortless campaign when he killed Onela.

7. A tribe within the larger kingdom of the Franks.
8. After Ohthere's death his brother Onela became king of the Swedes. Ohthere's sons
   Eadgils and Eanmund went into exile and found refuge with the Geats. See the sum-
   mary on p. 102.

And so the son of Ecgtheow had survived
every extreme, excelling himself
in daring and in danger, until the day arrived
when he had to come face to face with the dragon.   2400
The lord of the Geats took eleven comrades
and went in a rage to reconnoiter.
By then he had discovered the cause of the affliction
being visited on the people. The precious cup
had come to him from the hand of the finder,   2405
the one who had started all this strife
and was now added as a thirteenth to their number.
They press-ganged and compelled this poor creature
to be their guide. Against his will
he led them to the earth-vault he alone knew,   2410
an underground barrow near the sea-billows
and heaving waves, heaped inside
with exquisite metalwork. The one who stood guard
was dangerous and watchful, warden of the trove
buried under earth: no easy bargain   2415
would be made in that place by any man.
    The veteran king sat down on the cliff-top.
He wished good luck to the Geats who had shared
his hearth and his gold. He was sad at heart,
unsettled yet ready, sensing his death.   2420
His fate hovered near, unknowable but certain:
it would soon claim his coffered soul,
part life from limb. Before long
the prince's spirit would spin free from his body.
    Beowulf, son of Ecgtheow, spoke: 2425
"Many a skirmish I survived when I was young
and many times of war: I remember them well.
At seven, I was fostered out by my father,
left in the charge of my people's lord.
King Hrethel kept me and took care of me,   2430
was openhanded, behaved like a kinsman.
While I was his ward, he treated me no worse
as a wean[9] about the place than one of his own boys,
Herebeald and Haethcyn, or my own Hygelac.
For the eldest, Herebeald, an unexpected   2435
deathbed was laid out, through a brother's doing,
when Haethcyn bent his horn-tipped bow
and loosed the arrow that destroyed his life.
He shot wide and buried a shaft

9. A young child [Translator's note].

in the flesh and blood of his own brother.   2440
That offense was beyond redress, a wrongfooting
of the heart's affections; for who could avenge
the prince's life or pay his death-price?[1]
It was like the misery endured by an old man
who has lived to see his son's body   2445
swing on the gallows. He begins to keen
and weep for his boy, watching the raven
gloat where he hangs: he can be of no help.
The wisdom of age is worthless to him.
Morning after morning, he wakes to remember   2450
that his child is gone; he has no interest
in living on until another heir
is born in the hall, now that his first-born
has entered death's dominion forever.
He gazes sorrowfully at his son's dwelling,   2455
the banquet hall bereft of all delight,
the windswept hearthstone; the horsemen are sleeping,
the warriors under ground; what was is no more.
No tunes from the harp, no cheer raised in the yard.
Alone with his longing, he lies down on his bed   2460
and sings a lament; everything seems too large,
the steadings and the fields.
                         Such was the feeling
of loss endured by the lord of the Geats
after Herebeald's death. He was helplessly placed
to set to rights the wrong committed,   2465
could not punish the killer in accordance with the law
of the blood-feud, although he felt no love for him.
Heartsore, wearied, he turned away
from life's joys, chose God's light
and departed, leaving buildings and lands   2470
to his sons, as a man of substance will.
    "Then over the wide sea Swedes and Geats
battled and feuded and fought without quarter.
Hostilities broke out when Hrethel died.[2]
Ongentheow's sons were unrelenting,   2475
refusing to make peace, campaigning violently
from coast to coast, constantly setting up
terrible ambushes around Hreosnahill.
My own kith and kin avenged

---

1. Even an accidental homicide demanded vengeance or compensation, but neither option
   is open to king Hrethel because two sons were involved. Unable to act, he succumbs to
   his grief.
2. See p. 102, Phases 1 and 2.

these evil events, as everybody knows,   2480
but the price was high: one of them paid
with his life. Haethcyn, lord of the Geats,
met his fate there and fell in the battle.
Then, as I have heard, Hygelac's sword
was raised in the morning against Ongentheow,   2485
his brother's killer. When Eofor cleft
the old Swede's helmet, halved it open,
he fell, death-pale: his feud-calloused hand
could not stave off the fatal stroke.

"The treasures that Hygelac lavished on me   2490
I paid for when I fought, as fortune allowed me,
with my glittering sword. He gave me land
and the security land brings, so he had no call
to go looking for some lesser champion,
some mercenary from among the Gifthas   2495
or the Spear-Danes or the men of Sweden.
I marched ahead of him, always there
at the front of the line; and I shall fight like that
for as long as I live, as long as this sword
shall last, which has stood me in good stead   2500
late and soon, ever since I killed
Dayraven the Frank in front of the two armies.
He brought back no looted breastplate
to the Frisian king but fell in battle,
their standard-bearer, highborn and brave.   2505
No sword blade sent him to his death:
my bare hands stilled his heartbeats
and wrecked the bone-house. Now blade and hand,
sword and sword-stroke, will assay the hoard."

[Beowulf Attacks the Dragon]

Beowulf spoke, made a formal boast   2510
for the last time: "I risked my life
often when I was young. Now I am old,
but as king of the people I shall pursue this fight
for the glory of winning, if the evil one will only
abandon his earth-fort and face me in the open."   2515
Then he addressed each dear companion
one final time, those fighters in their helmets,
resolute and highborn: "I would rather not
use a weapon if I knew another way
to grapple with the dragon and make good my boast   2520

as I did against Grendel in days gone by.
But I shall be meeting molten venom
in the fire he breathes, so I go forth
in mail-shirt and shield. I won't shift a foot
when I meet the cave-guard: what occurs on the wall   2525
between the two of us will turn out as fate,
overseer of men, decides. I am resolved.
I scorn further words against this sky-borne foe.
    "Men-at-arms, remain here on the barrow,
safe in your armor, to see which one of us   2530
is better in the end at bearing wounds
in a deadly fray. This fight is not yours,
nor is it up to any man except me
to measure his strength against the monster
or to prove his worth. I shall win the gold   2535
by my courage, or else mortal combat,
doom of battle, will bear your lord away."
    Then he drew himself up beside his shield.
The fabled warrior in his war-shirt and helmet
trusted in his own strength entirely   2540
and went under the crag. No coward path.
    Hard by the rock face that hale veteran,
a good man who had gone repeatedly
into combat and danger and come through,
saw a stone arch and a gushing stream   2545
that burst from the barrow, blazing and wafting
a deadly heat. It would be hard to survive
unscathed near the hoard, to hold firm
against the dragon in those flaming depths.
Then he gave a shout. The lord of the Geats   2550
unburdened his breast and broke out
in a storm of anger. Under gray stone
his voice challenged and resounded clearly.
Hate was ignited. The hoard-guard recognized
a human voice, the time was over   2555
for peace and parleying. Pouring forth
in a hot battle-fume, the breath of the monster
burst from the rock. There was a rumble under ground.
Down there in the barrow, Beowulf the warrior
lifted his shield: the outlandish thing   2560
writhed and convulsed and viciously
turned on the king, whose keen-edged sword,
an heirloom inherited by ancient right,
was already in his hand. Roused to a fury,
each antagonist struck terror in the other.   2565

Unyielding, the lord of his people loomed
by his tall shield, sure of his ground,
while the serpent looped and unleashed itself.
Swaddled in flames, it came gliding and flexing
and racing toward its fate. Yet his shield defended   2570
the renowned leader's life and limb
for a shorter time than he meant it to:
that final day was the first time
when Beowulf fought and fate denied him
glory in battle. So the king of the Geats   2575
raised his hand and struck hard
at the enameled scales, but scarcely cut through:
the blade flashed and slashed yet the blow
was far less powerful than the hard-pressed king
had need of at that moment. The mound-keeper   2580
went into a spasm and spouted deadly flames:
when he felt the stroke, battle-fire
billowed and spewed. Beowulf was foiled
of a glorious victory. The glittering sword,
infallible before that day,   2585
failed when he unsheathed it, as it never should have.
For the son of Ecgtheow, it was no easy thing
to have to give ground like that and go
unwillingly to inhabit another home
in a place beyond; so every man must yield   2590
the leasehold of his days.
                              Before long
the fierce contenders clashed again.
The hoard-guard took heart, inhaled and swelled up
and got a new wind; he who had once ruled
was furled in fire and had to face the worst.   2595
No help or backing was to be had then
from his highborn comrades; that hand-picked troop
broke ranks and ran for their lives
to the safety of the wood. But within one heart
sorrow welled up: in a man of worth   2600
the claims of kinship cannot be denied.
    His name was Wiglaf, a son of Weohstan's,
a well-regarded Shylfing warrior
related to Aelfhere.[3] When he saw his lord

---

3. Wiglaf is said to be a Swede (Shylfing, line 2603) and a Waegmunding (line 2607), which is also Beowulf's family among the Geats. There is no problem with this dual identity if, for example, the family shifted allegiance at some point or if a marriage united families from two different tribes. Nothing else is known of Aelfhere.

tormented by the heat of his scalding helmet,   2605
he remembered the bountiful gifts bestowed on him,
how well he lived among the Waegmundings,
the freehold he inherited from his father[4] before him.
He could not hold back: one hand brandished
the yellow-timbered shield, the other drew his sword—   2610
an ancient blade that was said to have belonged
to Eanmund, the son of Ohthere, the one
Weohstan had slain when he was an exile without friends.
He carried the arms to the victim's kinfolk,
the burnished helmet, the webbed chain-mail   2615
and that relic of the giants. But Onela returned
the weapons to him, rewarded Weohstan
with Eanmund's war-gear. He ignored the blood-feud,
the fact that Eanmund was his brother's son.[5]
Weohstan kept that war-gear for a lifetime,   2620
the sword and the mail-shirt, until it was the son's turn
to follow his father and perform his part.
Then, in old age, at the end of his days
among the Weather-Geats, he bequeathed to Wiglaf
innumerable weapons.
                    And now the youth   2625
was to enter the line of battle with his lord,
his first time to be tested as a fighter.
His spirit did not break and the ancestral blade *braveness*
would keep its edge, as the dragon discovered
as soon as they came together in the combat.   2630
    Sad at heart, addressing his companions,
Wiglaf spoke wise and fluent words:
"I remember that time when mead was flowing,
how we pledged loyalty to our lord in the hall,
promised our ring-giver we would be worth our price,   2635
make good the gift of the war-gear,
those swords and helmets, as and when
his need required it. He picked us out
from the army deliberately, honored us and judged us
fit for this action, made me these lavish gifts—   2640
and all because he considered us the best
of his arms-bearing thanes. And now, although

---

4. I.e., Weohstan.
5. Because Weohstan killed King Onela's nephew Eanmund, he might have expected ret-
   ribution from a less dysfunctional family. But the Swedish royal family was already
   embroiled in a deadly power struggle, so to say that Onela "ignored the blood-feud" is
   deeply ironic: he rewarded Weohstan for removing a rival claimant to the throne. See
   p. 102, Phase 3.

he wanted this challenge to be one he'd face
by himself alone—the shepherd of our land,
a man unequaled in the quest for glory   2645
and a name for daring—now the day has come
when this lord we serve needs sound men
to give him their support. Let us go to him,
help our leader through the hot flame
and dread of the fire. As God is my witness,   2650
I would rather my body were robed in the same
burning blaze as my gold-giver's body
than go back home bearing arms.
That is unthinkable, unless we have first
slain the foe and defended the life   2655
of the prince of the Weather-Geats. I well know
the things he has done for us deserve better.
Should he alone be left exposed
to fall in battle? We must bond together,
shield and helmet, mail-shirt and sword."   2660
Then he waded the dangerous reek⁶ and went
under arms to his lord, saying only:
"Go on, dear Beowulf, do everything
you said you would when you were still young
and vowed you would never let your name and fame   2665
be dimmed while you lived. Your deeds are famous,
so stay resolute, my lord, defend your life now
with the whole of your strength. I shall stand by you."
    After those words, a wildness rose
in the dragon again and drove it to attack,   2670
heaving up fire, hunting for enemies,
the humans it loathed. Flames lapped the shield,
charred it to the boss, and the body armor
on the young warrior was useless to him.
But Wiglaf did well under the wide rim   2675
Beowulf shared with him once his own had shattered
in sparks and ashes.
                         Inspired again
by the thought of glory, the war-king threw
his whole strength behind a sword stroke
and connected with the skull. And Naegling snapped.   2680
Beowulf's ancient iron-gray sword
let him down in the fight. It was never his fortune
to be helped in combat by the cutting edge

---

6. The Old English compound *wæl-rec* literally means "slaughter-smoke." Heaney preserves
   the element "reek" even though today the primary meaning of the noun is "stench."

of weapons made of iron. When he wielded a sword,
no matter how blooded and hard-edged the blade,   2685
his hand was too strong, the stroke he dealt
(I have heard) would ruin it. He could reap no advantage.
    Then the bane of that people, the fire-breathing dragon,
was mad to attack for a third time.
When a chance came, he caught the hero   2690
in a rush of flame and clamped sharp fangs
into his neck. Beowulf's body
ran wet with his life-blood: it came welling out.
    Next thing, they say, the noble son of Weohstan
saw the king in danger at his side   2695
and displayed his inborn bravery and strength.
He left the head alone, but his fighting hand
was burned when he came to his kinsman's aid.
He lunged at the enemy lower down
so that his decorated sword sank into its belly   2700
and the flames grew weaker.
                              Once again the king
gathered his strength and drew a stabbing knife
he carried on his belt, sharpened for battle.
He stuck it deep in the dragon's flank.
Beowulf dealt it a deadly wound.   2705
They had killed the enemy, courage quelled his life;
that pair of kinsmen, partners in nobility,
had destroyed the foe. So every man should act,
be at hand when needed; but now, for the king,
this would be the last of his many labors   2710
and triumphs in the world.
                            Then the wound
dealt by the ground-burner earlier began
to scald and swell; Beowulf discovered
deadly poison suppurating inside him,
surges of nausea, and so, in his wisdom   2715
the prince realized his state and struggled
toward a seat on the rampart. He steadied his gaze
on those gigantic stones, saw how the earthwork
was braced with arches built over columns.
And now that thane unequaled for goodness   2720
with his own hands washed his lord's wounds,
swabbed the weary prince with water,
bathed him clean, unbuckled his helmet.
    Beowulf spoke: in spite of his wounds,
mortal wounds, he still spoke   2725
for he well knew his days in the world

had been lived out to the end—his allotted time
was drawing to a close, death was very near.
"Now is the time when I would have wanted
to bestow this armor on my own son,   2730
had it been my fortune to have fathered an heir
and live on in his flesh. For fifty years
I ruled this nation. No king
of any neighboring clan would dare
face me with troops, none had the power   2735
to intimidate me. I took what came,
cared for and stood by things in my keeping,
never fomented quarrels, never
swore to a lie. All this consoles me,
doomed as I am and sickening for death;   2740
because of my right ways, the Ruler of mankind
need never blame me when the breath leaves my body
for murder of kinsmen. Go now quickly,
dearest Wiglaf, under the gray stone
where the dragon is laid out, lost to his treasure;   2745
hurry to feast your eyes on the hoard.
Away you go: I want to examine
that ancient gold, gaze my fill
on those garnered jewels; my going will be easier
for having seen the treasure, a less troubled letting-go   2750
of the life and lordship I have long maintained."
      And so, I have heard, the son of Weohstan
quickly obeyed the command of his languishing
war-weary lord; he went in his chain-mail
under the rock-piled roof of the barrow,   2755
exulting in his triumph, and saw beyond the seat
a treasure-trove of astonishing richness,
wall-hangings that were a wonder to behold,
glittering gold spread across the ground,
the old dawn-scorching serpent's den   2760
packed with goblets and vessels from the past,
tarnished and corroding. Rusty helmets
all eaten away. Armbands everywhere,
artfully wrought. How easily treasure
buried in the ground, gold hidden   2765
however skillfully, can escape from any man!
      And he saw too a standard, entirely of gold,
hanging high over the hoard,
a masterpiece of filigree; it glowed with light
so he could make out the ground at his feet   2770
and inspect the valuables. Of the dragon there was no

remaining sign: the sword had dispatched him.
Then, the story goes, a certain man
plundered the hoard in that immemorial howe,[7]
filled his arms with flagons and plates,   2775
anything he wanted; and took the standard also,
most brilliant of banners.
                    Already the blade
of the old king's sharp killing-sword
had done its worst: the one who had for long
minded the hoard, hovering over gold,   2780
unleashing fire, surging forth
midnight after midnight, had been mown down.
   Wiglaf went quickly, keen to get back,
excited by the treasure. Anxiety weighed
on his brave heart—he was hoping he would find   2785
the leader of the Geats alive where he had left him
helpless, earlier, on the open ground.
   So he came to the place, carrying the treasure
and found his lord bleeding profusely,
his life at an end; again he began   2790
to swab his body. The beginnings of an utterance
broke out from the king's breast-cage.
The old lord gazed sadly at the gold.
   "To the everlasting Lord of all,
to the King of Glory, I give thanks   2795
that I behold this treasure here in front of me,
that I have been allowed to leave my people
so well endowed on the day I die.
Now that I have bartered my last breath
to own this fortune, it is up to you   2800
to look after their needs. I can hold out no longer.
Order my troop to construct a barrow
on a headland on the coast, after my pyre has cooled.
It will loom on the horizon at Hronesness[8]
and be a reminder among my people—   2805
so that in coming times crews under sail
will call it Beowulf's Barrow, as they steer
ships across the wide and shrouded waters."
   Then the king in his great-heartedness unclasped
the collar of gold from his neck and gave it   2810
to the young thane, telling him to use
it and the war-shirt and gilded helmet well.

---

7. A hollow place in the earth, a depression.
8. Literally "Whale's headland."

"You are the last of us, the only one left
of the Waegmundings. Fate swept us away,
sent my whole brave highborn clan   2815
to their final doom. Now I must follow them."
   That was the warrior's last word.
He had no more to confide. The furious heat
of the pyre would assail him. His soul fled from his breast
to its destined place among the steadfast ones.   2820

[Beowulf's Funeral]

   It was hard then on the young hero,
having to watch the one he held so dear
there on the ground, going through
his death agony. The dragon from underearth,
his nightmarish destroyer, lay destroyed as well,   2825
utterly without life. No longer would his snakefolds
ply themselves to safeguard hidden gold.
Hard-edged blades, hammered out
and keenly filed, had finished him
so that the sky-roamer lay there rigid,   2830
brought low beside the treasure-lodge.
Never again would he glitter and glide
and show himself off in midnight air,
exulting in his riches: he fell to earth
through the battle-strength in Beowulf's arm.   2835
There were few, indeed, as far as I have heard,
big and brave as they may have been,
few who would have held out if they had had to face
the outpourings of that poison-breather
or gone foraging on the ring-hall floor   2840
and found the deep barrow-dweller
on guard and awake.
                    The treasure had been won,
bought and paid for by Beowulf's death.
Both had reached the end of the road
through the life they had been lent.
                            Before long   2845
the battle-dodgers abandoned the wood,
the ones who had let down their lord earlier,
the tail-turners, ten of them together.
When he needed them most, they had made off.
Now they were ashamed and came behind shields,   2850
in their battle outfits, to where the old man lay.

They watched Wiglaf, sitting worn out,
a comrade shoulder to shoulder with his lord,
trying in vain to bring him round with water.
Much as he wanted to, there was no way   2855
he could preserve his lord's life on earth
or alter in the least the Almighty's will.
What God judged right would rule what happened
to every man, as it does to this day.
    Then a stern rebuke was bound to come   2860
from the young warrior to the ones who had been cowards.
Wiglaf, son of Weohstan, spoke
disdainfully and in disappointment:
"Anyone ready to admit the truth
will surely realize that the lord of men   2865
who showered you with gifts and gave you the armor
you are standing in—when he would distribute
helmets and mail-shirts to men on the mead-benches,
a prince treating his thanes in hall
to the best he could find, far or near—   2870
was throwing weapons uselessly away.
It would be a sad waste when the war broke out.
Beowulf had little cause to brag
about his armed guard; yet God who ordains
who wins or loses allowed him to strike   2875
with his own blade when bravery was needed.
There was little I could do to protect his life
in the heat of the fray, but I found new strength
welling up when I went to help him.
Then my sword connected and the deadly assaults   2880
of our foe grew weaker, the fire coursed
less strongly from his head. But when the worst happened
too few rallied around the prince.
    "So it is good-bye now to all you know and love
on your home ground, the open-handedness,   2885
the giving of war-swords. Every one of you
with freeholds of land, our whole nation,
will be dispossessed, once princes from beyond
get tidings of how you turned and fled
and disgraced yourselves. A warrior will sooner   2890
die than live a life of shame."
    Then he ordered the outcome of the fight to be reported
to those camped on the ridge, that crowd of retainers
who had sat all morning, sad at heart,
shield-bearers wondering about   2895
the man they loved: would this day be his last

or would he return? He told the truth
and did not balk, the rider who bore
news to the cliff-top. He addressed them all:
"Now the people's pride and love,   2900
the lord of the Geats, is laid on his deathbed,
brought down by the dragon's attack.
Beside him lies the bane of his life,
dead from knife-wounds. There was no way
Beowulf could manage to get the better   2905
of the monster with his sword. Wiglaf sits
at Beowulf's side, the son of Weohstan,
the living warrior watching by the dead,
keeping weary vigil, holding a wake
for the loved and the loathed.

                          Now war is looming   2910
over our nation, soon it will be known
to Franks and Frisians, far and wide,
that the king is gone. Hostility has been great
among the Franks since Hygelac sailed forth
at the head of a war-fleet into Friesland: 2915
there the Hetware harried and attacked
and overwhelmed him with great odds.
The leader in his war-gear was laid low,
fell among followers: that lord did not favor
his company with spoils. The Merovingian king   2920
has been an enemy to us ever since.[9]
    "Nor do I expect peace or pact-keeping
of any sort from the Swedes. Remember:
at Ravenswood Ongentheow
slaughtered Haethcyn, Hrethel's son,   2925
when the Geat people in their arrogance
first attacked the fierce Shylfings.
The return blow was quickly struck
by Ohthere's father.[1] Old and terrible,
he felled the sea-king and saved his own   2930
aged wife, the mother of Onela
and of Ohthere, bereft of her gold rings.
Then he kept hard on the heels of the foe
and drove them, leaderless, lucky to get away
in a desperate rout into Ravenswood.   2935
His army surrounded the weary remnant

---

9. The Merovingians were the royal family of the Frankish kingdom.
1. I.e., Ongentheow. The messenger traces back the animosity of the Swedes to the battle
   of Ravenswood. See p. 102.

where they nursed their wounds; all through the night
he howled threats at those huddled survivors,
promised to axe their bodies open
when dawn broke, dangle them from gallows   2940
to feed the birds. But at first light
when their spirits were lowest, relief arrived.
They heard the sound of Hygelac's horn,
his trumpet calling as he came to find them,
the hero in pursuit, at hand with troops.   2945
   "The bloody swathe that Swedes and Geats
cut through each other was everywhere.
No one could miss their murderous feuding.
Then the old man made his move,
pulled back, barred his people in: 2950
Ongentheow withdrew to higher ground.
Hygelac's pride and prowess as a fighter
were known to the earl; he had no confidence
that he could hold out against that horde of seamen,
defend his wife and the ones he loved   2955
from the shock of the attack. He retreated for shelter
behind the earthwall. Then Hygelac swooped
on the Swedes at bay, his banners swarmed
into their refuge, his Geat forces
drove forward to destroy the camp.   2960
There in his gray hairs, Ongentheow
was cornered, ringed around with swords.
And it came to pass that the king's fate
was in Eofor's hands,[2] and in his alone.
Wulf, son of Wonred, went for him in anger,   2965
split him open so that blood came spurting
from under his hair. The old hero
still did not flinch, but parried fast,
hit back with a harder stroke:
the king turned and took him on.   2970
Then Wonred's son, the brave Wulf,
could land no blow against the aged lord.
Ongentheow divided his helmet
so that he buckled and bowed his bloodied head
and dropped to the ground. But his doom held off.   2975
Though he was cut deep, he recovered again.
   "With his brother down, the undaunted Eofor,
Hygelac's thane, hefted his sword

2. Eofor's killing of Ongentheow is related more sparingly in lines 2486–89. For a summary
   of the wars between the Swedes and Geats, see p. 102.

and smashed murderously at the massive helmet
past the lifted shield. And the king collapsed,   2980
the shepherd of people was sheared of life.
Many then hurried to help Wulf,
bandaged and lifted him, now that they were left
masters of the blood-soaked battle-ground.
One warrior stripped the other,   2985
looted Ongentheow's iron mail-coat,
his hard sword-hilt, his helmet too,
and carried the graith to King Hygelac,
he accepted the prize, promised fairly
that reward would come, and kept his word.   2990
For their bravery in action, when they arrived home,
Eofor and Wulf were overloaded
by Hrethel's son, Hygelac the Geat,
with gifts of land and linked rings
that were worth a fortune. They had won glory,   2995
so there was no gainsaying his generosity.
And he gave Eofor his only daughter
to bide at home with him, an honor and a bond.
    "So this bad blood between us and the Swedes,
this vicious feud, I am convinced,   3000
is bound to revive; they will cross our borders
and attack in force when they find out
that Beowulf is dead. In days gone by
when our warriors fell and we were undefended,
he kept our coffers and our kingdom safe.   3005
He worked for the people, but as well as that
he behaved like a hero.
                    We must hurry now
to take a last look at the king
and launch him, lord and lavisher of rings,
on the funeral road. His royal pyre   3010
will melt no small amount of gold:
heaped there in a hoard, it was bought at heavy cost,
and that pile of rings he paid for at the end
with his own life will go up with the flame,
be furled in fire: treasure no follower   3015
will wear in his memory, nor lovely woman
link and attach as a torque around her neck—
but often, repeatedly, in the path of exile
they shall walk bereft, bowed under woe,
now that their leader's laugh is silenced,   3020
high spirits quenched. Many a spear
dawn-cold to the touch will be taken down

and waved on high; the swept harp
won't waken warriors, but the raven winging
darkly over the doomed will have news,   3025
tidings for the eagle of how he hoked[3] and ate,
how the wolf and he made short work of the dead."
   Such was the drift of the dire report
that gallant man delivered. He got little wrong
in what he told and predicted.
                 The whole troop   3030
rose in tears, then took their way
to the uncanny scene under Earnaness.[4]
There, on the sand, where his soul had left him,
they found him at rest, their ring-giver
from days gone by. The great man   3035
had breathed his last. Beowulf the king
had indeed met with a marvelous death.
   But what they saw first was far stranger:
the serpent on the ground, gruesome and vile,
lying facing him. The fire-dragon   3040
was scaresomely[5] burned, scorched all colors.
From head to tail, his entire length
was fifty feet. He had shimmered forth
on the night air once, then winged back
down to his den; but death owned him now,   3045
he would never enter his earth-gallery again.
Beside him stood pitchers and piled-up dishes,
silent flagons, precious swords
eaten through with rust, ranged as they had been
while they waited their thousand winters under ground.   3050
That huge cache, gold inherited
from an ancient race, was under a spell—
which meant no one was ever permitted
to enter the ring-hall unless God Himself,
mankind's Keeper, True King of Triumphs,   3055
allowed some person pleasing to Him—
and in His eyes worthy—to open the hoard.
   What came about brought to nothing
the hopes of the one who had wrongly hidden

3. Rooted about [*Translator's note*]. The gathering of the raven, the eagle, and the wolf in anticipation of a battle, where they can expect to scavenge on the dead flesh afterward, is a common motif in Germanic heroic poetry. It suggests that fate is so strong that even wild animals can sense it.
4. Literally "Eagles' headland," the place of the dragon's barrow.
5. Terrifyingly; a Hibernicism (T. P. Dolan, personal communication).

riches under the rock-face. First the dragon slew   3060
that man among men, who in turn made fierce amends
and settled the feud.[6] Famous for his deeds
a warrior may be, but it remains a mystery
where his life will end, when he may no longer
dwell in the mead-hall among his own.   3065
So it was with Beowulf, when he faced the cruelty
and cunning of the mound-guard. He himself was ignorant
of how his departure from the world would happen.
The highborn chiefs who had buried the treasure
declared it until doomsday so accursed   3070
that whoever robbed it would be guilty of wrong
and grimly punished for their transgression,
hasped in hell-bonds in heathen shrines.
Yet Beowulf's gaze at the gold treasure
when he first saw it had not been selfish.   3075
  Wiglaf, son of Weohstan, spoke:
"Often when one man follows his own will
many are hurt. This happened to us.
Nothing we advised could ever convince
the prince we loved, our land's guardian,   3080
not to vex the custodian of the gold,
let him lie where he was long accustomed,
lurk there under earth until the end of the world.
He held to his high destiny. The hoard is laid bare,
but at a grave cost; it was too cruel a fate   3085
that forced the king to that encounter.
I have been inside and seen everything
amassed in the vault. I managed to enter
although no great welcome awaited me
under the earthwall. I quickly gathered up   3090
a huge pile of the priceless treasures
handpicked from the hoard and carried them here
where the king could see them. He was still himself,
alive, aware, and in spite of his weakness
he had many requests. He wanted me to greet you   3095
and order the building of a barrow that would crown
the site of his pyre, serve as his memorial,
in a commanding position, since of all men
to have lived and thrived and lorded it on earth
his worth and due as a warrior were the greatest.   3100
Now let us again go quickly

6. The dragon gave Beowulf a mortal wound before Beowulf killed it.

and feast our eyes on that amazing fortune
heaped under the wall. I will show the way
and take you close to those coffers packed with rings
and bars of gold. Let a bier be made   3105
and got ready quickly when we come out
and then let us bring the body of our lord,
the man we loved, to where he will lodge
for a long time in the care of the Almighty."
    Then Weohstan's son, stalwart to the end,   3110
had orders given to owners of dwellings,
many people of importance in the land,
to fetch wood from far and wide
for the good man's pyre:
                 "Now shall flame consume
our leader in battle, the blaze darken   3115
round him who stood his ground in the steel-hail,
when the arrow storm shot from bowstrings
pelted the shield-wall. The shaft hit home.
Feather-fledged, it finned the barb in flight."
    Next the wise son of Weohstan   3120
called from among the king's thanes
a group of seven: he selected the best
and entered with them, the eighth of their number,
under the God-cursed roof; one raised
a lighted torch and led the way.   3125
No lots were cast for who should loot the hoard
for it was obvious to them that every bit of it
lay unprotected within the vault,
there for the taking. It was no trouble
to hurry to work and haul out   3130
the priceless store. They pitched the dragon
over the cliff-top, let tide's flow
and backwash take the treasure-minder.
Then coiled gold was loaded on a cart
in great abundance, and the gray-haired leader,   3135
the prince on his bier, borne to Hronesness.

    The Geat people built a pyre for Beowulf,
stacked and decked it until it stood foursquare,
hung with helmets, heavy war-shields
and shining armor, just as he had ordered.   3140
Then his warriors laid him in the middle of it,
mourning a lord far-famed and beloved.
On a height they kindled the hugest of all
funeral fires; fumes of woodsmoke
billowed darkly up, the blaze roared   3145
and drowned out their weeping, wind died down
and flames wrought havoc in the hot bone-house,
burning it to the core. They were disconsolate
and wailed aloud for their lord's decease.
A Great woman too sang out in grief;   3150
with hair bound up, she unburdened herself
of her worst fears, a wild litany
of nightmare and lament: her nation invaded,
enemies on the rampage, bodies in piles,
slavery and abasement. Heaven swallowed the smoke.   3155
    Then the Geat people began to construct
a mound on a headland, high and imposing,
a marker that sailors could see from far away,
and in ten days they had done the work.
It was their hero's memorial; what remained from the fire   3160
they housed inside it, behind a wall
as worthy of him as their workmanship could make it.
And they buried torques in the barrow, and jewels
and a trove of such things as trespassing men
had once dared to drag from the hoard.   3165
They let the ground keep that ancestral treasure,
gold under gravel, gone to earth,
as useless to men now as it ever was.
Then twelve warriors rode around the tomb,
chieftains' sons, champions in battle,   3170
all of them distraught, chanting in dirges,
mourning his loss as a man and a king.
They extolled his heroic nature and exploits
and gave thanks for his greatness; which was the proper thing,
for a man should praise a prince whom he holds dear   3175
and cherish his memory when that moment comes
when he has to be convoyed from his bodily home.
So the Geat people, his hearth-companions,
sorrowed for the lord who had been laid low.
They said that of all the kings upon earth   3180
he was the man most gracious and fair-minded,
kindest to his people and keenest to win fame.

Him ðā gegiredan   Gēata lēode
ād on corðan   unwāclicne
helmum behongen   hilde-bordum,
beorhtum byrnum   swā hē bēna wæs.   3140
Ālegdon ðā tōmiddes   mærne þēoden
hæleð hīofende   hlāford lēofne.
Ongunnon þā on beorge   bæl-fýra mæst
wigend weccan;   wudu-rec astah
sweart ofer swioðole   swōgende lēg   3145
wōpe bewunden   —wind-blond gelæg—
oð þæt hē ðā bān-hūs   gebrocen hæfde
hāt on hreðre.   Higum unrōte
mōd-ceare mændon   mon-dryhtnes cwealm.
Swylce giōmor-gyd   Gēatisc mēowle   3150
æfter Bīowulfe   bunden-heorde
song sorg-cearig   sæde geneahhe
þæt hīo hyre hearm dagas   hearde ondrēde
wælfylla worn,   wigendes egesan,
hýnðo ond hæft-nýd.   Heofon rēce swealg.   3155
   Geworhton ðā   Wedra lēode
hlǣw on hliðe,   se wæs hēah ond brād,
wǣg-līðendum   wīde gesýne,
ond betimbredon   on týn dagum
beadu-rōfes bēcn,   bronda lāfe   3160
wealle beworhton   swā hyt weorðlicost
fore-snotre men   findan mihton.
Hī on beorg dydon   bēg ond siglu,
eall swylce hyrsta   swylce on horde ǣr
nīð-hēdige men   genumen hæfdon.   3165
Forlēton eorla gestrēon   eorðan healdan
gold on grēote,   þǣr hit nū gēn lifað
eldum swā unnyt   swā hit ǣror wæs.
Þā ymbe hlǣw riodan   hilde-dīore
æþelinga bearn   ealra twelfe,   3170
woldon ceare cwīðan   ond kyning mǣnan,
word-gyd wrecan   ond ymb wer sprecan.
Eahtodan eorlscipe   ond his ellen-weorc
duguðum dēmdon,   swā hit gedēfe bið
þæt mon his wine-dryhten   wordum herge,   3175
ferhðum frēoge   þonne hē forð scile
of līc-haman   lǣded weorðan.
Swā begnornodon   Gēata lēode
hlāfordes hryre   heorð-genēatas.
Cwǣdon þæt hē wǣre   wyruld-cyninga   3180
manna mildust   ond mon-ðwǣrust,
lēodum līðost   ond lof-geornost.

CONTEXTS

BRUCE MITCHELL AND FRED C. ROBINSON

The *Beowulf* Manuscript[†]

§1 *Beowulf* is preserved in a single manuscript in the British Library in London. Since the early seventeenth century it has been known as MS Cotton Vitellius A. xv,[1] or, more informally, simply as 'the *Beowulf* manuscript'. Since the vast majority of Old English manuscripts perished during the Anglo-Saxon period and in the centuries immediately following, it is by lucky chance that this one is still extant. There may once have been many copies of the poem, but only Cotton Vitellius A. xv survives. Palaeographers have determined from characteristics of the scribal hands that wrote the text that the manuscript was copied down in the late tenth century or perhaps the first decade of the eleventh.

§2 Originally the poem *Beowulf* seems to have been the last in a series of narratives about wondrous creatures gathered together to make the book that is Cotton Vitellius A. xv. The first text in the manuscript is a fragmentary homily on St. Christopher in Old English prose. The saint is said to have been twelve fathoms tall and is in other respects quite out of the ordinary, and so he qualifies as a wondrous creature. *The Wonders of the East* and a putative *Letter of Alexander to Aristotle*, both also in Old English prose, follow. Like *The Passion of St. Christopher* these are translations of Latin texts which tell of marvellous creatures and places. *Beowulf* follows *Alexander's Letter*, and the last leaf of *Beowulf* is scuffed in a way that suggests that it was for a time the final page in the collection of narratives. But a fragment of another vernacular poem on the apocryphal Old Testament heroine Judith has been added to the collection following *Beowulf*. It is written by the same scribe who wrote the last portion of *Beowulf*, and so these five texts would appear to have been gathered together in the scriptorium where they were copied out. We may say, then, that *Beowulf* is preserved

---

† From *Beowulf: An Edition*, ed. Bruce Mitchell and Fred C. Robinson (London: Blackwell, 1998), pp. 3–6. Reprinted with the permission of John Wiley & Sons, Inc.

1. 'Cotton' is the name of the collector, Sir Robert Bruce Cotton (1571–1631), who owned and named the manuscript. Cotton kept his manuscripts in bookcases, each of which had a bust of a Roman emperor (or other notable) on top of it. The *Beowulf* manuscript was kept on shelf A of the bookcase surmounted by a bust of Emperor Vitellius. It was the fifteenth book (xv) on shelf A. This volume actually comprises two separate and unrelated manuscripts, *Beowulf* and the four texts accompanying it (all written at about the same period) and a completely unrelated twelfth-century manuscript which Cotton had bound together with it. When one examines the volume in the British Library, it is the later manuscript, beginning with an Old English version of the *Soliloquies* of St. Augustine, that one encounters first, the *Beowulf* manuscript beginning only some ninety leaves into the volume.

in a book containing texts about marvellous creatures combined with a narrative about a heroic woman saving her nation in Old Testament times. Taking note of the contents of the manuscript in which *Beowulf* is found provides us with just about the only context we have for judging what the poem may have meant to its original audience—i.e. it was one of a group of stories about men and monsters.[2]

§3 What do we know about the history of this manuscript? Before it came to rest in the British Library, where it is now displayed as a chief treasure of the English nation, the *Beowulf* manuscript belonged to Sir Robert Bruce Cotton (1571–1631), who kept his library in a building ominously named Ashburnam House. Fire swept through the library in 1731, and the *Beowulf* manuscript was badly singed * * *. Before Cotton owned the manuscript, it had passed through the hands of Lawrence Nowell, a sixteenth-century antiquary who signed his name on the first surviving leaf of the St. Christopher homily, dating the signature 1563. Nowell or a contemporary also wrote the word *feared* (i.e. 'terrified' in sixteenth-century English) over the Old English word *egsode* in 1.6 of *Beowulf*, thus showing that this part of the text was being read with understanding at this time. Before the manuscript came into Nowell's possession it had probably lain in a monastic library since monastic libraries are where most of the manuscripts from Anglo-Saxon England reposed between 1066 and the Reformation. We know that during this period someone took an interest in the *Beowulf* manuscript, for two readers have scribbled a few Middle English translations (or 'modernizations') of Old English words in the interlinear spaces of *The Wonders of the East*. We know nothing about the manuscript's history before this time. Some, it is true, have speculated that *Beowulf* II. 1357–76 was a source for a somewhat similarly phrased description of hell by a tenth-century homilist,[3] but it is hazardous to assume a direct connection between two similar passages when so much has been lost.

§4 We may be sure that Cotton Vitellius A. xv is not an author's holograph but rather a scribe's copy made from a pre-existing exemplar. Wax tablets rather than vellum and ink would have been what an author would probably use to compose a text, but aside from this there are numerous indications in the manuscript that it

---

2. Andy Orchard, *Pride and Prodigies: Studies in the Monsters of the Beowulf-Manuscript* (Cambridge, 1995) provides a discussion of the monster-theme of Cotton Vitellius A. xv together with text and translations of *The Wonders of the East* and *The Letter of Alexander to Aristotle*.
3. Richard Morris, ed., *The Blickling Homilies*, Early English Text Society o.s. 58, 63, 73 (London, 1880), pp. 208–10.

is a copy of a copy. Two different scribes wrote out the texts. Scribe A copied *St. Christopher, The Wonders of the East, Alexander's Letter,* and ll. 1–1939 (through the word *scyran*) of *Beowulf.* The remainder of *Beowulf* and all of *Judith* are written in the hand of scribe B.* * * In copying texts scribes were free to follow the spelling of their exemplar or to adapt the spelling to their own habitual practice as they liked. The two scribes of *Beowulf* show different spelling habits in some respects * * *, but they are not very different. It is important to note that their spelling habits change from text to text. Thus scribe B's habit of writing *io* for *eo* is characteristic only of his copying of *Beowulf*; in *Judith* he writes *eo*. This suggests that the *io* spellings were characteristic of his exemplar of *Beowulf* but not of his exemplar of *Judith*. Similarly scribes A and B both frequently use the abbreviation *þōn* for *þonne,* but this abbreviation never occurs in the first two texts copied by A and it occurs only once each in *Alexander's Letter* and *Judith*. From this we can surmise with some confidence that the exemplar of *Beowulf* from which the scribes copied made frequent use of *þōn*. Sometimes metre tells us that the two scribes' way of writing the text of *Beowulf* could not have been the way the original text read. The contracted forms throughout the poem often suggest that our manuscript is a late copy of an earlier text * * * and the scribes' occasional tendency to substitute synonyms for original words which must be restored to provide alliteration (e.g. *hand gripe* 965, *hild plegan* 1073, *side reced* 1981) is a typical copyist's error, as are the instances where the scribes simply confuse similarly formed letters (e.g. *hetlic* 780, *mid* 976, *að* 1107, *speop* 2854, *wræce* 3060).

§ 5 Correcting scribal errors and trying to recover the reading of the poet's original text is the task of every editor of an Old English text, but the editor of *Beowulf* faces yet another challenge. In consequence of the fire that swept through Sir Robert Bruce Cotton's library in 1731, the pages of Cotton Vitellius A. xv containing *Beowulf* were badly scorched, as we have said in §3 above. Some letters of the text were burned away, and over succeeding years more crumbling of the charred edges of the pages and further loss have taken place. Lines 1–19 and 53–73 were copied down and published by Humfrey Wanley in 1705 before the fire took place,[4] and so we have these lines intact (except for *le* of *aldorlease* in l. 15, which was apparently missing before the fire). Another valuable witness to original manuscript reading now lost is the Thorkelin transcripts.

---

4. *Antiquæ Literaturæ Septentrionalis Liber Alter . . . seu Humphredi Wanleii . . . Catalogus Historico-Criticus* in George Hickes, *Linguarum Vett. Septentrionalium Thesaurus,* vol. 3 (Oxford, 1705), pp. 218–19.

Grímur Jónsson Thorkelin (1752–1829), an Icelander living in Copenhagen, began a research trip to England in 1786, and while there he hired a professional copyist to make a complete transcription of the poem *Beowulf* for him. Later Thorkelin himself made a second copy of the manuscript text of the poem. These two transcriptions survive and are of primary importance because at the time Thorkelin's copies were made the charred manuscript pages had not deteriorated as far as they have today. In 1815 Thorkelin published the first edition of *Beowulf*, using his transcripts as his source for the text. His *editio princeps* is a crude edition with many inaccuracies, but other early scholars (such as N. S. F. Grundtvig, J. M. Kemble, Frederic Madden, and Benjamin Thorpe) made careful collations of Thorkelin's edition with the manuscript, and these often provide further witnesses to the manuscript in an earlier state of preservation.[5] Eventually the progressive deterioration of the manuscript leaves was arrested in August 1845 when Sir Frederic Madden, Keeper of Manuscripts in the British Museum, had the codex rebound and the separate folios inlaid in such a way as to stop the chipping of vellum edges.[6]

* * *

Genesis 4.1–16[†]

[Cain and Abel]

And Adam knew Eve, his wife, who conceived and brought forth Cain, saying, "I have gotten a man through God." [2]And again she brought forth his brother, Abel. And Abel was a shepherd, and Cain a husbandman.

[3]And it came to pass after many days that Cain offered of the fruits of the earth gifts to the Lord. [4]Abel also offered of the firstlings of his flock and of their fat, and the Lord had respect to Abel and to his offerings. [5]But to Cain and his offerings he had no respect, and Cain was exceedingly angry, and his countenance fell.

---

5. J. R. Hall of the University of Mississippi * * * has kindly made many of his findings available for our use in preparing this edition.
6. Kevin Kiernan, *Beowulf and the Beowulf Manuscript* (New Brunswick, NJ, 1981), p. 69, n. 7.
† From *The Vulgate Bible: Douay-Rheims Translation*, Vol. 1: *The Pentateuch*, ed. Swift Edgar, Dumbarton Oaks Medieval Library (Cambridge: Harvard UP, 2010), pp. 19, 21. Copyright © 2010 by the President and Fellows of Harvard College. Reprinted by permission of the publisher. The Latin Bible, or Vulgate, was known to the medieval audience of *Beowulf*; the Douay-Rheims translation of the Old Testament into English dates from 1609.

6And the Lord said to him, "Why art thou angry? And why is thy countenance fallen? 7If thou do well, shalt thou not receive? But if ill, shall not sin forthwith be present at the door? But the lust thereof shall be under thee, and thou shalt have dominion over it."

8And Cain said to Abel, his brother, "Let us go forth abroad." And when they were in the field, Cain rose up against his brother, Abel, and slew him.

9And the Lord said to Cain, "Where is thy brother, Abel?"

And he answered, "I know not: am I my brother's keeper?"

10And he said to him, "What hast thou done? The voice of thy brother's blood crieth to me from the earth. 11Now, therefore, cursed shalt thou be upon the earth, which hath opened her mouth and received the blood of thy brother at thy hand. 12When thou shalt till it, it shall not yield to thee its fruit. A fugitive and a vagabond shalt thou be upon the earth."

13And Cain said to the Lord, "My iniquity is greater than that I may deserve pardon. 14Behold! Thou dost cast me out this day from the face of the earth, and I shall be hidden from thy face, and I shall be a vagabond and a fugitive on the earth. Every one, therefore, that findeth me shall kill me."

15And the Lord said to him, "No, it shall not be so, but whosoever shall kill Cain shall be punished sevenfold." And the Lord set a mark upon Cain that whosoever found him should not kill him.

16And Cain went out from the face of the Lord and dwelt as a fugitive on the earth at the east side of Eden.

Hall-Feasts and the Queen[†]

From an Old English Poem

A king must obtain a queen at a price, with flagons and rings. First of all, both must be generous with gift-giving. War-skills must flourish in a man, and a woman must grow to be beloved among her people, must be cheerful, keep counsel, be generous with horses and treasure; at every banquet, before the troop of warriors, she must first greet the protector of princes, put the first cup right away into the lord's hand, and she must know what advice to give for both of them as masters of the house together.

---

† "Maxims I," lines 81–92, translated by the Editor of this Norton Critical Edition from *The Anglo-Saxon Poetic Records*, Vol. 3: *The Exeter Book*, ed. G. P. Krapp and E. V. K. Dobbie (New York: Columbia UP, 1936), pp. 159–60.

Grettir the Strong and the Trollwoman[†]

from an Icelandic Saga (c. 1300–1320)

[After being declared an outlaw, Grettir steals away and assumes the name "Gest." He offers his help to a woman whose farmstead has been attacked by a trollwoman for the past two years on Christmas Eve.]

* * * [T]owards midnight [Grettir] heard a great noise, then a huge trollwoman entered the room. She was holding a trough in one hand and a big knife in the other. She looked around when she was inside and, seeing Gest lying there, made a rush for him. He leapt up to confront her, and they attacked each other ferociously and struggled for a long time in the room. She was stronger but he dodged her cleverly. They smashed everything that was in their way, even the partition which divided the room crossways. She dragged him out through the door and towards the front door, where he made a firm stand against her. She wanted to drag him outside the farmhouse, but could not manage it until they had broken down the entire doorframe and took it with them around their necks. Then she lugged him off down to the river, right up to the chasm. Gest was exhausted, but either had to brace himself or let her hurl him into it. They struggled all night and he felt he had never fought such a powerful beast before. She was pressing him so tightly to her body that he could do nothing with either of his arms except clutch at her waist. When they were on the edge of the chasm he lifted her off her feet and swung her off balance, freeing his right arm. At once he grabbed for the short-sword he was wearing, drew it, swung it at her shoulder and chopped off her right arm. He was released the moment she plunged into the chasm and under the waterfall.

Gest the visitor was left stiff and exhausted and lay on the edge of the cliff for a long time. He went back at daybreak and lay down on the bed, swollen and bruised.

When the farmer's wife came back from the mass she saw the mess in her house, went over to Gest and asked him what had happened there that everything was broken and smashed. He told her about the entire episode, and she found it remarkable and asked him his name. He told her his real name and told her to fetch the priest, saying that he wanted to talk to him. This was done.

† From "The Saga of Grettir the Strong," trans. Bernard Scudder, in *The Complete Sagas of Icelanders*, Vol. 2, ed. Viðar Hreinsson et al. (Reykjavik: Leifur Eiriksson Publishing, 1997), pp. 152–55. Reprinted by permission of Leifur Eiriksson Ltd.

When Stein the priest arrived at Sandhaugar he realised at once that it was Grettir Asmundarson who called himself Gest. The priest asked him what he thought might have happened to the men who had vanished, and Grettir said he assumed they had gone into the chasm. The priest said he could not believe his stories without seeing any proof, but Grettir said they would find out for sure later. Then the priest went home. Grettir lay in bed for many days, the farmer's wife treated him very well and Christmas went by.

According to Grettir, the trollwoman plunged into the chasm when she received her wound, but the people of Bardardal claim she turned to stone at daybreak while they were wrestling and died when he chopped off her arm, and is still standing there on the cliff, as a rock in the shape of a woman. The people who lived in the valley hid Grettir there that winter.

One day after Christmas Grettir went to Eyjardalsa, and when he saw the priest he said to him, "I notice that you don't have much faith in my accounts, so I want you to go down to the river with me and see how probable you think it is."

The priest agreed. When they reached the waterfall they saw a cave in the cliff face, which was so sheer that no one could climb it and was almost ten fathoms down to the water. They had taken a rope with them.

The priest said, "It looks way beyond what you can manage, to go down there."

Grettir replied, "There is a way, and all the greater for great men. I shall take a look at what's in the cave while you keep an eye on the rope."

The priest said it was up to him, drove a peg into the top of the cliff and piled rocks around it.

Next, Grettir looped the end of the rope around a rock and lowered it down to the water.

"How do you plan to get down there now?" asked the priest.

"I don't want to be tied to anything when I enter the waterfall," said Grettir. "I have an intuition."

Afterwards he prepared himself to set off. He took off most of his clothes and girded on his short-sword but did not take any other weapons. Then he leapt over the side of the cliff and down into the waterfall. The priest watched the soles of his feet disappear, then had no idea what had become of him. Grettir dived under the waterfall, which was no easy task because to avoid the swirling current he had to dive right down to the bottom before he could resurface on the other side. There was a ledge that he climbed onto. Behind the waterfall, where the river plunged over the side of the cliff, was a huge cave.

He entered the cave and a great log fire was burning there. Grettir saw a giant lying there, monstrous in size and terrible to behold.

When Grettir approached it, the giant snatched up a pike and swung a blow at the intruder. Known as a shafted sword, this pike was equally suited for striking or stabbing, and had a wooden shaft. Grettir returned the blow with his short-sword, striking the shaft and chopping through it. The giant tried to reach behind him for a sword that was hanging on the wall of the cave, but as he did so Grettir struck him on the breast, slicing his lower ribs and belly straight off and sending his innards gushing out into the river where they were swept away.

The priest, sitting by the rope, saw some slimy, bloodstained strands floating in the current. He panicked, convinced that Grettir was dead, abandoned the rope and went home. It was evening by then. The priest said that Grettir was certainly dead and described it as a great loss.

To turn to Grettir, he struck a few quick blows at the giant until he was dead, then went inside the cave. He lit a flame and looked around. It is not said how much treasure he found there, but people assume that it was a great hoard. He stayed there into the night, found the bones of two men and put them into a bag. Then he made his way out of the cave, swam back to the rope and shook it, expecting the priest to be there. When he realised that the priest had gone, he had to clamber up it with his hands, and finally made it to the cliff top.

Then he headed back to Eyjardalsa, went to the church porch and left the bag there, which had the bones in it and a rune-stick beautifully carved with this verse:

I entered the black chasm where
the plummeting rock face gaped
with its cold spraying mouth
at the maker of sword-showers.   *sword-showers:* battle
The plunging current pressed hard
at my breast in the trollwoman's hall;   *trollwoman's hall:* cave?
the wife of the god of poets   *wife of the god of poets:*
burdened my shoulders with her hate.   Idunn, wife of Bragi; a
                                          concealed pun on a
                                          word for "eddy"

And also this one:

The trollwoman's ugly lover
came at me from his cave,
made his long and bold
struggle with me, for certain.
I snapped his hard-edged pike
away from its shaft—my sword,
ablaze with battle, split
open his breast and black belly.

The runes also stated that Grettir had taken these bones from the cave. When the priest went to church the next morning he found the stick and all the rest, and read the runes. By then, Grettir had gone back to Sandhaugar.

Sigemund's Exploits†

During the celebrations following Beowulf's defeat of Grendel, "a traditional singer deeply schooled / in the lore of the past" (lines 868–69) recounts stories of the legendary hero Sigemund as a way to praise and flatter Beowulf. This allusive and relatively brief account in *Beowulf* suggests that the poem's early audience would be able to fill in the details of Sigemund's solo fight with a dragon and the far-ranging exploits with his son and his nephew Fitela (whose mother is Signy, Sigemund's sister). The most recent critical edition of *Beowulf* conveniently summarizes the various strands of the larger tradition.

[The exploits of Sigemund and Fitela are] fully illuminated by the 13th-century *Vǫlsunga saga*, chs. 3–8. Sigmundr, we are told, is the eldest son of King Vǫlsungr, a descendant of Óðinn. His twin sister Signý is married against her will to Siggeirr, king of Gautland. While on a visit to Siggeirr's court, Vǫlsungr and his men are treacherously slain (cf. the Finnsburg legend); his sons are taken prisoners, put in stocks in a forest, and are devoured one by one by a she-wolf. Sigmundr kills the wolf and escapes, and he and Signý separately brood over revenge. Seeing that her sons by Siggeirr are not courageous enough for the task and that only a true Vǫlsung son will be able to help in the work of revenge, Signý, impelled by a desperate resolve, disguises herself as a witch and visits her brother in the forest. He finds her attractive, sleeps with her for three nights, and when her time comes, she gives birth to a son, who is named Sinfjǫtli [Fitela]. Ten years old, the boy at his mother's bidding joins Sigmundr (who does not know until the final catastrophe that Sinfjǫtli is his son) and is trained by him in deeds of strength and hardship. "For some summers they roved far and wide through the forest and killed people for plunder"; living for a time as werewolves (eating corpses and nearly killing each other while in wolf form), they engage in "many daring exploits in King Siggeirr's territory."[1] * * * Finally Sigmundr and Sinfjǫtli take revenge

† From R. D. Fulk, Robert E. Bjork, and John D. Niles, eds., *Klaeber's Beowulf and the Fight at Finnsburg*, 4th ed., Toronto Old English Series 21 (Toronto: U of Toronto P, 2008), pp. 166–67. © University of Toronto Press 2008. Reprinted by permission of the publisher.
1. R. Finch, ed. and trans., *The Saga of the Volsungs* (London: Nelson, 1965), pp. 10, 12.

by setting fire to Siggeirr's hall. Signý voluntarily meets her death in the flames.

How far the version known to the author of *Beowulf* agreed with this part of *Vǫlsunga saga* is impossible to determine. The reference to Fitela as Siġemund's *nefa* [nephew] (881) may reflect Siġemund's own ignorance of their true relation, or the use here may be euphemistic. * * * But we do not know whether the Anglo-Saxons were acquainted with a story answering to the Sigmundr-Signý story. * * *

Siġemund's dragon fight is peculiar to *Beowulf.* It naturally suggests the far-famed dragon fight of his still greater son, [Old Norse] Sigurðr, [Middle High German] Sigfrit. * * * But there are differences between the two stories, quite apart from the greater explicitness of detail to be found in the narrative of Sigurðr's exploit. The manner of the fight itself is not, after all, the same, Siġemund's deed appearing the more genuinely heroic one because he faces the dragon, whereas Sigurðr ambushes it. Other noteworthy incidents of the *Beowulf* version are the dissolving of the dragon in its own heat (897) and the carrying away of the hoard in a boat (895). * * *

The Frisian Slaughter: Episode and Fragment[†]

Beginning on line 1070, where Heaney's verse adopts a different rhythm, Hrothgar's poet recites a legendary story as part of the celebration following Beowulf's victory over Grendel. It has traditionally been called the Finnsburg Episode, though the *Beowulf* poet calls it *Freswæl* or the Frisian Slaughter. The narrative's oblique allusiveness makes sense only if one assumes that the audience was already familiar with the story, an idea that gains some support from the survival of a fragment of another Old English poem (see below). The events concern a devastating skirmish between the followers of the Frisian king Finn and a Danish party led by Hnaef, who was in Frisia for peaceful purposes, perhaps by invitation. Hnaef had good reason to visit, because his sister Hildeburh was married to Finn. Ideally such a marriage would secure diplomatic ties between two tribes, perhaps to settle a feud but not always for that reason.[1] Sometime during the Danes' visit, a party of Jutes in the service of Finn attack them in their guest-hall and kill Hnaef. At some point Hildeburh's son (not named) is also killed. After extensive fighting and mounting casualties a truce is

---

[†] The Editor's translation printed here follows the Old English text of J. R. R. Tolkien in *Finn and Hengest*, ed. Alan Bliss (Boston: Houghton Mifflin, 1983), pp. 19–20, which indulges in some bold reconstructions.

1. Tolkien, *Finn and Hengest*, ed. Alan Bliss (Boston: Houghton Mifflin, 1983), p. 159.

called and, because winter is coming, terms are negotiated so that Hengest (now the leader of the Danes) is given a hall and his men are treated with the same privileges as Finn's. A funeral pyre is erected for Hnaef, and Hildeburh orders her Frisian son placed beside her Danish brother. When spring arrives, a sword (Heaney's "Dazzle-the-Duel" for the Old English *Hildeleoma*) is laid ceremoniously on Hengest's lap as a reminder of his duty for vengeance. Overcoming his reluctance to renew the bloodshed, Hengest capitulates and leads the Danes against the Frisians. They kill Finn, take Hildeburh, and ransack Finn's hall. Yet another, more descriptive name for the episode might be "Hildeburh's Grief," a perspective the *Beowulf* poet takes pains to emphasize.

One possible explanation for the initial attack is that Jutes in Frisia had an old score to settle with the Danes, which Finn was powerless to stop; another is that Jutes were present in the retinues of *both* the Danes and the Frisians, and an old feud between them flared up, drawing Hnaef's and Finn's men into the fighting against their better judgment and dynastic interests. The generous terms that Finn proposes suggest that he was not in favor of hostilities in the first place and wanted to bring them to an honorable end, but either scenario would explain why "Hildeburh / had little cause / to credit the Jutes." In the end the feud stirred up by the Jutes cost her not only her brother and son, but also her husband Finn. She bears the greatest grief of any, but the episode underscores the constant danger of violence erupting in an honor-bound warrior society, despite the most prudent efforts to suppress the imperative for retribution.

A single leaf from a codex once housed in the Lambeth Palace Library in London contained more lines of poetry concerning the same event. The manuscript survived long enough to be printed in 1705 but was subsequently lost.[2] Because "The Finnsburg Fragment," as it is called, lacks a beginning and end, it is unknown how long the original poem was, but its tone is different from the episode in *Beowulf*. The imagery is visually arresting. In the first lines, for example, as Hnaef looks out of the hall and spots weapons glinting in the moonlight, he uses an expanded antithesis to alert his men about the imminent attack.

*　　*　　*

The young battle-king Hnaef then spoke: "This is not the dawning in the east, nor is a dragon flying here, nor are gables of this hall burning; on the contrary deadly enemies are carrying war-gear in readiness. Carrion birds sing, the gray-coated wolf howls; spears clang, shield answers shaft. Now that this wandering moon shines under the clouds, evil deeds will arise that will inflict violence on

<hr />

2. George Hickes, ed., *Linguarum Vett. Septentrionalium Thesaurus Grammatico-criticus et Archaeologicus*, vol. 3 (Oxford, 1705).

this people. But wake up now, my warriors! Take your coats of mail, contemplate courage, grow enraged in the vanguard, be resolute!"

When many gold-trimmed valiant warriors were getting up from their sleep and buckling their sword, the noble warriors Sigeferth and Eaha advanced to the door and drew their swords, and Ordlaf and Guthlaf went to the other doors, and Hengest himself followed close behind. Yet Garulf still admonished Guthhere that he should not take such a noble life, armed, to the hall door at the first onrush, now that a stern enemy wanted to deprive him of it; but unabashedly the brave hero asked above it all who held the door. "Sigeferth is my name," he said, "I am a Secga prince, a famous adventurer; I have endured much strife, harsh battles; here one of two outcomes you wish to seek for yourself is now ordained for you."

There was the clash of deadly slaughter in the hall: the hollow shield, the body's protector, was to shatter in the hand of brave ones; the hall-floor resounded until Garulf, Guthulf's son, was the first of all the inhabitants to perish—around him the bodies of many virtuous ones. The shadowy dark-brown raven circled. Sword-gleam stood out as if all Finnsburg was aflame. I have never heard sixty victory-warriors conduct themselves better, more worthily in a conflict of men, nor did followers and war-comrades ever make a better repayment for their bright mead than his young warriors tendered to Hnaef. For five days they fought so that none of the champions fell; no, they held the doors.

Then a wounded warrior was about to pass away. He said that his chain-mail was broken through, his armor useless, and his helmet was also pierced. Right away then the people's leader asked him how the warriors endured their wounds . . .

ALCUIN

"What has Ingeld to do with Christ?"†

Shortly before the year 800 C.E., an Anglo-Saxon abbot and scholar named Alcuin wrote a letter to a Mercian bishop known to us only by his pen-name "Speratus." Alcuin was one of the foremost scholars of Western Europe and a luminary in the constellation drawn to Charlemagne's court in the late eighth century. By the time of his death (804 C.E.) he had been made abbot of the monastery in Tours, but

---

† Translation from Donald A. Bullough, "What Has Ingeld to Do with Lindisfarne?" *Anglo-Saxon England* 22 (1993): 93–125 at 124. Reprinted with the permission of Cambridge University Press. For discussion, see Fred C. Robinson, *Beowulf and the Appositive Style* (Knoxville: U of Tennessee P, 1985), pp. 8–9 and notes.

during all the years he lived on the continent he kept up a steady correspondence with religious institutions in England. Many of Alcuin's letters survive, which, like the one to Speratus, display his command of Latin rhetoric. What is of interest in the passage excerpted below, however, is Alcuin's accusation that Bishop Speratus and his retinue would listen to "pagan song" about pre-Christian Germanic heroes. The old hero specifically mentioned, Hinield, may be the same as the Ingeld who briefly figures in *Beowulf* as a Heatho-Bard betrothed to Hrothgar's daughter Freawaru. Alcuin's accusation suggests that the pagan stories continued circulating well after the Anglo-Saxons converted to Christianity. Such habits help explain how the *Beowulf* poet could make passing allusions to figures such as Sigemund, Ongentheow, Hengest, and Ingeld with some assurance that the audience would be knowledgeable enough to fill in the details. Alcuin's immediate concern, of course, is to discourage such practices as inappropriate for a bishop's household. The contrast between Christ and Ingeld is a rhetorical antithesis that the early Christian church fathers Jerome and Tertullian deployed in various ways and which they in turn probably derived from Paul: "Bear not the yoke together with unbelievers. For what participation hath justice with injustice? Or what fellowship hath light with darkness? And what concord hath Christ with Belial? Or what part hath the faithful with the unbeliever? And what agreement hath the temple of God with idols?" (II Corinthians 6:14–16). It is not known how Speratus received Alcuin's admonition, but even two hundred years later the foremost churchmen of England, Abbot Aelfric and Archbishop Wulfstan, felt compelled to renew the condemnation of listening to "heathen songs." The passage printed below includes more than the "Hinield" reference to give a sense of Alcuin's rhetorical style and his pastoral concerns.

☩   ☩   ☩

It is surely better that Christ's bishop is more praised for his performance in church than for the pomp of his banquets. What kind of praise is it that your table is loaded so high that it can hardly be lifted and yet Christ is starving at the door? Who will then be saying on the day to be feared, 'Inasmuch as you did it to one of the least of mine you did it to me'. You should certainly have in your retinue an experienced steward, to see to the care of the poor with proper concern. It is better that the poor should eat at your table than entertainers and persons of extravagant behaviour. Avoid those who engage in heavy drinking, as blessed Jerome says, 'like the pit of Hell'. There are two evils here: firstly acting against God's commandment 'Keep a watch on drunkenness and dissipation'; secondly, to seek praise for an action when it is penitence that is called for. Blessed is the man who does not look to deceptions and false enthusiasms. Splendour in dress and the continual pursuit of drunkenness are insanity: in the words of the prophet, 'Shame on you, you mighty wine-drinkers and bold men in mixing your drinks'. Whoever takes pleasure in such things will, as Solomon says, never be wise. May you be the example of all sobriety and self-control.

Let God's words be read at the episcopal dinner-table. It is right that a reader should be heard, not a harpist, patristic discourse, not pagan song. What has Hinield to do with Christ? The house is narrow and has no room for both. The Heavenly King does not wish to have communion with pagan and forgotten kings listed name by name: for the eternal King reigns in Heaven, while the forgotten pagan king wails in Hell. The voices of readers should be heard in your dwellings, not the laughing rabble in the courtyards.

*   *   *

GREGORY OF TOURS

History of the Franks[†]

[Hygelac's Raid into Frisia]

[Book 3 Chapter 1] After the death of King Clovis, his four sons Theodoric, Chlodomer, Childebert, and Lothar, inherited his kingdom and divided it equally among themselves. By then Theodoric already had a son named Theodobert, graceful and well-trained.

*   *   *

[Chapter 3] * * * [T]he Danes with their king named Hygelac [Chlochilaicus] crossed the sea in ships and attacked Gaul. Upon landing they ransacked a region of Theodoric's kingdom and took captives. After loading their ships with captives and the rest of the spoils, they were eager to return to their homeland. The king, however, remained on the shore when the ships took to the deep sea, intending to follow them later. When it was announced to Theodoric that his region had been ransacked by foreigners, he sent his son Theodobert to those areas with a strong, well-equipped army. After killing the king [Hygelac], he overwhelmed the enemy in a naval battle and restored all the spoils to the country.

[†] Translated by the Editor of this Norton Critical Edition from *Gregorii Episcopi Turonensis Libri historiarum X*, ed. B. Krusch and W. Levison (Hanover: Impensis Bibliopolis Hahniani, 1937), I.1, book 3, as printed in *Klaeber's Beowulf*, ed. Fulk et al., pp. 310–11. Hygelac's ill-fated raid is mentioned several times in *Beowulf*. Unlike other, historically dubious tales that the poet weaves into the narrative, this story is based on an event that took place around 520 C.E. and was recorded shortly thereafter by the Frankish prelate Gregory of Tours (538–94 C.E.).

WILLIAM OF MALMESBURY

[Genealogy of the Royal Family of Wessex]†

The twelfth-century historian William of Malmesbury, drawing on several sources from the Anglo-Saxon period, gives the following genealogy of Æthelwulf, king of Wessex (d. 855 C.E.). What is of interest among the list that traces the West Saxon royal family through Woden and ultimately back to Noah is the presence of several names found in *Beowulf*, such as Finn and Geat, and the sequence Beow, Sceld, and Sceaf. It also includes a short excursus on Sceaf's miraculous arrival on the shores of Denmark. In *Beowulf* it is Shield who arrives as a foundling (l. 4–52), but otherwise the two accounts are remarkably similar.

* * *

Æthelwulf was the son of Ecgberht; Ecgberht of Ealhmund; Ealhmund of Eafa; Eafa of Eoppa; Eoppa of Ingild brother of King Ine and both of them sons of Cenred; Cenred of Ceolwald; Ceolwald of Cutha; Cutha of Cuthwine; Cuthwine of Ceawlin; Ceawlin of Cynric, Cynric * * * of Cerdic, who was the first king of the West Saxons; Cerdic of Elesa; Elesa of Esla; Esla of Gewis; Gewis of Wig; Wig of Freawine; Freawine of Fredegar; Fredegar of Brond; Brond of Bældæg; Bældæg of Woden, from whom, as I have often said, are descended the kings of many nations; Woden was the son of Fridewald; Fridewald of Frealaf; Frealaf of Finn; Finn of Godwulf; Godwulf of Geat; Geat of Tetti; Tetti of Beow; Beow of Sceld; Sceld of Sceaf. (This Sceaf, they say, landed on an island in Germany called Scandza mentioned by Jordanes the historian of the Goths, as a small child in a ship without a crew, sleeping with a sheaf of wheat laid by his head, and hence was called Sheaf. The men of that country welcomed him as something miraculous and brought him up carefully, and on reaching manhood he ruled a town then called *Slaswic* but now Hedeby. The name of that region is Old Anglia, and it was from there that the Angles came to Britain; it lies between the Saxons and the Goths.) Sceaf was the son of Heremod; Heremod of Stermon; Stermon of Hathra; Hathra of Gwala; Gwala of Bedwig; Bedwig of Streph who was, they say, a son of Noah, born in the Ark.

† From *Gesta Regum Anglorum*, ed. and trans. R. A. B. Mynors, completed by R. M. Thomson and M. Winterbottom, 2 vols. (Oxford: Clarendon, 1998), bk. 2, para. 116. © Estate of R. A. B. Mynors, R. M. Thomson, and M. Winterbottom, 1998. Reprinted by permission of Oxford University Press.

On the Wars between the Swedes and the Geats[†]

Lying ominously behind the action in the last thousand lines of *Beowulf* are the long-simmering hostilities between the Geats and the Swedes. The poem's references do not follow a chronological order and are allusive enough that it is difficult for a reader today to keep the main players and events straight. The following summary by Alfred David breaks up the events into five phases.

> *Phase 1:* After the death of the Geat patriarch, King Hrethel (lines 2462–70), Ohthere and Onela, the sons of the Swedish king Ongentheow, invade Geat territory and inflict heavy casualties in a battle at Hreosnahill (lines 2472–78).
>
> *Phase 2:* The Geats invade Sweden under Haethcyn, King Hrethel's son, who has succeeded him. At the battle of Ravenswood, the Geats capture Ongentheow's queen, but Ongentheow counter-attacks, rescues the queen, and kills Haethcyn. Hygelac, Haethcyn's younger brother, arrives with reinforcements; Ongentheow is killed in savage combat with two of Hygelac's men; and the Swedes are routed (lines 2479–89 and 2922–90).
>
> *Phase 3:* Eanmund and Eadgils, the sons of Ohthere (presumably dead), are driven into exile by their uncle Onela, who is now king of the Swedes. They are given refuge by Hygelac's son Heardred, who has succeeded his father. Onela invades Geatland and kills Heardred; his retainer Weohstan kills Eanmund; and after the Swedes withdraw, Beowulf becomes king (lines 2204–8 and 2379–90).
>
> *Phase 4:* Eadgils, supported by Beowulf, invades Sweden and kills Onela (lines 2391–96).
>
> *Phase 5* can be anticipated after the events of *Beowulf*. Despite Beowulf's alliance with Eadgils, the unnamed Geatish messenger predicts that "this bad blood between us and the Swedes . . . is bound to revive" (lines 2999–3007). The Swedes will attack the Geats once they learn that Beowulf is dead.

[†] From *The Norton Anthology of English Literature*, 10th ed., Vol. A: *The Middle Ages*, ed. Stephen Greenblatt et al. (New York: Norton, 2018), p. 89, n. 6. Reprinted, with revisions, by permission of W. W. Norton & Company, Inc. See also Michael Lapidge's summary on p. 253, n. 5 of this Norton Critical Edition.

Genealogies of the Royal Families in *Beowulf*†

The Danes or Shieldings ("Shield's sons")

Shield Sheafson

Beow

Halfdane

Heorogar — Hrothgar *m.* Wealhtheow (Helming) — Halga — daughter *m.* Onela (Swede)

Hrothulf

Hrethric — Hrothmund — Freawaru *m.* Ingeld (Heatho-Bard)

The Geats

Hrethel

Herebeald — Haethcyn — Hygelac *m.* Hygd — daughter *m.* Ecgtheow

Heardred — daughter *m.* Eofor — Beowulf

Swedes or Shylfings ("Shylf's sons")

Ongentheow

Ohthere — Onela *m.* daughter of Halfdane (Dane)

Eanmund — Eadgils

† Prepared by the Editor for the first Norton Critical Edition.

The Scandinavian Setting of *Beowulf*

The Kingdoms and Tribes of *Beowulf*[†]

Many of the kingdoms mentioned in *Beowulf* can be located with some confidence; others involve educated guesses.[1] While the *Beowulf* poet probably did not have a precise knowledge of the geography of early sixth-century Scandinavia, his narrative moves with remarkable assurance among the tribes that populate it.

The poem identifies some kingdoms by several names. The **Danes** are called Bright-Danes, Spear-Danes, Ring-Danes, South-Danes, West-Danes; also the patronymic **Shieldings** ("Shield's sons"), Victory-Shieldings and Ingwins ("Ing's friends"). The **Geats** are called War-Geats, Sea-Geats, Weather-Geats.[2] And the **Swedes** are sometimes called the **Shylfings**, or "Shylf's sons." Smaller tribes can form part of larger kingdoms; Beowulf, for example, is from the Waegmunding family, under the Geatish king. Other tribes are listed below with some of the prominent characters noted in parentheses:

Angles (Offa, Eomer)
Brondings (Beanstan, Breca)
Franks—a large kingdom ruled by the Merovingians
Frisians (Folcwalda, Finn)
Gifthas—a tribe east of the Danes
Heatho-Bards (Ingeld)
Heatho-Reams—in present-day Norway
Hetware—a tribe of the Frankish kingdom (Dayraven)
Jutes—involved in the fighting during the Finn episode
Waegmundings (Beowulf, Ecgtheow, Wiglaf)
Wendel (Wulfgar)
Wulfings = Helmings (Wealhtheow)

R. D. FULK AND JOSEPH HARRIS

Beowulf's Name[‡]

Most contemporary scholars will say that Beowulf's name is probably a kenning (a native Germanic form of metaphorical periphrasis) meaning "bee-wolf," where the wolf or foe of the bee is the

---

[†] Prepared by the Editor for the first Norton Critical Edition.
1. See *Klaeber's Beowulf*, pp. xvii and li–lxvii for maps and a discussion of people and places, and Sam Newton, *The Origins of Beowulf* (Woodbridge, Suffolk: D. S. Brewer, 1993), endleaves.
2. The Old English pronunciation of Beowulf's tribe begins with a *y*-sound, roughly "YEAH-ots" run together as one syllable.
‡ Written for the first Norton Critical Edition. Reprinted by permission of the authors. For a fuller discussion, see R. D. Fulk, "The Etymology and Significance of Beowulf's Name," *Anglo-Saxon* 1 (2007): 109–36; accessible at http://mypage.iu.edu/~fulk/Name.pdf.

honey-seeking bear. This inviting explanation of the hero's rare name arose in 1910 out of Friedrich Panzer's important investigations into the links between *Beowulf*, together with its Nordic analogues, and a type of folktale he calls "the Bear's Son Tale" and connected the hero, who shows some bear-like qualities, to the Bjarki "little bear" of one of the Norse analogues. But the analysis of the elements of the name goes back to Jacob Grimm (1836, hinted at already in 1823), for whom a "bee-wolf" was a woodpecker, a figure, Grimm shows, of more dignity in early myth than modern students might expect. Before Panzer there were several other explanations of the name, some (like Panzer's) coinciding in an essentially allegorical way with the interpreter's understanding of the myth (usually a nature or seasonal myth) underlying the epic, many building on very questionable etymological bases.

The authors of this note believe that an explanation better than the standard one from Grimm via Panzer is to be sought in a normal Germanic theophoric naming-type. (A theophoric name "bears" the name of a god, e.g., Gott-fried, Gott-lieb [which Mozart changed to Amadeus], Trau-gott, Torsten [Thor + "stone"], Jesús.) By contrast names derived from kennings appear to be very scarce indeed, and no good parallel for "bee-wolf," whether meaning woodpecker or bear, has ever been offered. The first element of the hero's name, then, is not *bēo* "bee" but *Bēow*, a pre-Christian god; and the structure of this name is the same as the very common Norse *Þór-ólfr* (from Thor + wolf) or the English *Tiu-wulf* (the god Tiu + wolf, as in *Tiuwulfingaceaster*). Beow appears (in variant spellings Beaw, Beowa, Bedwig, Beowius, etc.) in the upper, divine levels of Anglo-Saxon royal genealogies. In lines 18 and 53, where Heaney and several editors print "Beow," the manuscript reads "Beowulf," a mistake easily attributable to a scribe's confusion or misinterpretation. Metrical reasons support the conclusion that the name of the god Beow once stood in these two passages, but even more conclusive is the fact that Beow/Beowulf of lines 18 and 53 occupies the same genealogical position as his namesake in the Old English king lists.[1] Outside the genealogies, forms that may or may not belong to the god Beow appear fairly frequently in place names, but only one other appearance of his name has potential relevance to the poem: in a charter (a legal description of a piece of property) of 931 a *Beowan hamm* "Beowa's enclosure" is found in the immediate vicinity of a *Grendles mere* "Grendel's lake." (The relationship between the names Beowulf and Beow cannot be reversed, i.e., Beow cannot be a short form of Beowulf as "bee-wolf" if only because the

---

1. For an example of the Old English genealogies see p. 101. See also *Klaeber's Beowulf*, ed. Fulk et al., pp. 291–93, and R. W. Chambers's *Beowulf: An Introduction*, pp. 195–204, both listed in the bibliography [*Editor*].

bee word has no -w- element and a hypocoristic "Beow" would show false division at a relatively early date.) Thus we can only have a "beewolf" at the cost of an unlikely disconnection from the Beow of the genealogies and place names and a nearly opaque name-formation.

Beow's own name coincides with the Old English common noun for "barley, grain" and has a firm Germanic etymology; in the genealogies he is a descendent of another apparent vegetation or fertility god, Scēaf (with variants), meaning "sheaf (as of wheat)." The English common noun *bēow* "barley" has its close equivalent (through regular and universally recognized phonological correspondences) in Old Norse *bygg* "barley," and so the Anglo-Saxon deity Beow is inevitably in some sense equivalent to the Norse grain god Byggvir who has a role in the mythological poem *Lokasenna*. The name of Byggvir is of the type known to linguists as a *ja*-stem, and the parent article of this note argues (in part following one of the early etymological commentators) that Beow too can be a *ja*-stem. This argument, though difficult, is crucial for reconciling the single occurrence of the name Beowulf in English outside the poem, the form *biu[u]lf* in the Durham *Liber Vitae*, an early ninth-century census of the brothers of a Northumbrian monastery. In the dialect represented by the *Liber Vitae*, the first element can only be "bee" or a *ja*-stem (or *i*-stem) form of the root of *bēow*-; in addition the *ja*-stem derivation explains some of the difficult forms in the genealogies (e.g., *Beowi* and *Bedwig*). The name of Beow/Byggvir has long been thought to be the source of the similar Finnish-Estonian barley god Pekko, and the *ja*-stem hypothesis appears to be no hindrance to this derivation, though the mythological derivation, no less than the philological one, is not uncontroversial.

"Beowulf," we believe, is not an almost unique little allegory but a *name* such as a man might bear—indeed one of the brothers at Durham did. Though rarely attested, it is constructed on a common model and is very similar to its closest parallel, the very common *Ingulf* (Ing + wolf) with variants in every Germanic language. The god Ing was, like Beow, known in a euhemerized form to the Anglo-Saxons, and Old Norse sources make it clear that he was or became a hypostasis or (like Byggvir) an adjunct of the most successful fertility god, Freyr. Historical names such as *Inguiomērus* show the same stem morphology necessary for generating Byggvir. Possibly the dearth of human names built on "Byggvir" and the rarity of them with "Beow" is to be explained by the success of names in "Ing." In any case, our aim is to fix the etymology and onomastic type of Beowulf's name, and we suspend judgment on matters of "legend history" (*Sagengeschichte*) raised by the connection with Beow (which so absorbed the early scholars) and by the removal of the name from the Bear's Son complex.

CRITICISM

J. R. R. TOLKIEN

Beowulf: The Monsters and the Critics[†]

In 1864 the Reverend Oswald Cockayne wrote of the Reverend Doctor Joseph Bosworth, Rawlinsonian Professor of Anglo-Saxon: 'I have tried to lend to others the conviction I have long entertained that Dr. Bosworth is not a man so diligent in his special walk as duly to read the books . . . which have been printed in our old English, or so-called Anglosaxon tongue. He may do very well for a professor.'[1] These words were inspired by dissatisfaction with Bosworth's dictionary, and were doubtless unfair. If Bosworth were still alive, a modern Cockayne would probably accuse him of not reading the 'literature' of his subject, the books written about the books in the so-called Anglo-Saxon tongue. The original books are nearly buried.

Of none is this so true as of *The Beowulf*, as it used to be called. I have, of course, read *The Beowulf*, as have most (but not all) of those who have criticized it. But I fear that, unworthy successor and beneficiary of Joseph Bosworth, I have not been a man so diligent in my special walk as duly to read all that has been printed on, or touching on, this poem. But I have read enough, I think, to venture the opinion that *Beowulfiana* is, while rich in many departments, specially poor in one. It is poor in criticism, criticism that is directed to the understanding of a poem as a poem. It has been said of *Beowulf* itself that its weakness lies in placing the unimportant things at the centre and the important on the outer edges. This is one of the opinions that I wish specially to consider. I think it profoundly untrue of the poem, but strikingly true of the literature about it. *Beowulf* has been used as a quarry of fact and fancy far more assiduously than it has been studied as a work of art.

It is of *Beowulf*, then, as a poem that I wish to speak; and though it may seem presumption that I should try with *swich a lewed mannes wit to pace the wisdom of an heep of lerned men*, in this department there is at least more chance for the *lewed man*. But there is so much that might still be said even under these limitations that I shall confine myself mainly to the *monsters*—Grendel and the Dragon, as they appear in what seems to me the best and most authoritative general criticism in English—and to certain considerations of the structure and conduct of the poem that arise from this theme.

† From "*Beowulf*: The Monsters and the Critics," Sir Israel Gollancz Memorial Lecture, *Proceedings of the British Academy* 22 (1936): 245–95; rpt. in "*The Monsters and the Critics" and Other Essays*, ed. Christopher Tolkien (London: HarperCollins Publishers, 2006), pp. 5–40. Copyright © The J. R. R. Tolkien Copyright Trust and the Tolkien Trust 1983. Reprinted by permission of HarperCollins Publishers Ltd.
1. *The Shrine*, p. 4.

There is an historical explanation of the state of *Beowulfiana* that I have referred to. And that explanation is important, if one would venture to criticize the critics. A sketch of the history of the subject is required. But I will here only attempt, for brevity's sake, to present my view of it allegorically. As it set out upon its adventures among the modern scholars, *Beowulf* was christened by Wanley Poesis—*Poeseos Anglo-Saxonicæ egregium exemplum*. But the fairy godmother later invited to superintend its fortunes was Historia. And she brought with her Philologia, Mythologia, Archaeologia, and Laographia.[2] Excellent ladies. But where was the child's name-sake? Poesis was usually forgotten; occasionally admitted by a side-door; sometimes dismissed upon the door-step. 'The *Beowulf*', they said, 'is hardly an affair of yours, and not in any case a protégé that you could be proud of. It is an historical document. Only as such does it interest the superior culture of today.' And it is as an historical document that it has mainly been examined and dissected. Though ideas as to the nature and quality of the history and information embedded in it have changed much since Thorkelin called it *De Danorum Rebus Gestis*, this has remained steadily true. In still recent pronouncements this view is explicit. In 1925 Professor Archibald Strong translated *Beowulf* into verse;[3] but in 1921 he had declared: '*Beowulf* is the picture of a whole civilization, of the Germania which Tacitus describes. The main interest which the poem has for us is thus not a purely literary interest. *Beowulf* is an important historical document.'[4]

I make this preliminary point, because it seems to me that the air has been clouded not only for Strong, but for other more authoritative critics, by the dust of the quarrying researchers. It may well be asked: why should we approach this, or indeed any other poem, mainly as an historical document? Such an attitude is defensible: firstly, if one is not concerned with poetry at all, but seeking information wherever it may be found; secondly, if the so-called poem contains in fact no poetry. I am not concerned with the first case. The historian's search is, of course, perfectly legitimate, even

---

2. Thus in Professor Chambers's great bibliography (in his *Beowulf: An Introduction*) we find a section, §8. Questions of Literary History, Date, and Authorship; Beowulf in the Light of History, Archaeology, Heroic Legend, Mythology, and Folklore. It is impressive, but there is no section that names Poetry. As certain of the items included show, such consideration as Poetry is accorded at all is buried unnamed in §8.

3. *Beowulf translated into modern English rhyming verse*, Constable, 1925.

4. *A Short History of English Literature*, Oxford Univ. Press, 1921, pp. 2–3. I choose this example, because it is precisely to general literary histories that we must usually turn for literary judgements on *Beowulf*. The experts in *Beowulfiana* are seldom concerned with such judgements. And it is in the highly compressed histories, such as this, that we discover what the process of digestion makes of the special 'literature' of the experts. Here is the distilled product of Research. This compendium, moreover, is competent, and written by a man who had (unlike some other authors of similar things) read the poem itself with attention.

if it does not assist criticism in general at all (for that is not its object), so long as it is not mistaken for criticism. To Professor Birger Nerman as an historian of Swedish origins *Beowulf* is doubtless an important document, but he is not writing a history of English poetry. Of the second case it may be said that to rate a poem, a thing at the least in metrical form, as mainly of historical interest should *in a literary survey* be equivalent to saying that it has no literary merits, and little more need in such a survey then be said about it. But such a judgement on *Beowulf* is false. So far from being a poem so poor that only its accidental historical interest can still recommend it, *Beowulf* is in fact so interesting as poetry, in places poetry so powerful, that this quite overshadows the historical content, and is largely independent even of the most important facts (such as the date and identity of Hygelac) that research has discovered. It is indeed a curious fact that it is one of the peculiar poetic virtues of *Beowulf* that has contributed to its own critical misfortunes. The illusion of historical truth and perspective, that has made *Beowulf* seem such an attractive quarry, is largely a product of art. The author has used an instinctive historical sense—a part indeed of the ancient English temper (and not unconnected with its reputed melancholy), of which *Beowulf* is a supreme expression; but he has used it with a poetical and not an historical object. The lovers of poetry can safely study the art, but the seekers after history must beware lest the glamour of Poesis overcome them.

Nearly all the censure, and most of the praise, that has been bestowed on *The Beowulf* has been due either to the belief that it was something that it was *not*—for example, primitive, pagan, Teutonic, an allegory (political or mythical), or most often, an epic; or to disappointment at the discovery that it was itself and not something that the scholar would have liked better—for example, a heathen heroic lay, a history of Sweden, a manual of Germanic antiquities, or a Nordic *Summa Theologica*.

I would express the whole industry in yet another allegory. A man inherited a field in which was an accumulation of old stone, part of an older hall. Of the old stone some had already been used in building the house in which he actually lived, not far from the old house of his fathers. Of the rest he took some and built a tower. But his friends coming perceived at once (without troubling to climb the steps) that these stones had formerly belonged to a more ancient building. So they pushed the tower over, with no little labour, in order to look for hidden carvings and inscriptions, or to discover whence the man's distant forefathers had obtained their building material. Some suspecting a deposit of coal under the soil began to dig for it, and forgot even the stones. They all said, 'This tower is most interesting.' But they also said (after pushing it over): 'What a

muddle it is in!' And even the man's own descendants, who might
have been expected to consider what he had been about, were heard
to murmur: 'He is such an odd fellow! Imagine his using these old
stones just to build a nonsensical tower! Why did not he restore the
old house? He had no sense of proportion.' But from the top of that
tower the man had been able to look out upon the sea.

I hope I shall show that that allegory is just—even when we con-
sider the more recent and more perceptive critics (whose concern is
in intention with literature). To reach these we must pass in rapid
flight over the heads of many decades of critics. As we do so a con-
flicting babel mounts up to us, which I can report as something after
this fashion.[5] 'Beowulf is a half-baked native epic the development
of which was killed by Latin learning; it was inspired by emulation
of Virgil, and is a product of the education that came in with Chris-
tianity; it is feeble and incompetent as a narrative; the rules of nar-
rative are cleverly observed in the manner of the learned epic; it is
the confused product of a committee of muddle-headed and prob-
ably beer-bemused Anglo-Saxons (this is a Gallic voice); it is a string
of pagan lays edited by monks; it is the work of a learned but inac-
curate Christian antiquarian; it is a work of genius, rare and sur-
prising in the period, though the genius seems to have been shown
principally in doing something much better left undone (this is a very
recent voice); it is a wild folk-tale (general chorus); it is a poem of
an aristocratic and courtly tradition (same voices); it is a hotchpotch;
it is a sociological, anthropological, archaeological document; it is a
mythical allegory (very old voices these and generally shouted down,
but not so far out as some of the newer cries); it is rude and rough; it
is a masterpiece of metrical art; it has no shape at all; it is singularly
weak in construction; it is a clever allegory of contemporary poli-
tics (old John Earle with some slight support from Mr Girvan, only
they look to different periods); its architecture is solid; it is thin and
cheap (a solemn voice); it is undeniably weighty (the same voice); it is
a national epic; it is a translation from the Danish; it was imported
by Frisian traders; it is a burden to English syllabuses; and (final
universal chorus of all voices) it is worth studying.'

It is not surprising that it should now be felt that a view, a deci-
sion, a conviction are imperatively needed. But it is plainly only in
the consideration of Beowulf as a poem, with an inherent poetic sig-
nificance, that any view or conviction can be reached or steadily
held. For it is of their nature that the jabberwocks of historical and
antiquarian research burble in the tulgy wood of conjecture, flitting

---

5. I include nothing that has not somewhere been said by someone, if not in my exact
words; but I do not, of course, attempt to represent all the *dicta*, wise or otherwise, that
have been uttered.

from one tum-tum tree to another. Noble animals, whose burbling
is on occasion good to hear; but though their eyes of flame may
sometimes prove searchlights, their range is short.

None the less, paths of a sort have been opened in the wood.
Slowly with the rolling years the obvious (so often the last revela
tion of analytic study) has been discovered: that we have to deal with
a poem by an Englishman using afresh ancient and largely tradi-
tional material. At last then, after inquiring so long whence this
material came, and what its original or aboriginal nature was (ques-
tions that cannot ever be decisively answered), we might also now
again inquire what the poet did with it. If we ask that question, then
there is still, perhaps, something lacking even in the major critics,
the learned and revered masters from whom we humbly derive.

The chief points with which I feel dissatisfied I will now approach
by way of W. P. Ker, whose name and memory I honour. He would
deserve reverence, of course, even if he still lived and had not *ellor
gehworfen on Frean wære*[6] upon a high mountain in the heart of that
Europe which he loved: a great scholar, as illuminating himself as a
critic, as he was often biting as a critic of the critics. None the less
I cannot help feeling that in approaching *Beowulf* he was hampered
by the almost inevitable weakness of his greatness: stories and plots
must sometimes have seemed triter to him, the much-read, than they
did to the old poets and their audiences. The dwarf on the spot some-
times sees things missed by the travelling giant ranging many coun-
tries. In considering a period when literature was narrower in range
and men possessed a less diversified stock of ideas and themes, one
must seek to recapture and esteem the deep pondering and profound
feeling that they gave to such as they possessed.

In any case Ker has been potent. For his criticism is masterly,
expressed always in words both pungent and weighty, and not least
so when it is (as I occasionally venture to think) itself open to criti-
cism. His words and judgements are often quoted, or reappear in
various modifications, digested, their source probably sometimes for-
gotten. It is impossible to avoid quotation of the well-known pas-
sage in his *Dark Ages*:

> A reasonable view of the merit of *Beowulf* is not impossible,
> though rash enthusiasm may have made too much of it, while
> a correct and sober taste may have too contemptuously refused
> to attend to Grendel or the Fire-drake. The fault of *Beowulf* is
> that there is nothing much in the story. The hero is occupied
> in killing monsters, like Hercules or Theseus. But there are
> other things in the lives of Hercules and Theseus besides the

6. "Turned elsewhere into the Lord's protection." Tolkien's invention, patterned after pas-
sages in *Beowulf* [Editor's translation].

lulling of the Hydra or of Procrustes. Beowulf has nothing else
to do, when he has killed Grendel and Grendel's mother in Den-
mark: he goes home to his own Gautland, until at last the roll-
ing years bring the Fire-drake and his last adventure. It is too
simple. Yet the three chief episodes are well wrought and well
diversified; they are not repetitions, exactly; there is a change
of temper between the wrestling with Grendel in the night at
Heorot and the descent under water to encounter Grendel's
mother; while the sentiment of the Dragon is different again.
But the great beauty, the real value, of Beowulf is in its dignity
of style. In construction it is curiously weak, in a sense prepos-
terous; for while the main story is simplicity itself, the merest
commonplace of heroic legend, all about it, in the historic allu-
sions, there are revelations of a whole world of tragedy, plots
different in import from that of Beowulf, more like the tragic
themes of Iceland. Yet with this radical defect, a disproportion
that puts the irrelevances in the centre and the serious things
on the outer edges, the poem of Beowulf is undeniably weighty.
The thing itself is cheap; the moral and the spirit of it can only
be matched among the noblest authors.[7]

This passage was written more than thirty years ago, but has
hardly been surpassed. It remains, in this country at any rate, a
potent influence. Yet its primary effect is to state a paradox which
one feels has always strained the belief, even of those who accepted
it, and has given to Beowulf the character of an 'enigmatic poem'.
The chief virtue of the passage (not the one for which it is usually
esteemed) is that it does accord some attention to the monsters,
despite correct and sober taste. But the contrast made between the
radical defect of theme and structure, and at the same time the dig-
nity, loftiness in converse, and well-wrought finish, has become a
commonplace even of the best criticism, a paradox the strangeness
of which has almost been forgotten in the process of swallowing it
upon authority.[8] We may compare Professor Chambers in his Wid-
sith, p. 79, where he is studying the story of Ingeld, son of Froda,

---

7. The Dark Ages, pp. 252–3.
8. None the less Ker modified it in an important particular in English Literature, Mediæval,
   pp. 29–34. In general, though in different words, vaguer and less incisive, he repeats
   himself. We are still told that 'the story is commonplace and the plan is feeble', or that
   'the story is thin and poor'. But we learn also at the end of his notice that: 'Those
   distracting allusions to things apart from the chief story make up for their want of pro-
   portion. They give the impression of reality and weight; the story is not in the air . . . it
   is part of the solid world.' By the admission of so grave an artistic reason for the proce-
   dure of the poem Ker himself began the undermining of his own criticism of its
   structure. But this line of thought does not seem to have been further pursued. Possi-
   bly it was this very thought, working in his mind, that made Ker's notice of Beowulf in
   the small later book, his 'shilling shocker', more vague and hesitant in tone, and so of
   less influence.

and his feud with the great Scylding house of Denmark, a story introduced in *Beowulf* merely as an allusion.

> Nothing [Chambers says] could better show the disproportion of *Beowulf* which 'puts the irrelevances in the centre and the serious things on the outer edges', than this passing allusion to the story of Ingeld. For in this conflict between plighted troth and the duty of revenge we have a situation which the old heroic poets loved, and would not have sold for a wilderness of dragons.

I pass over the fact that the allusion has a dramatic purpose in *Beowulf* that is a sufficient defence both of its presence and of its manner. The author of *Beowulf* cannot be held responsible for the fact that we now have only his poem and not others dealing primarily with Ingeld. He was not selling one thing for another, but giving something new. But let us return to the dragon. 'A wilderness of dragons.' There is a sting in this Shylockian plural, the sharper for coming from a critic, who deserves the title of the poet's best friend. It is in the tradition of the Book of St. Albans, from which the poet might retort upon his critics: 'Yea, a desserte of lapwyngs, a shrewednes of apes, a raffull of knaues, and a gagle of gees.'

As for the poem, one dragon, however hot, does not make a summer, or a host; and a man might well exchange for one good dragon what he would not sell for a wilderness. And dragons, real dragons, essential both to the machinery and the ideas of a poem or tale, are actually rare. In northern literature there are only *two* that are significant. If we omit from consideration the vast and vague Encircler of the World, Miðgarðsormr, the doom of the great gods and no matter for heroes, we have but the dragon of the Völsungs, Fáfnir, and Beowulf's bane. It is true that both of these are in *Beowulf*, one in the main story, and the other spoken of by a minstrel praising Beowulf himself. But this is not a wilderness of dragons. Indeed the allusion to the more renowned worm killed by the Wælsing is sufficient indication that the poet selected a dragon of well-founded purpose (or saw its significance in the plot as it had reached him), even as he was careful to compare his hero, Beowulf son of Ecgtheow, to the prince of the heroes of the North, the dragon-slaying Wælsing. He esteemed dragons, as rare as they are dire, as some do still. He liked them—as a poet, not as a sober zoologist; and he had good reason.

But we meet this kind of criticism again. In Chambers's *Beowulf and the Heroic Age*—the most significant single essay on the poem that I know—it is still present. The riddle is still unsolved. The folktale motive stands still like the spectre of old research, dead but unquiet in its grave. We are told again that the main story of *Beowulf*

is a *wild folk-tale*. Quite true, of course. It is true of the main story
of *King Lear*, unless in that case you would prefer to substitute *silly*
for *wild*. But more: we are told that the same sort of stuff is found
in Homer, yet there it is kept in its proper place. 'The folk-tale is a
good servant', Chambers says, and does not perhaps realize the
importance of the admission, made to save the face of Homer and
Virgil; for he continues: 'but a bad master: it has been allowed in
Beowulf to usurp the place of honour, and to drive into episodes and
digressions the things which should be the main stuff of a well-
conducted epic.'[9] It is not clear to me why good *conduct* must depend
on the main *stuff*. But I will for the moment remark only that, if it is
so, *Beowulf* is evidently not a well-conducted epic. It may turn out to
be no epic at all. But the puzzle still continues. In the most recent
discourse upon this theme it still appears, toned down almost to a
melancholy question-mark, as if this paradox had at last begun to
afflict with weariness the thought that endeavours to support it. In
the final peroration of his notable lecture on *Folk-tale and History in
Beowulf*, given last year, Mr. Girvan said:

> Confessedly there is matter for wonder and scope for doubt, but
> we might be able to answer with complete satisfaction some of
> the questionings which rise in men's minds over the poet's pre-
> sentment of his hero, if we could also answer with certainty the
> question why he chose just this subject, when to our modern
> judgment there were at hand so many greater, charged with the
> splendour and tragedy of humanity, and in all respects worthier
> of a genius as astonishing as it was rare in Anglo-Saxon England.

There is something irritatingly odd about all this. One even dares
to wonder if something has not gone wrong with 'our modern judge-
ment', supposing that it is justly represented. Higher praise than is
found in the learned critics, whose scholarship enables them to
appreciate these things, could hardly be given to the detail, the tone,
the style, and indeed to the total effect of *Beowulf*. Yet this poetic
talent, we are to understand, has all been squandered on an unprofit-
able theme: as if Milton had recounted the story of Jack and the
Beanstalk in noble verse. Even if Milton had done this (and he might
have done worse), we should perhaps pause to consider whether his
poetic handling had not had some effect upon the trivial theme;
what alchemy had been performed upon the base metal; whether
indeed it remained base or trivial when he had finished with it. The
high tone, the sense of dignity, alone is evidence in *Beowulf* of the
presence of a mind lofty and thoughtful. It is, one would have said,
improbable that such a man would write more than three thousand

---

9. *Foreword* to Strong's translation, p. xxvi: see note 3.

lines (wrought to a high finish) on matter that is really not worth serious attention; that remains thin and cheap when he has finished with it. Or that he should in the selection of his material, in the choice of what to put forward, what to keep subordinate 'upon the outer edges', have shown a puerile simplicity much below the level of the characters he himself draws in his own poem. Any theory that will at least allow us to believe that what he did was of design, and that for that design there is a defence that may still have force, would seem more probable.

It has been too little observed that all the machinery of 'dignity' is to be found elsewhere. Cynewulf, or the author of *Andreas*, or of *Guthlac* (most notably), have a command of dignified verse. In them there is well-wrought language, weighty words, lofty sentiment, precisely that which we are told is the real beauty of *Beowulf*. Yet it cannot, I think, be disputed, that *Beowulf* is more beautiful, that each line there is more significant (even when, as sometimes happens, it is the same line) than in the other long Old English poems. Where then resides the special virtue of *Beowulf*, if the common element (which belongs largely to the language itself, and to a literary tradition) is deducted? It resides, one might guess, in the theme, and the spirit this has infused into the whole. For, in fact, if there were a real discrepancy between theme and style, that style would not be felt as beautiful but as incongruous or false. And that incongruity is present in some measure in all the long Old English poems, save one—*Beowulf*. The paradoxical contrast that has been drawn between matter and manner in *Beowulf* has thus an inherent *literary* improbability.

Why then have the great critics thought otherwise? I must pass rather hastily over the answers to this question. The reasons are various, I think, and would take long to examine. I believe that one reason is that the shadow of research has lain upon criticism. The habit, for instance, of pondering a summarized plot of *Beowulf*, denuded of all that gives it particular force or individual life, has encouraged the notion that its main story is wild, or trivial, or typical, *even after treatment*. Yet all stories, great and small, are one or more of these three things in such nakedness. The comparison of skeleton 'plots' is simply not a critical literary process at all. It has been favoured by research in comparative folk-lore, the objects of which are primarily historical or scientific.[1] Another reason is, I

---

1. It has also been favoured by the rise of 'English schools', in whose syllabuses *Beowulf* has inevitably some place, and the consequent production of compendious literary histories. For these cater (in fact, if not in intention) for those seeking knowledge about, and ready-made judgements upon, works which they have not the time, or (often enough) the desire, to know at first hand. The small literary value of such summaries is sometimes recognized in the act of giving them. Thus Strong (op. cit.) gives a fairly complete

think, that the allusions have attracted curiosity (antiquarian rather than critical) to their elucidation; and this needs so much study and research that attention has been diverted from the poem as a whole, and from the function of the allusions, as shaped and placed, in the poetic economy of *Beowulf* as it is. Yet actually the appreciation of this function is largely independent of such investigations.

But there is also, I suppose, a real question of taste involved: a judgement that the heroic or tragic story on a strictly human plane is by nature superior. Doom is held less literary than ἁμαρτία.[2] The proposition seems to have been passed as self-evident. I dissent, even at the risk of being held incorrect or not sober. But I will not here enter into debate, nor attempt at length a defence of the mythical mode of imagination, and the disentanglement of the confusion between myth and folk-tale into which these judgements appear to have fallen. The myth has other forms than the (now discredited) mythical allegory of nature: the sun, the seasons, the sea, and such things. The term 'folk-tale' is misleading; its very tone of depreciation begs the question. Folk-tales in being, as told—for the 'typical folktale', of course, is merely an abstract conception of research nowhere existing—do often contain elements that are thin and cheap, with little even potential virtue; but they also contain much that is far more powerful, and that cannot be sharply separated from myth, being derived from it, or capable in poetic hands of turning into it: that is of becoming largely significant—as a whole, accepted unanalysed. The significance of a myth is not easily to be pinned on paper by analytical reasoning. It is at its best when it is presented by a poet who feels rather than makes explicit what his theme portends; who presents it incarnate in the world of history and geography, as our poet has done. Its defender is thus at a disadvantage: unless he is careful, and speaks in parables, he will kill what he is studying by vivisection, and he will be left with a formal or mechanical allegory, and, what is more, probably with one that will not work. For myth is alive at once and in all its parts, and dies before it can be dissected. It is possible, I think, to be moved by the power of myth and yet to misunderstand the sensation, to ascribe it wholly to something else that is also present: to metrical art, style, or verbal skill. Correct and sober taste may refuse to admit that there can be an interest for

one, but remarks that 'the short summary does scant justice to the poem'. Ker in *E. Lit.* (*Med.*) says: 'So told, in abstract, it is not a particularly interesting story.' He evidently perceived what might be the retort, for he attempts to justify the procedure in this case, adding: 'Told in this way the story of Theseus or Hercules would still have much more in it.' I dissent. But it does not matter, for the comparison of two plots 'told in this way' is no guide whatever to the merits of literary versions told in quite different ways. It is not necessarily the best poem that loses least in précis.

2. Hamartia, the Aristotelian term for a hero's tragic flaw [*Editor*].

us—the proud *we* that includes all intelligent living people—in ogres and dragons; we then perceive its puzzlement in face of the odd fact that it has derived great pleasure from a poem that is actually about these unfashionable creatures. Even though it attributes 'genius', as does Mr Girvan, to the author, it cannot admit that the monsters are anything but a sad mistake.

It does not seem plain that ancient taste supports the modern as much as it has been represented to do. I have the author of *Beowulf*, at any rate, on my side: a greater man than most of us. And I cannot myself perceive a period in the North when one kind alone was esteemed: there was room for myth and heroic legend, and for blends of these. As for the dragon: as far as we know anything about these old poets, we know this: the prince of the heroes of the North, supremely memorable— *hans nafn mun uppi meðan veröldin stendr*[3]—was a dragon-slayer. And his most renowned deed, from which in Norse he derived his title Fáfnisbani, was the slaying of the prince of legendary worms. Although there is plainly considerable difference between the later Norse and the ancient English form of the story alluded to in *Beowulf*, already there it had these two primary features: the dragon, and the slaying of him as the chief deed of the greatest of heroes—*he wæs wreccena wide mærost*.[4] A dragon is no idle fancy. Whatever may be his origins, in fact or invention, the dragon in legend is a potent creation of men's imagination, richer in significance than his barrow is in gold. Even to-day (despite the critics) you may find men not ignorant of tragic legend and history, who have heard of heroes and indeed seen them, who yet have been caught by the fascination of the worm. More than one poem in recent years (since *Beowulf* escaped somewhat from the dominion of the students of origins to the students of poetry) has been inspired by the dragon of *Beowulf*, but none that I know of by Ingeld son of Froda. Indeed, I do not think Chambers very happy in his particular choice. He gives battle on dubious ground. In so far as we can now grasp its detail and atmosphere the story of Ingeld the thrice faithless and easily persuaded is chiefly interesting as an episode in a larger theme, as part of a tradition that had acquired legendary, and so dramatically personalized, form concerning moving events in history: the arising of Denmark, and wars in the islands of the North. In itself it is not a supremely potent story. But, of course, as with all tales of any sort, its literary power must have depended mainly upon how it was handled. A poet may have made

3. "And his [Sigurd's] name will endure while the world remains," ch. 12, *The Saga of the Volsungs*, trans. Jesse L. Byock (Berkeley: U of California P, 1990), p. 54 [*Editor*].
4. "He was the most famous of exiles," *Beowulf*, lines 898–99 [*Editor's translation*].

a great thing of it. Upon this chance must be founded the popularity of Ingeld's legend in England, for which there is some evidence.[5] There is no inherent magical virtue about heroic-tragic stories as such, and apart from the merits of individual treatments. The same heroic plot can yield good and bad poems, and good and bad sagas. The recipe for the central situations of such stories, studied in the abstract, is after all as 'simple' and as 'typical' as that of folktales. There are in any case many heroes but very few good dragons.

Beowulf's dragon, if one wishes really to criticize, is not to be blamed for being a dragon, but rather for not being dragon enough, plain pure fairy-story dragon. There are in the poem some vivid touches of the right kind—as *þa se wyrm onwoc, wroht wæs geniwad; stonc æfter stane*, 2285[6]—in which this dragon is real worm, with a bestial life and thought of his own, but the conception, none the less, approaches *draconitas* rather than *draco*: a personification of malice, greed, destruction (the evil side of heroic life), and of the undiscriminating cruelty of fortune that distinguishes not good or bad (the evil aspect of all life). But for *Beowulf*, the poem, that is as it should be. In this poem the balance is nice, but it is preserved. The large symbolism is near the surface, but it does not break through, nor become allegory. Something more significant than a standard hero, a man faced with a foe more evil than any human enemy of house or realm, is before us, and yet incarnate in time, walking in heroic history, and treading the named lands of the North. And this, we are told, is the radical defect of *Beowulf*, that its author, coming in a time rich in the legends of heroic men, has used them afresh in an original fashion, giving us not just one more, but something akin yet different: a measure and interpretation of them all.

We do not deny the worth of the hero by accepting Grendel and the dragon. Let us by all means esteem the old heroes: men caught in the chains of circumstance or of their own character, torn between duties equally sacred, dying with their backs to the wall. But *Beowulf*, I fancy, plays a larger part than is recognized in helping us to esteem them. Heroic lays may have dealt in their own way—we have little enough to judge by—a way more brief and vigorous, perhaps, though perhaps also more harsh and noisy (and less thoughtful), with the actions of heroes caught in circumstances that conformed more or less to the varied but fundamentally simple recipe for an heroic

5. Namely the use of it in *Beowulf*, both dramatically in depicting the sagacity of Beowulf the hero, and as an essential part of the traditions concerning the Scylding court, which is the legendary background against which the rise of the hero is set—as a later age would have chosen the court of Arthur. Also the probable allusion in Alcuin's letter to Speratus: see Chambers's *Widsith*, p. 78.
6. "When the dragon awoke, strife was renewed; he sniffed along the stone," lines 2287–88 [*Editor's translation*].

situation. In these (if we had them) we could see the exaltation of undefeated will, which receives doctrinal expression in the words of Byrhtwold at the battle of Maldon.[7] But though with sympathy and patience we might gather, from a line here or a tone there, the background of imagination which gives to this indomitability, this paradox of defeat inevitable yet unacknowledged, its full significance, it is in *Beowulf* that a poet has devoted a whole poem to the theme, and has drawn the struggle in different proportions, so that we may see man at war with the hostile world, and his inevitable overthrow in Time.[8] The particular is on the outer edge, the essential in the centre.

Of course, I do not assert that the poet, if questioned, would have replied in the Anglo-Saxon equivalents of these terms. Had the matter been so explicit to him, his poem would certainly have been the worse. None the less we may still, against his great scene, hung with tapestries woven of ancient tales of ruin, see the *hæleð* walk. When we have read his poem, as a poem, rather than as a collection of episodes, we perceive that he who wrote *hæleð under heofenum* may have meant in dictionary terms 'heroes under heaven', or 'mighty men upon earth', but he and his hearers were thinking of the *eormengrund*, the great earth, ringed with *garsecg*, the shoreless sea, beneath the sky's inaccessible roof; whereon, as in a little circle of light about their halls, men with courage as their stay went forward to that battle with the hostile world and the offspring of the dark which ends for all, even the kings and champions, in defeat. That even this 'geography', once held as a material fact, could now be classed as a mere folk-tale affects its value very little. It transcends astronomy. Not that astronomy has done anything to make the island seem more secure or the outer seas less formidable.

Beowulf is not, then, the hero of an heroic lay, precisely. He has no enmeshed loyalties, nor hapless love. *He is a man, and that for him and many is sufficient tragedy.* It is not an irritating accident that the tone of the poem is so high and its theme so low. It is the theme in its deadly seriousness that begets the dignity of tone: *lif is læne: eal scæceð leoht and lif somod.*[9] So deadly and ineluctable is the underlying thought, that those who in the circle of light, within

---

7. This expression may well have been actually used by the *eald geneat*, but none the less (or perhaps rather precisely on that account) is probably to be regarded not as new-minted, but as an ancient and honoured *gnome* of long descent.
8. For the words *hige sceal þe heardra, heorte þe cenre, mod sceal þe mare þe ure mægen lytlað* are not, of course, an exhortation to simple courage. They are not reminders that fortune favours the brave, or that victory may be snatched from defeat by the stubborn. (Such thoughts were familiar, but otherwise expressed: *wyrd oft nereð unfægne eorl, þonne his ellen deah.*) The words of Byrhtwold were made for a man's last and hopeless day.
9. "Life is transitory: all light and life departs together." Tolkien's invention, patterned after Old English gnomic verse [*Editor's translation*].

the besieged hall, are absorbed in work or talk and do not look to the
battlements, either do not regard it or recoil. Death comes to the
feast, and they say He gibbers: He has no sense of proportion.

I would suggest, then, that the monsters are not an inexplicable
blunder of taste; they are essential, fundamentally allied to the under-
lying ideas of the poem, which give it its lofty tone and high serious-
ness. The key to the fusion-point of imagination that produced this
poem lies, therefore, in those very references to Cain which have
often been used as a stick to beat an ass—taken as an evident sign
(were any needed) of the muddled heads of early Anglo-Saxons. They
could not, it was said, keep Scandinavian bogies and the Scriptures
separate in their puzzled brains. The New Testament was beyond
their comprehension. I am not, as I have confessed, a man so diligent
as duly to read all the books about *Beowulf*, but as far as I am aware
the most suggestive approach to this point appears in the essay
Beowulf and the Heroic Age to which I have already referred.[1] I will
quote a small part of it.

> In the epoch of *Beowulf* a Heroic Age more wild and primitive
> than that of Greece is brought into touch with Christendom,
> with the Sermon on the Mount, with Catholic theology and
> ideas of Heaven and Hell. We see the difference, if we compare
> the wilder things—the folk-tale element—in *Beowulf* with the
> wilder things of Homer. Take for example the tale of Odysseus
> and the Cyclops—the No-man trick. Odysseus is struggling
> with a monstrous and wicked foe, but he is not exactly thought
> of as struggling with the powers of darkness. Polyphemus, by
> devouring his guests, acts in a way which is hateful to Zeus
> and the other gods: yet the Cyclops is himself god-begotten and
> under divine protection, and the fact that Odysseus has maimed
> him is a wrong which Poseidon is slow to forgive. But the gigan-
> tic foes whom Beowulf has to meet are identified with the foes
> of God. Grendel and the dragon are constantly referred to in
> language which is meant to recall the powers of darkness with
> which Christian men felt themselves to be encompassed. They[2]
> are the 'inmates of Hell', 'adversaries of God', 'offspring of Cain',
> 'enemies of mankind'. Consequently, the matter of the main
> story of *Beowulf*, monstrous as it is, is not so far removed from
> common mediaeval experience as it seems to us to be from our
> own. . . . Grendel hardly differs[3] from the fiends of the pit who
> were always in ambush to waylay a righteous man. And so
> Beowulf, for all that he moves in the world of the primitive

1. *Foreword* to Strong's translation, p. xxviii. See note 3.
2. This is not strictly true. The dragon is not referred to in such terms, which are applied to Grendel and to the primeval giants.
3. He differs in important points, referred to later.

Heroic Age of the Germans, nevertheless is almost a Christian knight.[4]

There are some hints here which are, I think, worth pursuing further. Most important is it to consider how and why the monsters become 'adversaries of God', and so begin to symbolize (and ultimately to become identified with) the powers of evil, even while they remain, as they do still remain in *Beowulf*, mortal denizens of the material world, in it and of it. I accept without argument throughout the attribution of *Beowulf* to the 'age of Bede'—one of the firmer conclusions of a department of research most clearly serviceable to criticism: inquiry into the probable date of the effective composition of the poem as we have it. So regarded *Beowulf* is, of course, an historical document of the first order for the study of the mood and thought of the period and one perhaps too little used for the purpose by professed historians.[5] But it is the mood of the author, the essential cast of his imaginative apprehension of the world, that is my concern, not history for its own sake; I am interested in that time of fusion only as it may help us to understand the poem. And in the poem I think we may observe not confusion, a half-hearted or a muddled business, but a fusion that has occurred *at a given point* of contact between old and new, a product of thought and deep emotion.

One of the most potent elements in that fusion is the Northern courage: the theory of courage, which is the great contribution of early Northern literature. This is not a military judgement. I am not asserting that, if the Trojans could have employed a Northern king and his companions, they would have driven Agamemnon and Achilles into the sea, more decisively than the Greek hexameter routs the alliterative line—though it is not improbable. I refer rather to the central position the creed of unyielding will holds in the North. With due reserve we may turn to the tradition of pagan imagination as it survived in Icelandic. Of English pre-Christian mythology we know practically nothing. But the fundamentally similar heroic temper of ancient England and Scandinavia cannot have been founded on (or perhaps rather, cannot have generated) mythologies divergent on this essential point. 'The Northern Gods', Ker said, 'have an exultant extravagance in their warfare which makes them more like Titans than Olympians; *only they are on the right side, though it is not the side that wins. The winning side is Chaos and Unreason*'—mythologically, the monsters—'*but the gods, who are defeated, think*

---

4. I should prefer to say that he moves in a northern heroic age imagined by a Christian, and therefore has a noble and gentle quality, though conceived to be a pagan.
5. It is, for instance, dismissed cursorily, and somewhat contemptuously in the recent (somewhat contemptuous) essay of Dr. Watson, *The Age of Bede* in *Bede, His Life, Times, and Writings*, ed. A. Hamilton Thompson, 1935.

that defeat no refutation'.[6] And in their war men are their chosen allies, able when heroic to share in this 'absolute resistance, perfect because without hope'. At least in this vision of the final defeat of the humane (and of the divine made in its image), and in the essential hostility of the gods and heroes on the one hand and the monsters on the other, we may suppose that pagan English and Norse imagination agreed.

But in England this imagination was brought into touch with Christendom, and with the Scriptures. The process of 'conversion' was a long one, but some of its effects were doubtless immediate: an alchemy of change (producing ultimately the mediaeval) was at once at work. One does not have to wait until all the native traditions of the older world have been replaced or forgotten; for the minds which still retain them are changed, and the memories viewed in a different perspective: *at once they become more ancient and remote, and in a sense darker.* It is through such a blending that there was available to a poet who set out to *write* a poem—and in the case of *Beowulf* we may probably use this very word—on a scale and plan unlike a minstrel's lay, both new faith and new learning (or education), and also a body of native tradition (itself requiring to be learned) for the changed mind to contemplate together.[7] The native 'learning' cannot be denied in the case of *Beowulf*. Its display has grievously perturbed the critics, for the author draws upon tradition at will for his own purposes, as a poet of later times might draw upon history or the classics and expect his allusions to be understood (within a certain class of hearers). He was in fact, like Virgil, learned enough in the vernacular department to have an historical perspective, even an antiquarian curiosity. He cast his time into the long-ago, because already the long-ago had a special poetical attraction. He knew much about old days, and though his knowledge—of such things as sea-burial and the funeral pyre, for instance—was rich and poetical rather than accurate with the accuracy of modern archaeology (such as that is), one thing he knew clearly: those days were heathen—heathen, noble, and hopeless.

But if the specifically Christian was suppressed,[8] so also were the old gods. Partly because they had not really existed, and had been

---

6. *The Dark Ages*, p. 57.
7. If we consider the period as a whole. It is not, of course, necessarily true of individuals. These doubtless from the beginning showed many degrees from deep instruction and understanding to disjointed superstition, or blank ignorance.
8. Avoidance of obvious anachronisms (such as are found in *Judith*, for instance, where the heroine refers in her own speeches to Christ and the Trinity), and the absence of all definitely *Christian* names and terms, is natural and plainly intentional. It must be observed that there is a difference between the comments of the author and the things said in reported speech by his characters. The two chief of these, Hrothgar and Beowulf, are again differentiated. Thus the only definitely Scriptural references, to Abel (108) and to Cain (108, 1261), occur where the poet is speaking as commentator. The theory

always, in the Christian view, only delusions or lies fabricated by the evil one, the *gasthona*, to whom the hopeless turned especially in times of need. Partly because their old names (certainly not forgotten) had been potent, and were connected in memory still, not only with mythology or such fairy-tale matter as we find, say, in *Gylfaginning*, but with active heathendom, religion and *wigweorþung*. Most of all because they were not actually essential to the theme.

The monsters had been the foes of the gods, the captains of men, and within Time the monsters would win. In the heroic siege and last defeat men and gods alike had been imagined in the same host. Now the heroic figures, the men of old, *hæleð under heofenum*, remained and still fought on until defeat. For the monsters do not depart, whether the gods go or come. A Christian was (and is) still like his forefathers a mortal hemmed in a hostile world. The monsters remained the enemies of mankind, the infantry of the old war, and became inevitably the enemies of the one God, *ece Dryhten*, the eternal Captain of the new. Even so the vision of the war changes. For it begins to dissolve, even as the contest on the fields of Time thus takes on its largest aspect. The tragedy of the great temporal defeat remains for a while poignant, but ceases to be finally important. It is no defeat, for the end of the world is part of the design of Metod, the Arbiter who is above the mortal world. Beyond there appears a possibility of eternal victory (or eternal defeat), and the real battle is between the soul and its adversaries. So the old monsters became images of the evil spirit or spirits, or rather the evil spirits entered into the monsters and took visible shape in the hideous bodies of the *þyrsas* and *sigelhearwan* of heathen imagination.

But that shift is not complete in *Beowulf*—whatever may have been true of its period in general. Its author is still concerned primarily with *man on earth*, rehandling in a new perspective an ancient theme: that man, each man and all men, and all their works shall die. A theme no Christian need despise. Yet this theme plainly would not be so treated, but for the nearness of a pagan time. The shadow of its despair, if only as a mood, as an intense emotion of regret, is still there. The worth of defeated valour in this world is deeply felt. As the poet looks back into the past, surveying the history of kings and warriors in the old traditions, he sees that all glory (or as we might say 'culture' or 'civilization') ends in night. The solution of that

---

of Grendel's origin is not known to the actors: Hrothgar denies all knowledge of the ancestry of Grendel (1355). The giants (1688 ff.) are, it is true, represented pictorially, and in Scriptural terms. But this suggests rather that the author identified native and Scriptural accounts, and gave his picture Scriptural colour, since of the two accounts Scripture was the truer. And if so it would be closer to that told in remote antiquity when the sword was made, more especially since the *wundorsmiþas* who wrought it were actually giants (1558, 1562, 1679): they would know the true tale. See [p. 131, n. 9].

tragedy is not treated—it does not arise out of the material. We get in fact a poem from a pregnant moment of poise, looking back into the pit, by a man learned in old tales who was struggling, as it were, to get a general view of them all, perceiving their common tragedy of inevitable ruin, and yet feeling this more *poetically* because he was himself removed from the direct pressure of its despair. He could view from without, but still feel immediately and from within, the old dogma: despair of the event, combined with faith in the value of doomed resistance. He was still dealing with the great temporal tragedy, and not yet writing an allegorical homily in verse. Grendel inhabits the visible world and eats the flesh and blood of men; he enters their houses by the doors. The dragon wields a physical fire, and covets gold not souls; he is slain with iron in his belly. Beowulf's *byrne* was made by Weland; and the iron shield he bore against the serpent by his own smiths: it was not yet the breastplate of righteousness, nor the shield of faith for the quenching of all the fiery darts of the wicked.

Almost we might say that this poem was (in one direction) inspired by the debate that had long been held and continued after, and that it was one of the chief contributions to the controversy: shall we or shall we not consign the heathen ancestors to perdition? What good will it do posterity to read the battles of Hector? *Quid Hinieldus cum Christo?*[9] The author of *Beowulf* showed forth the permanent value of that *pietas* which treasures the memory of man's struggles in the dark past, man fallen and not yet saved, disgraced but not dethroned. It would seem to have been part of the English temper in its strong sense of tradition, dependent doubtless on dynasties, noble houses, and their code of honour, and strengthened, it may be, by the more inquisitive and less severe Celtic learning, that it should, at least in some quarters and despite grave and Gallic voices, preserve much from the northern past to blend with southern learning, and new faith.

It has been thought that the influence of Latin epic, especially of the *Aeneid*, is perceptible in *Beowulf*, and a necessary explanation, if only in the exciting of emulation, of the development of the long and studied poem in early England. There is, of course, a likeness in places between these greater and lesser things, the *Aeneid* and *Beowulf*, if they are read in conjunction. But the smaller points in which imitation or reminiscence might be perceived are inconclusive, while the real likeness is deeper and due to certain qualities in the authors independent of the question whether the Anglo-Saxon had read Virgil or not. It is this deeper likeness which makes things, that are either the inevitabilities of human poetry or the accidental

9. Alcuin, "What does Ingeld have to do with Christ?" see pp. 98–100 in this Norton Critical Edition [*Editor*].

congruences of all tales, ring alike. We have the great pagan on
the threshold of the change of the world; and the great (if lesser)
Christian just over the threshold of the great change in his time and
place: the backward view: *multa putans sortemque animo miseratus
iniquam.*[1]

But we will now return once more to the monsters, and consider
especially the difference of their status in the northern and south-
ern mythologies. Of Grendel it is said: *Godes yrre bær.*[2] But the
Cyclops is god-begotten and his maiming is an offence against his
begetter, the god Poseidon. This radical difference in mythological
status is only brought out more sharply by the very closeness of the
similarity in conception (in all save mere size) that is seen, if we com-
pare *Beowulf*, 740 ff., with the description of the Cyclops devouring
men in *Odyssey*, ix—or still more in *Aeneid*, iii. 622 ff. In Virgil,
whatever may be true of the fairy-tale world of the Odyssey, the
Cyclops walks veritably in the historic world. He is seen by Aeneas in
Sicily, *monstrum horrendum, informe, ingens,*[3] as much a perilous
fact as Grendel was in Denmark, *earmsceapen on weres wæstmum . . .
næfne he wæs mara þonne ænig man oðer;*[4] as real as Acestes or
Hrothgar.[5]

At this point in particular we may regret that we do not know more
about pre-Christian English mythology. Yet it is, as I have said, legit-
imate to suppose that in the matter of the position of the monsters
in regard to men and gods the view was fundamentally the same as in
later Icelandic. Thus, though all such generalizations are naturally
imperfect in detail (since they deal with matter of various origins,
constantly reworked, and never even at most more than partially sys-
tematized), we may with some truth contrast the 'inhumanness' of
the Greek gods, however anthropomorphic, with the 'humanness'
of the Northern, however titanic. In the southern myths there is also
rumour of wars with giants and great powers not Olympian, the *Tita-
nia pubes fulmine deiecti,*[6] rolling like Satan and his satellites in the
nethermost Abyss. But this war is differently conceived. It lies in a

---

1. In fact the real resemblance of the *Aeneid* and *Beowulf* lies in the constant presence of
   a sense of many-storied antiquity, together with its natural accompaniment, stern and
   noble melancholy. In this they are really akin and together differ from Homer's flatter,
   if more glittering, surface. ["Thinking many things and in his mind pondering their
   unequal lot," *Aeneid* 6.332—*Editor's translation.*]
2. "He carried God's wrath," line 711 [*Editor's translation*].
3. "A terrible monster, misshapen, huge," *Aeneid* 3.662 [*Editor's translation*].
4. "Wretchedly shaped in the form of a man . . . except that he was bigger than any other
   person," lines 1351–53 [*Editor's translation*].
5. I use this illustration following Chambers, because of the close resemblance between
   Grendel and the Cyclops in kind. But other examples could be adduced: Cacus, for
   instance, the offspring of Vulcan. One might ponder the contrast between the legends
   of the torture of Prometheus and of Loki: the one for assisting men, the other for assist-
   ing the powers of darkness.
6. "The Titanian youth hurled down by a thunderbolt," *Aeneid* 6.580 [*Editor's translation*].

chaotic past. The ruling gods are not besieged, not in ever-present peril or under future doom.[7] Their offspring on earth may be heroes or fair women; it may also be the other creatures hostile to men. The gods are not the allies of men in their war against these or other monsters. The interest of the gods is in this or that man as part of their individual schemes, not as part of a great strategy that includes all good men, as the infantry of battle. In Norse, at any rate, the gods are within Time, doomed with their allies to death. Their battle is with the monsters and the outer darkness. They gather heroes for the last defence. Already before euhemerism saved them by embalming them, and they dwindled in antiquarian fancy to the mighty ancestors of northern kings (English and Scandinavian), they had become in their very being the enlarged shadows of great men and warriors upon the walls of the world. When Baldr is slain and goes to Hel he cannot escape thence any more than mortal man.

This may make the southern gods more godlike—more lofty, dread, and inscrutable. They are timeless and do not fear death. Such a mythology may hold the promise of a profounder thought. In any case it was a virtue of the southern mythology that it could not stop where it was. It must go forward to philosophy or relapse into anarchy. For in a sense it had shirked the problem precisely by not having the monsters in the centre—as they are in *Beowulf* to the astonishment of the critics. But such horrors cannot be left permanently unexplained, lurking on the outer edges and under suspicion of being connected with the Government. It is the strength of the northern mythological imagination that it faced this problem, put the monsters in the centre, gave them victory but no honour, and found a potent but terrible solution in naked will and courage. 'As a working theory absolutely impregnable.' So potent is it, that while the older southern imagination has faded for ever into literary ornament, the northern has power, as it were, to revive its spirit even in our own times. It can work, even as it did work with the *goðlauss* viking, without gods: martial heroism as its own end. But we may

---

7. There is actually no final principle in the legendary hostilities contained in classical mythology. For the present purpose that is all that matters: we are not here concerned with remoter mythological origins, in the North or South. The gods, Cronian or Olympian, the Titans, and other great natural powers, and various monsters, even minor local horrors, are not clearly distinguished in origin or ancestry. There could be no permanent policy of war, led by Olympus, to which human courage might be dedicated, among mythological races so promiscuous. Of course, nowhere can absolute rigidity of distinction be expected, because in a sense the foe is always both within and without; the fortress must fall through treachery as well as by assault. Thus Grendel has a perverted human shape, and the giants or *jötnar,* even when (like the Titans) they are of super-divine stature, are parodies of the human-divine form. Even in Norse, where the distinction is most rigid, Loki dwells in Asgarðr, though he is an evil and lying spirit, and fatal monsters come of him. For it is true of man, maker of myths, that Grendel and the Dragon, in their lust, greed, and malice, have a part in him. But mythically conceived the gods do not recognize any bond with *Fenris úlfr,* any more than men with Grendel or the serpent.

remember that the poet of *Beowulf* saw clearly: the wages of heroism is death.

For these reasons I think that the passages in *Beowulf* concerning the giants and their war with God, together with the two mentions of Cain (as the ancestor of the giants in general and Grendel in particular) are specially important.

They are directly connected with Scripture, yet they cannot be dissociated from the creatures of northern myth, the ever-watchful foes of the gods (and men). The undoubtedly scriptural Cain is connected with *eotenas* and *ylfe*, which are the *jötnar* and *álfar* of Norse. But this is not due to mere confusion—it is rather an indication of the precise point at which an imagination, pondering old and new, was kindled. At this point new Scripture and old tradition touched and ignited. It is for this reason that these elements of Scripture alone appear in a poem dealing of design with the noble pagan of old days. For they are precisely the elements which bear upon this theme. Man alien in a hostile world, engaged in a struggle which he cannot win while the world lasts, is assured that his foes are the foes also of Dryhten, that his courage noble in itself is also the highest loyalty: so said thyle and clerk.

In *Beowulf* we have, then, an historical poem about the pagan past, or an attempt at one—literal historical fidelity founded on modern research was, of course, not attempted. It is a poem by a learned man writing of old times, who looking back on the heroism and sorrow feels in them something permanent and something symbolical. So far from being a confused semi-pagan—historically unlikely for a man of this sort in the period—he brought probably *first* to his task a knowledge of Christian poetry, especially that of the Cædmon school, and especially *Genesis*.[8] He makes his minstrel sing in Heorot of the Creation of the earth and the lights of Heaven. So excellent is this choice as the theme of the harp that maddened Grendel lurking joyless in the dark without that it matters little whether this is anachronistic or not.[9] *Secondly*, to his task the poet brought a considerable learning in native lays and traditions: only by learning and

8. The *Genesis* which is preserved for us is a late copy of a damaged original, but is still certainly in its older parts a poem whose composition must be referred to the early period. That *Genesis A* is actually older than *Beowulf* is generally recognized as the most probable reading of such evidence as there is.
9. Actually the poet may have known, what we can guess, that such creation-themes were also ancient in the North. *Völuspá* describes Chaos and the making of the sun and moon, and very similar language occurs in the Old High German fragment known as the *Wessobrunner Gebet*. The song of the minstrel Iopas, who had his knowledge from Atlas, at the end of the first book of the *Aeneid* is also in part a song of origins: *hic canit errantem lunam solisque labores, unde hominum genus et pecudes, unde imber et ignes*. In any case the Anglo-Saxon poet's view throughout was plainly that true, or truer, knowledge was possessed in ancient days (when men were not deceived by the Devil); at least they knew of the one God and Creator, though not of heaven, for that was lost. See [p. 126, n. 8].

training could such things be acquired, they were no more born naturally into an Englishman of the seventh or eighth centuries, by simple virtue of being an 'Anglo-Saxon', than ready-made knowledge of poetry and history is inherited at birth by modern children.

It would seem that, in his attempt to depict ancient pre-Christian days, intending to emphasize their nobility, and the desire of the good for truth, he turned naturally when delineating the great King of Heorot to the Old Testament. In the *folces hyrde* of the Danes we have much of the shepherd patriarchs and kings of Israel, servants of the one God, who attribute to His mercy all the good things that come to them in this life. We have in fact a Christian English conception of the noble chief before Christianity, who could lapse (as could Israel) in times of temptation into idolatry.[1] On the other hand, the traditional matter in English, not to mention the living survival of the heroic code and temper among the noble households of ancient England, enabled him to draw differently, and in some respects much closer to the actual heathen *hæleð*, the character of Beowulf, especially as a young knight, who used his great gift of *mægen* to earn *dom* and *lof* among men and posterity.

Beowulf is not an actual picture of historic Denmark or Geatland or Sweden about A.D. 500. But it is (if with certain minor defects) on a general view a self-consistent picture, a construction bearing clearly the marks of design and thought. The whole must have succeeded admirably in creating in the minds of the poet's contemporaries the illusion of surveying a past, pagan but noble and fraught with a deep significance—a past that itself had depth and reached backward into a dark antiquity of sorrow. This impression of depth is an effect and a justification of the use of episodes and allusions to old tales, mostly darker, more pagan, and desperate than the foreground.

To a similar antiquarian temper, and a similar use of vernacular learning, is probably due the similar effect of antiquity (and melancholy) in the *Aeneid*—especially felt as soon as Aeneas reaches Italy and the *Saturni gentem . . . sponte sua veterisque dei se more tenentem.*[2] *Ic þa leode wat ge wið feond ge wið freond fæste geworhte, æghwæs untæle ealde wisan.*[3] Alas for the lost lore, the annals and old

1. It is of Old Testament lapses rather than of any events in England (of which he is not speaking) that the poet is thinking in lines 175 ff., and this colours his manner of allusion to knowledge which he may have derived from native traditions concerning the Danes and the special heathen religious significance of the site of Heorot (*Hleiðrar, æt hærgtrafum*, the tabernacles)—it was possibly a matter that embittered the feud of Danes and Heathobards. If so, this is another point where old and new have blended. * * *
2. "A race of Saturn . . . ruled by their own will, and guiding themselves by the law of an ancient god," *Aeneid* 7.201–3 [*Editor's translation*].
3. "I know the people are resolutely disposed toward both enemies and friends, in every respect beyond reproach in the old manner," lines 1863–65 [*Editor's translation*].

poets that Virgil knew, and only used in the making of a new thing! The criticism that the important matters are put on the outer edges misses this point of artistry, and indeed fails to see why the old things have in *Beowulf* such an appeal: it is the poet himself who made antiquity so appealing. His poem has more value in consequence, and is a greater contribution to early mediaeval thought than the harsh and intolerant view that consigned all the heroes to the devil. We may be thankful that the product of so noble a temper has been preserved by chance (if such it be) from the dragon of destruction.

The general structure of the poem, so viewed, is not really difficult to perceive, if we look to the main points, the strategy, and neglect the many points of minor tactics. We must dismiss, of course, from mind the notion that *Beowulf* is a 'narrative poem', that it tells a tale or intends to tell a tale sequentially. The poem 'lacks steady advance': so Klaeber heads a critical section in his edition.[4] But the poem was not meant to advance, steadily or unsteadily. It is essentially a balance, an opposition of ends and beginnings. In its simplest terms it is a contrasted description of two moments in a great life, rising and setting; an elaboration of the ancient and intensely moving contrast between youth and age, first achievement and final death. It is divided in consequence into two opposed portions, different in matter, manner, and length: A from 1 to 2199 (including an exordium of 52 lines); B from 2200 to 3182 (the end). There is no reason to cavil at this proportion; in any case, for the purpose and the production of the required effect, it proves in practice to be right.

This simple and *static* structure, solid and strong, is in each part much diversified, and capable of enduring this treatment. In the conduct of the presentation of Beowulf's rise to fame on the one hand, and of his kingship and death on the other, criticism can find things to question, especially if it is captious, but also much to praise, if it is attentive. But the only serious weakness, or apparent weakness, is the long recapitulation: the report of Beowulf to Hygelac. This recapitulation is well done. Without serious discrepancy[5] it retells rapidly the events in Heorot, and retouches the account; and it serves to illustrate, since he himself describes his own deeds, yet more vividly

---

4. Though only explicitly referred to here and in disagreement, this edition is, of course, of great authority, and all who have used it have learned much from it.
5. I am not concerned with minor discrepancies at any point in the poem. They are no proof of composite authorship, nor even of incompetent authorship. It is very difficult, even in a newly invented tale of any length, to avoid such defects; more so still in rehandling old and oft-told tales. The points that are seized in the study, with a copy that can be indexed and turned to and fro (even if never read straight through as it was meant to be), are usually such as may easily escape an author and still more easily his natural audience. Virgil certainly does not escape such faults, even within the limits of a single book. Modern printed tales, that have presumably had the advantage of proof correction, can even be observed to hesitate in the heroine's Christian name.

the character of a young man, singled out by destiny, as he steps
suddenly forth in his full powers. Yet this is perhaps not quite suf-
ficient to justify the repetition. The explanation, if not complete
justification, is probably to be sought in different directions.

For one thing, the old tale was not first told or invented by this
poet. So much is clear from investigation of the folk-tale analogues.
Even the legendary association of the Scylding court with a maraud-
ing monster, and with the arrival from abroad of a champion and
deliverer was probably already old. The plot was not the poet's; and
though he has infused feeling and significance into its crude mate-
rial, that plot was not a perfect vehicle of the theme or themes that
came to hidden life in the poet's mind as he worked upon it. Not an
unusual event in literature. For the contrast—youth and death—it
would probably have been better, if we had no journeying. If the sin-
gle nation of the *Geatas* had been the scene, we should have felt the
stage not narrower, but symbolically wider. More plainly should we
have perceived in one people and their hero all mankind and its
heroes. This at any rate I have always myself felt in reading *Beowulf*;
but I have also felt that this defect is rectified by the bringing of the
tale of Grendel to Geatland. As Beowulf stands in Hygelac's hall and
tells his story, he sets his feet firm again in the land of his own
people, and is no longer in danger of appearing a mere *wrecca*, an
errant adventurer and slayer of bogies that do not concern him.

There is in fact a double division in the poem: the fundamental
one already referred to, and a secondary but important division at
line 1887. After that the essentials of the previous part are taken up
and compacted, so that all the tragedy of Beowulf is contained
between 1888 and the end.[6] But, of course, without the first half
we should miss much incidental illustration; we should miss also the
dark background of the court of Heorot that loomed as large in glory
and doom in ancient northern imagination as the court of Arthur:
no vision of the past was complete without it. And (most important)
we should lose the direct contrast of youth and age in the persons
of Beowulf and Hrothgar which is one of the chief purposes of this
section: it ends with the pregnant words *oþ þæt hine yldo benam
mægenes wynnum, se þe oft manegum scod.*[7]

In any case we must not view this poem as in intention an excit-
ing narrative or a romantic tale. The very nature of Old English
metre is often misjudged. In it there is no single rhythmic pattern

6. The least satisfactory arrangement possible is thus to read only lines 1–1887 and not
   the remainder. This procedure has none the less been, from time to time, directed or
   encouraged by more than one 'English syllabus'.
7. "Until old age, which has often robbed many, deprived him of the delights of physical
   vigor," lines 1886–87 [*Editor's translation*].

progressing from the beginning of a line to the end, and repeated with variation in other lines. The lines do not go according to a tune. They are founded on a balance; an opposition between two halves of roughly equivalent[8] phonetic weight, and significant content, which are more often rhythmically contrasted than similar. They are more like masonry than music. In this fundamental fact of poetic expression I think there is a parallel to the total structure of *Beowulf*. *Beowulf* is indeed the most successful Old English poem because in it the elements, language, metre, theme, structure, are all most nearly in harmony. Judgement of the verse has often gone astray through listening for an accentual rhythm and pattern: and it seems to halt and stumble. Judgement of the theme goes astray through considering it as the narrative handling of a plot: and it seems to halt and stumble. Language and verse, of course, differ from stone or wood or paint, and can be only heard or read in a time-sequence; so that in any poem that deals at all with characters and events some narrative element must be present. We have none the less in *Beowulf* a method and structure that within the limits of the verse-kind approaches rather to sculpture or painting. It is a composition not a tune.

This is clear in the second half. In the struggle with Grendel one can as a reader dismiss the certainty of literary experience that the hero will not in fact perish, and allow oneself to share the hopes and fears of the Geats upon the shore. In the second part the author has no desire whatever that the issue should remain open, even according to literary convention. There is no need to hasten like the messenger, who rode to bear the lamentable news to the waiting people (2892 ff.). They may have hoped, but we are not supposed to. By now we are supposed to have grasped the plan. Disaster is foreboded. Defeat is the theme. Triumph over the foes of man's precarious fortress is over, and we approach slowly and reluctantly the inevitable victory of death.[9]

'In structure', it was said of *Beowulf*, 'it is curiously weak, in a sense preposterous,' though great merits of detail were allowed. In structure actually it is curiously strong, in a sense inevitable, though there are defects of detail. The general design of the poet is not only defensible, it is, I think, admirable. There may have previously

---

8. Equivalent, but not necessarily *equal*, certainly not as such things may be measured by machines.
9. That the particular bearer of enmity, the Dragon, also dies is important chiefly to Beowulf himself. He was a great man. Not many even in dying can achieve the death of a single worm, or the temporary salvation of their kindred. Within the limits of human life Beowulf neither lived nor died in vain—brave men might say. But there is no hint, indeed there are many to the contrary, that it was a war to end war, or a dragon-fight to end dragons. It is the end of Beowulf, and of the hope of his people.

existed stirring verse dealing in straightforward manner and even
in natural sequence with Beowulf's deeds, or with the fall of Hygelac;
or again with the fluctuations of the feud between the houses of
Hrethel the Geat and Ongentheow the Swede; or with the tragedy
of the Heathobards, and the treason that destroyed the Scylding
dynasty. Indeed this must be admitted to be practically certain: it
was the existence of such connected legends—connected in the
mind, not necessarily dealt with in chronicle fashion or in long
semi-historical poems—that permitted the peculiar use of them in
Beowulf. This poem cannot be criticized or comprehended, if its
original audience is imagined in like case to ourselves, possessing
only *Beowulf* in splendid isolation. For *Beowulf* was not designed to
tell the tale of Hygelac's fall, or for that matter to give the whole biog-
raphy of Beowulf, still less to write the history of the Geatish king-
dom and its downfall. But it used knowledge of these things for its
own purpose—to give that sense of perspective, of antiquity with a
greater and yet darker antiquity behind. These things are mainly on
the outer edges or in the background because they belong there, if
they are to function in this way. But in the centre we have an heroic
figure of enlarged proportions.

Beowulf is not an 'epic', not even a magnified 'lay'. No terms bor-
rowed from Greek or other literatures exactly fit: there is no reason
why they should. Though if we must have a term, we should choose
rather 'elegy'. It is an heroic-elegiac poem; and in a sense all its first
3,136 lines are the prelude to a dirge: *him þa gegiredan Geata leode
ad ofer eorðan unwaclicne*[1] one of the most moving ever written. But
for the universal significance which is given to the fortunes of its
hero it is an enhancement and not a detraction, in fact it is neces-
sary, that his final foe should be not some Swedish prince, or treach-
erous friend, but a dragon: a thing made by imagination for just
such a purpose. Nowhere does a dragon come in so precisely where
he should. But if the hero falls before a dragon, then certainly he
should achieve his early glory by vanquishing a foe of similar order.

There is, I think, no criticism more beside the mark than that
which some have made, complaining that it is monsters in both
halves that is so disgusting; one they could have stomached more
easily. That is nonsense. I can see the point of asking for *no* mon-
sters. I can also see the point of the situation in *Beowulf*. But no
point at all in mere reduction of numbers. It would really have been
preposterous, if the poet had recounted Beowulf's rise to fame in a
'typical' or 'commonplace' war in Frisia, and then ended him with a

---

1. "The Geatish people then prepared a magnificent pyre on the ground," lines 3137–38
   [*Editor's translation*].

dragon. Or if he had told of his cleansing of Heorot, and then brought him to defeat and death in a 'wild' or 'trivial' Swedish invasion! If the dragon is the right end for Beowulf, and I agree with the author that it is, then Grendel is an eminently suitable beginning. They are creatures, *feond mancynnes*, of a similar order and kindred significance. Triumph over the lesser and more nearly human is cancelled by defeat before the older and more elemental. And the conquest of the ogres comes at the right moment: not in earliest youth, though the nicors are referred to in Beowulf's *geogoðfeore* as a presage of the kind of hero we have to deal with; and not during the later period of recognized ability and prowess;[2] but in that first moment, which often comes in great lives, when men look up in surprise and see that a hero has unawares leaped forth. The placing of the dragon is inevitable: a man can but die upon his death-day.

I will conclude by drawing an imaginary contrast. Let us suppose that our poet had chosen a theme more consonant with 'our modern judgement'; the life and death of St Oswald. He might then have made a poem, and told first of Heavenfield, when Oswald as a young prince against all hope won a great victory with a remnant of brave men; and then have passed at once to the lamentable defeat of Oswestry, which seemed to destroy the hope of Christian Northumbria; while all the rest of Oswald's life, and the traditions of the royal house and its feud with that of Deira might be introduced allusively or omitted. To any one but an historian in search of facts and chronology this would have been a fine thing, an heroic-elegiac poem greater than history. It would be much better than a plain narrative, in verse or prose, however steadily advancing. This mere arrangement would at once give it more significance than a straightforward account of one king's life: the contrast of rising and setting, achievement and death. But even so it would fall far short of *Beowulf*. Poetically it would be greatly enhanced if the poet had taken violent liberties with history and much enlarged the reign of Oswald, making him old and full of years of care and glory when he went forth heavy with foreboding to face the heathen Penda: the contrast of youth and age would add enormously to the original theme, and give it a more universal meaning. But even so it would still fall short of *Beowulf*. To match his theme with the rise and fall of poor 'folk-tale' Beowulf the poet would have been obliged to turn

---

2. We do, however, learn incidentally much of this period: it is not strictly true, even of our poem as it is, to say that after the deeds in Heorot Beowulf 'has nothing else to do'. Great heroes, like great saints, should show themselves capable of dealing also with the ordinary things of life, even though they may do so with a strength more than ordinary. We may wish to be assured of this (and the poet has assured us), without demanding that he should put such things in the centre, when they are not the centre of his thought.

J. R. R. Tolkien

Cadwallon and Penda into giants and demons. It is just because the main foes in *Beowulf* are inhuman that the story is larger and more significant than this imaginary poem of a great king's fall. It glimpses the cosmic and moves with the thought of all men concerning the fate of human life and efforts; it stands amid but above the petty wars of princes, and surpasses the dates and limits of historical periods, however important. At the beginning, and during its process, and most of all at the end, we look down as if from a visionary height upon the house of man in the valley of the world. A light starts— *lixte se leoma ofer landa fela*[3]—and there is a sound of music; but the outer darkness and its hostile offspring lie ever in wait for the torches to fail and the voices to cease. Grendel is maddened by the sound of harps.

And one last point, which those will feel who to-day preserve the ancient *pietas* towards the past: *Beowulf* is not a 'primitive' poem; it is a late one, using the materials (then still plentiful) preserved from a day already changing and passing, a time that has now for ever vanished, swallowed in oblivion; using them for a new purpose, with a wider sweep of imagination, if with a less bitter and concentrated force. When new *Beowulf* was already antiquarian, in a good sense, and it now produces a singular effect. For it is now to us itself ancient; and yet its maker was telling of things already old and weighted with regret, and he expended his art in making keen that touch upon the heart which sorrows have that are both poignant and remote. If the funeral of Beowulf moved once like the echo of an ancient dirge, far-off and hopeless, it is to us as a memory brought over the hills, an echo of an echo. There is not much poetry in the world like this; and though *Beowulf* may not be among the very greatest poems of our western world and its tradition, it has its own individual character, and peculiar solemnity; it would still have power had it been written in some time or place unknown and without posterity, if it contained no name that could now be recognized or identified by research. Yet it is in fact written in a language that after many centuries has still essential kinship with our own, it was made in this land, and moves in our northern world beneath our northern sky, and for those who are native to that tongue and land, it must ever call with a profound appeal—until the dragon comes.

*　　*　　*

---

3. "Its brilliance shone over many land," line 311 [*Editor's translation*].

MARIJANE OSBORN

The Great Feud:
Scriptural History and Strife in *Beowulf*[†]

Beowulf is the story of a culture hero who fights in succession three monsters that threaten the fabric of his society. Each fight takes place at a farther remove from the lighted center of that society—in darkened hall, cave-hall, and barrow—and each antagonist is more nonhuman than the last. The primary concern of the poet is with the heroic response to the encroachment of an unformed, nonhuman outer darkness upon the formal grace of life in the hall.[1] But there is an element in *Beowulf* beyond this primal encounter. There is history.

The history in *Beowulf*, which makes up most of the famous digressions in the poem, is chiefly concerned with feuds. Dorothy Whitelock remarks that the historical Scandinavian feuds are

> referred to so frequently that it is obvious that the poet wishes them to be present in his hearers' thoughts as he tells his tale. The tragic stories of family strife within the Scylding dynasty, and of the wars fought by the kings of the Geats against the Swedes or Franks, attain almost to the position of sub-plots to the two parts of *Beowulf* respectively.[2]

The heaviest reference to these Scandinavian feuds comes in the second half of the poem. But in the first half of the poem, the mythic beginnings of the Scyldings, of Heorot, and of strife in Heorot evoke a series of "historical" references to feuds of quite a different order—the feuds of sacred history. While Scandinavian history is accessible within the world of the poem (sometimes as political prophecy),[3] this scriptural history is of course unknowable to the ancient

† From *PMLA* 93.5 (October 1978): 973–81. Reprinted by permission of the copyright owner, the Modern Language Association of America.

1. Andreas Haarder's view of the poem is representative of that of many scholars:

   > *Beowulf* presents a picture of a hall-life that is forever at stake, confronted as it is by the threat of the monster-world. . . . The hall of *Beowulf* is the basis of man's existence and the motivation of his actions. The hall is in focus, not the before and after that the Christian preacher will point to. . . . The monster is man's existential problem which has to be solved again and again. (Beowulf: *The Appeal of a Poem* [Viborg: Akademisk Forlag, 1975], pp. 239, 241, 279)

   Such a description is accurate so far as it goes, but it does not go far enough.

2. Dorothy Whitelock, *The Audience of* Beowulf (Oxford: Clarendon, 1951), p 34.

3. Even as Beowulf saves the Danes and the Geats from monsters, secular history, in the form of retribution for feuds, is working against these two nations. But this drama is not "in" the story; it is in the future of the story, implied by the poet or guessed by perceptive characters. Kenneth Sisam casts doubts upon the importance of such historicity in the poem and upon the interpretations that modern historians put upon the passages of foresight, in *The Structure of* Beowulf (Oxford: Clarendon, 1965), pp. 51–59. For the counterargument that it is thematically important for these two sets of feuds to

Scandinavians in *Beowulf*, for Christianity has not yet penetrated to their lands. With decorum and subtlety the Christian poet introduces a perspective inaccessible to his protagonists, in such a way that it will enhance, but not interfere with, his tale of noble (and in some sense ancestral) pagans. He establishes two complementary frames of reference, one heroic and one cosmic. The former aligns us, the audience, with the native Germanic world within the poem, while the latter aligns us with the Christian world of the poet.

The poet distinguishes between the heroic and the cosmic frames of reference primarily by assigning to the monsters who attack Heorot a scriptural history recognizable only to his audience. But even before introducing Old Testament referents for the archetypically evil monsters, he has distinguished between two levels of knowledge, that bound by the secular world of the poem and that perceived from our initiated Christian perspective.

I. Scyld's Destiny

A recent critic remarks that the "before and after" of the hall world is not a major concern of the poem (Haarder, p. 241); yet it is very much a central theme in the Scyld episode that sets the stage and the tone for the story about Beowulf to follow. The episode is presented in two passages of nearly equal length, each concluding with a statement about Scyld's destiny after death. These two statements offer contrasting views, one certain and the other uncertain.

The first half of the episode deals with Scyld's glorious reign, establishes the beginning of dynastic history, which is the beginning of "time" in the story, and concludes with Scyld's death. Within these twenty-four lines the poet makes three almost casual references to God (*God, Liffrea*, and *Wealdend*), so that it is hard to interpret the destination described for Scyld at the end of the passage as anything but favorable, if not as Heaven at least as the bosom of some Germanic Abraham:

> Him ða Scyld gewat   to gescæphwile
> felahror feran   on Frean wære.

> Then Scyld went forth at his destined time,
> very old, to go into the Lord's keeping.[4]
>   (ll. 26–27)

---

end tragically see Stanley J. Kahrl, "Feuds in *Beowulf*: A Tragic Necessity?" *Modern Philology*, 69 (1972), 189–98.
4. All quotations from *Beowulf* are from Fr. Klaeber, ed., Beowulf *and the* Fight at Finnsburg, 3rd. ed. (Boston: Heath, 1950). The translations are my literal renderings. * * *

Although the concept itself is formulaic—when St. Andrew dies his spirit goes *on Godes wære* (*Menologium*, l. 218a) and Beowulf's own spirit goes *on ðæs Waldendes wære* (l. 3109)—the poet uses it to make a firm authorial statement about Scyld's destiny directly to us, the audience outside the story. The Danes in *Beowulf* perceive Scyld's fate differently, as the second passage tells us.

The second half of the episode, concerned with the burial at sea, emphasizes the people's adoration of Scyld and their adornment of his "comely ship." This personal involvement sets the elegaic tone for the secular history to follow and presents, as it were, a closeup view of life in the poem, bringing us down into that world. Scyld's *swæse gesiþas* 'dear companions' place him in the treasure-filled ship and finally give him to the sea with mourning hearts, but their view of his destiny is in contrast to what the poet, as omniscient narrator, has already told us. The passage concludes:

> Men ne cunnon
> secgan to soðe,   selerædende,
> hæleð under heofenum,   hwa þæm hlæste onfeng.

> Men do not know how
> to say for certain, hall-councillors,
> heroes under the heavens, who received that load.
> (ll. 50–52)

Pagan Danes and Christians alike would know that the important part of that ship's cargo was neither body nor treasure, but spirit. The death ship was a familiar metaphor in both ecclesiastical and secular traditions; the native tradition is attested by folklore, by excavated ship burials, and by such stone carvings as the magnificent Götland picture stones (often arranged much like the Scyld sequence, with battle and victory scenes above and a death ship below). Those who launched Scyld's ship had some concept of the soul setting forth to the Land of the Dead; but the most significant feature of Scyld's departure in *Beowulf* is that, while the poet assures us of his precise (and safe) journey's end, within the world of the story that destination is not known. Hall-councillors, heroes under Heaven, have only pagan knowledge, like Edwin's councillor as recorded by Bede: "This life of man appears but for a moment; what follows or indeed what went before, we know not at all."[5]

---

5. *Ecclesiastical History of the English People*, ed. Bertram Colgrave and R. A. B. Mynors (Oxford: Clarendon, 1969), p. 185. Bede's story of the conversion of Edwin and his vivid symbol of pagan ignorance were probably as well known in the *Beowulf* poet's time as in our own, and perhaps the poet was counting on his hearers' having the image of the fleeting sparrow in the backs of their minds, or perhaps he himself was inspired by it in

This double point of view in *Beowulf*—what they know in the
poem and what we know outside it—has been noted in passing by
previous scholars, two of whom take the audience specifically into
account. Donahue mentions that the poet is "playing the limited
hope of his protagonists against the fuller Christian knowledge of
his audiences,"[6] and Renoir astutely observes that this disparity in
knowledge is the chief source of dramatic tension in the poem. This
tension, he says,

> is not exclusively intrinsic to the action, but is primarily due to
> a divergence in points of view between the audience and the
> participants in the action. From our position outside the poem,
> we know far more about the participants than they do about
> each other, and we have access to information necessarily
> unavailable to them. . . . [7]

This disparity in knowledge, most striking in connection with Gren-
del's scriptural ancestry, occurs throughout those three passages
that a recent commentator, Greenfield, has called "explicit scriptur-
izing": "having the scop in Heorot paraphrase Genesis, the placing of
Grendel in the race of Cain, and Hrothgar's sermon."[8] Surprisingly,
what has not been remarked at all is that in these passages *the explic-
itly scriptural element is carefully kept separate from the perception of
persons in the poem and is presented solely as a gloss for the audience.*

It must be noted, however, that the poet is not concerned about
suppressing Christian doctrine, as opposed to scriptural history, in
Beowulf's world. Concepts like judgment (see ll. 978 and possibly
2330 and 2820) and damnation (ll. 588–89) are elements of an
inherent moral understanding known theologically as "natural
knowledge," the law inscribed upon the hearts of righteous pagans
(Rom. 2:15). Scriptural history, like any other history, is intellectual
knowledge, conveyed by human instruction and hence unavailable
to even the noblest pagan in the world of the poem.

II. The Creation Song in Heorot

The distinction first introduced in the Scyld episode between what
those of us outside the story can perceive and what those within it

---

his account of Scyld. But there is an important difference between Scyld's departure
and the sparrow's: in *Beowulf* it is not the horror of not knowing but the mystery that is
stressed. The image of Scyld emerging from the unknown and fading back into it at his
death is romantic rather than frightening.

6. Charles Donahue, "*Beowulf* and Christian Tradition: A Reconsideration from a Celtic
Stance," *Traditio*, 21 (1965), 81.

7. Alain Renoir, "The Heroic Oath in *Beowulf*, the *Chanson de Roland*, and the *Nibelun-
genlied*," *Studies in Old English Literature in Honor of Arthur G. Brodeur*, ed. Stanley B.
Greenfield (Eugene: Univ. of Oregon Press, 1963), p. 245.

8. Stanley B. Greenfield, *The Interpretation of Old English Poems* (London: Routledge and
Kegan Paul, 1972), p. 158.

can know is further elaborated by the first of the three "scripturiz-
ing" passages, the creation song in Heorot together with what fol-
lows it. The passage known as the creation song (ll. 92–98) has often
been cited as evidence for the essentially Christian character of
Hrothgar's court; the scop is said to paraphrase Genesis. But this
observation misses the poet's point completely. For those listening
in Heorot the song cannot be a paraphrase because they do not know
Genesis. For us it is a paraphrase because we do know Genesis—
but the echoes we hear extend beyond the song.

The creation song is not much more "Christian" than the hymn
of Iopas in Book I of the *Aeneid*, to which Klaeber compares it
(p. 131); the chief difference is the presence of the Creator himself
in the *Beowulf* song (as in the Scyld passage). In the *Aeneid*, "long-
haired Iopas" makes the hall ring with his cithara, then

> Hic canit errantem lunam, solisque labores,
> unde hominum genus et pecudes, unde imber et ignes . . .

> He sang of the wandering moon, and the sun's labors,
> whence came the creation of men and beasts, of rain and fire . . .
> (I.742–43)

In Heorot the scop sounds his harp, says that the Almighty made
the earth, then

> gesette sigehreþig   sunnan ond monan
>
> . . .   lif eac gesceop
> cynna gehwylcum   þara ðe cwice hwyrfaþ.—

> set victorious the sun and moon
>
> . . .   and also made life
> for every kind of being that moves.—
> (ll. 94, 97–98)

The song ends here for those listening in Heorot. But for those of
us outside the story it does not precisely come to an end at all. Rather,
it dissolves back into the hall scene where it is being sung:

> Swa ða drihtguman   dreamum lifdon,
> eadiglice,   oð ðæt an ongan
> fyrene frem(m)an,   feond on helle.

> So the noble beings dwelt in joy,
> happily, until a certain one began
> to do wicked deeds, a fiend from Hell.
> (ll. 99–101)

C. J. E. Ball would have the song in Heorot end after these three lines, with the scop in the hall having sung from the creation of the world into the story of Adam and Eve.[9] But these lines, hovering between the song in the hall and the scene in the hall, are an example of the classical figure of *synchysis*, liquid syntax, where "we do not know," explains Bede, "whether the thought ends with the words which have preceded . . . or with the words which follow."[1]

If we read the song as continuing from the creation of the world into the story of Adam and Eve, those "noble people" who "lived happily until a certain adversary from Hell began to perform wicked deeds" (as Ball translates), then we fully expect to hear next of Satan's arrival in Eden. What we get is:

> Wæs se grimma gæst   Grendel haten.

> That grim spirit was called Grendel.

> (l. 102)

With this pronouncement the fictive world of the creation song modulates conclusively back into that of Heorot, even from our alerted point of view. By following the song with explicit scriptural allusions, the poet reinforces our sense of it as a paraphrase, and we hear in it much more than the Danes can. But most important, through the synchysis that introduces the adversary of Heorot in a scriptural context, the poet has offered an archetypal referent for Grendel that is accessible to us but not to those in the story.

III. Grendel and the Race of Cain

Tolkien urges the importance of considering

> how and why the monsters become 'adversaries of God,' and so begin to symbolize (and ultimately to become identified with) the powers of evil, even while they remain, as they do still remain in *Beowulf*, mortal denizens of the material world, in it and of it.[2]

The poet contrives this dual vision by carefully presenting the monsters and their attack upon Heorot within a context of cosmic history. After the creation song and the introduction of Grendel, the

9. "*Beowulf* 99–101," *Notes and Queries*, 18 (1971), 163. When I first mentioned the transitional nature of these lines, in *Thoth*, 10 (1969), 26–27, I did not comment on what now seems the most important point about this transition, mentioned by Ball: "Lines 90–114 of *Beowulf* thus contain a rapid summary of the main points of Genesis chapters i–iv."
1. Bede, *De Schematibus et Tropis, Patrologia Latina*, ed. J. P. Migne (Paris: n.p., 1844–65), Vol. XC, cols. 175–86.
2. J. R. R. Tolkien, "*Beowulf*: The Monsters and the Critics," *Proceedings of the British Academy*, 22 (1936), 20.

allusions to Genesis are continued until the end of the first fit, providing us with much we need to know about the Great Feud, the cosmic battle between good and evil that controls the three main actions of the poem in a manner barely glimpsed by its chief protagonists. Early scholars of *Beowulf* proposed that the scriptural allusions were interpolated, but here one could almost say that the poet "interpolates" Grendel himself, at lines 102–05, into his scriptural summary. As we have seen, however, his method is not to interpolate but to interweave. The introduction of Grendel is thematically interwoven with the creation song and the Cain passage (ll. 86–114), so that he is totally identified with the Adversary of Mankind.

But all this background information from Genesis is given only to the poet's audience, those who have the understanding to grasp it; the Danes who are beset by a monster have no notion of this cosmic setting. They have what may be described as a sense of myth and the idea of reversal: within the world of Heorot light challenges darkness, and it is felt that the bright hall of friendship and harp song calls up the envious *grimma gæst* from his misery. But after twelve long years of sorrow the Danes *know* only that Grendel is openly feuding against Hrothgar and that he will not abide by their legal codes (ll. 146–58). In the world of the poem this most evil of monsters, though he dwells by night in Heorot, cannot approach the *gifstol*, the center of giving and fellowship in that hall; this too makes mythic sense, just as it follows (within the logic of paradox) that the Devil cannot approach an altar.

The lines stating the inability of the demonic being to approach the hall's numinous center are probably the most discussed crux of the poem:

> No he þone gifstol   gretan moste,
> maþðum for metode,   ne his myne wisse.

> He could not approach that gift-throne,
> the treasure (before/on account of) the lord,
> nor know his love.
>   (ll. 168–69)

C. L. Wrenn believes that these lines "probably have been misplaced in the MS. from their proper position between 110 and 111"[3]—an opinion that Kevin Crossley-Holland tacitly follows in his translation.[4] These interpreters would "restore" the lines about the *gifstol*

3. C. L. Wrenn, ed., *Beowulf with the Finnesburg Fragment*, rev. ed. (London: Harrap, 1958), p. 188.
4. Kevin Crossley-Holland, trans., *Beowulf* (New York: Farrar, 1968), p. 35.

to the end of the account of the banishing of Cain in the first fit.
Wrenn translates the passage as follows, inserting the *gifstol* lines
168–69 between lines 110 and 111:

> He (Cain) had no joy of that act of enmity, but the Creator ban-
> ished him afar off from mankind because of that wickedness.
> He (Cain) could not draw near to God's throne (as he could have
> done before his slaying of Abel), that precious thing (bejewelled
> as in *Ezekiel* or the *Apocalypse*), in the Creator's presence, nor
> did he feel his love.
>
> (p. 69)

A reorganization of the received text is not necessary, however,
once we are alerted to the double vision that is carefully being
prepared for us. In neither line 109 nor line 168 does the *he* that
Wrenn glosses "Cain" refer exclusively to an individual. The Danes
know that Grendel (*he*, l. 168) cannot approach their *gifstol*; the
audience outside the poem can observe that the direct antecedent of
the pronoun *he* is *feond mancynnes* 'mankind's enemy' (l. 164) and
that Grendel is thus once more identified with the Antagonist of
scripture.

Lest we miss the dual perspective at this point, the "crux" is brack-
eted between narrative comments about the ignorance of the Danes
concerning cosmic matters: "Men do not know whither hell-
creatures go in their wanderings" (ll. 162–63), but what is worse,
"the Danes did not know the Lord" (l. 180); they understand neither
the demonic nor the holy. (This is clearly not true of those Danes
who, like the scop in Heorot, know God through his creation.) The
word for Lord here, *Metod* (l. 180), appears also in the *gifstol* pas-
sage (l. 169) and firmly establishes the dual focus of that passage.

Through this use of dual focus, the limited knowledge of the
Danes in Heorot (their understanding of Grendel's strife against
Hrothgar in terms of Germanic feud) is encompassed within the
larger history of the Great Feud. When the Danes, not knowing how
to worship the Lord, seek help from the "slayer of souls" (l. 177),
they are unwittingly aligning themselves with those adversaries of
God enumerated at the end of the first fit. At the end of the second
fit the poet follows his account of the most overtly heathen ritual in
the poem (the Danes' devil worship) with strong Christian admoni-
tion, in language recalling the Feud:

> Wa bið þæm ðe sceal
> þurh sliðne nið   sawle bescufan
> in fyres fæþm,   frofre ne wenan,
> wihte gewendan!   Wel bið þæm þe mot

æfter deaðdæge   Drihten secean
ond to Fæder fæþmum   freoðo wilnian!

> Woe be to him who must
> through terrible hostility shove his soul
> into the fire's embrace; he may not expect comfort
> or change at all! Well it will be for him who may
> seek the Lord after the day of his death
> and in the Father's embrace ask for peace!
> (ll. 183–88)

On the whole the poet maintains his two frames of reference less overtly than this. When he again "scripturizes" the lineage of Grendel (ll. 1261b–67a), he first puts the warriors in Heorot to sleep, secure in their faulty knowledge that no "demon created of old" will move upon Heorot to bring "reversal to men." As in the first fit, he then interweaves the introduction of the monster, now Grendel's mother, with scriptural commentary to evoke the perspective of cosmic archetypes. Grendel's mother, at the heroic level of the Scandinavian feud, comes only to avenge her son (ll. 1276–78), but the coming of the Grendel kind at all is part of a feud more ancient and malicious.

IV. *The Giant Hilt and Hrothgar's Sermon*

This vision of evil intention is, like the scriptural history, an element added to the heroic level of the story; more hangs on the impeccability of the warrior than he can possibly realize. To the Germanic concepts of blind fate (*wyrd*) and the disaster that strikes the unwary, the poet adds the malice of a supernatural agent, first by recalling to us the ancient beginnings of the recurrent feud that exploded upon the Danes as they slept, then by associating this feud with Hrothgar's evocation of the soul-slayer who comes upon men asleep in spirit.

The third and last of the "scripturizing" passages in *Beowulf* moves again into the ancient history of the Grendel kind, but it does not concern them personally. It gives the "lineage" of the giant sword hilt that Beowulf brings back from the mere. When the hilt is given into Hrothgar's hand, the poet tells us more or less parenthetically that it came to Hrothgar after the "fall of devils," specifically after the deaths of Grendel and his mother (ll. 1679–83). The poet then completes the rhetorical figures of envelope pattern and variation by delivering a two-line eulogy to Hrothgar. He finally says that "Hrothgar spoke" (l. 1687a)—but the speech does not in fact begin until fourteen lines later (l. 1700). The delay, as we watch Hrothgar

looking at the hilt, is significant.[5] It may be compared to the long
look that occurs later when the poet stops all action to give the pedi-
gree of the sword that Wiglaf has just drawn against the dragon.
Attached to Wiglaf's sword is a tradition about ordinary feuding in
the world of the poem, like that attached to the swords in the Hengest
and Ingeld digressions; the political history of Wiglaf's sword will
have repercussions after the dragon lies dead. But the golden hilt of
Grendel's mere, the work of wondersmiths, gives information of a
different order. Hrothgar "looks upon the hilt"—and while Hrothgar
gazes, considering what to say, the poet tells *us* what is written on
the hilt.

There are two inscriptions: the first refers to the beginning of
the ancient fight; the second gives the name of the first owner of the
sword, in runes. The latter is archeologically quite credible; there is
a rune-inscribed sword pommel in Liverpool City Museum.[6] What
is written about the ancient fight suggests that the poet has in his
mind's eye a combination of runic and nonrunic inscriptions, which
is quite possible in his own time but improbable in Beowulf's. Hence
Klaeber notes the suggestion that the writing about the ancient fight
was a graphic illustration.[7] But a fifth-century Scandinavian weapon
would be unlikely to document, either in pictures or in writing, "the
ungodly acts of the giants which preceded the deluge" (Klaeber), and
one mode of inscription would be as unintelligible as the other to a
reader with no knowledge of scriptural history. But we are not told
that Hrothgar reads what he is looking at. He gazes upon the hilt,
and the information with which the poet provides *us* during this
pause gives a scriptural context for the wisdom that Hrothgar sub-
sequently reveals about the recurrent feud with mankind's enemy
within the human breast. This context is chiefly what makes his
speech seem like a Christian homily.

Even quite recently an exclusively secular interpretation of
Hrothgar's speech has been proposed:

5. The technique of stopping the story is superficially reminiscent of the Homeric tech-
   nique discussed by Erich Auerbach in *Mimesis* (trans. Willard R. Trask [Princeton:
   Princeton Univ. Press, 1953]) in the chapter "Odysseus' Scar." But whereas (according
   to Auerbach) in Homer everything, including digressions, is equally "foregrounded," in
   Beowulf the two major digressions about swords introduce additional historical perspec-
   tives, scriptural in the passage about the golden hilt and Scandinavian in the one on
   Wiglaf's sword. Both confirm a perspective outside the sphere of awareness of the actors
   in the story, to whom the larger moral context of the monster fights and the future of
   their own continuing tribal identity are equally mysterious.
6. The inscription is reproduced by R. I. Page in *An Introduction to English Runes* (Lon-
   don: Methuen, 1973), p. 170.
7. Klaeber, p. 189. Wrenn assumes that the story of the flood is graphic and runic, in a
   combination of "Christian and pre-Christian styles which reminds one of the Franks
   Casket" (p. 56). "It is worth noticing," he adds, "how the Biblical story has been used in
   exactly the same way as the Germanic legends proper." That this is *not* so is precisely
   what I am trying to show.

> Hrothgar concerns himself with the duties and proper con-
> duct of Germanic lords, and with the glory which they may
> lose if they fail to fulfill the ideals upon which that glory is
> founded. The speech is not a Christian homily, even though it
> may contain echoes of the poet's Christian background. . . .
> Hrothgar's "sermon" is important, perhaps central to the poem,
> not because it reveals a Christian view of life, but because it
> gives expression to secular ideals which control the conduct of
> Germanic heroes.[8]

But surely the speech is most relevant to the poem as a whole because
it shows, through contextual allusion, how the highest conduct of
Germanic heroes is not in opposition to that of any hero aligned
with God's forces in the Great Feud. The speech reveals Hrothgar's
character and perhaps relates to Beowulf's motives at the end of
the poem, because it shows, again through contextual allusion, how
the Germanic ethos of wise magnanimity supports the will of God.
From the first, Hrothgar has been presented to us as more con-
cerned with the binding social function of ring-giving than with
the performance of heroic deeds; his purpose in building Heorot
was to provide a hall in which to imitate God's generosity with his
own. This "cosmic" connection is stressed both in the introduction
of Hrothgar (ll. 70–73) and in his speech, for Hrothgar has a vision
of giving as a kind of stability in the world of change, the world
where *wyrd* strikes against honor and dignity and, as a matter of
course, against avarice, the miserly hoarding of that treasure which
is the lifeblood of Germanic society.

Hrothgar's vision reaches beyond the bounds of the heroic world
until he seems able to accept (if not precisely to imagine) a gener-
ous God superior to *wyrd*, a Boethian ruler of the universe. Though
Hrothgar is not, as Klaeber maintains he is, "depicted as a good
Christian" (p. 135), he may be compared to Augustine's pagan phi-
losophers who have recognized God: "Whoever they may have
been, we rank such thinkers above all others and acknowledge
them as representing the closest approximation to our Christian
position."[9] Snorri Sturlusson, too, recognizes such minds among his
pagan ancestors. God granted men earthly gifts, worldly wealth and
prosperity, Snorri explains in the Prologue to his *Prose Edda*, "and
he also bestowed on them wisdom so that they understood all earthly
things, they guessed that there must be someone who ruled the

---

8. Michael D. Cherniss, *Ingeld and Christ: Heroic Concepts and Values in Old English
   Christian Poetry* (The Hague: Mouton, 1972), p. 149. In *The Mode and Meaning of
   Beowulf* (London: Athlone, 1970), Margaret Goldsmith argues precisely the opposite:
   "There is a discernible Augustinian pattern of thought throughout Hrothgar's speech"
   (p. 188).
9. Augustine, *City of God*, trans. Henry Bettenson (Harmondsworth, Eng.: Penguin, 1972),
   p. 311 (VIII, 9).

stars. . . . They understood everything in a material sense, however, since they had not been given spiritual understanding."[1] Hrothgar is among those Danes who guessed (like his scop) that "there must be someone who ruled the stars." He is grateful to Beowulf, with whom he promises to share treasures, but he thanks God, not Beowulf, that he may now look on Grendel's severed head after his "ancient struggle" (l. 1791).

In the context of the inscribed hilt and the meditation it inspires, this struggle has a meaning beyond the hero fight that we have witnessed in the story. But, as with the creation song, it is the accompanying scriptural allusions that lend Hrothgar's discourse a special meaning for us, different from the meaning it has for those listening in Heorot, who have not "been given spiritual understanding." It is what we are told of the sword's biblical history that elevates the ensuing discourse on generosity, *wyrd*, and vigilance to the level of a "sermon" for our Christian understanding and alerts us to the homiletic allusions throughout. The speaker himself, however, does not recognize that level in the words he speaks.

V. Levels of Knowledge in Beowulf

The poet controls his two perspectives simply by distinguishing between the natural wisdom possible to pagans and the revealed knowledge he shares with us. "In the persons of Beowulf and Hrothgar," writes A. D. Horton, "the poet is setting before us examples of noble pagans, virtuous in the practice of a natural religion."[2] He suggests that Paul's letter to the Romans, describing the ways in which pagans can know God and the degree to which they are culpable for their sins of ignorance, was influential in the *Beowulf* poet's time because it offered a means of justifying one's valued pagan ancestors that did not conflict with Germanic *pietas*. The line between what the ancient Scandinavians of Beowulf's world can and cannot have known may be charted from the Pauline doctrine expressed in Romans 1 and 2. First, all men can know the Creator through his works. Certain persons in *Beowulf* give evidence of this knowledge, just as Snorri Sturlusson acknowledges that some pagans have guessed at theistic truth. Second, all men have the natural law written in their hearts; so the freedom of right choice is not unduly affected by limited knowledge. The Danes are therefore culpable for deciding, in their despair, to worship the "soul-slayer." Both these kinds of knowledge, the principles of deity and of ethics, are said by Paul to be the "natural" knowledge available to pagans.

1. *The Prose Edda*, trans. Jean I. Young (Berkeley: Univ. of California Press, 1964), p. 24.
2. "Religious Attitudes in *Beowulf*," in *Essays and Poems Presented to Lord David Cecil* (London: Constable, 1970), p. 10.

What is not available to the pagans in the story is revealed knowledge: eschatology and the scriptures. The destiny of the soul is of concern to the Danes, but it remains a mystery to them, as the Scyld prologue makes clear. The value of the scriptural references is to point to a cosmic history of feuds that a postrevelation audience may see repeated in the action of the story and may align with pre-Christian native tradition. For an audience in a royal hall, the biblical overtones would reaffirm the native culture, whose values had been called into question by the arrival of Roman Christianity; for a cloister audience, the archetypal reflection of scriptural history in Beowulf's fights with demonic monsters would serve to "redeem" the native past.[3]

There is a patristic precedent for the nonallegorical method by which the *Beowulf* poet fuses the native historical and folklore materials of his story with the scriptural history of the beginnings of good and evil among mankind. Augustine "scripturizes" Romulus in much the same way as the *Beowulf* poet does Grendel, but with an entirely different purpose:

> The first founder of the earthly city was, as we have seen, a fratricide; for, overcome by envy, he slew his own brother, a citizen of the Eternal City, on pilgrimage in this world. Hence it is no wonder that long afterwards this first precedent—what the Greeks call an *archetype*—was answered by a kind of reflection, by an event of the same kind. . . . For this is how Rome was founded, when Remus, as Roman history witnesses, was slain by his brother Romulus.[4]

Augustine is using his theory of archetypes to defend his religion against the charge that it has corrupted his culture; the *Beowulf* poet is using a similar method to redeem his native and pagan culture by reconciling secular history to sacred "by a kind of reflection."[5] The text demonstrates that the poet had a firm grasp of this idea. His

---

3. Two such divergent experiences are still offered to the audience of the poem today, allowing one scholar to find the "meaning" of *Beowulf* "already complete within the Germanic heroic ethos" and another to read the poem as "the first great medieval allegory of human life and death based on the beliefs of the Western Church." The first is G. W. Smithers, quoted by Greenfield, *Interpretation*, p. 156; the second is Goldsmith, p. viii.

4. *City of God*, p. 600 (xv, 5). This concept of the archetype may well have been familiar to influential thinkers among the Anglo-Saxons. J. D. A. Ogilvy, in *Books Known to the English 597–1066* (Cambridge, Mass.: Medieval Academy of America, 1967), says, "The *Civitas Dei* was one of the most popular, if not the most popular, of Augustine's works among the English. . . . The fifteenth book seems to have been especially popular, being used almost as much as all the other books combined" (p. 82).

5. Citing Augustine's *City of God*, but not this passage, Marie Padgett Hamilton advances much the same interpretation in "The Religious Principle in *Beowulf*," *An Anthology of Beowulf Criticism*, ed. Lewis E. Nicholson (Notre Dame: Univ. of Notre Dame Press, 1963): "One is tempted to surmise that the author of *Beowulf*, in the manner of Bede and Augustine, envisioned the race of Cain in its timeless as well as temporal state . . ." (p. 124). When she goes on, however, to ascribe to the poet a deep concern with Augustine's doctrine of Grace, she seems to me to be over-reading the poem.

curiously unmedieval concern with anachronism, with what may be known "now" (in Christian England) but not "then" (in pagan Scandinavia), is necessary if he is to present Christian and secular themes as fused for us, as a kind of reflection of the archetype, while keeping these themes carefully separated, with the Christian element suppressed, for those in the story.

There is no need for further scriptural references after the two kinsfolk of Cain have been destroyed. We have had Hrothgar's warning that calamity continues to come unexpected upon mankind: strife is *always* renewed. "That feud with mankind has been going on since the earth first swallowed Abel's blood," proclaims the *Exeter Book* maximist, "that is not the hostility of a single day."[6] The advent of another adversary of mankind is inevitable. But the dragon's awakening is unexpected and misunderstood within the world of the story[7] because men there have little or no understanding of the Great Feud, continuous in cosmic history from Cain's blow until the monster fight of the apocalypse.

There is no pagan-Christian "problem" in *Beowulf*, as scholars have argued for over a century and a half, usually showing their prejudices by taking one side or the other. Rather than being in opposition, these two elements form an epistemological scheme embracing both secular and spiritual understanding like that presented more traditionally in *The Wanderer*.[8] Whereas some movement from the secular level toward the spiritual occurs within the Wanderer's experience, no such progression occurs within Beowulf's world, where the two levels are used for a different purpose. Our scriptural knowledge of the Great Feud gives us a framework within which to set particular feuds (both historical and monstrous) and to estimate men's valor. This cosmic dimension does not detract from, but instead supports, the native grandeur of the human soul as it is understood by the noblest pagans in *Beowulf*. By carefully maintaining two separate frames of reference, the poet allows us to "look down as if from a visionary height upon the house of man in the

6. *The Exeter Book*, ed. George Philip Krapp and Elliott van Kirk Dobbie, Vol. III of *The Anglo-Saxon Poetic Records* (New York: Columbia Univ. Press, 1936), p. 163 (*Maxims I*, ll. 192–93).

7. When the dragon burns the gift-throne of the Geats, Beowulf wonders whether this is divine retribution for some crime he has unwittingly committed (ll. 2327–32); curiously, Margaret Goldsmith takes this as a proof of Beowulf's "worldly outlook" (p. 226), which, through a misreading of the text of the poem, she sees as culminating in avarice (p. 239) and ultimately damnation (p. 262 et passim). There is in fact a great difference between Grendel's attack upon Heorot and the dragon's upon the Geats: whereas Grendel cannot approach the gift-throne of Hrothgar, the dragon burns Beowulf's. In heroic terms this is equivalent to the murder of a kingdom, and in such circumstances the dutiful hero-king has little choice: he must avenge the kingdom and obtain an honorable *eðel-gyld* (my word).

8. See Marijane Osborn, "Classical Meditation and *The Wanderer*," *Comparison*, 1 (1975), 67–101; . . . reprinted (condensed) in *Studia Mystica*, 1 (1978).

valley of the world" (Tolkien), and thereby to understand something more than may those heroes under Heaven, without intruding our Christian knowledge into Beowulf's world, where it is not relevant.

JANE CHANCE

The Structural Unity of *Beowulf*: The Problem of Grendel's Mother[†]

The episode in *Beowulf* involving Grendel's Mother has been viewed as largely extraneous, a blot upon the thematic and structural unity of the poem. If the poem is regarded as two-part in structure, balancing contrasts between the hero's youth and old age, his rise as a retainer and his fall as a king, his battles with the Grendel family and his battle with the dragon, then her episode (which includes Hrothgar's sermon and Hygelac's welcoming court celebration with its recapitulation of earlier events) lengthens the first "half" focusing on his youth to two-thirds of the poem (lines 1–2199).[1] If the poem is regarded as three-part in structure, with each part centering on one of the three monsters or the three fights, then the brevity of her episode again mars the structural balance: her section, roughly 500 lines (1251–1784), is not as long as Grendel's, roughly 1100–1200 lines (86–1250), or the dragon's, 1000 lines (2200–3182).[2] Even if her episode is lengthened to a thousand lines (from

---

† From *Texas Studies in Literature and Language* 22.3 (Fall 1980): 287–303. Copyright © 1980 by the University of Texas Press. All rights reserved. Reprinted by permission of the publisher.

1. This view of the structure as two-part has generally prevailed since its inception in J. R. R. Tolkien's "*Beowulf*: The Monsters and the Critics," in *Proceedings of the British Academy* 22 (1936): 245–95, rpt. in *An Anthology of Beowulf Criticism*, ed. Lewis E. Nicholson (Notre Dame: University of Notre Dame Press, 1963), pp. 51–104. The edition used throughout is Fr. Klaeber, *Beowulf and the Fight at Finnsburg*, 3rd ed. (Boston: D. C. Heath and Co., 1936, with supplements in 1941 and 1950).

2. This increasingly popular view of the structure as tripartite has been advanced by H. L. Rogers, "Beowulf's Three Great Fights," *Review of English Studies* 6 (1955): 339–55, rpt. in Nicholson, *Anthology*, pp. 233–56; John Gardner, "Fulgentius' *Expositio Vergiliana Continentia* and the Plan of *Beowulf*: Another Approach to the Poem's Style and Structure," *Papers in Language and Literature* 6 (1970): 227–62; and most recently, Kathryn Hume, "The Theme and Structure of *Beowulf*," *Studies in Philology* 72 (1975): 1–27. Hume's fine analysis includes an extensive survey of the various approaches to and interpretations of structural and thematic unity in *Beowulf* (see pp. 2–5). She declares, p. 3, "That critics should disagree over whether the structure has two parts or three is hardly surprising. Those concentrating on the hero tend to see two, those on action usually prefer three. But neither camp has produced a structural analysis which does not, by implication, damn the poet for gross incompetence, or leave the critic with a logically awkward position." For example, William W. Ryding, *Structure in Medieval Narrative* (The Hague: Mouton, 1971), first regards the middle of *Beowulf* as "a point of maximum logical discontinuity," p. 40, and then, contradicting himself, as a more difficult, more intense, more exciting combat than the fight with Grendel, illustrating a "varied repetition" of the same narrative motif, therefore implying logical continuity (p. 88).

line 1251 to 2199) so as to include Hrothgar's sermon and Hygelac's court celebration, still Grendel's Mother hardly dominates these events literally or symbolically as Grendel and the dragon dominate the events in their sections.

But her battle with Beowulf (and this middle section of the poem) is more than merely a "transition between two great crises," even though it is "linked with both the Grendel fight and the Dragon fight."[3] The key to her significance[4] may indeed derive from her links with the other two monsters in a way Bonjour did not envision when he made these statements.

Grendel and the dragon have been interpreted recently as monstrous projections of flaws in Germanic civilization portrayed by the poet as "Negative Men."[5] Grendel is introduced as a mock

3. Adrien Bonjour, "Grendel's Dam and the Composition of *Beowulf,*" *English Studies* 30 (1949): 117. Other early *Beowulf* studies similarly ignored Grendel's Mother or treated her as a type of Grendel. See also Tolkien, "Monsters," in which he declares, "I shall confine myself mainly to the monsters—Grendel and the Dragon . . . ," in Nicholson, *Anthology,* p. 52. Similar treatments occur in T. M. Gang, "Approaches to *Beowulf,*" *Review of English Studies* 3 (1952): 1–12; Bonjour, "Monsters Crouching and Critics Rampant: or the *Beowulf* Dragon Debated," *Publications of the Modern Language Association* 68 (1953): 304–12; and even more recently, in Margaret Goldsmith, *The Mode and Meaning of Beowulf* (London: Athlone Press, 1970), e.g., p. 144; Alvin A. Lee, *The Guest-Hall of Eden* (New Haven: Yale University Press, 1972), pp. 171–223; and Daniel G. Calder, "Setting and Ethos: The Pattern of Measure and Limit in *Beowulf,*" *Studies in Philology* 69 (1972): 21–37.
4. Recently interpretations have stressed her significance in Germanic social terms, but without developing the implications of such insights: a Jungian analysis views her as symbolic of the "evil latent in woman's function, as Grendel symbolizes the destructive element hidden in Beowulf's *maegen.* . . . Grendel's Mother symbolizes the feud aspect of the web of peace. . . ." Further, as a destroyer she signifies "the obverse of the women we meet in the two banqueting scenes which precede Beowulf's descent into Grendelsmere," both of whom combine to form the dual mother image. See Jeffrey Helterman, "*Beowulf*: The Archetype Enters History," *ELH* 35 (1968): 12–13, 14. To other critics she represents vengeance (Nist, Irving, Hume), false loyalty (Gardner), revenge (Leyerle). See John A. Nist, *The Structure and Texture of Beowulf* (Língua e Literatura Inglése, vol. 1; São Paulo: Universidade de São Paulo, Faculdade de Filosofia, Ciências, e Letres, 1959), p. 21; Edward B. Irving, Jr., *A Reading of Beowulf* (New Haven: Yale University Press, 1968), p. 113, and *Introduction to Beowulf* (Englewood Cliffs, N.J.: Prentice-Hall, 1969), p. 57; Kathryn Hume, "The Theme and Structure of *Beowulf,*" p. 7; Gardner, "Fulgentius' *Expositio Vergiliana Continentia* and the Plan of *Beowulf,*" p. 255; and John Leyerle, "The Interlace Structure of *Beowulf,*" *University of Toronto Quarterly* 37 (1967–68): 11–12.
   Other recent interpretations have explored not only Jungian but also Scandinavian and Celtic mythic and legendary parallels, sources, or analogues of this figure: for the Scandinavian parallels, see Nora K. Chadwick, "The Monsters and *Beowulf,*" in *The Anglo-Saxons: Studies in Some Aspects of their History and Culture Presented to Bruce Dickins,* ed. Peter Clemoes (London: Bowes and Bowes, 1959), pp. 171–203, and Larry D. Benson, "The Originality of *Beowulf,*" in *The Interpretation of Narrative: Theory and Practice,* ed. Morton W. Bloomfield (Harvard English Studies, vol. 1; Cambridge, Mass.: Harvard University Press, 1970), pp. 1–43; for the Celtic parallels, see Martin Puhvel, "The Might of Grendel's Mother," *Folklore* 80 (1969): 81–88; and for amalgamated parallels—English, German, Latin, and Scandinavian—viewing Grendel and his mother as incubus and succubus, see Nicolas K. Kiessling, "Grendel: A New Aspect," *Modern Philology* 65 (1968): 191–201.
5. Groundwork for this interpretation of the monsters as enemies of man was first laid by Arthur E. Dubois, "The Unity of *Beowulf,*" *Publications of the Modern Language Association* 49 (1934): 391 (Grendel and his mother become "the Danes' liability to punishment" for the secular sins of weakness, pride, and treachery; the dragon, "a variation

"hall-retainer" (*renweard*, 770; *healðegn*, 142) who envies the men of Heorot their joy of community; he subsequently attacks the hall in a raid that is described through the parodic hall ceremonies of feasting, ale-drinking, gift-receiving, and singing.[6] The dragon is introduced as a mock "gold-king" or *hord-weard* (2293, 2303, 2554, 2593) who avariciously guards his barrow or "ring-hall" (*hringsele*, 3053),[7] and attacks Beowulf's kingdom after he discovers the loss of a single cup. The envy of the evil hall-retainer and the avarice of the evil gold-king antithesize the Germanic *comitatus* ideal first enunciated in Tacitus' *Germania* and pervading heroic and elegiac Anglo-Saxon literature: the *comitatus'* well-being depended upon the retainer's valor in battle and loyalty to his lord and the lord's protection and treasure-giving in return.[8]

Like these monsters, Grendel's Mother is also described in human and social terms. She is specifically called a *wīf unhȳre* "a monstrous woman" (2120), and an *ides āglǣcwīf* "a lady monster-woman" (1259). *Ides* elsewhere in *Beowulf* denotes "lady" and connotes either a queen or a woman of high social rank; outside *Beowulf*, primarily in Latin and Old English glosses, *ides* pairs with *virgo* to suggest maidenhood, as when *on idesan* equals *in virgunculam*.[9] In addition, as if the poet wished to stress her maternal role, she is characterized usually as Grendel's *mōdor* or kinswoman (*māge*, 1391), the former a word almost exclusively reserved for her, although other mothers appear in the poem.[1] It seems clear from these epithets that Grendel's Mother inverts the Germanic roles of the mother and queen, or lady. She has the form of a woman (*idese onlīcnes*, 1351) and is weaker than a man (1282ff) and more cowardly, for she flees in fear

---

upon Grendel," is "internal discord"). More recently they have been understood as adversaries of both man and God: see Richard N. Ringler, "Him Sōo Wōn Gelēah: The Design for Irony in Grendel's Last Visit to Heorot," *Speculum* 41 (1966): 64, in which Grendel represents *ofermōd* or *forträwung*, "held suspect by both Germanic instinct and Christian doctrine." See also Lee, *Guest-Hall*, p. 186.
6. For this interpretation of Grendel, see especially Edward B. Irving, Jr., "*Ealuscerwen*: Wild Party at Heorot," *Tennessee Studies in Literature* 11 (1966): 161–68, and *A Reading*, p. 16; also William A. Chaney, "Grendel and the *Gifstol*: A Legal View of Monsters," *Publications of the Modern Language Association* 77 (1962): 513–20; Joseph L. Baird, "Grendel the Exile," *Neuphilologische Mitteilungen* 67 (1966): 375–81.
7. Irving, *A Reading*, p. 209; Lee, *Guest-Hall*, pp. 215–16.
8. Tacitus, *Germania*, ed. Rodney Potter Robinson (Philological Monographs, vol. 5; Middletown, Conn.: American Philological Association, 1935), p. 291 (cap. 14).
9. In *Beowulf*: in 620, 1168, and 1649 used of Wealhtheow, lady of the Helmings or Scyldings; in 1075 and 1117 of Hildeburh; in 1941 of Queen Thryth. Outside *Beowulf*: see "Kentish Glosses" (ca. ninth century) in Thomas Wright, *Anglo-Saxon and Old English Vocabularies*, ed. Richard Paul Wülcker, 2nd ed. (London: Trübner and Co., 1884), vol. 1, p. 88. For *on idesan* paired with *in virgunculam*, see *in iuuenculam* in the gloss on Aldhelm's *De Laudibus Virginitatis* 29.14, in *Old English Glosses*, ed. Arthur S. Napier (Oxford: Oxford University Press, 1900), p. 57; also for *ides* as *virguncula* see the gloss on Aldhelm's *De Laudibus Virginum* 191.7 and 191.14, pp. 181, 183.
1. Used of Grendel's Mother in 1258, 1276, 1282, 1538, 1683, 2118, and 2139. In 2932 *mōdor* refers to the mother of Onela and Ohthere.

for her life when discovered in Heorot (1292–93). But unlike most mothers and queens, she fights her own battles. *Maxims I* testifies that, "Battle, war, must develop in the man, and the woman must flourish beloved among her people, must be light-hearted."[2]

Because the poet wishes to stress this specific inversion of the Anglo-Saxon ideal of woman as both monstrous and masculine he labels her domain a "battle-hall" (*nīðsele*, 1513; *gūðsele*, 2139).[3] (The dragon's barrow he describes equally appropriately, given the monster's avaricious symbolic nature, as a "ring-hall," as we saw previously.) In addition, he occasionally uses a masculine pronoun in referring to her (*sē þe* instead of *sēo þe* in 1260, 1497; *hē* instead of *hēo* in 1392, 1394). Such a change in pronoun occurs elsewhere in the poem only in reference to abstract feminine nouns used as personifications and to concrete feminine nouns used as synecdoches.[4] Other epithets applied to her are usually applied to male figures: warrior, *sinnige secg*, in 1379; destroyer, *mihtig mānscaða*, in 1339; and [male] guardian, *gryrelīcne grundhyrde*, in 2136. Indeed, in the phrase *ides āglǣcwīf* applied to Grendel's Mother as a "lady monster-woman" the *āglǣca* not only means "monster," as it does when directed at Grendel (159, 425, 433, 556, 592, 646, 732, 739, 816, 989, 1000, 1269) or the water monsters (1512), but also "fierce combatant" or "strong adversary," as when directed at Sigemund in line 893 and Beowulf and the dragon in line 2592.[5] Such a woman might be wretched or monstrous because she insists on arrogating the masculine role of the warrior or lord.

Her episode is thus appropriately divided like her monstrous but human nature and her female but male behavior into two parts to illustrate the various feminine roles—of the mother or kinswoman (*mōdor*) and queen or lady (*ides āglǣcwīf*)—she inverts. The poet constantly contrasts the unnatural behavior of Grendel's dam with that of the feminine ideal by presenting human examples as foils in each of the two parts. We turn first to an examination of the female ideal in *Beowulf*, then to a detailed analysis of the episode involving

2. George Philip Krapp and Elliott Van Kirk Dobbie, eds., *The Exeter Book*, vol. 3 of *The Anglo-Saxon Poetic Records* (New York: Columbia University Press, 1936), p. 159 (lines 83–85).
3. Bosworth-Toller's *Anglo-Saxon Dictionary* lists *hringsele* and *nīðsele* as compounds singular to *Beowulf*, underscoring the intentionality of the poet's irony.
4. Masculine pronouns refer to the feminine personifications of Old Age (1887) and Change or Death (2421), and to the feminine synecdoche "hand" (1344).
5. *Āglǣca* apparently means "fierce adversary" in *Juliana* 268 and 319 where the Devil in the garb of an angel brings tidings to the maiden; when she asks who sent him, *Hyre se aglæca ageaf ondsware* 'The fierce adversary answered her' (319) in *The Exeter Book*, p. 122. Because he no longer appears to be a "wretch, monster, miscreant," the term *āglǣca* must denote "foe" in this passage. Indeed, Juliana addresses him in line 317 as *feond moncynnes*, "foe" or "enemy of mankind."

Grendel's Mother and its two parts, and finally to some conclusions regarding the structural unity of the entire poem.

I

The role of woman in *Beowulf* primarily depends upon "peace-making," either biologically through her marital ties with foreign kings as a peace pledge or mother of sons, or socially and psychologically as a cup-passing and peace-weaving queen within a hall. Wealhtheow becomes a peace-pledge or *friðusibb folca* (2017) to unite the Danes and Helmings; Hildeburh similarly unites the Danes and Frisians through her marriage; and Freawaru at least intends to pledge peace between the Danes and Heathobards. Such a role is predicated upon the woman's ability to bear children, to create blood ties, bonds to weave a "peace kinship."

In addition, woman functions domestically within the nation as a cup-passer during hall festivities of peace (*freoþo*) and joy (*drēam*) after battle or contest. The mead-sharing ritual and the cup-passer herself come to symbolize peace-weaving and peace because they strengthen the societal and familial bonds between lord and retainers. First, the literal action of the *freoðuwebbe* "peace-weaver" (1942) as she passes the cup from warrior to warrior weaves an invisible web of peace: the order in which each man is served, according to his social position, reveals each man's dependence upon and responsibility toward another. For example, after Wealhtheow gives the cup to Hrothgar, she bids him to be joyful at drinking as well as loving to his people (615ff). Then she offers it to the *duguð* "old retainers," then to the *geoguð* "young retainers," and finally to the guest Beowulf. Second, her peace-weaving also takes a verbal form: her speeches accompanying the mead-sharing stress the peace and joy contingent upon the fulfillment of each man's duty to his nation. At the joyous celebration after Grendel's defeat, Wealhtheow concludes her speeches with a tribute to the harmony of the present moment by reminding her tribe of its cause, that is, adherence to the *comitatus* ethic. Each man remains true to the other, each is loyal to the king, the nation is ready and alert, the drinking warriors attend to the ale-dispenser herself (1228–31). Yet minutes before she attempted to forestall future danger to her family and nation by preventive peace-weaving, she advised Hrothgar to leave his kingdom to his sons, and then, as if sensing the future, she reminded Hrothulf, his nephew, of his obligations to those sons (obligations he will later deny). Third, the peace-weaver herself emblematizes peace, for she appears in the poem with her mead-vessel only after a contest has been concluded. Thus Wealhtheow

enters the hall only after the contest between Unferth and Beowulf
(612); she does not appear again until after Beowulf has overcome
Grendel, when the more elaborate feasting invites the peace-making
speeches mentioned above. After Grendel's Mother is defeated the
poet preserves the integrity of the pattern of feminine cup-passing
after masculine contest by describing the homecoming banquet at
Hygelac's court, where Hygd conveys the mead-vessel. This struc-
tural pattern to which we shall return simultaneously weaves
together the Danish part of the poem with its Geatish part.

Most of the other female characters figure as well in this middle
section so that the female monster's adventures are framed by
descriptions of other women for ironic contrast. The role of mother
highlights the first half of the middle section with the scop's men-
tion of Hildeburh (1071ff) and the entrance of Wealhtheow, both of
whom preface the first appearance of Grendel's dam (1258) in her
role as avenging mother. Then the introduction of Hygd, Thryth, and
Freawaru after the female monster's death (1590) stresses the role
of queen as peace-weaver and cup-passer to preface Beowulf's final
narration of the female monster's downfall (2143). The actual adven-
tures of Grendel's Mother cluster then at the middle of the middle
section of the poem.

II

In the first part of the female monster's section, the idea is stressed
that a kinswoman or mother must passively accept and not actively
avenge the loss of her son. The story of the mother Hildeburh is
recited by the scop early on the evening Grendel's Mother will visit
Heorot. The lay ends at line 1159; Grendel's Mother enters the poem
a mere hundred lines later when she attacks the Danish hall, as the
Frisian contingent attacked the hall lodging Hildeburh's Danish
brother in the *Finnsburh Fragment*. The *Beowulf* poet alters the
focus of the fragment: he stresses the consequences of the surprise
attack rather than the attack itself in order to reveal Hildeburh's
maternal reactions to them.

Hildeburh is unjustly (*unsynnum*, 1072) deprived of her Danish
brother and Frisian son, but all she does, this sad woman (*geōmuru
ides*, 1075), is to mourn her loss with dirges and stoically place her
son on the pyre. In fact, she can do nothing, caught in the very web
she has woven as peace-pledge: her husband's men have killed her
brother, her brother's men have killed her son. Later the Danish
Hengest will avenge the feud with her husband Finn, whether she
approves or not, by overwhelming the Frisians and returning Hilde-
burh to her original tribe. The point remains: the peace-pledge must
accept a passive role precisely because the ties she knots bind

her—she *is* the knot, the pledge of peace. Her fate interlaces with
that of her husband and brothers through her role as a mother
bearing a son: thus Hildeburh appropriately mourns the loss of her
symbolic tie at the pyre, the failure of herself as peace-pledge, the
loss of her identity. Like Hildeburh Grendel's dam will also lose her
identity as mother, never having had an identity as peace-pledge to
lose.

As if reminded of her own role as mother by hearing of Hilde-
burh's plight, Wealhtheow demonstrates her maternal concern in
an address to Hrothgar immediately after the scop sings this lay. In
it she first alludes to Hrothgar's adoption of Beowulf as a son: appar-
ently troubled by this, she insists that Hrothgar leave his kingdom
only to his actual kinsmen or descendants when he dies (1178–79).
Then she urges her foster "son" Hrothulf (actually a nephew) to
remember his obligations to them so that he will "repay our sons
with liberality" (1184–85). Finally, she moves to the mead-bench
where the adopted Beowulf sits, rather symbolically, next to her sons
Hrethric and Hrothmund (1188–91). The *past* helplessness of the
first mother, Hildeburh, to requite the death of her son counter-
points the anxiously maternal Wealhtheow's attempts to weave the
ties of kinship and obligation, thereby forestalling *future* danger to
her sons. Later that night, Grendel's Mother intent on avenging the
loss of her son in the *present* attacks Heorot, her masculine aggres-
sion contrasting with the feminine passivity of both Hildeburh and
Wealhtheow. Indeed, she resembles a grieving human mother: like
Hildeburh she is guiltless and *galgmōd* "gloomy-minded" (1277); her
journey to Heorot must be sorrowful (1278) for she "remembered her
misery" (1259). But a woman's primary loyalty as peace pledge was
reserved for her husband, not her son, according to the Danish his-
tory of Saxo Grammaticus.[6] Perhaps for this reason Grendel's Mother
is presented as husbandless and son-obsessed—to suggest to an
Anglo-Saxon audience the dangers inherent in woman's function as
friðusibb "pledge of peace".

However, her attempts to avenge her son's death could be justi-
fied if she were human and male, for no *wergild* "man price" has
been offered to her by the homicide Beowulf.[7] The role of the mas-
culine avenger is emphasized throughout the passage (1255–78) in

6. See the stories of the treacherous wife but loyal mother Urse in the twelfth-century
Saxonis Grammatici Gesta Danorum, ed. Alfred Holder (Strassburg: K. J. Trübner, 1886),
pp. 53–55; (*The First Nine Books of the Danish History of Saxo Grammaticus*, tr. Oliver
Elton [London: D. Nutt, 1894], pp. 64–65 [II, 53–55]).
7. Dorothy Whitelock, *The Beginnings of English Society* (Baltimore: Penguin Books, 1952),
p. 41; on duty to one's kin, see pp. 38–47; on duty to one's lord, see pp. 31ff. Duty to
one's lord superseded duty to one's kin (p. 37). See also *Saxonis Grammatici Gesta Dan-
orum*, p. 254 (VII), for the retainer's duty to lord; in cases of blood revenge the son
remained most deeply obligated to his father, pp. 75, 96 (III), then to his brother or sister,
pp. 53, 280 (II, VIII), finally to his grandfather, p. 301 (IX).

defining her motivation to attack: she performs the role of avenger (*wrecend*, 1256) "to avenge the death of her son" (1278). Whatever her maternal feelings, she actually fulfills the duty of the kinsman. Unlike Hildeburh, she cannot wait for a Hengest to resolve the feud in some way; unlike Freawaru, she cannot act as a peace-pledge to settle the feud. Tribeless, now kinless, forced to rely on her own might, she seizes and kills Aeschere, Hrothgar's most beloved retainer, in an appropriate retribution for the loss of her own most beloved "retainer" and "lord"—her son.

The monstrosity of her action is at first not evident. Hrothgar suspects she has carried the "feud" too far (1339–40). And from the Danish and human point of view she possesses no legal right to exact compensation for her kinsman's loss because Grendel is himself a homicide. However, Beowulf later implies that the two feuds must remain separate, as she desires her own "revenge for injury" (*gyrn-wracu*, 2118). Because she is legally justified in pursuing her own feud given the tribal duty of the retainer to avenge the death of his lord, regardless of the acts he has committed, she behaves monstrously then in only one way. For a mother to "avenge" her son (2121) as if she were a retainer, he were her lord, and avenging more important than peace-making, is monstrous. An analogy conveying her effect on the men in Heorot when she first appears suggests how unusual are her actions in human terms. Her horror "is as much less as is the skill (strength) of maidens, the war-horror of a woman, in comparison to a (weaponed) man, when the bound sword shears the one standing opposite" (*Wæs se gryre læssa / efne swā micle,   swā bið mægþa cræft, / wīggryre wīfes   þe wæpnedmen, / þonne heoru bunden . . . / . . . / . . . andweard sireð*, 1282–87). In their eyes recognizably female, she threatens them physically less than her son. But because female "peacemakers" do not wage war, the analogy implies, by litotes, that her unnatural behavior seems *more* horrible.

In the second part of her adventure she no longer behaves solely as an avenging monster, antitype of Hildeburh and Wealhtheow, who are both through marriage "visitors" to a hall like Grendel and his dam. Such hall-visitors contrast with the hall-rulers of this second part: the *merewīf* as queen or guardian (*grundhyrde*, 2136) protects her "battle-hall," the cave-like lair, from the visiting hero like the regal dragon guarding his ring-hall, and like King Beowulf his kingdom, in the last section of the poem. Accordingly, the stress on the relationship between mother and son delineated in the first part of her adventure changes to a stress on the relationship between host and guest.

As a tribeless queen or lady (*ides āglǣcwīf*) she rudely receives her "hall-guest" Beowulf (*selegyst*, 1545; *gist*, 1522) by "embracing" him and then "repaying him" for his valor not with treasure but with "grim grips" (*Hēo him eft hraþe   andlean forgeald / grimman grapum*, 1541–42) just as the dragon will "entertain" him in the future.[8] Indeed, the parody of the hall-ceremony of treasure-giving is complete when a "scop" (Beowulf's sword, acting as bard) sings a fierce "war song" off the side of her head (*hire on hafelan   hringmǣl āgōl / grǣdig gūðlēoð*, 1521–22). It is interesting to note that this "hall-celebration" of the mock peace-weaver to welcome her valorous guest Beowulf following her attack on Heorot and her curiously listless "contest" with Aeschere duplicates the pattern of mead-sharing ceremonies involving peacemakers which follow masculine contests throughout the poem.

It is also interesting to note that the contest between this apparently lordless "queen" and her "guest" contrasts in its mock-sensual embracing and grasping with the other two major battles of the hero—the briefly described arm-wrestling between Grendel and Beowulf and the conventional sword-wielding of Beowulf against the fire-breathing dragon. Indeed, before Beowulf arrives at the "battle-hall" Hrothgar introduces the possibility of a Grendel's father in addition to the mother, even though they do not know of such a father (1355), and of possible additional progeny of such a father or even of Grendel himself (through an incestuous union with his mother?): *hwæþer him ǣnig wæs   ǣr ācenned / dyrnra gāsta* (1356–57). His ostensible point is to warn Beowulf of additional monsters lurking nearby, but it serves as well to remind the reader that Grendel's Mother has an animal nature very different from that of a human lady. For during the passage describing their battle the poet exploits the basic resemblance between sexual intercourse and battle to emphasize the inversion of the feminine role of the queen or hall-ruler by Grendel's Mother. This is achieved in three steps: first, the emphasis upon clutching, grasping, and embracing while they fight; second, the contest for a dominant position astride the other; and third, the use of fingers, knife, or sword to penetrate clothing or the body, the latter always accompanied by the implied figurative kinship between the sword and the phallus and between decapitation and castration.

8. The poet uses similar wordplay in describing the "reception" of the guest Beowulf in the "hall" of the gold-lord dragon. First, Beowulf does not dare attack (or more figuratively, "approach") the gold-lord dragon in his ring-hall (*hringsele*, 2840, 3053); Wiglaf admits *hē ne grētte goldweard þone* 'he did not approach the guardian of the gold' (3081), literally because of the danger from fire, figuratively because of the dragon's avarice. Instead, *wyrd* 'fate' will dispense or distribute his "soul's hoard" for which Beowulf has paid with his life (*wyrd* will seek his *sāwle hord,   sundur gedǣlan / līf wið līce* 'soul's hoard, separate his life from his body', 2422–23a; he "buys" the hoard with his life in 2799–800). After this "treasure-giving," the cup-passer—Wiglaf—pours water from the cup—Beowulf's helmet.

First, she welcomes him to the *mere* with an almost fatal embrace similar to the "embrace" (*fæðm*, 1218) to which Aeschere has succumbed. She "grasped then towards him" (1501), seizing him with "horrible grips" (1502–03) envisioned earlier by the hero as a "battle-grip" (1445) and a "malicious grasp" (1447). Second, inside the "castle" (*hof*, 1507) where she has transported him, both grapple for a superior position over the other. After his sword fails him, for example, he "grasped her by the shoulder," hurling her to the ground. The poet, conscious of the monster's sex and Beowulf's definitely unchivalrous behavior, drily protests that in this case "the lord of the Battle-Geats did not at all lament the hostile act" (1537–38). Then, as "reward" for his valor, this lady "repaid" him with the treasure of her *grimman grāpum* "fierce graspings," forcing him to stumble and fall (1541–44), after which she climbs, rather ludicrously, on top of her "hall-guest" (*selegyst*, 1545), intent on stabbing him and thereby (again) avenging her only offspring (1546–47). Third, the battle culminates in very suggestive swordplay, and wordplay too. Earlier her "hostile fingers" (1505) tried to "penetrate" (*ðurhfōn*, 1504) his locked coat-of-mail; now she tries unsuccessfully to pierce the woven breast-net with her knife. Previously Beowulf discovered his own weapon was impotent against the spell or charm of the "sword-greedy" woman (*heorogīfre*, 1498), who collects the swords of giants. Now the "sword-grim" hero substitutes one of these swords, an appropriate tool to quell such a woman. The "sword entirely penetrated (*ðurhwōd*) the doomed-to-die body" (1567–68). After this final "embrace" of the "grasping" of her neck, the sword *wæs swātig secg weorce gefeh* "was bloody, the warrior rejoiced in the work" (1569). The alliteration links *sweord* with *secg*, to identify the bloody sword with the rejoicing, laboring "man-sword" (*secg*); the "battle" appropriately evokes erotic undertones. The equation of the sword and warrior, with the subsequent sexual connotations, resembles the synedoche controlling Riddle Twenty, "The Sword," in which the sword becomes a retainer who serves his lord through celibacy, forgoing the "joy-game" of marriage and the "treasure" of children, and whose only unpleasant battle occurs with a woman, because he must overcome her desire while she voices her terror, claps her hands, rebukes him with words, and cries out *ungod* "not good."[9] Similarly in *Beowulf* once the sword finally penetrates the body its blade miraculously melts—like ice into water—either from

9. *The Exeter Book*, pp. 190–91. The sword declares:

                              Ic wiþ bryde ne mot
        hæmed habban,   ac me þæs hyhtplegan
        geno wyrneð,   se mec geara on
        bende legde;   forþon ic brucan sceal
        on hagostealde   hæleþa gestreona.
        Oft ic wirum dol   wife abelge,

the poison of Grendel's blood or of his mother's, the poem does not specify which (1601). And even the *mere* itself, approached through winding passageways, slopes, and paths, and in whose stirred-up and bloody waters sea monsters lurk and the strange battle-hall remains hidden, almost projects the mystery and danger of female sexuality run rampant.

Such erotic overtones in descriptions of battles between a male and a female adversary are not especially common in Anglo-Saxon literature but can be found in various saints' lives in the Old English *Martyrology* (ca. 850) and in Ælfric's *Lives of the Saints* (ca. 994– early eleventh century), and in another epic poem also contained in the same manuscript as *Beowulf, Judith*. In the saints' lives a large group of thirty-four portrays a physical conflict between a Christian woman and a pagan man wishing to seduce her physically or spiritually. The description of the torture the saint undergoes to preserve her chastity often veils with obvious sexual symbolism the act of intercourse, or else it lovingly lingers over the description of the virgin's rape (see, for example, the life of St. Lucia).[1] The reason for such descriptions should be clear to those acquainted with the *Canticum Canticorum* and its celebration of the love of the Sponsa for the Sponsus (of man's soul for God, of the Church for Christ), providing an analogous basis for the holy sacrament of marriage. The woman saint as a type of the soul longs to be joined, as in intercourse, with her spouse Christ; the threat of seduction by a human male must be read as an assault on the soul by the Devil.

In *Judith*, a work like *Beowulf* contained in MS Cotton Vitellius A.xv,[2] the fragmentary epic portrays similar sexual overtones in Judith's "battle" with Holofernes. As in *Beowulf* a warrior battles a monster: the blessed maiden grapples with the "drunken, vicious

---

wonie hyre willan;   heo me worn spreceð,
floceð hyre folmum,   firenaþ mec wordum,
ungod gæleð.   Ic ne gyme þæs compes.

(I may not have sexual intercourse with a bride, but he who formerly laid bonds on me denies me still the joy-game; therefore I must enjoy the treasures of heroes while living in my lord's house. Often I, foolish in ornaments, anger the woman, diminish her will; she speaks evil to me with words, cries out "not good." I do not care for the contest.)

Similarly erotic riddles include no. 21, "Plow"; no. 44, "Key", no. 53, "Battering Ram"; no. 62, "Poker" or "Burning Arrow"; and no. 91, "Key."

1. When St. Lucia resists the advances of the pagan Paschasius and he condemns her to be 'defiled' (*bysmrian*) in a whorehouse as punishment, she retorts, 'To me intercourse with thy slave is not more pleasant than if an adder would hurt me' (*nis me þynes weales hæmed næfre þe leofre þe me nædre toslyte*). See *An Old English Martyrology*, ed. George Herzfeld (Early English Text Society, o.s., vol. 116; London: The Early English Text Society, 1900), p. 218.

2. Although the poems were written by different poets, *Beowulf* in the late seventh or eighth century and *Judith* in the middle or late tenth century, the second *Beowulf* scribe did transcribe all of the *Judith* fragment, probably in the late tenth century. All references to *Judith* derive from Elliott Van Kirk Dobbie, ed., *Beowulf and Judith*, vol. 4 of *The Anglo-Saxon Poetic Records* (New York: Columbia University Press, 1953).

monster" (se inwidda 'the evil one', 28) Holofernes. However, the
sexual role behavior of Beowulf occurs in reverse in Judith: Holofernes
parallels Grendel's dam, but whereas the wīf is aggressive and sword-
greedy, Holofernes seems slightly effete (his bed enclosed by gold
curtains, for example) and impotent from mead-drinking: "The lord
fell, the powerful one so drunken, in the middle of his bed, as if he
knew no reason in his mind" (67–69). These hypermetrical lines
heighten the irony of his situation, for the warrior swoons on the
very bed upon which he intended to rape the maiden. Having lost
his head to drink in a double sense he himself is penetrated by the
virgin's sharp sword, "hard in the storm of battle" (79), thereafter
literally losing his head. But first Judith draws the sword from its
sheath in her right hand, seizes him by the hair in a mock loving
gesture (98–99), then "with her hands pulls him toward her shame-
fully" (teah hyne folmum wið hyre weard / bysmerlice, 99b–100a). The
"b" alliteration in line 100 (bysmerlice, ond þone bealofullan) draws
attention to bysmerlice, which as a verb (bysmrian) elsewhere sug-
gests the act of "defiling" (intercourse).[3] In this line what seems
shameful is apparently her embrace of the warrior's body while she
moves it to a supine position. As in Beowulf, the female assumes
the superior position; she lays him down so that she may "control"
(gewealdan, 103) him more easily in cutting off his head. The ironic
embrace and mock intercourse of this couple parallels that of Beowulf
and the ides āglæcwīf: the aggressive and sword-bearing "virgin" con-
trasts with the passive and swordless man (Holofernes, Aeschere, and
even Beowulf are all momentarily or permanently swordless). The
poet's point in each case is that a perversion of the sexual roles signals
an equally perverse spiritual state. Holofernes' impotence is as unnat-
ural in the male as the wīf's aggression is unnatural in the female; so
the battle with the heroine or hero in each case is described with
erotic overtones to suggest the triumph of a right and natural sexual
(and social and spiritual) order over the perverse and unnatural one.
In the latter case Grendel's dam and her son pose a heathen threat to
Germanic society (the macrocosm) and to the individual (Beowulf
the microcosm) as Holofernes and the Assyrians pose a heathen
threat to Israelite society (the macrocosm) and to the individual
(Judith the microcosm).[4]

In this second part of her adventure, Hygd and Freawaru contrast
with the wīf as queen or cup-passer as Hildeburh and Wealhtheow
contrasted with Grendel's dam as mother in the first. Hygd, the first

3. See, for example, the life of St. Lucia in the Martyrology, p. 218.
4. For a discussion of these planes of correspondence in Judith, see James F. Doubleday,
   "The Principle of Contrast in Judith," Neuphilologische Mitteilungen 72 (1971): 436–41.

woman encountered after the defeat of Grendel's Mother, as truly
fulfills the feminine ideal of *Maxims* I as does Wealhtheow. Her
name, which means "Thought" or "Deliberation," contrasts her nature
with that of the bellicose *wīf* and possibly that of the war-like Thryth,
whose actions, if not her name, suggest "Strength" (only in the physi-
cal sense; the alternate form of her name, "Modthrytho" or "Mind-
Force," implies in a more spiritual sense stubbornness or pride).[5]
Although Hygd like the *wīf* and Thryth will be lordless after Hygelac's
death, she does not desire to usurp the role of king for herself: doubt-
ing her son's ability to prevent tribal wars she offers the throne to
Beowulf (2369ff). In addition, this gracious queen bestows treasure
generously (1929–31), unlike the *wīf* and Thryth, the latter of whom
dispense only "grim grips" and sword blows upon their "retainers."

The Thryth digression is inserted after Hygd enters to pass the
cup upon Beowulf's return to Hygelac. Its structural position invites
a comparison of this stubborn princess and the other two "queens,"
Hygd and the *wīf*. She appears to combine features of both: she
begins as a type of the female monster, but upon marriage to Offa
changes her nature and becomes a much-loved queen. According to
the poet, Thryth commits a "terrible crime"; she condemns to death
any retainer at court caught staring at her regal beauty. That she
abrogates her responsibilities as a queen and as a woman the poet
makes clear: "Such a custom—that the peace-weaver after a pre-
tended injury deprive the dear man of life—is not queenly for a
woman to do, although she be beautiful" (*Ne bið swylc cwēnlīc þeaw
/ idese tō efnanne, þeah ðe hīo ænlicu sȳ, / þætte freoðuwebbe fēores
onsæce / æfter ligetorne lēofne mannan*, 1940b–43). The label "peace-
weaver" (*freoðuwebbe*) seems ironic in this context, especially as
she does not weave but instead severs the ties of kinship binding her
to her people and the bonds of life tying the accused man to this
world. That is, for any man caught looking at her "the deadly bonds,

5. See Klaeber's discussion of Thryth's possible prototypes, 1931–62nn. Thryth's name
resembles that of Quendrida (Queen Thryth?) and that of the Scottish Queen Her-
mutrude, whose story is related in Saxo Grammaticus' *Danish History*, p. 124 (*Gesta
Danorum*, pp. 101–102 [IV]). Hermutrude, loved by Amleth, remains unmarried because
of her cruelty and arrogance, similar to Thryth's. Finally, note the similarity between
the following descriptions and those in *Beowulf*: Offa murdered many without distinc-
tion, including King Ethelbert, "thereby being guilty of an *atrocious outrage* against the
suitor of his daughter," in William of Malmesbury's *Chronicle of the Kings of England:
From the Earliest Period to the Reign of King Stephen*, tr. J. A. Giles (London: H. G. Bohn,
1847), p. 238; in Latin "nefarium rem *in procum filiae operatus*," in *Willelmi Malmes-
biriensis Monachi De Gestis Regum Anglorum Libri Quinque, Historiae Novellae Libri
Tres*, ed. William Stubbs, 2 vols. (Rerum Britannicarum Medii Aevii Scriptores, vol. 90;
London: Eyre and Spottiswoode, 1887), p. 262 (II, 210). Compare *Beowulf*: *Modþrȳðo
wæg fremu folces cwēn, firen' ondrysne* 'Modthrytho, the excellent queen of the people,
carried on terrible wickedness' (1931–32). Did the *Beowulf* poet confuse the father of
Modthrytho with the daughter herself?

hand-woven, were in store; after his arrest it was quickly determined that the sword, the damascened sword, must shear, make known death-bale" (*ac him wælbende   weotode tealde / handgewriþene; hraþe seoþðan wæs / æfter mundgripe   mēce geþinged, / þæt hit sceādenmæl   scȳran mōste / cwealmbealu cȳðan*, 1936–40a). If she weaves at all then she weaves only "deadly hand-woven bonds" binding him to a grisly end. The "peace-weaver" *cuts* these bonds— imprisoning ropes—with a sword, simultaneously shearing the bonds of life to "make known death-bale." She resembles that other ironic peace-weaver, the *wīf*, who tried to penetrate the braided breast-net of Beowulf with her knife.

Both antitypes of the peace-weaving queen behave like kings, using the sword to rid their halls of intruders or unwanted "hall-guests." Unlike Thryth, the monstrous *wīf* remains husbandless, having lost her son, "wife" only to the *mere* she inhabits both in life and in death. At this moment in the poem, both Thryth and Grendel's Mother belong to the past. If they represent *previous* inversions of the peace-weaver and cup-passer, and Hygd who is now passing the mead-cup to Beowulf's weary men in celebration signifies a *present* cup-passer, so the poet introduces a final queen, this time a cup-passer of the *future*, who will fail in her role as the first woman, Hildeburh, failed in hers.

Freawaru, like Hildeburh, seems innocent of any crime. She is envisioned by Beowulf as a queen married to Ingeld of the Heathobards in a digression (2032–69) immediately preceding his summary of the battles with Grendel and with his mother. She will fail in her role as peace-weaver because of an underlying hostility—an old Heathobard warrior's bitterness over ancient Heathobard treasure acquired through previous wars and worn by a young Danish man accompanying the new queen. The fragility of this role is heightened even further when, in the third section involving the dragon, Beowulf inhabits a queenless kingdom and when Wiglaf must become the cup-passer, pouring water from the "cup" of Beowulf's helmet in a futile attempt to revive his wounded lord.

Indeed, three women characters appear outside this middle section to convey dialectically the idea that woman cannot ensure peace in this world. First, Wealhtheow, unlike other female figures, appears in the first (or Grendel) section of the poem to pour mead after Grendel's challenge has been answered by the hero. This first entrance symbolizes the ideal role of Germanic woman as a personification of peace, as we have seen. In antithesis, Beowulf's account of the fall of the *wīf unhȳre* "monstrous woman" appropriately ends the poem's second (Grendel's Mother) section which has centered on this role: the personification of discord, the antitype of the feminine ideal, has been destroyed. But in the poem's third section a synthesis emerges. The nameless and unidentified Geat woman who appears, like the other female characters, after a battle—this one between Beowulf and the dragon—mourns at the pyre. That is, the efforts of the peacemaker, while valuable in worldly and social terms, ultimately must fail because of the nature of this world. True peace exists not in woman's but in God's 'embrace' (*fæþm*, 188).

III

This idea is implied in Hrothgar's sermon (1700–84); like the court celebration of Hygelac, it is a part of the middle section belonging to Grendel's Mother but apparently unrelated to it. In it Hrothgar describes three Christian vices in distinctly Germanic terms. Impelled by envy like Grendel, Heremod kills his "table-companions" (1713–14). Next, the wealthy hall-ruler in his pride is attacked by the Adversary while his guardian conscience sleeps within the hall of his soul (1740–44). So the monster that specifically epitomizes pride in *Beowulf*, as in Genesis, is female—Grendel's Mother—thematically related to Thryth or Modthrytho, whose name (if it can be said to exist in manuscript in that form) means "pride." Grendel's Mother substitutes war-making for the peace-weaving of the queen out of a kind of selfish pride—if she were capable of recognizing it as such. Finally, this same hall-ruler "covets angry-minded" (*gȳtsað gromhȳdig*, 1749) the ornamented treasures God had previously given him by refusing to dispense any to his warriors. So the mock gold-king dragon avariciously guards his treasure. Although the poet portrays the monsters as antitypes of Germanic ideals, his integument conceals a Christian idea. The city of man, whether located in a Germanic or Christian society, is always threatened by sin and failure.

Such sin alienates Christian man from self, neighbor, and God; it alienates Germanic man primarily from other men. Note that although in *Beowulf* each of the three monsters is described as guarding or possessing a hall, whether Heorot, a watery cavern, or a barrow, each remains isolated from humanity (and from each other—Grendel and his mother live together, but they never appear together in the poem until he is dead). Ideally when the retainer, the queen, and the gold-lord cooperate they constitute a viable nucleus of Germanic society: a retainer must have a gold-lord from whom to receive gold for his loyalty in battle; the peace-weaver must have a "loom"—the band of retainers and their lord, or two nations—upon which to weave peace.

Despite the poet's realization that these roles cannot be fulfilled in this world, this Germanic ideal provides structural and thematic unity for *Beowulf*. Grendel's Mother does occupy a transitional position in the poem: as a "retainer" attacking Heorot she resembles Grendel, but as an "attacked ruler" of her own "hall" she resembles the dragon. As a monstrous mother and queen she perverts a role more important socially and symbolically than that of Grendel, just as the queen as peace-pledge or peace-weaver ultimately becomes more valuable than the retainer but less valuable than the gold-giver himself.

If it seems ironic that a Germanic ideal that cannot exist in this world *can* exist in art, unifying the theme and structure of the poem, then Grendel's Mother, warring antitype of harmony and peace, must seem doubly ironic. The structural position of her episode in the poem, like woman's position as cup-passer among members of a nation, or as a peace-pledge between two nations, is similarly medial and transitional, but successfully so.

ROBERTA FRANK

The *Beowulf* Poet's Sense of History†

Awareness of historical change, of the pastness of a past that itself has depth, is not instinctive to man; there is nothing natural about a sense of history. Anthropologists report that the lack of historical perspective is a feature of primitive thought, and historians that its absence characterizes medieval thinking: Herod in the Wakefield Cycle swears "by Mahoun in heaven," the medieval Alexander is a knight, and heathen Orléans boasts a university.[1] Morton Bloomfield has shown that a sense of history, even a tentative, under-developed one, was a rare thing in fourteenth-century England, and that Chaucer's attention to chronology and his preoccupation with cultural diversity have affinities with aspects of the early Italian Renaissance.[2] But what in the Anglo-Saxon period stimulated a monastic author to stress the differences between ancient days and his own, to paint the past as if it were something other than the present?[3] The *Beowulf* poet's reconstruction of a northern heroic age is

† From *The Wisdom of Poetry: Essays in Early English Literature in Honor of Morton W. Bloomfield*, ed. Larry D. Benson and Siegfried Wenzel (Kalamazoo, MI: Medieval Institute Publications, 1982), pp. 53–65. Reprinted by permission of the Board of the Medieval Institute.
1. Peter Burke, *The Renaissance Sense of the Past* (London, 1969), pp. 1–6; Michael Hunter, "Germanic and Roman Antiquity and the Sense of the Past in Anglo-Saxon England," *Anglo-Saxon England* 3 (1974), 45–48.
2. "Chaucer's Sense of History," *Journal of English and Germanic Philology* 51 (1952), 301–13; rpt. in Morton Bloomfield, *Essays and Explorations: Studies in Ideas, Language, and Literature* (Cambridge, Mass., 1970), pp. 13–26.
3. In assuming that literate composition indicates authorship by a cleric, I am following, among others, C. P. Wormald, "The Uses of Literacy in Anglo-Saxon England and its Neighbours," *Transactions of the Royal Historical Society.* 5th ser., 27 (1977), 95–114.

chronologically sophisticated, rich in local color and fitting speeches. The poet avoids obvious anachronisms and presents such an internally consistent picture of Scandinavian society around A.D. 500 that his illusion of historical truth has been taken for the reality.[4]

The poet's heroic age is full of men both "emphatically pagan and exceptionally good," men who believe in a God whom they thank at every imaginable opportunity.[5] Yet they perform all the pagan rites known to Tacitus, and are not Christian. The temporal distance between past and present, acknowledged in the opening words of the poem—"in geardagum" ("in days of yore")—is heard again when Beowulf, as yet unnamed, makes his entrance. He is the strongest of men "on þæm dæge þysses lifes" ("on that day of this life" 197, 790).[6] The alliterating demonstratives stress the remoteness of the past, here and later when a hall-servant in Heorot looks after all the visitors' bedtime needs "swylce þy dogore heaþoliðende habban scoldon" ("such as in those days seafarers were wont to have" 1797–98). The descriptive clause distances but also glosses over, shadowing with vagueness an unknown corner of the past. The poet is so attracted by the aristocratic rituals of life in the hall, so intent on historical verisimilitude, that he imagines everything, even basic human needs, to have changed over time. His proposition that golden tapestries hanging in the hall were a wondrous sight for the partying sixth-century retainers is quickly modified in the direction of reality: "þara þe on swylc starað" ("for those who look upon such things" 996); even in Heorot not all beefy breakers-of-rings in their cups would have had an eye for interior design. The vividness of the past underlines, paradoxically, its distance.

The *Beowulf* poet has a strong sense of cultural diversity, as strong perhaps as Chaucer's. Three times in the "Knight's Tale" Chaucer explains the behavior of characters with the clause "as was tho the gyse"; in "The Legend of Cleopatra" he has Anthony sent out to win kingdoms and honor "as was usance"; and in "The Legend of Lucrece" he notes approvingly that Roman wives prized a good name

4. On the use of *Beowulf* as a historical document, see J. R. R. Tolkien, "*Beowulf*: The Monsters and the Critics," *Proceedings of the British Academy* 22 (1936), 245–51; sep. rpt. (London, 1937, 1958, 1960), pp. 1–6; Robert T. Farrell, "*Beowulf*, Swedes and Geats," *Saga-Book* (Viking Society for Northern Research) 18 (1972), 225–86. Kemp Malone found the most remarkable feature of *Beowulf* to be its "high standard of historical accuracy": the anachronisms "that one would expect in a poem of the eighth century" are missing ("Beowulf," *English Studies* 29 [1948], 161–72, esp. 164). But the *Beowulf* poet occasionally nodded; see Walter Goffart, "Hetware and Hugas: Datable Anachronisms in *Beowulf*" in *The Dating of Beowulf,* ed. Colin Chase, Toronto Old English Series, 6 (1981), pp. 83–100.
5. Larry D. Benson, "The Pagan Coloring of *Beowulf*" in *Old English Poetry: Fifteen Essays,* ed. Robert P. Creed (Providence, 1967), p. 194.
6. The same line is used to place Grendel's downfall in the distant past (806). Citations of *Beowulf* refer to Frederick Klaeber, ed., *Beowulf and The Fight at Finnsburg,* 3rd ed. (Boston, 1950).

"at thilke tyme."[7] The Old English poet maintains a similar perspective. He praises the Geats for their ancient custom of keeping armor and weapons at their sides at all times: "They were always prepared for war, whether at home or in the field, as their lord required" (1246–50). He has Hrothgar admire their steadfastness, the dependability of men who live blameless "ealde wisan" ("in the old fashion" 1865). When the dragon's ravages begin, the poet makes the aged Beowulf fear that he has transgressed "ofer ealde riht" ("against ancient law" 2330): pagans have their own moral code, separating them from the author and us. The poet emphasizes cultural differences not only between present and past but also between coeval peoples. He depicts the Swedes and Geats as more authentically primitive, more pagan in outlook and idiom, than the Danes. When a roughhewn Beowulf arrives at the Danish court he puts himself in the hands of a skilled local who "knew the custom of the retainers" (359). Ongentheow, the grizzled king of the Swedes, threatens to pierce ("getan" 2940) captives on the gallows for the pleasure of carrion birds.[8] The Geats consult auspices (204); Beowulf, like the Scandinavian heroes of old, trusts in his own might (418, 670, 1270, 1533); the messenger imagines a raven boasting to an eagle of carnage-feasts (3024–27); and Hæthcyn's slaying of Herebeald (2435–43) imitates a fratricide in the Norse pantheon: euhemerism becomes, in the poet's hands, an aid to historical research.[9]

The poet's sense of anachronism is revealed in his characters' speeches, utterances that avoid all distinctively Christian names and terms. The actors themselves have a sense of the past and of the future. They are able to look back two generations, tracing the origins of the feud between the Geats and the Swedes (2379–96, 2472–89, 2611–19, 2379–96). They can also forecast the feuds of the next generation. There is a fine display of chronological wit when Beowulf, on the basis of a piece of information picked up at the Danish court, turns the Ingeld legend into a political prophecy, a sequence of events likely to occur in the near future (2024–69). The poet's sense

7. Morton W. Bloomfield observes that Chaucer employs "as was tho the gyse" to qualify pagan funeral customs (line 993), sacrificial rites (line 2279), and cremations (line 2911) (*Essays and Explorations*, p. 21). Citations from *The Legend of Good Women* are to lines 586 and 1813 in the second edition of F. N. Robinson (Boston, 1957).

8. Hans Kuhn relates Ongentheow's threat (*getan* = **gautian*) to a boast by the pagan tenth-century skald Helgi trausti Ólafsson: "I paid to the gallows-prince [Odin] Gautr's [Odin's] sacrifice" ("Gaut," *Festschrift für Jost Trier zu seinem 60. Geburtstag*, ed. Benno von Wiese and Karl Heinz Borck [Meisenheim, 1954], pp. 417–33).

9. Ursula Dronke points out that *Beowulf* contains human analogues for two additional mythological incidents recorded in Norse poetry ("*Beowulf* and Ragnarǫk," *Saga-Book* (Viking Society for Northern Research) 17 [1969], 322–25). On Scandinavian heroes' faith in their own *megin* (OE *mægen*), see Peter Foote and David M. Wilson, *The Viking Achievement* (London, 1970), p. 404. A raven, "oath-brother of the eagle," converses again in a section of the tenth-century pagan Norse *Hrafnsmál* (or *Haraldskvæði*) attributed to the skald Þórbjǫrn Hornklofi.

of historic succession is so strong and the internal chronology of the poem so carefully worked out that his audience knows why Hrothulf and Heoroweard have to be kept in the wings a little while longer. After Beowulf's death, it is clear even to the messenger that Eadgils is not likely to sit for long on the Swedish throne without avenging his brother's murder on the new king of the Geats, son of the slayer. The poet does not make earlier Danish and Germanic heroes like Scyld, Heremod, Finn, Offa, Sigemund, Eormenric and Hama contemporaneous with the sixth-century events narrated, but sets them in a distant mirror, conveying the illusion of a many-storied long-ago. Such chronological tidiness is all the more remarkable for its appearance in a poetic vernacular that has no distinctive future tense, and whose chief adverbs of recollection and continuation— "þa" and "siððan" ("thereupon": looking forward; "at that time," "from the time that": looking back)—are almost always ambiguous.[1]

Philosophically, in order to have a sense of history at all, the *Beowulf* poet had to hold certain premises about man and his role on earth. Despite his professional concern with the timeless, he had to be engaged to some extent with the things of this world; he needed a positive attitude toward secular wisdom and some notion of natural law. Above all, he had to believe that pagan Germanic legend had intellectual value and interest for Christians. These concepts were available to twelfth-century humanists. Christian Platonists like William of Conches, Bernard Silvestris, and Alan of Lille shared an unpolemical attitude toward the pagan past and stressed the importance of earthly understanding as the base of all human knowledge.[2] But in the central theological traditions of the early medieval West and, more specifically, in the teachings of Aldhelm, Bede, and Alcuin, there is no trace of this liberal mentality.[3] No contemporary of these three concerned himself with man on earth, looking upon heathen virtues and customs with an indulgent eye, and had his vision survive. The patristic tradition that pagan story is diabolically inspired, that unbaptized pagans lie lamenting in hell, was too strong.

Purely from the perspective of the history of ideas, the *Beowulf* poet's chronological acrobatics and fascination with cultural diversity, his positive view of those who lived "while men loved the lawe

1. Noted by E. G. Stanley, "The Narrative Art of *Beowulf*," in *Medieval Narrative: A Symposium,* ed. Hans Bekker-Nielsen et al. (Odense, 1979), pp. 59–60.
2. See Ursula and Peter Dronke, "The Prologue of the Prose *Edda*: Explorations of a Latin Background" in *Sjötíu ritgerðir helgaðar Jakobi Benediktssyni* (Reykjavik, 1977), pp. 169–70.
3. See H. M. and N. K. Chadwick, *The Growth of Literature* (Cambridge, Eng., 1932–40), 1.556–57; Patrick Wormald, "Bede, *Beowulf*, and the Conversion of the Anglo-Saxon Aristocracy" in *Bede and Anglo-Saxon England*, ed. Robert T. Farrell, British Archaeological Reports, 46 (1978), pp. 42–49.

of kinde," needs explanation.[4] We cannot, wielding editorial knives, remove these ideas from the text the way other late-seeming growths have been excised solely on the grounds that the poem is early.[5] "It is a dangerous principle to adopt in literary investigation that nothing we do not readily understand can be rationally explained. We must as a working principle assume that everything in a work of art is capable of explanation even at the cost of oversubtlety and even error. . . . We must not assume, unless we are finally forced to it, that the writer or composer did not know what he was doing."[6] Professor Bloomfield offered this guidance in a review of Kenneth Sisam's *The Structure of Beowulf*. Sisam contends that "great difficulties stand in the way of all explanations that make the poet a deep thinker, attempting themes and ways of conveying them that might be tried on a select body of readers in a more advance age."[7] The fact remains, however, that the poem, for an early composition, is full of oddly advanced notions. Twenty years ago Morton Bloomfield observed that "ealde riht" ("old law" 2330) in *Beowulf* referred not to the Mosaic Code, the Old Law, but to natural law, and noted that the moral laws of the Old Testament were often equated with this natural law, "although in general this equation is later than the early Middle Ages."[8] More recently, he has seen behind Beowulf's single combat with Grendel the concept of the *iudicium Dei*, a calling upon God to decide the justice of an action: "Let wise God, the holy Lord, adjudge the glory to whichever side he thinks fit," says Beowulf (685–87); the champion will rely in the coming struggle on the judgment of God (440–41).[9] Something like the judicial duel appears to have been a feature of medieval Scandinavian society. Yet all the early evidence for trial by combat from Tacitus to Pope Nicholas I

---

4. Chaucer, *The Book of the Duchess*, line 56 (*The Works of Geoffrey Chaucer*, ed. F. N. Robinson, 2nd ed. [Boston, 1957]).
5. Kenneth Sisam long ago interpreted the Scyld Scefing preamble to *Beowulf* as a contemporary allusion to the West Saxon dynasty; but since he took *Beowulf* as a whole to be seventh or eighth century, the opening episode had to be a late, post-Alfredian addition: better a composite poem than a Viking one. See Sisam, "Anglo-Saxon Royal Genealogies," *Proceedings of the British Academy* 39 (1953), 287–346, esp. 339. The Offa digression of *Beowulf*—a probable allusion to the great ancestor of the Mercian house—would have flattered not only Offa of Mercia but also the descendants of Alfred who had succeeded to the rule of Mercia and who were themselves descendants of the Mercian royal line. But commentators, reluctant to look outside the age of Bede, either reject the Mercian associations of this digression or declare it, too, a later interpolation. See the important article by Nicolas Jacobs, "Anglo-Danish Relations, Poetic Archaism and the Date of *Beowulf*: A Reconsideration of the Evidence," *Poetica* (Tokyo) 8 (1977) [1978], 23–43. Jacobs demonstrates that no linguistic or historical fact compels us to anchor *Beowulf* before the tenth century.
6. *Speculum* 41 (1966), 368–71.
7. *The Structure of Beowulf* (New York and Oxford, 1965), p. 77.
8. "Patristics and Old English Literature: Notes on Some Poems," *Comparative Literature* 14 (Winter 1962), 36–43; rpt. twice in its entirety, and partially in *An Anthology of Beowulf Criticism*, ed. Lewis E. Nicholson (Notre Dame, 1963), p. 370.
9. "Beowulf, Byrhtnoth, and the Judgment of God: Trial by Combat in Anglo-Saxon England," *Speculum* 44 (1969), 545–59.

is Continental; there is no documentation for multilateral ordeal in England before the Norman Conquest. The *Beowulf* poet's use of the form and spirit of the judicial duel, whether he derived the concept from Tacitus, from the Franks, or from the Danelaw, emphasizes—like his auguries, sacrifices, and exotic cremations—the temporal and cultural distance between the pagan Scandinavian past and the England of his own day. His backward glance is both admiring and antiquarian.

Anglo-Saxon scholarship has done its best to read *Beowulf* as the seventh and eighth centuries would have. Because Aldhelm and Bede insisted that the only suitable subject for poetry was a religious one, and because secular epics and long historical poems only started to appear in the later ninth century, Margaret Goldsmith had little choice but to interpret *Beowulf* allegorically.[1] Alcuin's only known comment on heroic literature in ecclesiastical contexts is an orthodox denunciation of it as a heathen distraction.[2] W. F. Bolton's new book on *Alcuin and Beowulf* discovers, predictably, that the great schoolmaster would have found Beowulf guilty, flawed, vengeful, incapable even of protecting his people.[3] Charles Donahue attempts to account for the existence of an eighth-century Old English poem about noble pagans by invoking Irish views of pre-Christian goodness, legends that tell of virtuous pagans and their natural knowledge of God.[4] Yet the stories of Cormac and Morand that he cites are not easy to date (that of Cormac is surely no earlier than the last quarter of the tenth century), and Donahue concedes that they are "later than *Beowulf* and can be viewed only as parallel developments of that early insular Christian humanism. . . ."[5] Patrick Wormald has recently located a social and cultural context for the composition of heroic literature in the aristocratic climate of early English Christianity, in the integration of monastic and royal houses.[6] Yet the aristocratic nature of the early English church is, if anything, more pronounced with the passage of time, reaching a kind of culmination under the successors of Alfred.[7] The "vast zone

1. *The Mode and Meaning of 'Beowulf'* (London, 1970).
2. *Alcuini Epistolae*, 124, ed. Ernest Dümmler, Monumenta Germaniae Historica, *Epistolae* IV. 2 (Berlin, 1895), p. 183.
3. *Alcuin and Beowulf: An Eighth-Century View* (New Brunswick, N.J., 1978), esp. pp. 152–54, 165–70.
4. "*Beowulf*, Ireland, and the Natural Good," *Traditio* 7 (1949–51), 263–77; "*Beowulf* and Christian Tradition: A Reconsideration from a Celtic Stance," *Traditio* 21 (1965), 55–116.
5. "*Beowulf*, Ireland, and the Natural Good," p. 277.
6. "Bede, *Beowulf*, and the Conversion of the Anglo-Saxon Aristocracy," esp. pp. 49–58.
7. According to Wormald, "the aristocratic climate of early English Christianity is, if anything, more apparent in the age of Offa than in the age of Bede" ("Bede, *Beowulf*, and the Conversion of the Anglo-Saxon Aristocracy," p. 94). Royal and monastic interests seem even more closely integrated in the age of Athelstan. Accompanying that king on his military expedition to Scotland in 934 were the two archbishops, fourteen bishops,

of silence" Wormald observes existing between Bede and the *Beowulf* poet[8] may be due not only to Bede's fundamentalism but also to the centuries separating the two authors.

When in the Anglo-Saxon period did pagans become palatable? A positive attitude toward the pagans of classical antiquity is visible in translations of the Alfredian period. While the real Orosius, writing in the first decades of the fifth century, was as reluctant as Bede to say anything good about those who lived before the Christian Era, the Old English paraphrase of *Orosius* from around 900 contemplates with pleasure the bravery, honorable behavior, and renown of several early Romans, adds references to Julius Caesar's clemency, generosity, and courage, and even suggests that in some of their customs the Romans of the Christian Era were worse than their pagan ancestors.[9] Unlike his source, the Old English translator does not think in an exclusively religious way: what matters is how rulers of the past served God's purpose, not whether they were Christians or pagans.[1]

Boethius' *Consolation of Philosophy,* translated by King Alfred himself, resorted to pre-Christian human history and to pagan mythology for some fifty illustrations, finding archetypal patterns in the behavior of a Nero or a Hercules just as the *Beowulf* poet locates exemplary models in Heremod and Beowulf. In the late ninth and early tenth centuries, the *Consolation* enjoyed a considerable vogue among Carolingian commentators, at least one of whom, Remigius of Auxerre, Alfred may have used.[2] Alfred thrusts aside

seven ealdormen, six jarls with Norse names, three Welsh kings, and twenty-four others including eleven royal thegns. One of Athelstan's laws commanded that every Friday at every monastery all monks were to sing fifty psalms "for the king and those who want what he wants . . ." See P. H. Sawyer, *From Roman Britain to Norman England* (New York, 1978), pp. 126, 192, 243. For a glimpse of aristocratic climates in tenth-century Saxony, see K. J. Leyser, *Rule and Conflict in an Early Medieval Society: Ottonian Saxony* (London, 1979).

8. "Bede, *Beowulf,* and the Conversion of the Anglo-Saxon Aristocracy," p. 36.
9. See Dorothy Whitelock, "The Prose of Alfred's Reign" in *Continuations and Beginnings: Studies in Old English Literature,* ed. E. G. Stanley (London, 1966), p. 91. For the Old English text, see *The Old English Orosius,* ed. Janet Bately, Early English Text Society, s. s. 6 (Oxford, 1980), p. xcix; for the Latin, *Pauli Orosii Presbyteri Hispani adversus Paganos Historiarum Libri Septem,* ed. Karl Zangemeister, Corpus Scriptorum Ecclesiasticorum Latinorum, 5 (Vienna, 1882).
1. See J. M. Wallace-Hadrill, *Early Germanic Kingship in England and on the Continent* (Oxford, 1971), pp. 145–46.
2. Kurt Otten surveys attempts from Schepss (1881) to Courcelle (1937) to locate the Remigian commentaries available to Alfred (*König Alfreds Boethius,* Studien zur englischen Philologie, N. F. 3 [Tübingen, 1964], pp. 4–9). See also Brian Donaghey, "The Sources of King Alfred's Translation of Boethius' *De Consolatione Philosophiae,*" *Anglia* 82 (1964), 23–57. Pierre Courcelle favors a ninth-century commentary by an anonymous monk of St. Gall (*La Consolation de Philosophie dans la tradition littéraire: antécédents et postérité de Boèce* [Paris, 1967]). But even if Alfred (d. 899) did not have access to Remigius' work in its final Parisian form (c. 902–908), he could have followed a version modelled on Remigius' earlier teaching at Auxerre and Rheims. See Diane Bolton, "Remigian Commentaries on the *Consolation of Philosophy* and their Sources," *Traditio* 33 (1977), 381–94, and "The Study of the *Consolation of Philosophy* in Anglo-Saxon England," *Archives d'histoire doctrinale et littéraire du Moyen Âge* 44 (1977), [1978], 33–78.

much of Remigius' Neoplatonic speculation along with his scientific and theological information, but is quick to insert commentary material having to do with classical myths. He occasionally gives a pagan analogy for a Christian concept, something Alcuin never managed to do.[3] Alfred's story of Orpheus teaches that a man who wishes to see the true light of God must not turn back to his old errors.[4] Boethius' tale of Jupiter overthrowing the giants who warred on heaven is shown by Alfred to reflect—*secundum fidem gentilium*—Nimrod's building of the Tower of Babel and God's subsequent division of tongues.[5] Alfred stresses the underlying truthfulness of Boethius' pagan fables. The details of Hercules' taming the Centaurs, burning the Hydra's poisonous heads, and slaying Cacus are skipped, but the myth itself is universalized into a philosophic reflection on life and on the meaning of victory and defeat: good men fight for honor in this world, to win glory and fame; for their deeds, they dwell beyond the stars in eternal bliss.[6] Circe in Alfred's paraphrase is no longer the wicked enchantress of Boethius, but a vulnerable goddess who falls violently in love with Odysseus at first sight; she turns his men into animals only after they, out of homesickness, plot to abandon their lord.[7] Alfred, like the *Beowulf* poet, looks for the moral and psychological laws of things, tries to understand and learn rather than condemn. Only once in his paraphrase does he abandon the world of classical paganism for a Germanic allusion; it is a small step, but full of significance for the future of Old English poetry. He translates Boethius' "Where now are the bones of faithful Fabricius?" as "Where now are the bones of the famous and wise goldsmith Weland?"[8]

When in the Anglo-Saxon period could a Christian author exploit pagan Germanic legend for its intellectual and moral values? Seventh- and eighth-century sources furnish evidence that English monks were overfond of harpists, secular tales, eating and drinking; but such worldly tastes provoked the scorn and hostility of their superiors: "What has Ingeld to do with Christ? The House is narrow, it cannot hold both. The King of Heaven wishes to have no

3. Bolton, *Alcuin and Beowulf*, pp. 139, 177.
4. *Anicii Manlii Severini Boethii Philosophiae Consolatio*, ed. L. Bieler, Corpus Christianorum, 94 (Turnhout, 1957), III, m. 12, lines 52–58; *King Alfred's Old English Version of Boethius' De Consolatione Philosophiae*, ed. W. J. Sedgefield (Oxford, 1900), p. 103, lines 14–16. Otten, *König Alfreds Boethius*, p. 133.
5. *De Consolatione Philosophiae*, III, pr. 12, lines 64–65; *King Alfred's Old English Version*, p. 99, lines 4–20. Otten, *König Alfreds Boethius*, pp. 129–32.
6. *De Consolatione Philosophiae*, IV, m. 7; *King Alfred's Old English Version*, p. 139, lines 5–18. Otten, *König Alfreds Boethius*, p. 38.
7. *King Alfred's Old English Version*, p. 116, lines 2–34.
8. *De Consolatione Philosophiae*, II, m. 7; *King Alfred's Old English Version*, p. 46, lines 16–17.

fellowship with so-called kings, who are pagan and lost."[9] But by the late ninth century, even an archbishop—Fulk of Rheims, who recruited Remigius of Auxerre, corresponded with King Alfred and sent Grimbald to him—could in one and the same sentence refer to a letter of Gregory the Great on kingship and to "Teutonic books regarding a certain King Hermenric."[1] A century and a half later, puritanical youth can be seen shaking its fist at reckless middle age in a letter that one cleric of Bamberg Cathedral wrote to another complaining of their bishop, Gunther, who spent all his time reading of Attila and Theodoric when not composing epics himself.[2]

The *Beowulf* poet insists on the virtue and paganism of his characters, and is unusually explicit about their heathen rites, describing them lovingly at length.[3] A slender tradition of extolling the good customs of Germanic pagans can be traced in Roman authors, but this tradition does not enjoy a continuous run through the medieval period. The first known use of Tacitus' *Germania* after Cassiodorus occurs in the mid-ninth-century *Translatio Sancti Alexandri* by the monk Rudolf of Fulda.[4] This work, commissioned by the aristocratic abbot of the monastery of Wildeshausen in Saxony, opens with a description of the moral practices and brave deeds of the early pagan ancestors of the Saxons. Bede, monk of Wearmouth-Jarrow and historian of the English church and people (c. 731), is reticent about the doings of the Anglo-Saxons before their conversion and shows no inclination to celebrate heathens or their habits.[5] Widukind, monk of Corvey and historian of the Continental Saxons (c. 967), does not hesitate to do so. He borrows Rudolf of Fulda's account of pagan institutions and shapes the heathen past of his nation into a carefully contoured whole. He develops a single thread of historical tradition into a complex narrative, incorporating heroic dialogue, vivid details, and dramatic scenes, in much the same way that the

9. See n. 2. The Council of Clovesho (746/7) specified that priests were not to chatter in church like secular poets (*Councils and Ecclesiastical Documents Relating to Great Britain and Ireland,* ed. A. W. Haddan and W. Stubbs [Oxford, 1869–78], 3:366); for additional examples, including one from the early eleventh century, see Wormald, "Bede, *Beowulf,* and the Conversion of the Anglo-Saxon Aristocracy," pp. 51–52.
1. The reference is to Eormenric of heroic legend and *Beowulf* (1201). Flodoard, *Historia Remensis Ecclesiae,* IV.5, ed. J. Heller and G. Waitz, Monumenta Germaniae Historica, Scriptores Rerum Germanicarum (in folio), 13 (Hanover, 1881), pp. 564, 574.
2. Carl Erdmann, *Studien zur Briefliteratur Deutschlands im elften Jahrhundert,* Schriften des Reichsinstituts für ältere deutsche Geschichtskunde (= Monumenta Germaniae Historica), 1 (Leipzig, 1938), p. 102; K. Leyser, "The German Aristocracy from the Ninth to the Early Twelfth Centuries: A Social and Cultural Survey," *Past and Present* 41 (1968), 25–53.
3. On the poet's featuring of pagan elements, see Benson, "Pagan Coloring," pp. 193–213.
4. Rudolf of Fulda, *Translatio Sancti Alexandri,* ed. B. Krusch, Nachrichten von der Gesellschaft der Wissenschaften zu Göttingen, Phil.-Hist. Klasse, 1933, pp. 405–36.
5. See Wormald, "Bede, *Beowulf,* and the Conversion of the Anglo-Saxon Aristocracy," pp. 58–63.

Beowulf poet seems to have worked.[6] Widukind saw his efforts in recording the deeds of the Saxon leaders (*principum nostrorum res gestae litteris . . . commendare*) as equal in value to the service he earlier performed with his two lives of saints. He wrote his history, he said, partly by virtue of his monastic calling, partly as a member of *gens Saxonum.*[7] One historical sense seems to beget another: Widukind, like the *Beowulf* poet, learned much from classical historians, including the art of depicting people whose behavior made sense within the framework of their age and culture.

The *Beowulf* poet's attribution of monotheism to his good heathens is sometimes taken as revealing his ignorance of Germanic paganism, sometimes as a sign of his inability to see the past as anything other than the present. Like Widukind, he mentions pagan error, briefly and in passing (175–88), before depicting noble pagan monotheists for some three thousand lines. In the Alfredian *Orosius,* as in the fifth-century original, God is shown to have always guided the world, even in pagan times. But the paraphraser adds a few touches of his own: the pagan Leonidas places his trust in God; even Hannibal is heard to lament that God would not allow him domination over Rome.[8] The *Beowulf* poet, too, makes his heroes refer again and again to the power and providence of a single God, and he takes Beowulf's victory as a sign that "God has always ruled mankind, as he still does" (700–02, 1057–58). The Danes' hymn in Heorot to a single Almighty (90–98) expresses a Boethian wonder at seeing an invisible God through his creation. Wiglaf's contention that the fallen Beowulf shall for a long time "abide in the Lord's keeping" (3109) suggests a Boethian philosophy of salvation, of individuals ascending by reason alone to a knowledge of one God. It was probably Remigius of Auxerre who around 900 compiled a short treatise on the gods of classical antiquity, announcing—in the final paragraph of his prologue—that a single divine being lay behind the multiplicity of Greek and Roman names for the gods.[9] Renewed contact with the texts of late antiquity, especially Macrobius, Martianus Capella, and Boethius, ended by making some men at least think in

6. Larry D. Benson, "The Originality of *Beowulf*" in *The Interpretation of Narrative: Theory and Practice,* Harvard English Studies, 1 (Cambridge, Mass., 1970), pp. 1–43.
7. *Widukindi Monachi Corbeiensis Rerum Gestarum Saxonicarum Libri Tres,* ed. H.-E. Lohmann and P. Hirsch, 5th ed., Monumenta Germaniae Historica, Scriptores Rerum Germanicarum in usum scholarum (Hanover, 1935), Bk. I, chs. 1–15. On Widukind, see especially Helmut Beumann, *Widukind von Korvei* (Weimar, 1950), and "Historiographische Konzeption und politische Ziele Widukinds von Korvei," *Settimane di studio del Centro Italiano di Studi sull'alto medioevo* 17 (Spoleto, 1970), 857–94.
8. The *Old English Orosius,* 49.1–3; 103.27–29.
9. *Scriptores Rerum Mythicarum Latini Tres,* ed. G. H. Bode (Cellis, 1834), 1:74. See Ursula and Peter Dronke, "The Prologue of the Prose *Edda,*" p. 166.

a less narrowly religious ways.[1] The *Beowulf* poet allows glimpses of a *paradiso terrestre* in the distant past—brief, transitory but glowing moments whose thrust is to remind his hearers of all the unfulfilled potential of their pre-Christian heritage.

What emerges from a sufficiently intense concern for history in any literary work is a series of projections inevitably focused by the particular anxieties of the writer. Alfred's *Boethius* reveals that king's fascination with the psychology of the tyrant, his concern for the proper uses of power and wealth, and his insistence, against Boethius, that temporal possessions can be put to good ends.[2] The *Beowulf* poet seems especially concerned to distinguish between justifiable and unjustifiable aggression, to place the warlike activities of his pagan hero in an ethical context. Beowulf resorts to arms out of concern for the defenseless and for the common good, not exclusively out of lust for conquest, ambition, or vengefulness. He is heroic and pious, a pagan prince of peace.[3] Christianity in the early barbarian West may have thought it was being assimilated by a warrior aristocracy, but it ended up—even before the Crusades—accommodating itself to the heroic values of the nobility. The blending of the two cultures would have begun at the time of conversion, but it was an extended process. At one stage, revelry in the hall, vowing oaths of fidelity to a lord; ambushes and plundering and slaughter, all the duties and responsibilities of heroic society were seen as demonic and damnable, as in the eighth-century *Life of Guthlac* by Felix of Crowland.[4] In the Old English *Guthlac A*, the poet even sends in devils to remind the royal saint and hermit of his secular obligations, to tempt him with the hall-delights long abandoned after a warlike youth (191–99). The heroic life is the opposite of the life that leads to salvation.

The synthesis of religious and heroic idealism present in *Beowulf* was probably not available to monastic authors at an early date. In the 930s, Odo of Cluny wrote his *Life of St. Gerald of Aurillac* in

1. John Scotus Eriugena, whose teaching is reflected in the school of Auxerre, wrote commentaries on all three authors. On his life, see E. Jeauneau, *Jean Scot, Homélie sur le Prologue de Jean*, Sources Chrétiennes, 151 (Paris, 1969), pp. 9–50, and *Jean Scot, Commentaire sur l'Evangile de Jean*, Sources Chrétiennes, 180 (Paris, 1972), pp. 11–21.
2. Otten, *König Alfreds Boethius*, pp. 99–118.
3. See especially Levin L. Schücking, "Das Königsideal im Beowulf" in *Modern Humanities Research Association Bulletin* 3 (1929), 143–54; rpt. *Englische Studien* 67 (1932), 1–14. English trans. as "The Ideal of Kingship in *Beowulf*" in *An Anthology of Beowulf Criticism*, ed. Nicholson, pp. 35–49. Robert E. Kaske, "*Sapientia et Fortitudo* as the Controlling Theme of *Beowulf*," *Studies in Philology* 55 (1958), 423–56; rpt. in *An Anthology of Beowulf Criticism*, pp. 269–310.
4. *Felix's Life of Saint Guthlac*, ed. and trans. Bertram Colgrave (Cambridge, Eng., 1956), pp. 81–83. See E. G. Stanley, "Hæthenra Hyht in *Beowulf*" in *Studies in Old English Literature in Honor of Arthur G. Brodeur*, ed. Stanley B. Greenfield (Eugene, Ore., 1963), pp. 136–51, and Colin Chase, "Saints' Lives, Royal Lives, and the Date of *Beowulf*" in *The Dating of Beowulf*, pp. 161–71.

order to demonstrate for his own aristocratic circle how a layman and noble lord, a man out in the world, could lead a holy existence.[5] Odo gives moral and religious dimensions to Gerald's lifelong martial career. The warrior soothes the suspicious, squelches the malicious, and puts down the violent who refuse to come to terms; he does this not for personal gain but in order to achieve peace for his society. So Beowulf restrains, one after the other, coastguard, Unferth, and Grendel, making friends of two potential foes and ridding Denmark of monsters who pay no wergild. Ottoman Saxony as portrayed by Widukind is—in the heroic cast of its values and the ferocity of its feuds—very close to the world of *Beowulf*.[6] Tenth-century monastic narratives seem, like *Beowulf*, able to find a place for heroic values—even fighting and the bonds of kinship—within a Christian framework. In Hrotsvitha's *Gongolfus* the ideals of a warrior's life are fused with the Christian goal of *caritas*, while Ruotger's *Life of Bruno*, archbishop of Cologne and brother of Otto the Great, reports with some understatement that "priestly religion and royal determination united their strength" in him.[7] Like these works, the Old English poems that we can date to the tenth century set up no unresolvable contradictions between piety and the heroic life. *The Battle of Maldon*, composed after 991 and regarded as the finest utterance of the Anglo-Saxon heroic age (and most "Germanic" since Tacitus), contains a prayer by a warlord soon to be venerated by the monks of Ely.[8] *The Battle of Brunanburh*, from around 937, is red with blood, God's rising and setting sun, and a historical perspective reminiscent of manifest destiny. *Judith*, probably from the same century, focuses on a prayerful heroine who chops off heads with only slightly less savoir-faire than Beowulf. Between *Bede's Death Song* and *Maldon* something happened to Old English poetry, whether we call this something rebarbarization or adapting Christian models for a new and only partly literate secular aristocracy. New syntheses were becoming possible. Unlike Anglian stone crosses of the eighth century, English religious sculpture after

5. Odo, *Vita S. Geradli Aureliacensis Comitis*, Patrologiae Cursus Completus, Series Latina 133:639–703. See Carl Erdmann (*Die Entstehung des Kreuzzugsgedankens* [Stuttgart, 1935]), trans. M. W. Baldwin and W. Goffart, *The Origin of the Idea of Crusade* (Princeton, 1977), pp. 87–89. Odo was among Remigius' students at Paris (*Vita Odonis Abbatis Cluniacensis*, ch. 19, in J. Mabillon and L. d'Achery, *Acta Sanctorum Ordinis S. Benedicti* [Paris, 1668–1701], VII. 124).

6. Leyser, passim.

7. *Hrotsvithae Opera*, ed. P. Winterfeld, Monumenta Germaniae Historica, Scriptores Rerum Germanicarum in usum scholarum (Berlin, 1902), pp. 35–51; *Ruotgeri Vita Brunonis Archiepiscopi Coloniensis*, ed. Irene Schmale-Ott, Monumenta Germaniae Historica, Scriptores Rerum Germanicarum, n. s. 10 (Weimar, 1951), p. 19.

8. See Rosemary Woolf, "The Ideal of Men Dying with their Lord in the *Germania* and in *The Battle of Maldon*," *Anglo-Saxon England* 5 (1976), 63–81.

the Danish invasions was able to draw, like *Beowulf,* on pagan myth and heroic legend.[9]

In still another area, the vision of the *Beowulf* poet seems to derive from contemporary concerns, from a need to establish in the present an ideological basis for national unity. I suggested in an earlier paper that the *Beowulf* poet's incentive for composing an epic about sixth-century Scyldings may have had something to do with the fact that, by the 890s at least, Heremod, Scyld, Healfdene, and the rest, were taken to be the common ancestors both of the Anglo-Saxon royal family and of the ninth-century Danish immigrants, the *Scaldingi.*[1] The *Beowulf* poet admires kings who, like Hrothgar, have regional overlordship of surrounding tribes and who, like Beowulf, are powerful enough to keep neighbors in check. A key political catchword—"þeodcyning" ("great" or "national king")—is prominently displayed by the poet in his opening sentence. He depicts the Danish nation's former glory in a time when powerful kings had been able to unite the various peoples of the land, something that did not occur with any permanence in Denmark or England until the tenth century.[2] The *Beowulf* poet does his best to attach his pagan champion to as many peoples as possible—Danes, Geats, Swedes, Wulfings, and Wægmundings—as if to make him the more authentically representative of the culture and traditions of central Scandinavia: an archetypal Northman. Epics have their propagandist appeal. There is a relationship, however indirect, between Virgil's account of the majesty of Rome's legendary past, the glory of her ancient traditions, and the Augustan program to bring back a "pristine" patriotism and code of morals. Both the *Aeneid* and *Beowulf* are in some sense historical novels, mythically presented, philosophically committed, and focused on the adventures of a new hero.[3] Both poets project onto the distant past features of the

---

9. E.g., Wayland in Leeds Parish Church, Thor in Gosforth Church, and Sigemund at Winchester Old Minster. See Richard N. Bailey, *Viking Age Sculpture in Northern England* (London, 1980).
1. "Skaldic Verse and the Date of *Beowulf*" in *The Dating of Beowulf,* pp. 123–39 and Alexander Murray, "*Beowulf,* the Danish Invasions, and Royal Genealogy," pp. 101–11 in the same volume.
2. See discussion in Horst Zettel, *Das Bild der Normannen und der Normanneneinfälle in westfränkischen, ostfränkischen und angelsächsischen Quellen des 8. bis 11. Jahrhunderts* (Munich, 1977), pp. 69–84. On West Saxon hegemonial tendencies during the first half of the tenth century, see E. E. Stengel, "Imperator und Imperium bei den Angelsachsen," *Deutsches Archiv für Erforschung des Mittelalters* 16 (1960), 15–72; J. L. Nelson, "Inauguration Rituals" in *Early Medieval Kingship,* ed. P. H. Sawyer and I. N. Wood (Leeds, 1977), pp. 68–70.
3. See Robert W. Hanning, *The Vision of History in Early Britain* (New York, 1966), p. 19. Tom Burns Haber makes one of several attempts to list verbal echoes and narrative parallels between the two poems (*A Comparative Study of the 'Beowulf' and the 'Aeneid'* [Princeton, 1931]). Recent publications demonstrating Virgilian influence on the narrative structure and perspective of *Beowulf* include Theodore M. Andersson, *Early Epic Scenery: Homer, Virgil, and the Medieval Legacy* (Ithaca, N. Y., 1976), pp. 145–59,

society of their own day, consciously and deliberately, in order to provide a sense of continuity. Virgil's Rome is grounded in an earlier Rome; the *Beowulf* poet anchors the West Saxon *imperium* in a brilliant North Germanic antiquity. By the twelfth century, the Normans were very French; yet the more French they became, the more they stressed their Danish ancestry and the heroic deeds of their founding dynasty.[4] By the first quarter of the tenth century, the Danes in England were working hard to be more Christian and English than the English: at mid-century both archbishops of England, Oda and Oskytel, were of Danish extraction.[5] An Old English poem about northern heathens and northern heroes, opening with the mythical figure of Scyld from whom the ruling houses of both Denmark and England were descended, fits nicely with the efforts of Alfred and his successors to promote an Anglo-Danish brotherhood, to see Dane and Anglo-Saxon as equal partners in a united kingdom.

The sadness, the poignancy, the *lacrimae rerum* we associate with *Beowulf* come from the epic poet's sense of duration, of how "time condemns itself and all human endeavor and hopes."[6] Yet though Heorot is snuffed out by flames and noble pagans and their works perish, the poet does not scorn the heroic fellowship whose passing he has had to tell. There is still something left worth ambition: "The task to be accomplished is not the conservation of the past, but the redemption of the hopes of the past."[7] The last word in the poem is uttered by sixth-century Geats who commend Beowulf as "lofgeornost" ("most intent on glory"). Lady Philosophy assured Boethius (II, pr. 7) that the praise won even by noble souls is of slight value: only a small part of a tiny earth is inhabited, and by nations differing in language, custom, and philosophy; even written eulogies fail because time veils them and their authors in obscurity. King Alfred did not entirely accept her last point. He argued that the fame of a great man can also fade through a kind of *trahison des clercs*—"þurh þa heardsælþa þara writera ðæt hi for heora slæwðe ond for gimeleste

and Alistair Campbell, "The Use in *Beowulf* of Earlier Heroic Verse" in *England before the Conquest: Studies in Primary Sources Presented to Dorothy Whitelock*, ed. Peter Clemoes and Kathleen Hughes (Cambridge, Eng., 1971), pp. 283–92.

4. R. H. C. Davis, *The Normans and their Myth* (London, 1976), pp. 27, 54.

5. Oda, bishop of Ramsbury under Athelstan and archbishop of Canterbury from 940–958, was the son of a Dane who came to England with the first settlers. Oskytel, kinsman of Oda, was the archbishop of York. Oda's nephew was St. Oswald, prominent founder and renovator of monasteries. See J. Armitage Robinson, *St. Oswald and the Church of Worcester*, British Academy Supplemental Papers, 5 (London, 1919), pp. 38–51. The Danes appear to have been widely accepted in English society from at least 927 onwards; see Jacobs, p. 40, and R. I. Page, "The Audience of *Beowulf* and the Vikings" in *The Dating of Beowulf*, pp. 113–22.

6. Bloomfield, "Chaucer's Sense of History" in *Essays and Explorations*, p. 25.

7. Max Horkheimer and Theodor Adorno, *Dialectic of Enlightenment*, tr. John Cumming (New York, 1972), p. xv.

ond eac for recceleste forleton unwriten þara monna ðeawas ond
hiora dæda, þe on hiora dagum formæroste ond weorðgeornuste
wæron"[8] ("through the bad conduct of those writers who—in their
sloth and in carelessness and also in negligence—leave unwritten
the virtues and deeds of those men who in their day were most
renowned and most intent on honor"). The purpose of *Beowulf*, as
Morton Bloomfield has often reminded us, is heroic celebration, to
present the deeds of a great man in order "to give his audience new
strength and a model."[9] Those of us who were privileged to be Pro-
fessor Bloomfield's students at Harvard know what such a model can
be worth.

FRED C. ROBINSON

The Tomb of Beowulf[†]

The Old English poem to which we have assigned the name *Beowulf*
was composed, apparently, by a Christian poet—some say a monk
or a priest—who was concerned to extol the virtues of ancient Ger-
manic heroes while acknowledging regretfully (for example, in lines
175–88) that they were deprived of the Christian revelation enjoyed
in his own era. This poignant intermingling of veneration and regret,
of pride in the Anglo-Saxons' Germanic ancestors shadowed by sad-
ness over the perilous state of their souls, permeates, I believe, the
poem's tone and lends it intellectual sophistication and complexity
which exceed mere admiration of a heroic past.[1] Young Beowulf's
achievements in the first part of the poem—his deliverance of the
Danes from the incursions of the Grendelkin, his farsighted diplo-
macy in committing his nation to an alliance with the Danish royal
family, and his discerning report to his own king Hygelac on the
state of the nation which he has just visited—are all circumscribed
by discreet reminders of the heathen status of the heroic partici-
pants; and the displays of wisdom, such as the speeches of Hroth-
gar, leave us simultaneously impressed by their loftiness of thought
and saddened by their always falling short of ultimate truth, which,
to a medieval English audience, would have been Christian truth. In
the last half of the poem we see the hero devoting his strength,

---

8. *King Alfred's Old English Version of Boethius*, p. 44, lines 1–4. [The abbreviation "7"
   has been expanded to "ond"—*Editor*.]
9. *Speculum* 41 (1966), 369.
† From *"The Tomb of Beowulf" and Other Essays on Old English* by Fred C. Robinson
   (Oxford: Blackwell Publishers, 1993), pp. 3–19. Reprinted by permission of John
   Wiley & Sons, Inc.
1. I have discussed this feature of the poem *in extenso* in *Beowulf and the Appositive Style*
   (Knoxville, TN, 1985).

courage, and wisdom to the protection of his nation until, at the end of his fifty-year reign as king, he protects them against the attacks of the dragon, which he slays at the cost of his own life. At his death he leaves to his people as a legacy a vast hoard of treasure, which he seems to think might ensure their survival in the militant and hostile world surrounding them:

Nū ic on māðma hord   mīne bebohte
frōde feorhlege,   fremmað gēna
lēoda þearfe;   ne mæg ic hēr leng wesan.[2]   (2799–801)

"Now that I have exchanged my old life for this hoard of treasures, they will now meet the needs of the people; I can be here no longer."[3] But, in a gesture which seems to express that sense of despair which darkens all the triumphs and hazards in the poem, the Geatas bury the treasure with the ashes of their king—a pagan ritual following upon the pagan rite of cremation—and the last words of the poem are the warriors' solemn encomia as they pace their horses around his splendid tomb.

The tomb of Beowulf and the rites enacted there make up a scene of strange and somber majesty which readers have often found reverberant with dark implications beyond the merely scenic. The hero's obsequies have also been regarded as problematic by scholars of the poem, who are troubled by the fact that Beowulf's funeral rites are not merely grander than the funerals of other characters described in the poem, but peculiarly complex in a way that makes them unique. The hero's obsequies begin with these verses:

Him ðā gegiredan   Gēata lēode
ad on eorðan   unwaclicne,
helm[um] behongen,   hildebordum,
beorhtum byrnum,   swā hē bēna wæs;
ālegdon ðā tōmiddes   mǣrne þēoden
hæleð hīofende,   hlāford lēofne.   (3137–42)

"The people of the Geatas erected then on the ground a splendid pyre hung about with helmets, with battle-shields, and with shining mail-coats, as he had asked; then the lamenting warriors laid in the midst the renowned king, their beloved lord." The poet then tells us that the roaring flames and dark smoke rise into the sky,

---

2. *Beowulf and the Fight at Finnsburg*, ed. Fr. Klaeber, 3rd edn with 1st and 2nd supplements (Boston, 1950). All quotations from the poem are from this edition. Quotations from other Old English poems will be from *The Anglo-Saxon Poetic Records*, ed. G. P. Krapp and E. V. K. Dobbie (New York: Columbia UP, 1931–1953).

3. Charles Donahue, "Potlatch and charity: notes on the heroic in *Beowulf*," in *Anglo-Saxon Poetry: essays in appreciation for John C. McGalliard*, ed. Lewis E. Nicholson and Dolores Warwick Frese (Notre Dame, 1975), p. 32, reminds us that the plural *fremmað* cannot be an imperative singular addressed to Wiglaf, as some have thought.

intertwined with the lamentations of the mourners. "With grief-stricken hearts they bemoaned their sorrow, the death of their king" (3148–49), he says, and following this a mysterious old woman steps forward and prophesies the doom of the nation now that their king and protector has fallen. The scene closes with the evocative detail *Heofon rēce swealg* ("Heaven swallowed up the smoke.")[4]

This impressive tableau with grieving comrades, a lamenting woman, and flames consuming the corpse and battle-gear is much the same as the ritual cremation which followed the fight at Finnsburg earlier in the poem. The peculiarity of Beowulf's last rites is that ten days after the very formal closure of the scene we have just examined, Beowulf's subjects initiate a whole new series of ceremonies. Having erected a magnificent *beorh* or tumulus, which they fill with sumptuous treasure together with their king's ashes, they surround it with a splendid wall devised by *foresnotere men* "exceedingly wise people," and then twelve mounted, chanting warriors circle the wall:

> Þā ymbe hlæw riodan   hildedēore,
> æþelinga bearn,   ealra twelfe,
> woldon (care) cwīðan,   [ond] kyning mænan,
> wordgyd wrecan,   ond ymb w(er) sprecan;
> eahtodan eorlscipe   ond his ellenweorc
> duguðum dēmdon,—   swā hit gedē(fe) bið,
> þæt mon his winedryhten   wordum herge,
> ferhðum frēoge,   þonne hē forð scile
> of līchaman   (læded) weorðan.
> Swā begnornodon   Gēata lēode
> hlāfordes (hry)re,   heorðgenēatas;
> cwædon þæt hē wære   wyruldcyning[a]
> manna mildust   ond mon(ðw)ærust,
> lēodum līðost   ond lofgeornost.   (3169–82)

"Then around the barrow rode twelve sons of noblemen, valiant in battle. They wanted to declare their sorrow and speak of their king, to utter a chant and speak of the man. They praised his nobility and his deeds of valor, proclaimed them majestically, as it is fitting that one should do—to extol with words and cherish in the heart one's

4. The prophesying woman and the rising smoke are among the details that scholars have found suggestive of some special significance. Several people have noted that the smoke from the cremation fire passing directly up to the heavens is a Germanic pagan motif documented in the *Ynglinga saga*; see for example Paul Beekman Taylor, "*Heofon riece swealg*: a sign of Beowulf's state of grace," *Philological Quarterly*, 42 (1963), 257–9. On the funeral in general see both text and bibliographical footnotes in Ute Schwab, *Servire il Signore Morto: Funzione e trasformazione di riti funebri germanici nell'epica medievale inglese e tedesca*, Università Catania: Collana di studi di filologia moderna 5 (Catania, 1990), pp. 22–5, 64–5.

lord and friend when he must be led forth from his garment of flesh.
Thus the people of the Geatas, the companions of his hearth,
bewailed the fall of their lord. They said that he was of all the kings
of the world the kindest and most mildhearted of men, the most gra-
cious to his people, and the most eager for praise." The sentiment
in this passage is so noble, the style so consciously sublime, that an
early translator of Beowulf and the only prominent poet ever to edit
the poem—N. S. V. Grundtvig—believed that the closing scene is
central to the meaning of Beowulf and therefore he named the poem
Beowulfes Beorh "the tomb of Beowulf" (cf. line 2807). Grundtvig
even composed a poem of his own in Old English and in Danish in
which he justifies this title, suggesting that the beorh of Beowulf is
analogous to the poem itself, both being monuments which preserve
the hero's name and fame in succeeding ages.[5] * * *

But however much we might agree with Grundtvig that the mem-
orable closing of Beowulf distills and reifies the sense of the whole
narrative, we cannot deny that it is also problematic. "It is the pecu-
liarity of the Beowulf account," says Klaeber, "that two distinct and,
as it were, parallel funeral ceremonies are related in detail, . . . and
that the greater emphasis is placed on the closing stage, which is
made the occasion of rehearsing solemn and inspiring songs."[6] The
archeologist Knut Stjerna found the two ceremonies such an
extraordinary departure from actual practice in pagan days that he
concluded the poet must have had two separate sources treating
Beowulf's funeral, one in which he was cremated and one in which
he was buried with treasure, and that he somewhat ineptly conflated
them in his poem; but R. W. Chambers disagrees, saying that the
double ceremony simply shows the Christian poet's ignorance of
pagan practice.[7] He would agree no doubt with a recent scholar's
judgment that "there must be some confusion of tradition."[8] No one
has ever doubted, so far as I am aware, that the ceremony around
the walled monument is simply a second funeral for Beowulf, a curi-
ous redundancy which, however impressive, means nothing more
than that the poet was confused about pagan burial customs.[9]

5. See F. C. Robinson, "The Afterlife of Old English: A Brief History of Composition in
   Old English after the Close of the Anglo-Saxon Period," in The Tomb of Beowulf,
   pp. 275–303 at 299–303 [Editor].
6. Klaeber, Beowulf and the Fight at Finnsburg, p. 229.
7. Chambers, Beowulf: an introduction to the study of the poem, 3rd edn with a supple-
   ment by C. L. Wrenn (Cambridge, 1959), p. 124.
8. Paula Loikala, "Funeral rites in Beowulf," Quaderni di Filologia Germanica della Facoltà
   di Lettere e Filosofia dell'Università di Bologna, 2 (1982), 287.
9. That the Geatas should erect a monument on the cliff as Beowulf wished (2802–8) is
   of course to be expected. But the consignment of a vast treasure to the beorh and (espe-
   cially) the ceremony of chants and marching seem to be a puzzling repetition and expan-
   sion of what went on at the cremation ten days before.

My purpose in this essay is to suggest that the second rite described at the end of *Beowulf* may have had a significance beyond confused redundancy. I shall supply evidence to suggest that at least some in the poet's audience would have seen in the final ceremony of the poem suggestions of an apotheosis. King Beowulf's bereaved subjects, I will suggest, are so overawed by their fallen leader's accomplishments and so unwilling to accept the finality of his death that they turn desperately to the pagan resources available to them to accord him ultimate veneration and, perhaps, recruit his protective force beyond the grave. Such an act would be a closing parallel with the act of the Danes at the beginning of the poem in lines 175–88, where in a time of crisis they turn to their heathen gods with propitiatory sacrifices.

My procedure will be to survey the cultural background of the Anglo-Saxons to determine how familiar they would have been with the concept of deifying a deceased hero and to see whether manifestations of apotheosis in their culture bear any resemblance to the events described at the end of *Beowulf.* And finally I shall consider what the attitude of at least a portion of a Christian Anglo-Saxon audience might have been toward a poem that implies that their ancestors may have ascribed divine status to a slain hero.[1]

Herotheism is attested fairly widely in the early stages of the western European culture of which Anglo-Saxon England forms a part. We might begin with a glance at the classical world.[2] Hector, whose funeral ceremony in the *Iliad* has so often been compared with that of Beowulf, was worshipped in the Troad and also at Tanagra, east

---

1. The verb "implies" is carefully chosen here. I am also careful to say that the implication would have been understood by "at least a portion of" the poet's audience. I am mindful of Bruce Mitchell's well-directed impatience with some scholars' "assumption that the audience of *Beowulf* was homogeneous; that all its members reacted in the same way, had all heard—or not heard—the story before hearing the poem, had all heard—or not heard—the poem before; were all equally intelligent and equally knowledgeable about theology or the Church Fathers or scriptural exegesis or whatever; were all equally sensitive and capable—or insensitive and incapable—of making such connexions." (See "1987: postscript on *Beowulf,*" in *On Old English* (Oxford, 1988), pp. 41–2.) On the other hand, I would not think that the point of this essay were worth making if I did not believe that the implication was likely to be a conscious element in the poet's design, available to that part of his audience which was knowledgeable and attentive enough to perceive it. As I have suggested elsewhere (see footnote 1, p. 182 of this Norton Critical Edition), a medieval Christian who addresses a Christian audience about their pagan ancestors will necessarily work more by implication than by overt declaration.
2. The ensuing examples (and many others) are cited in *Paulys Realencyclopädie der classischen Altertumswissenschaft,* neue Bearbeitung begonnen von Georg Wissowa, vol. 14 (Stuttgart, 1912), pp. 2814–15, s.v. *Heros,* and vol. 15, pp. 1119–27, s.v. *Heros . . . Der Kultus;* also *The Oxford Classical Dictionary,* ed. N. G. L. Hammond and H. H. Scullard, 2nd edn (Oxford, 1970), p. 491, s.v. *Hector,* and p. 506, s.v. *Hero-cult.* In Greek, it should be mentioned, a hero was less powerful than the primary gods but had divine status, and cult was paid to him, usually at his tomb or *heroön.* Conceived of as mortals who had died and were apotheosized, heroes in this sense were not the same as the heroes of Homer—Ajax, Odysseus, etc.—although some (e.g. Hector) were in both groups. In the case of Hercules the distinction between god and hero was uncertain, as it was in some others.

of Thebes, and later poetry speaks of him as a god. Theseus was worshipped in Athens, and there were cults of Oedipus, while the Argive hero Adrastus of Sicyon was venerated at a *heroön* (a shrine to a hero, which is usually located at or identical with his tomb) in the marketplace of that city, with tragic choruses recounting his sad fate being sung in his honor. Turning to the Romans, an Anglo-Saxon who read Virgil would have seen that in book VI of the *Aeneid* Palinurus is assured that he will be deified and worshipped at his tomb, and Dardanus in book VII is similarly deified and worshipped. In book XII Juno says that Aeneas has his niche as a god in heaven. Pliny discusses the *heroön*, using the Latinized name *heroum*. These instances are all from the realm of classical legend or literature, but, as is well known, the deification of mortals was also a part of ancient history. Alexander the Great, after he was hailed as the son of Amon-Zeus by the oracle of Amon in 332 BC, became increasingly convinced that he was a god and as such began demanding veneration from his subjects. The Spartans' cynical response to this demand ("If Alexander wants to be a god, let him be a god") finds an echo in the Old English *Orosius,* where Alexander's claims to divinity are similarly scorned. But the example of Alexander was not lost on the Roman emperors, who came to make similar pretensions. Later we shall return to these historical examples as they impinged on the Anglo-Saxon consciousness.

In the Germanic world texts both early and late attest to deification of heroes.[3] Jordanes tells us that during the reign of Domitian (one of the self-deified Roman emperors) the Goths so venerated the generals who had led them to victory that they elevated them to the status of demigods. The Latin word Jordanes uses is *semideos,* which he translates for his Gothic audience, "id est ansis."[4] *Ansis* is the Gothic word for "gods," cognate with Old Icelandic *Æsir* (and Old English *ōs,* preserved in personal names and the rune-name). The Gothic royal family known as the Amali always claimed to be the descendants of the *ansis.* More deifications of kings occur in Scandinavia. The eleventh-century historian Adam of Bremen reports that the Swedes made gods out of men who had accomplished extraordinary deeds, and he cites the example of a King Eric, who,

3. Among the works of reference I have drawn on are Richard M. Meyer, *Altgermanische Religionsgeschichte* (Leipzig, 1910), esp. pp. 90–2, Wolfgang Golther, *Handbuch der germanischen Mythologie* (Leipzig, 1895), esp. pp. 92–5, and Hilda Roderick Ellis, *The Road to Hel: a study of the conception of the dead in Old Norse literature* (Cambridge, 1943), esp. pp. 99–111.

4. Jordanes, *Getica,* XIII, 78: "iam proceres suos, quorum quasi fortuna vincebant, non puros homines, sed semideos, id est ansis, vocaverunt." Herwig Wolfram, *History of the Goths,* tr. Thomas Dunlap (Berkeley, CA, 1987), p. 324, points out that Theodoric continued to encourage the belief in the divinity of the Amali rulers. See also Walter Goffart's comments on barbarian *memoria* in *Barbarians and Romans: techniques of accommodation* (Princeton, 1980), esp. pp. 21–4.

according to the *Vita Anskarii* of Rimbert, was deified by his people
after his death and worshipped by them with prayers and sacrifices at
his *heroön*.[5] Another king who was deified and served with sacri-
fices after his death was King Olaf, brother of Halfdan, who accord-
ing to the Icelandic *Flateyarbók* is laid in a mound with a certain
amount of silver coin and venerated there as *geirstaðaálfr* by his sub-
jects.[6] Icelandic sagas tell us that King Guðmundr was proclaimed
a god and worshipped after his death, as was another Icelander
named Barðr.[7] In the *Skáldskaparmál* Snorri Sturlusson says, "That
king who is called Helgi, after whom Halogaland is named, was the
father of Þorgerðr Hölgabrúðr; they were both worshipped with
sacrifice, and a mound was reared for Helgi, one layer being of gold
and silver—that was the sacrificial wealth—and the other of earth
and stones."[8]

"Die Apotheose bleibt in der Regel auf Könige beschränkt,"
observes Richard Meyer, but he notes that others too are deified
from time to time.[9] The *Landnámabók* tells of a Norwegian chief-
tain named Grimr who was so popular among his people that after
his death he was worshipped with sacrifices.[1] We have already seen
that Þorgerðr Hölgabrúðr was worshipped as a goddess along with
her father, King Helgi. Another woman who was regarded by the
common people as a kind of goddess is a prophetess mentioned by
Gregory of Tours in the *Historia Francorum*.[2]

The Frankish prophetess was apparently venerated during her life-
time, but worship of mortals among the Germanic peoples was nor-
mally accorded only to select persons among the dead, a practice
which is documented from the early eighth century on, primarily in
ecclesiastical prohibitions. In his letter to the people of Hesse and
Thuringia Pope Gregory III lists sacrifices to the dead among the
pagan Germanic customs which they must reject absolutely, and in
his letter to the bishops in Bavaria and Alemania he tells the mis-
sionary bishops that they must make the people stop sacrificing to
the dead.[3] In his publication of the decrees of the synod of 742, Karl-
mann, palace mayor of the Eastern Franks, says that every bishop
within his own diocese must root out all the filth of the heathen,

5. Golther, *Handbuch*, pp. 93–4, supplies full Latin text with translation.
6. Golther, *Handbuch*, pp. 94–5, and Ellis, *The Road to Hel*, pp. 100–2, who draws atten-
   tion also to the sacrifices offered after the death of Halfdan the Black at the burial
   mounds containing his remains.
7. Ellis, *The Road to Hel*, p. 102.
8. Quoted in Ellis, *The Road to Hel*, p. 105.
9. Meyer, *Altgermanische Religionsgeschichte*, p. 91.
1. Golther, *Handbuch*, p. 94.
2. *Gregoire de Tours: Histoire des Francs*, ed. Henri Omont and Gaston Collon, 2 vols (Paris,
   1886–93), VII, 44.
3. *Die Briefe des heiligen Bonifatius und Lullus*, ed. Michael Tangl (Berlin, 1916), XXXIII,
   43, and XXXIV, 44.

such as sacrifices to the dead.[4] The *Indiculus superstitionum et Paganiarum* (AD 743) has prohibitions "de sacrilegio ad sepulchra mortuorum" and "de sacrilegio super defunctos, id est, dadsisas"—thus supplying the native Germanic word for veneration of the dead.[5] The phrase *ad sepulchrum* is noteworthy, for it reminds us that worship of the dead was normally conducted at the tomb (or *heroön*) of the apotheosized mortal.[6]

Conforming with the widespread reports of deified kings and heroes in early Germanic times was the euhemeristic explanation of the origin of pagan gods, a theory that became increasingly popular as Christianity took root in Germanic lands. Euhemerus was a Sicilian mythographer who, in the third century BC, advanced the theory that the Greek gods had all been human kings or heroes who were deified after their deaths by the people they had ruled over or benefited. Early Christians seized eagerly on the euhemeristic rationale since it provided a simple explanation for how so many different pagan gods could have come into existence among so many different peoples. The Icelander Snorri Sturlusson provides euhemeristic origins for Odin and Frey, and the manner in which their deification took place has some remarkable similarities to Beowulf's death and funeral.[7] In the *Ynglinga Saga*, chapter 10, we are told that Odin was a king, and when he died after a long and prosperous reign, his subjects prepared a sumptuously provided pyre for him and cremated his remains. After the cremation they believed he was a god in Asgaard and prayed to him. Snorri explains that the smoke of the funeral pyre rising into the air was a sign to the people that Odin was being exalted. In chapters 12 and 13 we learn that Frey became king in later days, and after a successful reign he died and was placed in a great mound with a lavish hoard of gold, silver, and copper. His Swedish subjects proclaimed him a god and made sacrifices to him. Saxo Grammaticus's *Gesta Danorum* explains the origin of Norse gods euhemeristically too, as do the *Historia Norvegiæ*, the *Íslendingabók*, and other Scandinavian writings. Outside of Scandinavia, Gregory's *History of the Franks*, II, 29, tells how Queen Clotild the Christian explains to her husband Clovis that his pagan gods are merely mortal men who came to be worshipped by the Germanic heathens. The euhemeristic explanation was codified in the broadly influential *Etymologiae* of Isidore of Seville and in the "De diis

4. Ibid., XLIV, 56.
5. Quoted from Francis B. Gummere, *Founders of England,* with a supplementary note by Francis B. Magoun, Jr (New York, 1930), p. 349. Gummere's entire chapter on "The worship of the dead," pp. 337–65, supplies a wealth of evidence for Germanic practices.
6. Ellis, *The Road to Hel*, pp. 100–5 provides a detailed survey of the evidence for worship at the grave-mound.
7. For a skillful survey and synopsis of euhemerism in the Germanic lands see Anthony Faulkes, "Descent from the gods," *Mediaeval Scandinavia*, 11 (1978–9), 92–125.

gentium" section of Rabanus Maurus's *De universo*, where he emphasizes that powerful men and founders of cities were especially venerated by pagan communities. The pervasive use by Christians of the euhemeristic account of the origin of pagan gods must have served as a constant reminder to Germanic Christians that their ancestors had been accustomed to deifying kings and heroes.

The evidence supplied thus far for Germanic apotheosis comes from a wide range of sources both Latin and vernacular, but we have not yet investigated the most important Germanic culture for our purposes—the Anglo-Saxon—except for our glances at certain passages in the eighth-century correspondence of Boniface. In fact, allusions to deification of heroes, to worship of the dead, and to the Germanic pantheon being mere deified rulers are prominent in Old English and Anglo-Latin writings right up to the end of the Anglo-Saxon period. In his *De falsis Deis*, Wulfstan tells how pagan men were not satisfied with the gods they had but took to worshipping "strenuous worldly men who had become mighty in worldly powers and were awesome when they were alive"—a formulation which would fit Beowulf admirably.[8] In his source-text, Ælfric's *De falsis Diis*, we are told that the pagans took for their gods powerful men and giants.[9] This view of pagan worship would no doubt have seemed to Ælfric and Wulfstan to be confirmed by Romans 1: 18–25. In his *Canons of Edgar* Wulfstan urges the priests to tell their congregations that the worship of human beings (*manweorðunga*) is expressly forbidden.[1] Clerics like Ælfric and Wulfstan become especially anxious about lapses into *manweorðung* when they discuss funerals; they evidently thought that it is when saying farewell to the deceased that an Anglo-Saxon is most likely to begin worshipping a mortal. Ælfric tells priests that if they are invited to ceremonies for the dead they must forbid heathen chants by the layfolk and must not participate in drinking and eating in the presence of the corpse.[2] A letter of Pope Zacharius to the Anglo-Saxon Boniface in the early eighth century shows what lies behind these prohibitions: the pope speaks of sacrilegious priests who lapsed into the heathen practice of eating the offerings to the dead.[3] Wulfstan admonishes that when someone dies the people must avoid any vain practices *æt þam lice*, and confessionals and penitentials both early and late forbid the burning of grain to the dead in order to heal living people who are

8. *The Homilies of Wulfstan*, ed. Dorothy Bethurum (Oxford, 1957), p. 222.
9. *Homilies of Ælfric: a supplementary collection*, ed. John C. Pope, Early English Text Society o.s. 260 (London, 1968), pp. 681–2.
1. *Wulfstan's Canons of Edgar*, ed. Roger Fowler, Early English Text Society o.s. 266 (London, 1972), p. 4.
2. *Die Hirtenbriefe Ælfrics*, ed. Bernhard Fehr, reprinted with a supplement to the introduction by Peter Clemoes (Darmstadt, 1966), p. 25.
3. *Die Briefe des heiligen Bonifatius*, LXIV, 80.

sick.[4] The Old English translator of the *Dicts of Cato* gives biblical authority to warnings against illicit commerce with the deceased by incorporating in his text the Old Testament prohibition against seeking truth from the dead (Deuteronomy 18: 12).[5] The assumption of preternatural powers of healing and omniscience on the part of the dead is like the Scandinavians' belief that their deified kings could provide abundant crops.[6]

As we shall see later on, all these practices and prohibitions which we have been examining could have a bearing on the obsequies of Beowulf. For the moment it may be sufficient to observe that while we have long recognized that the cremation of Beowulf and the burial of him with lavish grave goods were flagrant violations of the church's teachings in the poet's day, it seems possible that the chants and processions of the warriors before the hero's grave-mound would have been seen as no less flagrant an infraction of Christian observance.

Deification of their rulers by the ancients in the classical world was known to the Anglo-Saxons both through King Alfred the Great and through the anonymous translator of the Orosius.[7] In one of his original insertions into the text of his translation of Boethius's *De consolatione philosophiae*, Alfred explains to his subjects that Apollo, Jupiter, and Saturn were simply mortals who were members of the royal family and whose foolish subjects (*dysige folc*) believed them when they claimed to be gods. The Orosius translator mentions both Alexander the Great's pretensions to divinity and the deification of the Roman emperor Domitian, who demanded that his people bow to him as to a god. The Anglo-Saxons' added comments about the arrogance of the rulers and the folly of the people may be the result not only of Christian piety but also of the fact that when their own pagan ancestors practiced deification it was almost always a rite performed after the death of the mortal who was to be deified and not a status rulers would assume during their lifetimes. The later Roman practice of deifying emperors posthumously by senatorial decrees would perhaps have seemed less absurd—though not less wicked— to Alfred and his contemporaries.

Euhemeristic explanations of the pagan gods were widespread among the Christian Anglo-Saxons both early and late. Daniel, bishop of Winchester from 705 to 744, writes a letter to Boniface advising him to inform the heathen Germanic tribes on the continent that

4. *Wulfstan's Canons*, p. 17.
5. R. S. Cox, "The Old English Dicts of Cato," *Anglia*, 90 (1972), 16.
6. Ellis, *The Road to Hel*, pp. 100–1.
7. *King Alfred's Old English Version of Boethius*, ed. Walter John Sedgefield (Oxford, 1899), pp. 115–16, and *The Old English Orosius*, ed. Janet Bately, Early English Text Society s.s. 6 (London, 1980), p. 139.

their gods were actually mortals, not gods.[8] In their treatises on false gods, which are the fullest euhemeristic analyses in a Germanic language, Ælfric and Wulfstan give detailed accounts of how each pagan god was originally a powerful or distinguished man who was declared a god after his death and venerated. Ælfric treats euhemerism further in *De initio creaturae*[9] and in his *Passion of St Sebastian, Martyr.*[1] In his life of King Alfred, Asser says that the king's ancestors Ingild and Ine were descendants of Geat, "whom the pagans worshipped for a long time as god."[2] (Nennius says people called Geat the son of a god.)[3] The life of St. Kentigern says, "Woden, whom the Angles worship as chief god, and from whom they derive their origin, was a mortal man, and king of the Saxons, and father of many races."[4]

Anglo-Saxon euhemerism, or, more specifically, the concept of pagan Germanic kings being deified, was woven into the fabric of the culture in yet another important way. The numerous surviving Anglo-Saxon royal genealogies, drawn up to establish the kings' ancestral right to rule, always include among the names of ancestors listed the names of pagan Germanic gods. Thus Woden (or Seaxnet) appears in the genealogies as an ancestor in the royal houses of Kent, Essex, Wessex, Deira, Bernicia, East Anglia, Mercia, and Lindsey.[5] Woden's ancestor Geata is also listed, and an annotation in one manuscript (Textus Roffensis) gives us an idea of how the Anglo-Saxons understood this curious incorporation of pagan gods in the lineage of their Christian kings: *Geata, ðene ða hæþena wurþedon for god* ("Geata, whom the heathens worshipped as a god").[6] Æthelweard too attests to the Christian Anglo-Saxons' assumptions about the Germanic god Woden's appearance in the

8. *Die Briefe des heiligen Bonifatius*, XV, 23.
9. *Homilies of the Anglo-Saxon Church*, ed. Benjamin Thorpe, vol. 1 (London, 1843), p. 82. Ælfric's euhemeristic account is widely adopted by later homilists: e.g. a sermon from a twelfth-century manuscript draws heavily on Ælfric's *De falsis diis*: see Rubie D. N. Warner, *Early English Homilies from the Twelfth Century MS. Vesp. D.XIV*, Early English Text Society o.s. 152 (London, 1910), pp. 34–41.
1. *Ælfric's Lives of Saints*, ed. W. W. Skeat, Early English Text Society o.s. 76 (1881), pp. 126–8.
2. This translation is from *Alfred the Great: Asser's Life of King Alfred and other contemporary sources*, tr. with an introduction and notes Simon Keynes and Michael Lapidge (Harmondsworth, Middlesex, 1983), p. 67. For the Latin text see Klaeber, *Beowulf and the Fight at Finnsburg*, p. 254.
3. "Geta, qui fuit, ut aiunt, filius dei:" John Morris, in his edition and translation, *Nennius: British history and the Welsh annals* (London, 1980), p. 26, mistakenly capitalizes *Dei* and *God* and mistranslates the passage: "Geta, who said they were son of God."
4. Gummere, *Founders of England*, p. 421.
5. Kenneth Sisam, "Anglo-Saxon royal genealogies," *Proceedings of the British Academy*, 39 (1953), 32. Cf. J. S. Ryan, "Othin in England," *Folklore*, 74 (1963), 462.
6. Chambers, *Beowulf: an introduction*, p. 202 (with *wuþedon* misprinted for *wurþedon*). The source of the comment in both Textus Roffensis and in Asser is presumably Nennius's *Historia Brittonum*; see Sisam, "Anglo-Saxon royal genealogies," pp. 313–14.

genealogies: he was actually a king of barbarian hordes whose fol-
lowers ignorantly deified him.[7] Anthony Faulkes is right, then, when
he says that "always when such genealogies are recorded by Chris-
tian writers (e.g. Bede, *Historia Ecclesiastica* I 15), the gods that
appear in them will have been interpreted euhemeristically, i.e. as
great kings or heroes who came to be worshipped as gods after their
deaths."[8] And, we might add, the same interpretation would presum-
ably have been made by those who read or heard the genealogies,
including the kings themselves.[9] It seems likely, moreover, that
Alistair Campbell was right in assuming that the *Beowulf* poet had
first-hand acquaintance with one or more of the many genealogies
in circulation, for they also contained the names of several impor-
tant characters in his poem—Scyld Scefing, Heremod, Beaw, Offa,
and perhaps Wermund and Eomær. Campbell argues in particular
that the account of Scyld Scefing at the beginning of the poem is
based on an annotation to a royal genealogy.[1]

This selective interrogation of the surviving records has yielded
more copious evidence than we might have expected that posthu-
mous deification of Germanic heroes in pre-Christian days was a
subject familiar to the Anglo-Saxons in later, Christian times. An
Anglo-Saxon audience contemplating the final scene of *Beowulf*
could possibly have had the euhemeristic accounts of deified hea-
thens preached at them in sermons, explained to them by their schol-
ars, and evoked in the genealogies of their kings. They were probably
aware that their missionaries tried to convert Germanic heathens
(whether Scandinavians in England or their Germanic cousins on
the continent) by explaining to them that their pagan deities were
mere mortals whom the misguided ancestors had proclaimed gods
at their deaths. The Anglo-Saxon audience had available the word
mannweorðung "worship of human beings" and knew that this was
something condemned in both canon and sermon. The sermons
also ring with warnings that funerals are flashpoints for outbreaks
of heathen practices among Germanic people, whether Anglo-
Saxon, Danish, or others. Is it not likely that an Anglo-Saxon con-
templating Beowulf's last rites—the pagan cremation followed by
the pagan interment of his ashes with lavish treasures as the war-
riors circle his *bēcn* chanting of his fame—might be reminded
of the men of old deifying their kings? The *praecognita* to an

7. Chambers, *Beowulf: an introduction*, p. 320, n. 1.
8. Faulkes, "Descent from the gods," p. 93.
9. For a convenient assemblage of the relevant genealogical texts, see Chambers, *Beowulf:
   an introduction*, pp. 195, 197–203, 311–12.
1. Alistair Campbell, "The use in *Beowulf* of earlier heroic verse," *England before the Con-
   quest: studies in primary sources presented to Dorothy Whitelock*, ed. Peter Clemoes and
   Kathleen Hughes (Cambridge, 1971), p. 290.

understanding of the closing ritual as a dark Germanic apotheosis
were to be found, as we have seen, not only in sermons but also in
Asser's biography of Alfred, in Nennius, in saints' lives, and in
annotations to royal genealogies.

Let us turn again to the actual words spoken by the twelve noble-
men who march their horses around the *bēcn*:

> Þā ymbe hlǣw riodan   hildedēore,
> æþelinga bearn,   ealra twelf*e*,
> woldon (care) cwīðan,   [ond] kyning mǣnan,
> wordgyd wrecan,   ond ymb w(er) sprecan;   (3169–72)

Their utterance is described as a *wordgyd*. This is a nonce-word
which Klaeber says means "elegy" and Clark Hall "dirge," but it
means nothing so specific as that.[2] Their chant is as much an
encomium as a lament and could just as well refer to *dadsisas*, the
heathen litany which the *Indiculus . . . paganiarum* forbids the
eighth-century Saxons to say in the presence of the dead. The noble-
men's chant continues:

> eahtodan eorlscipe   ond his ellenweorc
> duguðum dēmdon,—   swā hit gedē(fe) bið,
> þæt mon his winedryhten   wordum herge,
> ferhðum frēoge,   þonne hē forð scile
> of līchaman   (lǣded) weorðan.   (3173–7)

"They praised his nobility and his deeds of valor, praised them fit-
tingly, as it is proper that one should do—to extol with words and
cherish in the heart one's friend and lord when he must be led forth
from the fleshly garment." Klaeber says of this passage, "The lines
setting forth the praise of Beowulf by his faithful thanes sound like
an echo of divine service, and closely resemble *Gen[esis]* 1ff, 15ff"
(p. 230). The verses in *Genesis A* to which he refers are the poem's
opening, which is based upon the Common Preface to the Mass—

> Us is riht micel   ðæt we rodera weard,
> wereda wuldorcining,   wordum herigen,
> modum lufien!

"It is right that we praise the Lord of heaven, the glorious King of
hosts, cherish him in our hearts"—and the angels' praise of God:

> Þegnas þrymfæste   þeoden heredon,
> sægdon lustum lof,   heora liffrean
> demdon drihtenes,   (15–17)

2. Klaeber, *Beowulf and the Fight at Finnsburg*, p. 428; John R. Clark Hall, *A Concise Anglo-Saxon Dictionary*, 4th edn with a supplement by Herbert D. Meritt (Cambridge, 1960), s. v. *wordgydd*.

which one translator has rendered, "Servants in glory worshipped the Prince, gladly uttered praise of their Lord of life, glorified God."[3] If we transfer these lexical renderings of *herian* and *deman* to the *Beowulf* passage, the import of the lines will be unambiguously devotional. In any case, the similarities are striking. The prayer-like quality of the *Beowulf* passage is also suggested by Klaeber's further observation that the phrase *manna mildust* in 3181 occurs in the Old High German *Wessobrun Prayer* with reference to God: *almahtico Cot, / manno miltisto.* Klaeber offers no surmise as to why the poet has the warriors' chant echo these prayers, but some modern scholars have suggested that these phrases impart a Christian tone to the passage and imply a Christian Beowulf. It is difficult to see what sense can be made of supposed Christian allusions in a speech made about a pagan hero by his pagan comrades at his emphatically pagan obsequies. But in making the chant prayer-like, the poet is not necessarily making it Christian. (The supplication *kyrie, eleison* was addressed by pagan Greeks to their pagan rulers long before it was transformed into a prayer to Christ, and it implies reverent entreaty in either context.) The chant is not Christian, but it does have a worshipful quality, and perhaps this is what has led more than one modern scholar to see godlike qualities in the hero.[4] And as for the phrase *manna mildust*, its closest analogue in Old English writings is a comment inserted by the Anglo-Saxon translator of *Orosius* into his text: *He wæs eallra monna mildheortast on þæm dagum* "He was the most mild-hearted of all men in those days"—a comment referring to a heathen ruler who was deified.[5]

Lines 3174–7, as they are usually read, are puzzling:

> swā hit gedē(fe) bið,
> þæt mon his winedryhten   wordum herge,
> ferhðum frēoge,   þonne hē forð scile
> of līchaman   (læded) weorðan.

3. R. K. Gordon, *Anglo-Saxon Poetry Selected and Translated* (London, 1926), pp. 95–6. Gordon's punctuation is used in both translation and original.

4. Robert P. Creed observes, "The *Beowulf*-poet even seems to have sensed, with disapproval, that Beowulf had been regarded as some sort of god. Now the Christian poet was not about to violate the First Commandment. If earlier people had regarded Beowulf as a god, they had simply been mistaken. . . . Beowulf the god seems always to have come from afar, probably at the request of suppliants": "The remaking of *Beowulf*," in *Oral Tradition in Literature: interpretation in context*, ed. John Miles Foley (Columbia, MO, 1986), pp. 144–5. Earlier, Edward B. Irving suggested much more tentatively that "a mysterious and half-mythic atmosphere surrounds the funeral rites [for Beowulf], perhaps largely because we half recognize the striking of those same notes of feeling we heard in the description of Scyld's funeral. . . . The similarity does not imply that Beowulf is a god, but it lays stress on the hero's role as a rescuer, protector, shield of his people, . . . and hints at some possible unknown order beyond the known seas of men": *Introduction to Beowulf* (Englewood Cliffs, NJ, 1969), p. 99. As for Scyld's funeral, Adrien Bonjour, *The Digressions in Beowulf* (Oxford, 1950), p. 9, says it "is almost an apotheosis."

5. *The Old English Orosius*, p. 128. The reference is to Julius Caesar.

They seem to imply that ten days after his cremation Beowulf's soul is still in his body, and only now, as the warriors chant Beowulf's praises, is his spirit departing. But a closer look at the text makes clear that this clause does not say "when his soul leaves his body" but rather "when *he* is transported from his physical covering."[6] Perhaps this vaguer statement—"when *he* must go on to another state"—gives latitude for a broader range of meanings so that we are not obliged to assume that the poet has carelessly forgotten that Beowulf's soul parted from his body more than ten days before; he could be referring, rather, to the hero's translation to a higher state.

Finally, let us turn to the actual tomb of Beowulf, the *beorh* on Hronesnæs. When Beowulf conceives of a monument for himself in lines 2802–8—

> Hātað heaðomǣre   hlǣw gewyrcean
> beorhtne æfter bǣle   æt brimes nosan;
> sē scel tō gemyndum   mīnum lēodum
> hēah hlīfian   on Hronesnæsse,
> þæt hit sǣlīðend   syððan hātan
> Bīowulfes biorh,   ðā ðe brentingas
> ofer flōda genipu   feorran drīfað,

his concern is that he be remembered after his death. He wants a monument *to gemyndum   minum leodum* "as a remembrance among my people," and he wishes to have it located so that seafarers will see it and, hearing that it is *Beowulfes beorh*, will carry his name to distant lands. This desire that a physical memorial keep his name alive in people's memory after his death is typical of early Germanic folk throughout their era. The great Rök column in Sweden, the Istaby memorial stone in Blekinge, Denmark, the Norse *bautasteinar* in general, and the many Anglo-Saxon memorial stones such as those at Hackness, Thorhill, Great Urswick, Yarm, and Overchurch bear witness to this concern. But the monument and ceremony that Beowulf's survivors provide go far beyond anything he requests in his dying speech. He says nothing about having a splendid wall built

---

6. *Beowulf*, 3176–7, is frequently compared with *Soul and Body II*, 20–1, "*to won þinre sawle sið siþþan wurde, / siþþan heo of lichoman   læded wære*," which is, in fact, the basis for editors' supplying *læded* for the manuscript lacuna in *Beowulf*, 3177. Kemp Malone, "Some *Beowulf* readings," *Franciplegius: medieval and linguistic studies in honor of Francis Peabody Magoun, Jr.*, ed. Jess B. Bessinger Jr, and Robert P. Creed (New York, 1965), pp. 122–3, rejects the reconstruction *læded* because, he says, the word is too long for the space available in the manuscript. But if this is so, we can simply assume that the scribe (who is everywhere economizing on space as he brings the poem to a close) used the reduced form (by syncopation and simplification of final double consonants) *læd*. In any case, it is significant that while the two passages are otherwise parallel, *heo* (the soul) is the subject of the subordinate clause in *Soul and Body II* while *he* (Beowulf) is the subject in *Beowulf*.

around his *becn* and enshrining his ashes within it; he says nothing about filling the structure with treasure and certainly nothing about ritual chants and processions. These elements are all conceived by his bereaved subjects, and it is these elements that make the structure seem like something more than a monument and the occasion something more than a second funeral.

The words *hlæw* and *beorh* used to designate the monument are quite general. By far the largest number of their documented occurrences are in charters or placenames, where they seem to mean "mountain, hill, mound" and refer to landmarks. They can also mean a hollow mound such as a dragon might occupy or such as men might use for a tomb. Placenames like *Wodnes beorh* "Woden's borrow," which occurs in the *Chronicle* (for 592 and 715) and in charters, and *Þunores hlæw* "Thor's barrow," which occurs in the life of St Mildred, suggest that these nouns could also refer to a place for worshipping pagan gods—a shrine or *heroön*.[7] The noun *bēcn* used of the monument in line 3160 lends it a numinous quality, since *bēcn* means "sign, portent, idol," and it is used in Christian times to refer to the Cross and to Christ's miracles.[8] It can designate memorial stones (especially in the inscriptions written on such stones) but never refers to a tomb in Old English. The *beorh* which the Geatas prepared for Beowulf is twice described as *heah* "high" (2805 and 3157), and of course it was, both because it stood on a lofty promontory and because the structure itself was built *hēah ond brād* (3157). High *beorgas* are mentioned also in Ælfric's *De falsis diis*, where it says of Woden, *þone macodan ða hæðenan him to mæran gode, . . . and to heagum beorgum him brohtan onsæg[ed]nysse* "the heathens made that one [that is, Woden] their famous god . . . and brought sacrifices to him on high *beorgas*."[9] Wulfstan's account of

7. "Association with a mound or tumulus occurs three times in the case of Woden, twice in the case of Thunor," according to Margaret Gelling. "Place-names and Anglo-Saxon paganism," *University of Birmingham Historical Journal*, 3 (1961), 15. Conjuncture of tomb and temple is not unusual. Clement of Alexandria in his *Exhortation to the Heathen*, chapter 3, states contemptuously that pagan temples are simply tombs at which the heathen began worshipping, and he provides a catalogue of people who had died and whose tombs became places of worship. (In chapter 2 he says that the native countries, the biographies, and especially the sepulchers of the heathen gods prove that they were nothing but human beings.) We have seen earlier that Snorri Sturlusson describes Germanic people worshipping at the tombs of their gods. Even in Christian times the tomb can serve as a shrine. In Spain there is a tradition that a tomb cult developed at the grave of the Cid; see W. J. Entwistle, "La Estoria del noble varón el Cid Ruiz Díaz," *Hispanic Review*, 15 (1947), 206–11, and P. E. Russell, "San Pedro de Cardeña and the heroic history of the Cid," *Medium Ævum*, 27 (1958), 57–79

8. See *Dictionary of Old English: B*, ed. Antonette diPaolo Healey (Toronto, 1991), s.v. *bēacen*. See also Elisabeth Okasha, "'Beacen' in Old English poetry," *Notes and Queries*, 221 (1976), 200–8. Among the senses established by Okasha are "idolatrous monument" (p. 205).

9. *Homilies of Ælfric: a supplementary collection*, p. 664.

the deification of Woden is much the same, noting that the heathens *to heagum beorgum him brohton oft mistlice loflac* "often brought manifold offerings to him on high *beorgas*."[1] Pope and Bethurum offer abundant evidence from other sources confirming that cult was paid to pagan Germanic gods at high mounds,[2] and the place-name *Wodnes beorh* itself would seem to offer some corroboration. These data in aggregate suggest, I believe, that the monument that the Geatas prepare for Beowulf is patient of an interpretation which would view it as a shrine or *heroön*.

This essay proposes, then, a possible rationale for the funeral rites' "mysterious and half-mythic atmosphere" which "hints at some possible unknown order beyond the known seas of men."[3] It suggests that some in the poet's audience might have sensed a darker purpose in the Geatas' ceremonies than that of having a redundant second funeral, a purpose which the poet intimates through muted hints, as is his wont in alluding to his characters' paganism. An overt statement that the Geatas proclaimed dead Beowulf a god would have alienated a Christian Anglo-Saxon audience,[4] but by appealing subtly to the knowledge he knew they shared about Germanic apotheosis, he could arouse suspicions that the somber majesty of the ceremonies was an expression of something more precise than the "mysterious and half-mythic," of something more disquieting than mere grief. For those in the audience who thought of pagan deification, the closing rites would have been a powerful culmination of the pervasive tension throughout the poem between inspiring heroism and the sad shame of heathenism. The poet reveres the exemplary conduct of Beowulf and his people while deploring the pagan darkness which leaves that whole world in danger of perdition. His moving depiction of the solemn ritual around Beowulf's *beorh* is his last, melancholy, admiring gaze back on a man so great that people would think him a god; on a people so benighted that they thought a man might become a god.[5]

1. *The Homilies of Wulfstan*, p. 223.
2. See the notes to these passages in the editions of Pope and Bethurum; cf. Ursula Dronke's note to *at Sigtýs bergi* on p. 64 of *The Poetic Edda*, vol. 1: *Heroic Poems* (Oxford, 1969).
3. See n. 4, p. 195, in this Norton Critical Edition.
4. Howell D. Chickering, Jr, *Beowulf Translated with an Introduction and Commentary* (Garden City, NY, 1977), p. 377, rightly observes that the pagan element "is strong without being explicitly cultic." Allusions to heathenism are common in the poem, but they are always restrained.
5. I wish to thank Robert E. Bjork of Arizona State University for some helpful suggestions he made after hearing this essay read as a lecture.

LESLIE WEBSTER

Archaeology and *Beowulf*†

1. Introduction

In his introduction to the 1925 Wyatt and Chambers edition of
Beowulf, Chambers wrote eloquently of the subtle pitfalls of editing
Old English, especially of being led astray by our knowledge of the
modern language.[1] Any study of the archaeological background to
Beowulf must be aware that this is even more true of attempts to
relate academic knowledge of the archaeology of early medieval
northwestern Europe to the poem. Marrying the specialized inten-
tions of poetic description and the complex history of the text to the
archaeological record with the intentions of those who created it
and to our own contemporary perceptions presents multiple oppor-
tunities for misunderstanding.[2] To take burials, for example: the
poetic account of Beowulf's burial and the great Sutton Hoo ship
burial are both carefully constructed messages for their respective
contemporary audiences, in which conceptions of the past play a
significant part, but they may not necessarily have had identical
aims in view.[3] Moreover, archaeology is a fragile and incomplete
witness; what survives in a burial is only a small part of what was
involved in the process, including intangible rituals and organic

† From *Beowulf: An Edition*, ed. Bruce Mitchell and Fred C. Robinson (Oxford: Black-
well, 1998), 183–94. © 1998 by Bruce Mitchell and Fred C. Robinson. Reprinted, with
authorial updates and revisions, by permission of Wiley.
1. A. J. Wyatt, ed., rev. R. W. Chambers, *Beowulf: With the Finnsburg Fragment* (Cam-
bridge: Cambridge UP, 1925), xxii–xxxv, especially xxxiv.
2. The most useful and comprehensive archaeological studies of *Beowulf* are those of K.
Stjerna, *Essays on Questions Connected with the Old English Poem of Beowulf*, trans. J. R.
Clark Hall, Viking Club Extra Series 3 (Coventry: Curtis & Beamish, 1912); R. J. Cramp,
"*Beowulf* and Archaeology," *Medieval Archaeology* 1 (1957): 57–77; R. J. Cramp, "The
Hall in *Beowulf* and in Archaeology," in *Heroic Poetry of the Anglo-Saxon Period: Essays
in Honor of Jess B. Bessinger, Jr.*, ed. H. Damico and J. Leyerle, Studies in Medieval
Culture 32 (Kalamazoo, Mich.: Medieval Institute Publications, 1993), 331–46; C. M.
Hills, "*Beowulf* and Archaeology," in *A Beowulf Handbook*, ed. R. E. Bjork and J. D.
Niles (Lincoln, Neb.: University of Nebraska, 1997), 291–310; and John D. Niles,
"Afterword: Visualizing *Beowulf*," in *Beowulf: An illustrated Edition*, trans. Seamus
Heaney, illustrations ed. J. D. Niles (New York: Norton, 2007), 213–48. Stjerna,
though now very outdated in both contents and use of evidence, remains a remarkable
survey. Cramp's excellent studies, though again to some extent overtaken by new dis-
coveries and research, are still essential reading; Hills's survey article gives a thorough-
going review of past and current archaeological approaches to the poem.
3. Indeed, Carver has argued that, in a sense, the Sutton Hoo Mound 1 burial is itself a
form of poem: M. O. H. Carver, "Ideology and Allegiance in East Anglia," in *Sutton
Hoo: Fifty Years After*, ed. R. Farrell and C. Neuman de Vegvar, American Early Medi-
eval Studies 2 (Oxford, Ohio: Miami University Department of Art, 1992), 173–82,
esp. 181. See also L. Webster, "Death's Diplomacy: Sutton Hoo in the Light of Other
Male Princely Burials," in *Sutton Hoo*, ed. Farrell and Neuman de Vegvar, 75–82, esp.
75–81; and L. Webster and M. P. Brown, eds., *The Transformation of the Roman World
AD 400–900* (London: British Museum Press, 1997), 222–23.

offerings that we can only guess at. In making sense of that partial evidence, we bring our own contemporary preconceptions, just as nineteenth-century archaeologists and editors interpreted the sources very differently from their twenty-first-century successors. How we relate these differing forms of evidence therefore needs delicacy and care. What follows aims to avoid too literal and dogmatic an approach in the hope of respecting the subtleties and ambiguities of both the poem and the archaeological evidence.

How the past was regarded is an important factor in this. Its own history was certainly important to the audience of *Beowulf*. The poem is, of course, set in the past; it reverberates not only with ancestral legend, but also with repeated reference to heirlooms, to the mighty works of forbears, long-dead smiths and giants, and to "ancient treasure," *ealde lāfe* (ll. 795, 1488, 1688) of all kinds; indeed, mention of *geārdagum* ("days of yore," l. 1) sets the scene in the opening line.[4] Significantly, however, descriptions of ancient treasures—the dragon's hoard, for example, though sometimes characterized as decayed (ll. 2253–62, 2758–64)—differ little from those of the possessions contemporary to Beowulf and his companions in the surviving text, which would themselves have been archaic in the late tenth century when the poem was written down. So, for Anglo-Saxons, the past was in a sense the present, and this too colors the way in which things are represented in the poem, and hence the way in which we need to look at them. There is little point, for example, in using archaeological evidence for attempting any sophisticated chronological analysis of the text,[5] nor in speculating why relevant practices known from the archaeological record, such as votive offerings of weapons and gold, find no reference in *Beowulf*. It is a poem, not an archaeological textbook.

2. *Warrior Culture*

Before going on to examine specific topics in more detail, a general word on the archaeology of aristocratic warrior culture and its place in the understanding of *Beowulf* is appropriate. Much stress is laid in the poem on the integrity and loyalty of the fighting troop, the virtues of the warrior hero on whom it depends, and the almost chivalric bonds between the two. Wiglaf's rallying speech to Beowulf's *comitatus* ("warrior-band," ll. 2633–60) is one of several

4. Quotations and definitions come from the edition of R. D. Fulk, Robert E. Bjork, and John D. Niles, *Klaeber's Beowulf and the Fight at Finnsburg*, Toronto Old English Series 21, 4th ed., (Toronto: University of Toronto Press, 2008). Long vowel marks are retained, but diacritics and other editorial signals are omitted.

5. Though it seems that the most detailed and concrete descriptions—those of swords and helmets especially—probably reached their present form no later than the eighth century.

such statements in the poem of *duguðe þēaw* ("the custom of noble warriors," l. 359). We know from many documentary sources of the importance of warrior culture in the Germanic world, and how the opportunistic getting and ritual dispensing of treasure, made easier in the fluid circumstances of post-Roman Europe, underpinned and sustained this power base.[6] Archaeology also reflects this, not only in the migration-period treasure-hoards of gold coins and neck-rings from Scandinavia and the Netherlands (Fig. 1)[7] but also much nearer home. We are familiar with ideas of treasure, and its dispensation, from the princely burials at Sutton Hoo (Suffolk), Taplow (Buckinghamshire), and the recently discovered (and magnificently preserved) chamber grave at Prittlewell (Essex).[8] The symbolic funerary deposits which accompany these dead leaders include—apart from precious accoutrements, gold coins, and what might be termed regalia—weapon sets and a multitude of vessels and other equipment that express the complex relationships between the lord and his followers, many of them the emblems of the feast that lay at the core of this bond.

In each of these three burials, the dead lord was accompanied by an array of vessels for the provisioning and feasting of his followers, including buckets, hanging cauldrons, and great tubs as well as vessels imported from Byzantium and the Celtic regions, which were probably used in hand washing at table. At Sutton Hoo, Roman and Byzantine silver tableware, treasure in itself, also emphasizes the ceremonial nature of the feast. But dominating the feasting equipment were drinking vessels of every kind, from elaborately mounted aurochs horns to tiny burr-wood cups for stronger stuff than ale.[9] Great drinking horns, like the equally unstable glass claw beakers from Taplow, were designed to be passed from hand to hand in formal drinking ceremonies of the kind described at Heorot and in Hygelac's hall, where Wealhtheow and Hygd went round the table,

6. For a general survey of the European historical context, see Webster and Brown, *Transformation of the Roman World*, passim.
7. M. Alkemade and A. Pol, "Elite Lifestyle and the Transformation of the Roman World in Northern Gaul" and "The Lifestyle of the Elite," in *Transformation of the Roman World*, ed. Webster and Brown, 180–93, esp. plates 50 and 51; A. Pesch, in collaboration with J. P. Lamm, M. Fecht, and B. Armbruster, *Die Kraft der Tiere. Völkerwanderungszeitliche Goldhalskragen und die Grundsätze germanischer Kunst / The Powers of Animals. Migration Period Gold Collars and the Fundamentals of Germanic Art*, Schriften des Archäologischen Landesmuseums 12 (Mainz: Verlag des Römisch-Germanischen Zentralmuseums, 2015).
8. A. C. Evans, *The Sutton Hoo Ship Burial* (London: British Museum, 1986); R. A. Smith, "Anglo-Saxon Remains," *Victoria History of the County of Buckinghamshire*, 4 vols. (London: Constable, 1905), vol. 1, 199–204; L. Webster, "The Taplow Barrow," in *The Blackwell Encyclopedia of Anglo-Saxon England*, ed. M. Lapidge et al., 2nd ed. (Oxford: Blackwell, 2014), 758–59; L. Blackmore, I. Blair, S. Hirst, and C. Scull, *The Prittlewell Princely Burial: Excavations at Priory Crescent, Southend-on-Sea, Essex* (London: MOLA Monograph Series, forthcoming 2018).
9. C. Fell, "Old English *Beor*," *Leeds Studies in English*, new series 8 (1975): 76–95.

Fig. 1. Gold neck-rings from a hoard, Olst, Netherlands, c. 400. d1953/2.1–4 courtesy of the National Museum of Antiquities, Leiden.

offering the horns to the warriors in courtly ritual (Figs. 2 and 3). Such ceremonies, like others at the feast, served to bond the war band. Other symbols of the joys and ceremonies of life in hall are to be seen in the lyres which accompany the dead in all three princely burials. In the ritual theater of burial, the lyre embodied the celebration of the deeds of the dead man in the afterlife, and those of his ancestors. A wooden lyre found in 2002, at Trossingen, Germany, in an Alemannic grave dated by dendrochronology to the summer of 580 C.E., is richly decorated with images of processing bands of warriors and intricately entwined serpents, in an echo of the symbolic warrior images and interlacing animal decoration seen on contemporary Anglo-Saxon and Scandinavian helmets (Fig. 4).[1] It graphically illustrates the role of the lyre, the *glēobēames*

---

1. B. Theune-Grosskopf, "Die vollständig erhaltene Leier des 6. Jahrhunderts aus Grab 58 von Trossingen, Ldkr. Tuttlingen, Baden-Württemberg," *Germania* 84 (2006): 93–142.

Fig. 2. Drinking horns from the Sutton Hoo ship burial, early seventh century. © The Trustees of the British Museum.

Fig. 3. Glass claw-beakers from the Taplow princely burial, early seventh century. © The Trustees of the British Museum.

Fig. 4. Reconstruction of wooden lyre from Trossingen, Baden-Württemberg, Germany. Original, before c. 580 C.E. Courtesy of Michael J. King, luthier, Warwickshire, England.

(l. 2263), *hearpan* (l. 89), *gomenwudu* (l. 1065) of *Beowulf*, as the essential accompaniment to the deeds of heroes sung in hall.

As noted, multiple weapon sets feature in these burials, symbolizing the arming of the warrior band. Our knowledge of what forms these weapons could take, and the underlying military organization, has now been greatly extended by the extraordinary Staffordshire Hoard, a seventh-century Anglo-Saxon battlefield treasure, which among other prestige items, contained the dismantled fittings from at least seventy-four gold and jeweled swords (Fig. 5).[2] As an insight into the wealth of elite warrior culture and the treasure that was its source, the hoard is very revealing, even though it lacks the iron sword blades, mail coats, shields, and spearheads that would have accompanied this dismantled war gear. They were presumably recycled in other ways. Most of the richly decorated sword pommels fall into a few distinctive groups, suggestive of particular fighting bands, perhaps serving different leaders. And, as a

2. C. Fern, T. Dickinson, and L. Webster, *The Staffordshire Hoard: An Anglo-Saxon Treasure* (London: Historic England and Society of Antiquaries, forthcoming 2019).

Fig. 5. The Staffordshire Hoard, selection of sword fittings, mid-seventh century. Photo © Birmingham Museums Trust.

glittering image of the treasure to be captured on the battlefield, it complements those treasures we are more familiar with, the offerings *nēan ond feorran* ("from near and far," l. 1174) that we see in burials. At Sutton Hoo, for instance, this took the shape of Frankish gold coins, Byzantine silver, Swedish armor, and Celtic precious vessels. In all these contexts we can see something of the leader of the war band as gainer and giver of gold, provider of battle gear, and of the joys of life in hall. It is time to turn to that center of lordly activity, the hall itself.

3. Halls

The *idea* of the hall plays a major part in the poem. It is presented as a symbol of power and rule, but also of warmth, companionship, joy, and safety; outside, the world could be cold, dark, and dangerous. It was the theater for the feast, where a king fed, sheltered, and rewarded his warrior band in return for their loyalty when it came to fighting. It was the focus for all the ceremonies of hospitality, fellowship, and allegiance that accompanied the feast; not just communal eating and drinking and other entertainments but the dispensing of rewards, the sealing of loyalties and alliances, the recounting of heroic deeds past, and praise of the lord and his ancestry.

Heorot, above all, symbolizes this; and recent work has now shown that its lofty splendor can be paralleled by archaeological examples from sixth- and seventh-century England and Scandinavia. In Anglo-Saxon England, Edwin of Northumbria's seventh-century kingly hall at Yeavering (Northumberland), some twenty-five meters long, is an excavated example of the kind of massive wooden halls described in the poem, while in the Scandinavian homelands of *Beowulf*, even grander structures are known.[3] At Gammel Lejre in Denmark, the great migration period and Viking hall complex is by tradition the home of the *Scylding* dynasty, and thus perhaps the site where the *Beowulf* poet locates Heorot, the royal hall of Hrothgar; its earliest hall (forty-seven meters long) has been radiocarbon dated to the mid-sixth century.[4] A comparable example from England is the recently discovered twenty-one-meter-long great hall from the seventh-century hall complex at Lyminge (Kent), radiocarbon dated to 560–613 C.E. (68 percent confidence); its excavators found ample evidence of feasting and other

3. Cramp, "*Beowulf* and Archaeology," 68–77; B. Hope-Taylor, *Yeavering: An Anglo-British Centre of Early Northumbria*, Department of the Environment Archaeological Reports 7 (London: H.M.S.O, 1977), 315; Hills, "*Beowulf* and Archaeology," 302–03.
4. T. Christensen, "Lejre beyond the Legend: The Archaeological Evidence," *Siedlungs-und Küstenforschung im südlichen Nordseegebiet* 33 (2010): 237–54; and *Lejre bag myten: de arkæologiske utgravninger*, Jutland Archaeological Society Publications 87 (Roskilde: Jysk Arkæologisk Selskab, 2015).

entertainments in the form of shattered glass drinking vessels and even a gaming piece, similar to ones found in the Taplow princely grave.[5] Among other recent discoveries of Anglo-Saxon halls, it is particularly worth noting the site at Rendlesham (Suffolk), not far from Sutton Hoo, where archaeologists have identified the probable location of a major East Anglian *vicus regius* ("royal estate") mentioned by Bede. High-status finds attest to its royal connection, and there is evidence of a large timber hall within the site.[6]

Some of these buildings have been reconstructed, at least on paper or in simulation, to flesh out the evidence of postholes and enable the halls to emerge in their grandeur. The computer simulation of the sixth-century "Heorot" at Gammel Lejre presents a dramatic illusion of a powerful place, safe from the dangers of the world outside (Fig. 6). The excavators of the Anglo-Saxon high-status hall complex at Cowdery's Down (Hampshire) have provided alternative versions of what Heorot might have looked like in the form of building C12, which is dated to the seventh to eighth century.[7] Various superstructures that could have fitted on the excavated ground plan are presented (Fig. 7). But common to all of them is the evidence for a wooden floor, which would have echoed to any step—*healwudu dynede* ("[the] hall-wood resounded," l. 1317)—and an elaborate scheme of external supporting timber braces. Could this latter be what is implied by the well-known crux of *stapol* ("flight of steps? pedestal?," l. 926), elsewhere in the poem unambiguously a pillar or support (l. 2178)? In that interpretation, Hrothgar would have had to stand at, not on, the *stapol* to look up at Grendel's hand hanging from the gable.[8] Fortunately, the Cowdery's Down building also provides support for the usual explanation of *stapol* as a step of some kind. The archaeological evidence may suggest that the raised floor of that elaborate structure could have had timber supports for a step to the entrance at its gable end. The excavators have also deduced from the complex and massive ground plan that

5. G. Thomas, "Monasteries and Places of Power in Pre-Viking England: Trajectories, Relationships and Interactions," in G. Thomas and A. Knox (eds.), *Early Medieval Monasticism in the North Sea Zone: Recent Research and New Perspectives*, Anglo-Saxon Studies in Archaeology and History 20 (Oxford: Oxford University School of Archaeology, 2017), 95–116.
6. C. Scull, F. Minter, and J. Plouviez, "Social and Economic Complexity in Early Medieval England: A Central Place Complex of the East Anglian Kingdom at Rendlesham, Suffolk," *Antiquity* 90 (2016): 1594–1612; C. Scull, F. Minter, and J. Plouviez, "Rendlesham Rediscovered," *British Archaeology* 137 (2014): 50–55.
7. M. Millett and S. James, "Excavations at Cowdery's Down Basingstoke, Hampshire, 1978–81," *Archaeological Journal* 140 (1983): 151–279, esp. 215–17, 233–46. Note that aspects of these reconstructions have been challenged; see N. W. Alcock and D. Walsh, "Architecture at Cowdery's Down: A Reconsideration," *Archaeological Journal* 150.1 (1993): 403–9.
8. The interpretation with "at" may stretch the literal meaning too far. For a survey of proposed interpretations see the note for line 926 in the edition of Fulk, Bjork, and Niles, *Klaeber's Beowulf and the Fight at Finnsburg*, 172–73.

Fig. 6. Digital reconstruction of the great hall at Gammel Lejre, Denmark. Niels Valentin, © Roskilde Museum, Denmark.

Fig. 7. Reconstruction of an eighth-century hall at Cowdery's Down, Hampshire. Fig. 70 in Martin Millett and Simon James, "Excavations at Cowdery's Down, Basingstoke, Hampshire, 1978–81," *Archaeological Journal* 140.1 (1983): 151–279. Reprinted by permission of the publisher, Taylor & Francis Ltd. www.tandfonline.com.

the building must have had a steeply pitched roof of gabled construction. Heorot's *stēapne hrōf* ("steep roof," l. 926) certainly finds a parallel here. The descriptions of Heorot as *horngēap* ("wide-gabled," l. 82) and *hornreced* ("a gabled house," l. 704) have also more usually been interpreted as references to gables, rather than to decoration with antlers or horns. From another perspective, however, *horn* could imply an architectural element invisible in excavation, but well-known from manuscripts and from the evidence of certain house-shaped shrines and oratories.[9] Some Irish stone

9. T. Ó Carragáin, *Churches in Early Medieval Ireland* (New Haven and London: Yale University Press, 2010), esp. 15–47; the Book of Kells (Trinity College Dublin, ms 58) fol. 202v depicts the Temptation of Christ, above a representation of the Heavenly Temple in the form of just such a gabled structure (http://digitalcollections.tcd.ie/home/index .php?DRIS_ID=MS58_003v, accessed August 22, 2018); L. Webster and J. Backhouse, eds., *The Making of England: Anglo-Saxon Art and Culture, AD 600–900* (London: British Museum Press, 1991), cat. no. 137.

churches, copying wooden building features, have projecting cross members at the peak of the gable, rather like a pair of horns. Could this be an explanation both of *horngēap* and even of that term opaque to archaeological scrutiny, *bānfāg* ("decorated with bone," l. 780)? This may be a speculation too far, but there are possible explanations for other descriptions of Heorot's external appearance, notably terms such as *goldfāh* ("ornamented with gold," l. 308) and *fǣtum fāhne* ("decorated with [gold] plate," l. 716). There is no archaeological evidence for the embellishment of Anglo-Saxon or any other Germanic halls with gold, but if the description is not simply pure hyperbole, it would not seem unreasonable to read in the description of the golden, shining-plated exterior a poetic image of thatch or of gleaming shingles, both attested in the archaeological record.

Among other constructional details, the references to iron fittings and door hinges (*īrenbendum, heorras,* ll. 998–99) can now find secure archaeological parallels: the *īrenbendum searoþoncum besmiþod* ("iron bands made with skill") that secured the hall *innan ond ūtan* ("from within and without," ll. 774–75) are well represented at Gamle Lejre and in the numerous clench bolts from sites such as York and Flixborough (Yorkshire), where they were clearly used in the construction of planked timber buildings.[1]

Inside the hall, the evidence for hangings and fittings is inevitably less good. Benches are known from excavated Scandinavian and continental timber buildings,[2] more ephemeral details such as wall hangings (*web,* ll. 994–95) hardly at all, though the presence of what seem to have been colored hangings in the burial chamber at Sutton Hoo Mound 1 clearly hints at the splendors of earthly halls.[3]

4. *Arms and Armor*

Essential to the conduct of warrior culture was the weapon set, more rarely accompanied in the archaeological record by armor. In the poem, it too is presented as a kit (e.g., ll. 1242–50), though the elements are different; the possession of swords, not uncommon in archaeological contexts, seems confined to those of the highest status in the poem, while helmets and chain mail, still exceptionally rare survivals, are depicted in the poem as the regular equipment of the warrior troop. It is uncertain whether this apparent discrepancy

1. P. Ottaway, *Anglo-Scandinavian Ironwork from 16–22 Coppergate,* The Archaeology of York, 17/6: The Small Finds (London: Council for British Archaeology, 1992), 615–18.
2. E. Roesdahl, *The Vikings,* trans. S. M. Margeson and K. Williams (London: Penguin Books, 1987), 45.
3. R. L. S. Bruce-Mitford, *The Sutton Hoo Ship-Burial,* Vol. 1: *Excavations, Background, the Ship, Dating and Inventory* (London: British Museum Publications, 1975), 480; Roesdahl, *Vikings,* 44–45.

arises from an artificial poetic convention, or from the practice of handing down such expensive prestige items rather than discarding them in graves. Nevertheless, the discovery of so many fine sword fittings in the Staffordshire Hoard has certainly altered our understanding of the conventional picture supplied by Anglo-Saxon burial assemblages, where the only gold filigree decorated sword pommel found in a grave is an unusual type from Middleham (Yorkshire)[4] and the only such gold and garnet mounted sword is from the Sutton Hoo Mound 1 royal burial. In addition, the complete absence from this hoard of sword blades and other iron war gear—including chain mail—seems to suggest that items such as these were indeed efficiently recycled and thus often did not make it into the grave. Recent discoveries of complete Anglo-Saxon helmets (see below), and the identification of fragments from others, tell a similar picture, suggesting that they were in more widespread use than was formerly apparent; the poem may indeed reflect the realities of *comitatus* equipment more accurately than had been imagined.

5. Helmets

The image *par excellence* of the Germanic warrior, the helmet is one of the dominant images of the poem. Like a number of late-sixth- to seventh-century Scandinavian helmets,[5] (Fig. 8), the helmet type described in the poem is explicitly a crested or combed helmet of the kind known from the seventh- and eighth-century Anglo-Saxon examples at Sutton Hoo, Wollaston (Northamptonshire), and Coppergate at York (Figs. 9–10).[6] To this roll call must now be added the remarkable gilded silver fragmentary helmet from the Staffordshire Hoard (Fig. 11).[7] These helmets have particularly prominent crests or combs (*wala*, l. 1030) that pass across the crown to reinforce the iron cap:

> Ymb þæs helmes hrōf   hēafodbeorge
> wīrum bewunden   wala ūtan hēold.   (ll. 1030–1)

> An embossed ridge, a band lapped with wire
> arched over the helmet, head-protection . . . (trans. Heaney)

4. Middleham sword pommel, Portable Antiquities Scheme number BM-7C4457 (https://finds.org.uk/database/artefacts/record/id/643932) (2014, accessed June 12, 2017).
5. D. Tweddle, *The Anglian Helmet from 16–22 Coppergate*, The Archaeology of York, 17/8: The Small Finds (London: Council for British Archaeology, 1992), 1104–25.
6. Cramp, "*Beowulf* and Archaeology," 60–63; Evans, *Sutton Hoo*, 46–49; I. Meadows, "The Pioneer Helmet," *Current Archaeology* 154 (1997): 391–95; Tweddle, *Anglian Helmet*.
7. C. Fern and G. Speake, *Beasts, Birds and Gods: interpreting the Staffordshire Hoard* (Alcester: West Midlands History Ltd., 2014), 34–7; Fern, Dickinson, and Webster, *The Staffordshire Hoard*, figs. 3.45–3.56.

Fig. 8. Iron helmet with ribbed crest from grave 5, Valsgärde, Uppland, Sweden, mid-seventh century. Courtesy of Gustavianum Uppsala University Museum. Fig. 9. Helmet from the Sutton Hoo ship burial, late sixth or early seventh century. © The Trustees of the British Museum. Fig. 10. The York helmet, late eighth century. Image © York Museums Trust (Yorkshire Museum).

Fig. 11. Silver-gilt helmet parts from the Staffordshire Hoard, mid-seventh century. Cheekpiece: Cotswold Archaeology © Barbican Research Associates. Crest: Photo by G. Evans © Barbican Research Associates.

In the case of the Wollaston and York examples, two such crests pass over the crown crosswise. The Sutton Hoo helmet's single iron comb is inlaid with twisted wires, *wīrum bewunden* ("wound with wires," l. 1031,), while the York helmet, like some of the Swedish examples, copies twisted wire in bronze. The elaborately decorated Staffordshire helmet has a different version of the single comb, with a central groove to hold some kind of organic crest, possibly boar-like bristles.

Another passage describes Beowulf's helmet as *befongen fréawrāsnum* ("encircled / set about with splendid chains," l. 1451). Rosemary Cramp's perceptive identification of this as a description of a mail curtain is now reinforced by the York helmet, with its neck guard of mail. These Anglo-Saxon helmets, and their Swedish counterparts, all had face masks (*heregrīman*, "war mask," l. 396, *grīmhelmas*, "mask-helmet," l. 334), cheek guards (*hléorbergan* l. 304), and neck protection, which derive from late antique parade models.[8] The descent from that particular helmet type is also significant, in that the archaeological evidence suggests that the type is confined to the peripheral areas of northwestern Europe—Anglo-Saxon England and Scandinavia. In the Frankish territories and beyond, a different kind of helmet was current. The archaeological evidence thus corresponds directly to the cultural milieu of the poem. These late antique prototypes were often gilded, and the Staffordshire, Sutton Hoo, and York helmets emulate them in being decorated with tinned or gilded elements—*brūnfāgne* ("of a brown reflective color, shining," l. 2615), *hwīta* ("white, shining," l. 1448), and *goldfāhne* ("ornamented with gold," l. 2811). *Beowulf* interestingly refers to the stripping of precious fittings from helmets (*hearda helm hyrsted golde . . . fǣtum befeallen*, "hard helmet, ornamented with gold . . . deprived of [its] gold plate," ll. 2255–56), a practice now visible in the number of stray finds of bronze helmet attachments that have been recognized in recent years and that can be seen at work in the dismantled and distorted elements prised from the precious gilded silver helmet in the Staffordshire Hoard (Fig. 11).[9] By contrast, the helmet discovered in a seventh-century warrior grave at Wollaston is a simple and sturdy all-iron construction—not a ceremonial item, but a highly functional piece of regular fighting equipment.

The most spectacular aspect of the Wollaston helmet is, however, the presence of a three-dimensional boar figure on its crown. Such images resonate throughout the poem—the *swȳn eal gylden, eofor īrenheard* ("swine all covered with gold, the boar iron-hard," ll. 1111–12) of Hnæf's funeral pyre, the *swīn ofer helme* ("swine above the helmet," l. 1286)—to the extent that the powerful image of the boar becomes a metaphor for the warriors themselves (l. 1328). The Wollaston helmet is not the only surviving example of this potent tradition; the differently constructed Benty Grange (Derbyshire) helmet also bears a fine boar figure on its crown (Fig. 12),[1] and a dismounted

8. Tweddle, *Anglian Helmet*, 1087–90; Webster and Brown, *Transformation of the Roman World*, 222.
9. Fern, Dickinson, and Webster, *The Staffordshire Hoard*, figs. 3.49–3.55.
1. R. L. S. Bruce-Mitford and M. R. Luscombe, "The Benty Grange Helmet and Some Other Supposed Anglo-Saxon Helmets," in *Aspects of Anglo-Saxon Archaeology: Sutton Hoo and Other Discoveries*, ed. R. L. S. Bruce-Mitford (London: Gollancz, 1974), 223–52.

Fig. 12. Helmet from Benty Grange, Derbyshire, showing the boar crest; seventh century. Courtesy of Museums Sheffield.

boar from a helmet crest comes from an old grave find at Guilden Morden (Cambridgeshire).[2] Depictions of warriors wearing helmets of this kind are also known from Swedish contexts; one of the best known occurs on a bronze die for impressing decorative metal helmet panels, from a seventh-century site at Torslunda, Gotland (Fig. 13). A rather later representation of a ferociously beaked quadruped on a helmet crest appears in an eighth-century Anglo-Saxon flyleaf drawing in a manuscript now in St. Petersburg, where it adorns the defeated Goliath's helmet.[3] Perhaps in such a context, and by that time, it was only possible to depict such a pagan image of courage and strength on the headgear of the unrighteous. In *Beowulf*, the motif is certainly one of strength and protection; it also appears (ll. 303–06, 1451–54) in contexts where it seems to be not a crest but an image on a helmet, protecting the wearer in a manner similar to the amuletic boar and beast heads that shield the brows of the Sutton Hoo and York helmets. A more ambiguous image is presented by the *eoforhēafodsegn* ("boar-head sign / banner," l. 2152) among the gifts from Hrothgar that Beowulf presents to Hygelac (ll. 2152–54a); it may be the same as the *segen gyldenne* ("golden banner," l. 1021) among Hrothgar's gifts to Beowulf earlier in the poem. If the reading of this as a boar ensign, a standard with a boar image, is correct (rather than another helmet epithet, in apposition to the *heaðostēapne helm*, "helmet towering in battle" of line 2153), it serves to remind us that archaeological evidence has its own limitations.

2. J. Foster, "A Boar Figurine from Guilden Morden, Cambs.," *Medieval Archaeology* 21 (1977): 166–67.
3. St. Petersburg, National Library of Russia, ms Cod. Q. v. XIV.1, fol. 1. M. J. Swanton, "The Manuscript Illustration of a Helmet of Benty Grange Type," *Journal of the Arms and Armour Society* 10 (1980): 1–5; Tweddle, *Anglian Helmet*, fig. 534.

Fig. 13. Bronze die with warriors wearing boar helmets, from Torslunda, Öland, Sweden; late sixth or seventh century. Courtesy of Swedish National Heritage Board/Antikvarisk-topografiska arkivet, Stockholm.

6. Mail-Coats

Like the helmet, the mail coat is a rarity in archaeological contexts, though, as we have already seen, this probably reflects burial practice rather than actual usage. Later Anglo-Saxon wills and the evidence of the Bayeux Tapestry suggest that mail coats were in widespread military use by the later tenth century.[4] The mail coat from the Sutton Hoo ship burial is an elaborate construction consisting of rows of riveted rings apparently alternating with rows of butt welded ones.[5] A similar technique is seen in the chain-mail neck guard on the York helmet in the later eighth century, where lapped and riveted rings are combined in alternate rows with welded ones (Fig. 11). The poetic accounts of these garments accord very precisely with the archaeological evidence. They are of gray steel (*grǣge syrcan*, l. 334), skillfully formed of rings in an intricate mesh (*hondlocen*, "linked by hand," l. 323, also 406, 550–53), and they clink and jingle on the move (*syrcan hrysedon*, "the mail-shirts rattled," l. 226).

4. S. A. O'Connor, "Technology and Dating of the Mail," in *Anglian Helmet*, ed. Tweddle, 1057–87, esp. 1059.
5. Evans, *Sutton Hoo*, 41.

Fig. 14. Shield of Swedish origin from the Sutton Hoo ship burial; late sixth century. © The Trustees of the British Museum.

7. Shields

Shields are a much more standard item of warrior equipment, as represented in Anglo-Saxon and other Germanic burials. They form, with the spear, the basic fighting kit of the member of a war band.[6] The poetic vocabulary of *Beowulf* highlights elements of the shield that have a certain archaeological reality (Fig. 14). They are characteristically described as broad, probably with a rim of some kind (e.g. *sīdrand*, "broad shield," l. 1289, *bordrand*, "shield," l. 2559) and they may possess a prominent central boss (*rondas regnheard*, "wonderfully strong shield boss," l. 326, *stēapne rond*, "towering shield boss," l. 2566). Each of these elements can be matched in archaeological material from the early Anglo-Saxon period, though metal edge bindings are rare. Sutton Hoo again provides the best

6. T. M. Dickinson and H. Härke, *Early Anglo-Saxon Shields*, Archaeologia 110 (London: Society of Antiquaries of London, 1992).

Fig. 15. Sword hilt elements from Market Rasen, Lincolnshire, first half of the seventh century. © The Trustees of the British Museum.

surviving example of this, and interestingly, a rare instance of the use of lime-wood in a shield.[7] The regular use of *lind* ("linden-wood," ll. 2341, 2610, 2365) and its compounds to denote shields or warriors in *Beowulf* may therefore depend on a notion of high-class rather than everyday shields, but it would be unwise to press the meaning of this trope too far.

8. Swords and Seaxes

The defining heroic weapon, the sword (Fig. 15), plays a large part in the poem and is described in considerable detail. Swords are arche-typally the *ealde lāfe* ("ancient treasures," l. 795), powerful heirlooms to be prized for their power and might; some are "the work of marvel-ous smiths" (*wundorsmiþa geweorc*, l. 1681), or *eotenisc* ("the work of

7. Ibid., 48.

218   LESLIE WEBSTER

Fig. 16. Detail of pattern-welding on a copy of the early seventh-century sword blade from the Sutton Hoo ship burial, made by Scott Lankton and Robert Engström. © The Trustees of the British Museum.

giants," l. 1558) from long ago. Swords have personalities; they may have names or carry owner inscriptions and images that tell of the mythic past (ll. 1688–98).[8] They have richly decorated hilts (*wreoþen-hilt*, "wrapped with twisted ornamentation," l. 1698) and bear intertwined, snakelike, or poisonous branching patterns (*brōdenmǣl*, "ornamented with a wavy pattern," l. 1616; *wyrmfāh*, "with serpentine ornamentation," l. 1698; *ātertānum fāh*, "decorated with poisonous stripe / serpentine patternings," l. 1459); their iron blades are fearsome double-edged weapons, which can need two hands to swing (l. 1461). Supporting archaeological evidence for much of this has long been recognized.[9] The descriptions of interlaced, snaking, and poisonous dendritic patterns have been thought to suggest the intricate twisted patterns produced by the pattern welding technique used to make the best and strongest of blades in the pre-Viking period (Fig. 16).[1] However, recent discoveries of gold sword hilts with decoration of serpentlike interlacing creatures, such as that from Market Rasen (Lincolnshire), and the numerous similar examples in the Staffordshire Hoard, support another explanation for two of

8. S. Brunning, "The 'Living' Sword in Early Medieval Northern Europe: An Interdisciplinary Study" (PhD diss., University College, London, 2013).
9. H. R. E. Davidson, *The Sword in Anglo-Saxon England: Its Archaeology and Literature* (Oxford: Clarendon Press, 1962).
1. Cramp, "*Beowulf* and Archaeology," 65; J. Lang and B. Ager, "Swords of the Anglo-Saxon and Viking Periods in the British Museum: A Radiographic Study," in *Weapons and Warfare in Anglo-Saxon England*, ed. S. C. Hawkes, Oxford University Committee for Archaeology Monograph 21 (Oxford: Oxford University Committee for Archaeology, 1989), 85–122; R. Engstrom, S. M. Lankton, and A. Lesher-Engstrom, *A Modern Replication Based on the Pattern-Welded Sword of Sutton Hoo* (Kalamazoo, Mich.: Medieval Institute Publications, 1989).

these serpentine epithets.[2] Filigree-decorated gold hilts such as these aptly fit the description *wreoþenhilt ond wyrmfāh* ("wrapped with a grip and serpentine ornamentation," l. 1698) of the sword hilt that Beowulf presented to Hrothgar; in this case the twisted hilt patterns and snake ornament do not refer to the blade, which had melted away in the scalding blood of Grendel and his mother (ll. 1615–16).

The word *hringmæl* ("ring-sword," ll. 1521, 1564), which occurs more than once as a description of swords, may also refer to the twisted coiling patterns sometimes seen in pattern-welded blades. An alternative explanation has been that this signifies the attached rings seen on certain Anglo-Saxon and other Germanic sword pommels (Fig. 17), which possibly denote a bond between lord and retainer.[3] Some appear to be later additions, perhaps given in recognition of some special service; other pommels were made with the ring in place, including two from the Staffordshire Hoard, which had two rings apiece (Fig. 18).[4] The reference to *fetelhilt* ("linked hilt," l. 1563) has also sometimes been taken to refer to a ring-bearing hilt, but the more probable and simpler explanation is that this term means "belted hilt," and denotes a sword harness such as one sees in very grand form in the Sutton Hoo burial (Fig. 19), as well as in more modest Anglo-Saxon and other Germanic examples.

A number of sixth-century sword hilts from Anglo-Saxon graves carry runic inscriptions that seem to include personal names,[5] like the hilt of the mighty sword that dispatched Grendel's mother, and while no surviving sword carries anything resembling the story of the downfall of the giants (ll. 1687–93), there are a number of elaborately decorated hilts dating from the sixth to the eighth century in both England and Scandinavia where the complex motifs may carry special meaning. Rosemary Cramp has drawn attention to the images on the gold-sheeted hilt of the early sixth-century sword from Snartemo, Norway,[6] while from Anglo-Saxon contexts, the gold and garnet depiction of Golgotha on a seventh-century garnet-inlaid sword pommel from Dinham (Shropshire) and the eloquent and complex animal decoration on an eighth-century silver pommel from near Beckley (Oxfordshire) present other examples of swords

2. A. C. Evans, "Market Rasen Area, Lincolnshire," Treasure Annual Report (London: Department of Culture, Media and Sport, Cultural Property Unit, 2002), nos. 58, 68–70; Fern, Dickinson and Webster, *The Staffordshire Hoard*, figs. 3.14 and 3.15.
3. Cramp, "*Beowulf* and Archaeology," 64; V. I. Evison, "The Dover Ring-Sword and Other Sword-Rings and Beads," *Archaeologia* 101 (1967): 63–118.
4. Fern, Dickinson, and Webster, eds., *The Staffordshire Hoard*, nos. 75 and 76, fig. 3.12.
5. S. C. Hawkes and R. I. Page, "Swords and Runes in South-East England," *Antiquaries Journal* 47 (1967): 11–18.
6. Cramp, "*Beowulf* and Archaeology," plate XIb.

Fig. 17. Ring-sword with silver mounts from Gilton, Kent; sixth century. Reproduced by kind permission of the Society of Antiquaries of London.

that may carry a visual message (Figs. 20 and 21).[7] There is even a certain amount of archaeological as well as documentary evidence for swords as heirlooms; some from graves show extreme wear, or have had their fittings removed; sometimes only the pommel is

7. For Dinham, see L. Webster, *Anglo-Saxon Art, a new History* (London: British Museum Press, 2012) 31; for Beckley, L. Webster, *"Wundorsmiþa geweorc*: A Mercian Sword-Pommel from the Beckley Area, Oxfordshire," in *Crossing Boundaries: Interdisciplinary Approaches to the Art, Material Culture, Language and Literature of the Early Medieval World*, ed. E. Cambridge and J. Hawkes (Oxford: Oxbow Books, 2017), 97–111.

Fig. 18. Sword pommel with double rings from the Staffordshire Hoard; mid-seventh-century. Courtesy of the Potteries Museum & Art Gallery, Stoke-on-Trent.

Fig. 19. Mounts from the Sutton Hoo sword harness. © The Trustees of the British Museum.

Fig. 20. Two sides of a sword pommel from Dinham, Shropshire, with Christian iconography; early seventh century. Photo © Friends of Ludlow Museum and Shropshire Museum Service.

Fig. 21. Sword pommel with ambiguous animal decoration from Beckley, Oxfordshire, late eighth century. © The Trustees of the British Museum.

Fig. 22. *Seax* inlaid with runic *fuþorc* from the River Thames at Battersea, London; tenth century. © The Trustees of the British Museum.

Fig. 23. Bronze die showing a warrior armed with a *seax* and sword, from Torslunda, Öland, Sweden; late sixth or seventh century. Courtesy of Swedish National Heritage Board/Antikvarisk-topografiska arkivet, Stockholm.

buried, the sword apparently kept for another generation.[8] These potent weapons were as significant in real life as in poetry.

The double-edged sword was a formidable weapon; but the *seax*, its single-edged counterpart, though a slighter weapon, was just as effective (Fig. 22). The "broad and bright-edged knife" that Grendel's mother draws on Beowulf (*seax . . . brād ond brūnecg*, ll. 1545–46) and the *wællseax* ("battle-knife," l. 2703) with which Beowulf dispatched the dragon were as deadly as swords. The weapon grew in popularity from the seventh century, and a particularly fine example from the Staffordshire Hoard, with gold and garnet fittings, has been reconstructed from its parts. A *seax* in action, seemingly drawn, like Beowulf's, from the mail coat (l. 2703), is shown on one of the Torslunda dies (Fig. 23). By the eighth century, they appear on Insular

---

8. Davidson, *The Sword in Anglo-Saxon England*, 13. The Sarre Anglo-Saxon cemetery contained at least two graves where pommels only seem to have been buried with the dead; J. Brent, "Account of the Society's Researches in the Anglo-Saxon Cemetery at Sarr," *Archaeologia Cantiana* 6 [1866]: 157–85, esp. 173.

224 LESLIE WEBSTER

figural sculpture as equipment proper to the highest rank; the Repton
warrior king bears one alongside his sword, and so does the mighty
figure of King David on the great Pictish St. Andrews Sarcophagus.[9]

9. Interlace and Ambiguity

The serpentine decoration described on swords such as those dis-
cussed above suggests a way in which Anglo-Saxon artifacts may pro-
vide analogues to the plot structure and syntax of *Beowulf*. Such
decoration is just one example of the distinctive interlacing animal
ornament prevalent in late sixth- and seventh-century Anglo-Saxon
culture, where it is a dominant element in prestige male and female
gold and silver jewelry, sword fittings, and other indicators of high
status such as helmets and horse trappings (Fig. 24). Parallels have
been drawn between the precision and complexity of the best
examples of this work, and the skillful interweaving of narrative
threads in *Beowulf* and other Anglo-Saxon poetry, in which struc-
tural complexity and intertwining patterns of allusion and prefigu-
ration seem to reflect a predisposition in the contemporary mindset
for presenting both verbal and visual narratives in a dense pattern-
ing of precisely interlaced strands.[1]

A parallel fondness for verbal and visual ambiguity can also be seen
in the shapeshifters and visual riddles that recur throughout Anglo-
Saxon art and the use of kennings and other devices that play on rid-
dling meanings in *Beowulf* and certain other Anglo-Saxon poems.[2]
Thus compounds such as *ban-hus* (ll. 2508, 3147, "bone-house" sig-
nifying "body"), *wig-heafola* (l. 2661, "war-head, helmet"), and *swan-
rade* (l. 200, "swan-road, sea") yoke together unlike elements to
create a mini-riddle, leading to a new mental image. In visual art, the
man/beast/bird/serpent hybrids of the early Anglo-Saxon animal
style and riddling images that can be read in two ways (Fig. 25; see
also Fig. 21) perform a similar conjuring trick of concealing and
revealing, in a visual image that has to be teased out to be under-
stood.[3] These formal devices, literary and artistic, are twin aspects

9. Webster and Brown, *Transformation of the Roman World*, 227, fig. 100; S. Foster, ed.,
The St Andrews Sarcophagus: A Pictish Masterpiece and its International Connections
(Dublin: Four Courts Press, 1998).
1. J. Leyerle "The interlace structure of Beowulf," *Toronto University Quarterly* 37 (1967): 1–17.
2. L. Webster, "Anglo-Saxon Art: Tradition and Transformation" in *Transformation in
Anglo-Saxon Culture: Toller Lectures on Art, Archaeology and Text*, ed. Charles Insley
and Gale R. Owen-Crocker (London and Philadelphia: Oxbow, 2017), 23–46, espe-
cially 41–42.
3. L. Webster, "Encrypted Visions: Style and Sense in the Anglo-Saxon Minor Arts, AD
400–900" in *Anglo-Saxon Styles*, ed. C. Karkov and George H. Brown; L. Webster,
Anglo-Saxon Art, 34–36, SUNY Series in Medieval Studies (Albany: State University
of New York Press, 2003), 11–30, esp. fig. 3, fig.4, g–i, and fig.5, g–h; and also Webster,
"*Wundorsmiða geweorc*," 106–07.

Fig. 24. Gold buckle and clasps with interlacing animal ornament from the princely burial at Taplow, Buckinghamshire, late sixth and early seventh century. © The Trustees of the British Museum.

Fig. 25. Silver-gilt brooch from Chessel Down, Isle of Wight, with ambiguous ornament designed to be read in more than one way; first half of the sixth century. © The Trustees of the British Museum.

Fig. 26. Reconstruction of a Viking ship at sea. Copyright: Vikingeskibs-museet i Roskilde (The Viking Ship Museum, Denmark). Photo: Werner Karrasch.

of a particular Anglo-Saxon tradition and sensibility that has its origins in a preliterate, oral and visual culture.[4]

10. Ships and Other Transport

The ship (Fig. 26) plays a prominent part in the poem in the rituals of death, which we shall turn to shortly, as well as in the life of these North Sea fighting bands. It is of tarred clinker-built construction, like the Sutton Hoo Mound 1 ship and other migration period boats, broad-beamed to accommodate the warriors and their fighting gear. Unlike the Sutton Hoo ship, however, it goes under sail, rather than propelled by oarsmen; Viking ships certainly used sail, and it was certainly in use during the later Saxon period, as the evidence of the tenth-century Graveney boat shows.[5] The ship is variously described as *hringedstefna* ("ring-prowed ship," l. 32), *hringnaca* ("ring-prowed ship," l. 1862), *bundenstefna* ("ship with bound prow," l. 1910), and *wundenstefna* ("ship with wound / curved prow," l. 220), all of them terms that have given rise to suggestions

4. Webster, *Anglo-Saxon Art*, 13–17.
5. V. H. Fenwick, ed., *The Graveney Boat: A Tenth-Century Find from Kent*, National Maritime Museum Archaeological Series 3, British Archaeological Reports British Series 53 (Oxford: British Archaeological Reports, 1978).

Fig. 27. Trappings from a bridle and other horse gear, from the high-status burial in Mound 17 at Sutton Hoo; early seventh century. © The Trustees of the British Museum.

that it had ring-decorated or twisted prows. More prosaically, these terms may rather describe a prow like the ship's stem post dredged from the River Scheldt at Moerzeke-Mariekerke,[6] which is radio-carbon dated to the mid-fourth century plus or minus seventy years. The curving neck of this open-jawed creature is encircled by a series of carved collars, a feature that evidently continued in use for centuries, as it can be seen on some of the English ships' prows on the Bayeux Tapestry.

Land-based transport, when not on foot, was by horse, and though the references in the poem are few, it is worth noting that the splendid equipment of these creatures finds echoes in the archae-ological record. The "gold-sheeted bridle plates" (*fǣtedhlēore*, l. 1036) of the horses presented by Hrothgar to Beowulf have a close parallel in the gilded bridle and other horse trappings from the prince's burial at Sutton Hoo Mound 17 (Fig. 27).[7] One of Hrothgar's horses was also equipped with a gleaming saddle, described as the high king's battle seat, "skillfully made and adorned with treasure"

6. R. L. S. Bruce-Mitford, "A New Wooden Ship's Figure-Head Found in the Scheldt, Moerzeke-Mariekerke," *Acta Archaeologica* 38 (1967): 199–209.
7. A. C. Evans, "The Pony-Bridle in Mound 17: Problems and Challenges," *Saxon: The Newsletter of the Sutton Hoo Society* 25 (1997): 1–3; and for a fine Frankish example, see R. Pirling, "Ein Fränkisches Fürstengrab aus Krefeld-Gellep," *Germania* 42 (1964): 188–216, esp. plates 47 and 52.

(*searwum fāh, since gewurþad*, l. 1038). Sixth- and seventh-century continental and Irish examples of decorative saddle fittings have been known for some time, including those from burials at Wesel-Bislich, Krefeld-Gellep, and Ravenna,[8] but once more, the Staffordshire Hoard has provided us with new Anglo-Saxon evidence for such saddles, in gold and garnet fittings from the high front board of a saddle. It is likely that a large gold mount with the powerful motif of two eagles grasping a fish was also mounted on a saddle board.[9]

11. Death and Burial

Death is a powerful theme in the poem; *Beowulf* begins and ends with a hero's funeral, and other burials play a significant part in the narrative, such as Hnaef's cremation and the ancient barrow burial guarded by the dragon. Each of these contexts recalls elements that can be matched with archaeological evidence, but in doing so, we should be aware that each is a literary construction, with its own purpose within the text, rather than any kind of documentary account. The burial of Scyld Scefing, with which the poem opens, has often attracted comparison with the great Sutton Hoo ship burial, and other boat burials from East Anglian and Swedish contexts.[1] Here too, the dead man is buried amidships surrounded by treasures and battle gear of all kinds. But Scyld's boat is consigned to the sea, not buried under a mound like the others. We cannot know whether this is a genuine or garbled tradition of the past, or a literary invention. It is however striking that each of the burials in the poem exemplifies a different theme, which suggests a conscious literary intention. Beowulf's own burial place, with which the poem ends, is, by contrast to Scyld's sea burial, a barrow on the headland *Hrones Næss*, visible for miles:

> hlǣw on hōe,   sē wæs hēah ond brād,
> wēglīðendum   wīde gesȳne,   (ll. 3157–58)

a mound on a headland, high and imposing,
a marker that sailors could see from far away (trans. Heaney)

8. J. Oexle, *Studien zu merowingerzeitlichen Pferdegeschirr am Beispiel der Trensen*, Germanische Denkmäler der Völkerwanderungszeit, Serie A, 16; 2 vols. (Mainz: P. von Zabern, 1992), vol. 2, Taf. 172; Pirling, "Ein Fränkisches Fürstengrab," plates 46 and 2.

9. Fern, Dickinson, and Webster, *The Staffordshire Hoard*, fig. 2.66. For the high front board of a saddle, see nos. 556–61; for the eagles and fish motif, see no. 538.

1. R. L. S. Bruce-Mitford, *The Sutton Hoo Ship Burial: A Handbook*, 3rd edition (London: British Museum Publications, 1979), 81–83.

Fig. 28. The princely burial mound at Taplow, Buckinghamshire, early seventh century. Courtesy of Leslie Webster.

This is exactly the kind of sentinel burial we see in a number of prominent barrow mounds, often sited near boundaries or waterways, like those at Taplow (Fig. 28) and at Sutton Hoo.[2] Beowulf's burial mound is an expression of power and fame—and a territorial statement—that is familiar from the archaeological evidence. But first, Beowulf is cremated, like Hnaef, with full battle equipment. This recalls the unusual case of the Asthall (Oxfordshire) barrow, where a rich cremation was buried in the mound,[3] but the placing of unburned treasure with the cremated remains in Beowulf's barrow finds no real archaeological parallel and suggests that the narrative is led by the need to consign the ill-gotten treasure back to the earth.

The account of the fated ancient barrow that became the dragon's lair is a particularly fascinating blend of, once again, archaeological verisimilitude and moral fable. The Anglo-Saxons certainly were

2. E. O'Brien, "Post Roman Britain to Anglo-Saxon England: the Burial Evidence Reviewed," vol. 1 (D.Phil. thesis, Oxford University, 1996).
3. T. M. Dickinson and G. Speake, "The Seventh-Century Cremation Burial in Asthall Barrow, Oxfordshire: A Reassessment," in *The Age of Sutton Hoo*, ed. M. O. H. Carver (Woodbridge: Boydell Press, 1992), 95–130, esp. 95–127.

not averse to robbing the graves of their own contemporaries.[4] They were equally aware of the ancient past, often choosing prehistoric burial sites for their own cemeteries in the pagan period. So the description of the stone barrow, *stānbeorh stēarcne* ("strong stone-barrow," l. 2213), with its chambers and elaborate masonry (ll. 2542–45, 2717–19) could certainly represent a contemporary awareness of the inside of a Neolithic tomb, such as Weland's Smithy. The ancient treasure it contains, with its goblets, helmets, swords, and mail coats, its jeweled gold artifacts and golden standard, is, however, an image of Anglo-Saxon, not prehistoric riches (e.g., ll. 2756–71, 3047–50; Figs. 15 and 24). Like the Staffordshire treasure, it is predominantly military in nature, recognizable to its audience. But, at the poem's conclusion, in Beowulf's burial, it remains an earthly treasure, consigned once again to the ground— gold that, in the end, was as useless to men as it ever was. In this final image, the past merges with its audience's present, as it has resonated throughout the poem.

DANIEL DONOGHUE

The Philologer Poet:
Seamus Heaney and the Translation of *Beowulf*†

That every translation is also an act of interpretation has been a commonplace at least since Cicero, Horace, and Augustine of Hippo. It arises in response to the notion that the word-for-word and sense-for-sense task that aims for "faithfulness" provides at best only a partial description of all that a good translation entails. Even the most literal effort, according to this commonplace, sets up a tension between the mechanical and the creative as when, for example, one metaphor substitutes for another. Such moments can become the despair of the philologist who detects a net loss when the changes are extensive, especially if the original is a literary masterpiece. In most cases the readers remain unaware of the specific changes. Presumably, they turn to the translation in the first place because they do not know the original language, and they trust that the rhetorical

---

4. A. M. Klevnäs, *Whodunnit? Grave Robbery in Anglo-Saxon England and the Merovingian Kingdoms*, British Archaeological Reports International Series 2582 (Oxford: British Archaeological Reports, 2013).

† From *Harvard Review* 19 (2000): 12–21; revised by the author for the first Norton Critical Edition. Reprinted by permission of the author. Line and page references refer to this Norton Critical Edition.

embellishments will not obscure the essential continuity with the source text. When a poet like Seamus Heaney turns his attention to translating *Beowulf*, however, readers pay special attention to the signs of his interpretive touches. What is presumed to be "literal" is taken in stride, perhaps necessary to understanding the narrative but inherently less interesting.

Some strands of literary criticism respond with another commonplace, which rejects the logic behind the mechanical/creative dualism. It questions whether literal accuracy is possible at all. The Old English *cyning*, for example, becomes *king* in Modern English and is always translated so, but what a male monarch meant to the Anglo-Saxons is necessarily different from our notions, which have been colored by later developments such as primogeniture, the divine right of succession, charismatic kingship, constitutional monarchies, and the like. In this case the superficial resemblance between *cyning* and *king* masks a semantic change over the centuries. Such subtle, perhaps imperceptible differences add up in a work of any length. This critical commonplace thus spreads the act of interpretation from a local effect to a universal condition, even in those places where translation seems most mechanical, because the literal meaning is always chimerical.

Without taking up the merits of the critical commonplace, this essay questions the mechanical/creative dualism from an opposite direction. Instead of dissolving the philological pole, it provisionally accepts the possibility of literal accuracy and asks whether "faithfulness" can be as innovative as the most radical reinterpretation. Heaney circles around the same idea in a poem from his 1975 collection *North*, in which he teases out traditional connotations of an Old English kenning for the human body, a compound literally meaning "bone-house":

> In the coffered
> riches of grammar
> and declensions
> I found *bān-hūs*,
>
> its fire, benches,
> wattle and rafters,
> where the soul
> fluttered a while
> in the roofspace. ("Bone Dreams")

The word's meaning is something to be "found" in philology, and while the sense of distance between then and now prompts the search, it does not open a gap of despair. The search extends beyond

the coffers of grammars and glossaries to the airier halls of culture
if one follows the allusion of the fluttering soul to its source, the
Anglo-Saxon historian Bede (d. 735). The second book of his *History of the English Church and People* tells how Edwin, king of Northumbria about a century before Bede, was deliberating whether to
accept Christianity. He turns to his advisers for their opinion. One
of them compares human life to "the swift flight of a single sparrow
through the banquetting-hall where you are sitting at dinner on a
winter's day with your thanes and counsellors. In the midst there is
a comforting fire to warm the hall; outside, the storms of winter rain
or snow are raging. This sparrow flies swiftly in through one door
of the hall, and out through another."[1] He goes on to compare the
bird's brief interval inside the hall to their old religion's conception
of human existence: Christianity promises something better than a
winter storm when the bird flies out.

Heaney turns the moral of Bede's metaphor from religion to
language. The "soul" of a living culture animates *bān-hūs* with
meaning for only a short interval before it passes into the oblivion of time. Death hovers in the not-too-distant background: the
coffer could turn at any moment from a treasure chest into a coffin
holding the lifeless "bone-house," and winter's darkness threatens
just outside the wattle walls. Yet to make poetry about the word's
transience is in a way to reverse the process, to breathe life back
into the body of language. Heaney's lines gesture toward a model
of translation that is optimistic even if it is precarious. It says that
literal accuracy does not arrive by a mechanical process but through
the translator's imaginative engagement with tradition. "Faithfulness" is capacious enough to include the interpretive moments that
every translation demands. Philology and poetry in this case
inform one another.

What applies in a local way for *bān-hūs* applies *in extenso* for
Heaney's translation of *Beowulf*, where the length and complexity
of the poem help generate its own cultural context. His Introduction speaks of the poem's "mythic potency" in terms of a movement
similar to Bede's sparrow. "Like Shield Sheafson," the eponymous
founder of a line of kings who arrived as a foundling washed up on
Denmark's shores aboard an abandoned ship, *Beowulf* "arrives from
somewhere beyond the known bourne of our experience, and having
fulfilled its purpose (again like Shield), it passes once more into the
beyond."[2] Two funeral scenes frame the plot of the poem; it ends
with Beowulf's, of course, but Shield's magnificent burial dominates

1. *A History of the English Church and People*, trans. Leo Sherley-Price, rev. R. E. Latham
   (Harmondsworth: Penguin, 1968) 127.
2. Translator's Introduction, p. xxv.

the first fifty lines. After his death the Danes pile treasures onto his funeral ship and push him back into the sea:

> They decked his body no less bountifully
> with offerings than those first ones did
> who cast him away when he was a child
> and launched him alone out over the waves.   (lines 43–46)

Shield earns such a lavish send-off because of his spectacular success as king, but the "life cycle" of his mysterious arrival, later triumphs, and mysterious departure sets a model for the poem itself. *Beowulf* comes to us from an unknown author, written in an unfamiliar language from an uncertain date. Like Shield's career or the sparrow's flight through the hall, the poem makes its mark on the reader in the interval between its mysterious arrival and departure.

Heaney makes an oblique allusion to Shield's funeral ship in "The Settle Bed," from his 1991 collection *Seeing Things*. It would call to mind an Anglo-Saxon clinker-built ship even if Heaney did not tip us off by including lines from it as an epigraph to his introduction to *Beowulf*:

> And now this is "an inheritance"
> Upright, rudimentary, unshiftably planked
> In the long ago, yet willable forward
>
> Again and again and again.[3]

The settle bed arrives as an unlooked for bequest: clumsy and heavy and bearing a history that can be heard in the "old sombre tide awash in the headboard." It is handed over to a new owner, becomes "'an inheritance,'" and finally is willed away in a cycle that repeats itself "again and again and again." But what matters more than its four-square presence is the lesson that "whatever is given / Can always be reimagined." It is reimagined not "cargoed with / its own dumb, tongue-and-groove worthiness / And un-get-roundable weight," but as "unkindled boards of a funeral ship" carrying Shield Sheafson piled over with gold. Or the bed/ship can be reimagined as a metaphor for the poem *Beowulf*, as Heaney's epigraph suggests, or more generally as any vehicle for the poet embarking on another exercise of *translatio*.

The vocabulary of "The Settle Bed" gives another hint that *Beowulf*'s Old English is part of the imaginative structure of the poem. The first tercet alone has five compound words, four of which are invented for the occasion: "Trunk-hasped," "cart-heavy," "pew-strait,"

---

3. *Seeing Things* (New York: Farrar, Straus and Giroux, 1991) 50–51; reprinted with small changes in *Opened Ground* (New York: Farrar, Straus and Giroux, 1998), p. 321.

and "bin-deep." They are hammer-blows of metaphors, announcing the categories "domestic," "rural," "religious," and "mercantile" almost with the force of allegorical figures assigned to the bed's four corners. The English language has always augmented its lexicon by generating compounds, although the preferred way to do so since the later Middle Ages has been through borrowing. But in lines such as these, Heaney's inventiveness rivals that of Gerard Manley Hopkins and the *Beowulf* poet, the most prolific compounder of all. Responding to the interpretive engagement that compounds demand, readers expand elements like "bin" and "deep" into an image of, say, an ample bin holding flour or nuts or nails in a shop. "Pew-strait," for example, calls to mind the upright wooden back of the pew (where "strait" meets "straight") as well as the narrowness of religious doctrine, so its meaning hovers between carpentry and catechism even though it appears within a catalogue of physical features. The inferred meaning of such compounds can be slippery because the relation between the elements is not always self-evident. From their constituent parts "firewall" and "fireplace" might seem to be similar in meaning, yet one stops a fire and the other allows it to burn. When explaining a compound we instinctively expand it into a phrase or a clause ("a wall designed to stop the spread of fire in a building"), but "pew-strait" is not so easy. Does it mean that the settle bed's headboard is "straight and confining like a pew" and therefore physically uncomfortable when one sits against it? Or is "pew" a metonym for "religion" so that the compound means "doctrinally narrow," thus more a commentary on the previous owners than the physical features? Few readers of "The Settle Bed" are likely to tease out the various possibilities for "pew-strait" because we are used to the interplay within compounds, and the context does not force a choice between the physical and the doctrinal. "Pew-strait" is in some essential way both.

"The Settle Bed" is by no means Heaney's only effort to exploit the vivid parallels, syntactic openness, and strong rhythm of compounds. He uses them in many other poems, even those inspired by Greek hexameters, for example: "That killing-fest, the life-warp and world-wrong / It brought to pass."[4] He admires their use by poets like Hopkins, Shakespeare, and Philip Larkin.[5] So when he turns to *Beowulf*, part of the translator's philological "faithfulness" shows itself through an inventiveness. Some passages restrict themselves to compounds already found in the English lexicon, as for example in the scene when Grendel attacks Beowulf in the hall:

4. "The Watchman's War" from "Mycenae Lookout," quoted from *Opened Ground*, p. 387.
5. See, for example, "Englands of the Mind," in *Preoccupations: Selected Prose 1968–1978* (New York: Farrar, Straus and Giroux, 1980), p. 166.

> he was bearing in
> with open claw when the alert hero's
> comeback and armlock forestalled him utterly.   (lines 746–48)

Some, like "hall-thane" and "neck-torque," are calques from Old English compounds. Just as often, though, newly minted creations glint here and there in the lines. An aging Swedish king dies when his "feud-calloused hand / could not stave off the fatal stroke." An arrow is "feather-fledged." Grendel is a "guilt-steeped, God-cursed fiend." The dragon coils its "snake-folds." Other compounds that may seem to be nonce inventions in *Beowulf* have been used by Heaney in earlier poems. Beowulf comes "first-footing" early in the morning, but so does "Servant Boy" in *Wintering Out* (1972). The dragon emerges from his home "underearth," but "the shut-eyed blank of underearth" also threatens St. Kevin in *The Spirit Level* (1996).[6]

Just as he reimagines the settle bed as a funeral ship, Heaney reanimates the *Beowulf*-poet's skillful use of compounds. Their potential as poetic devices has always been present in English literature, although the *Beowulf*-poet had at his command a wealth of traditional poetic elements to combine. The example of *bān hūs* is illustrative again. One of the two times it appears in *Beowulf* is near the end of the poem, when the Geats have lit Beowulf's funeral pyre. The fire swells, hot to its core, *oð þæt hē ðā bān-hūs gebrocen hæfde*.[7] Heaney translates, "and flames wrought havoc in the hot bone-house." To liken Beowulf's body to a house consumed by flames is more than a passing metaphoric touch. Earlier the poem alludes to the fate of the Dane's great hall Heorot, which was destined to burn to the ground as a result of the treachery of King Hrothgar's nephew. Just as Heaney reimagines the wooden "benches / wattle and rafters" of *bān-hūs*, the metaphor of a house consumed by fire links the disastrous events suffered by the Danes and the Geats: both the burning of Heorot and the death of Beowulf contribute to a deeper theme concerning the limits of heroic action which dominates the end of the poem. However formidable the hero, however magnificent the hall, the depredations of time and human weakness will bring them down. To aspire to the *Beowulf*-poet's allusiveness in compounding becomes another measure of the translator's philological faithfulness, whether in preserving the elements *bān-hūs* or in forging analogous compounds.

---

6. "Servant Boy," *Opened Ground*, p. 48, and "St. Kevin and the Blackbird," *The Spirit Level* (London: Faber and Faber, 1996), p. 20–21.
7. Bruce Mitchell and Fred C. Robinson, ed., *Beowulf: An Edition with Relevant Shorter Texts* (Oxford: Blackwell, 1998), line 3147. All Old English quotations come from this edition.

The simple placement of elements side by side in compounds like *bān-hūs* is mirrored in larger syntactic structures using parallel phrases and clauses. The half-line structure of the verse seems to have encouraged a mode of expression where ideas are repeated incrementally. Sometimes the effect is simply cumulative; at other times the repetition allows shifting perspectives to examine the same idea. For example, at the crucial moment in Beowulf's fight with Grendel's mother, when his sword has failed him and he despairs for his life, he spots a weapon that may help him:

> Geseah ðā on searwum   sigeēadig bil
> ealdsweord eotenisc   ecgum þȳhtig
> wigena weorðmynd.   (lines 1557–59)

A literal translation: "Then he saw among the war-gear a victory-blessed sword, an ancient sword made by giants, strong in its edges, of warriors the glory." The three phrases for "sword" do not exactly repeat one another: one hints that it will bring Beowulf success, the second is more than a comment on its enormous size because giants were thought to have superior metalworking skills, and the third draws a correlation between splendid arms and the worthiness of the warrior. The most searching discussion of such constructions is Fred C. Robinson's *Beowulf and the Appositive Style*, which demonstrates how apposition informs much of the poem's theme and structure. Despite the apparent simplicity of the "proximate and parallel status" of the elements in apposition, the rhetorical effect can become complex.[8] The three epithets for sword, for example, have the same referent within a sentence and are not linked syntactically by a function word such as a conjunction. Such appositive constructions are not only ubiquitous in Old English poetry, they are its defining rhetorical trope, much like the long-tailed simile in classical epic. But more to the point they demand inferential judgment on the part of the reader to make connections, and at times those connections are more various than conjunctions alone can indicate.

Translating appositive constructions can be especially challenging, because Modern English prefers the disambiguating touches of grammatical function words and punctuation. A passage like that describing the gigantic sword, for example, might make use of separate clauses in Modern English; e.g., ". . . the victory blessed sword, which was the ancient work of giants . . ." Adding to

8. Fred C. Robinson, *Beowulf and the Appositive Style* (Knoxville: U of Tennessee P, 1985), p. 3.

the difficulty of translation is the common practice of scattering the apposed elements about the sentence rather than lining them up one after the other as in the "sword" passage. The sentence just before it (lines 1550–56) has five separate elements of apposition, including a triplet for God (as a nod to the doctrine of the Trinity). Such constructions are no longer idiomatic in Modern English. The closest parallels are simple catalogs, as (famously) in Shakespeare's sonnet,

> Th' expense of spirit in a waste of shame
> Is lust in action; and till action, lust
> Is perjured, murd'rous, bloody, full of blame,
> Savage, extreme, rude, cruel, not to trust . . .

And so on.[9] The catalog is also a favorite device of Heaney, and it shares some of the "parallel and proximate" qualities of *Beowulf*ian apposition. In "The Pitchfork," for example, an entire stanza sacrifices syntax for a list:

> Riveted steel, turned timber, burnish, grain,
> Smoothness, straightness, roundness, length and sheen.
> Sweat-cured, sharpened, balanced, tested, fitted.
> The springiness, the clip and dart of it.[1]

What could give a better description than the accumulation of modifiers flowing together without the help of syntax? In other instances the bare juxtaposition of words can deliver a sudden shock. In "The Strand at Lough Beg," some spent shotgun shells discovered on the ground are "Acrid, brassy, genital, ejected." The cumulative effect has less to do with description than evoking the feeling of revulsion at the moment of discovery—almost a sense of violation. The effect of apposition is completely different a few lines later in "The Strand at Lough Beg," in a passage introducing some of Heaney's relatives on his father's side, who (he reveals in his Introduction) supplied him with the imaginative voice for his translation of *Beowulf*:

> Big-voiced scullions, herders, feelers round
> Haycocks and hindquarters, talkers in byres,
> Slow arbitrators of the burial ground.[2]

In their formal and slightly old-fashioned way, these epithets come closest to *Beowulf*ian apposition. It is intriguing to think that *Beowulf*

---

9. Sonnet 129; quoted from Helen Vendler, *The Art of Shakespeare's Sonnets* (Cambridge, Mass: Harvard UP, 1997), p. 549.
1. *Opened Ground*, p. 320.
2. From *Field Work* (1979); quoted from *Opened Ground*, p. 145; see Introduction, p. xxxvi of this Norton Critical Edition.

may have supplied the appositive syntax of these lines years before Heaney returned to the Scullions to find a language for his translation which could be "speakable by one of those relatives." In any case Heaney's parallel phrases in these lines finds a point of congruence with Old English syntax.

When translators of *Beowulf* do not retain appositive constructions, they usually smooth out the idiom by incorporating them into separate clauses or merging some together. Grendel, for example, is introduced into the narrative with the apposed epithets *grimma gǣst* (grim creature) and *mǣre mearcstapa* (notorious border-prowler), who held *mōras . . . fen ond fǣsten* (the moors, fen and fastness). Heaney's translation removes the apposition by means of a participial phrase and a conjunction:

> Grendel was the name of this grim demon
> haunting the marches, marauding round the heath
> and the desolate fens; . . .   (lines 102–104)

In at least one case, however, Heaney makes a passage more appositive than the Old English:

> Afterwards a boy-child was born to Shield,
> a cub in the yard, a comfort sent
> by God to that nation.   (lines 12–14)

Here "boy-child," "cub," and "comfort" are parallel nominals, where in the Old English they are part of different constructions:

> Ðǣm eafera wæs   æfter cenned
> geong in geardum   þone god sende
> folce tō frōfre.   (lines 12–14)

The Old English *geong* ("young") can be taken as a modifier for *eafera* ("son") rather than as a substantive like "cub." A literal translation preserving the word order of Old English would be: "To that one [Shield] a son was later born young in the yards whom God sent to the people as a comfort." The strong impression throughout the poem, however, is that Heaney preserves the rich layering of apposition in the poem without doing violence to his idiom. And as Robinson convincingly points out, apposition extends beyond the sentence boundary to characterization, episodes, and even theology. For example, just after introducing Hygd, the queen of the Geats, the poem plunges into the story of Thryth, a queen who was famous for her vicious retribution. The implicit lesson is that Hygd is unlike Thryth, although there is no narrative instruction to that effect.

Even images can be apposed. Near the end of the poem, for example, after Beowulf has ruled the Geats for fifty years, he decides to seek out the dragon that has decimated his land. With the help of the warrior Wiglaf, he manages to kill the dragon, but not before it sinks its poisonous fangs into his neck. As Beowulf lies with his life ebbing away, he asks to examine some of the treasure from the dragon's hoard, which he receives with a prayer of thanks. Witnessing the moment of death a short while later brings unbearable anguish for Wiglaf:

> It was hard then on the young hero,
> having to watch the one he held so dear
> there on the ground, going through
> his death agony. The dragon from underearth,
> his nightmarish destroyer, lay destroyed as well,
> utterly without life. No longer would his snakefolds
> ply themselves to guard gold in the hoard:
> Hard-edged blades hammered out
> and keenly filed, had finished him
> so that the sky-roamer lay there rigid,
> brought low beside the treasure-lodge.   (lines 2821–31)

The dramatic intensity of the passage gains from its narrative restraint. It dwells less on Beowulf than on Wiglaf and the dragon. There is no maudlin wailing, no memorable expostulation from Wiglaf: just a king quietly dying beside his distraught follower. A narrative technique that the poet employs to great effect here and throughout *Beowulf* is to reveal a character's emotional response before describing the event that provokes it. Learning of Wiglaf's anguish creates a moment of suspense that makes the revelation of its cause—Beowulf's death agonies—all the more poignant.

In the fourth line a sentence break shifts the focus from Beowulf's "death agony" to the "dragon," where alliteration on the *d*-sound and the repeated syllables of *agon* link the two adversaries across a sentence boundary: on one side a virtuous king who defends his people; on the other, a monstrous creature determined to destroy them. The aural link goes even deeper because the repeating syllables *agon* call to mind Heaney's observation that the plot of *Beowulf* is structured around the three great agons in the hero's life.[3]

Even though the juxtaposition of the hero and dragon in death seems straightforward, what it signifies raises questions: is good fated to succumb to evil in the end? Is the dragon morally equivalent to the hero? Is Beowulf's life too high a price for the Geats to pay? Which is more ruinous: the monster alive or the hero dead?

---

3. Introduction, pp. xxv, xxvii of this Norton Critical Edition.

It is not just the posture of death that unites them, but the treasure as well. Here again there is no definitive guidance from the poem: is the treasure a good thing or not? To whom does it belong? We learn later that the treasure will be buried with Beowulf "as useless to men now as it ever was" (line 3168). Yet earlier the sight of it cheers the dying Beowulf because he sees it buying security for the Geats when he is no longer there to protect them (lines 2794–98).

The technique of juxtaposing references to the dragon and hero without giving interpretive clues is part of a pervasive narrative technique in *Beowulf*. In this case the syntax drives the visual impact of the scene: Beowulf and the dragon side by side in death. Interpretive judgments are not entirely absent— Beowulf is "dear" and the dragon is a "nightmarish destroyer"— but another writer in another century might offer a more specific evaluation about their relative worth. Heaney finds an affinity in the deftness of *Beowulf*'s appositive style, which opens up rich possibilities by leaving a great deal of the interpretive work up to the reader.

But in a way Heaney's instinct for apposition is hardly surprising. It is as much Heaney's "voice-right" as Hibernicisms like "kesh" and English archaisms like "thole."[4] It is as familiar as the alliteration, stressed lines, and compounding in his verse, because it is as familiar as T. S. Eliot's *Wasteland*, Yeats's hollow moon in "Adam's Curse," and Wallace Stevens's jar in Tennessee. Apposition is as much a master trope of twentieth-century poetry as it is of Old English. Heaney's "Flight Path" from *The Spirit Level* (1996), for example, combines chronology and travel as its organizing principle, but its immediate structure consists of six numbered segments with no overt indication about their relation to one another. Among other things, the use of apposition allows the poem to explore the volatile subject of Heaney's political affiliations in Northern Ireland. The fourth part begins with language that withholds personal judgment in the most familiar official jargon:

> The following for the record, in the light
> Of everything before and since:
> One bright May morning . . .

From this apparently neutral beginning, it slips into the language of the innocence and exhilaration of home-coming. But it is shattered by a blunt-spoken sectarian who finds him on the train back to Belfast:

4. Introduction, pp. xxxiii–xxxvi of this Norton Critical Edition.

> So he enters and sits down
> Opposite and goes for me head on.
> "When, for fuck's sake, are you going to write
> Something for us?"

The poem's immediate answer is equivocal; the deeper response waits for the next stanza, which apposes a haunting reference to the protest in Long Kesh and a quotation from Heaney's "Ugolino." Dante's journey through Inferno thus comments on Heaney's journey, but just how the apposed segments comment on one another is left up to the reader. Every part of "The Flight Path," not just the segments outlined here, requires the reader to make the kind of inferential judgments that *Beowulf* does.

There are even more such correspondences. "The Settle Bed," for example, has a series of modifiers—"unkindled," "unwilling," "unbeaten," "unshiftably," "un-get-roundable"—which work by negating an attribute so that the resulting image calls to mind the absence of something that might otherwise be present. It is hard to say what "unkindled" means except as something that is not ignited, but it cannot do so without suggesting fire in the first place. Such negative modifiers are, again, a favorite device of the *Beowulf* poet. When Grendel attacks Heorot at night, *lēoht unfæger* or "unbeautiful light" shines from his eyes. Because a person's eyes and light itself are strongly associated with beauty, to deny it categorically makes the light from Grendel's eyes worse than ugly. When Wiglaf gazes on his dying king he is described as *unfrōd*—meaning both "un-aged" and "un-wise"—which makes a brief but telling comparison with Beowulf, who after fifty years as king has become *frōd*. It is probably pointless to ask whether the many levels of affinity between Heaney's poetic voice and *Beowulf* is the result of his study of Old English, or somehow gathered indirectly through other poets like Hopkins and W. H. Auden, or by a more anonymous transmission of prosodic devices that have survived the centuries. Most of what has been written about Heaney's translation of *Beowulf*, including his own essays, dwell on the foreignness of Old English, the labor of translation, the difficulty of finding the right voice or the right turn of phrase. But there is another dynamic at work. The many affinities already existing between his poetry and *Beowulf* enables Heaney to enter the old clinker-built ship as familiarly as an inherited settle bed, so that his interpretation is measured not merely by the changes imposed from the outside but also by shaping and reshaping the tradition from within.

MICHAEL LAPIDGE

Beowulf and Perception[†]

The story of *Beowulf* is well known, even to those who have never read the poem.[1] It concerns a courageous young warrior from Geatland (in southern Sweden) who travels to Denmark to confront a monster that has been ravaging the hall of the Danish king Hrothgar for many years; after successfully destroying the monster, the hero is obliged to destroy the monster's mother, which he does with somewhat greater difficulty; and finally, in his declining years back home in Geatland, his confrontation with a marauding dragon proves fatal for him and, by implication, for the Geatish people. The story of *Beowulf* has been well studied for a century or more, to the point that (for example) we are well informed, and perhaps over-informed, about analogues in many languages to each of the three confrontations, but also about the poet's design in contrasting the hero's youth with his old age, about pervasive themes in the poem such as kingship and the nature of early Germanic society, and so on.[2] But what has not been well studied is the *way* the story is told, the poem's diegesis or narrative discourse, to borrow a useful term from the French structuralists.[3] For the story is told in anything but a straightforward manner. Although the poet was undoubtedly able to narrate a story in a straightforward linear manner (as he does, for example, when recounting through Beowulf's mouth the story of Ingeld, 2024–69), his characteristic method of narration is oblique and allusive. The principal character himself is introduced when first he hears of the monster (194) at home in Geatland, but we are not told his name until he has reached Heorot, the Danish king's hall,

---

† From the Sir Israel Gollancz Memorial Lecture, *Proceedings of the British Academy* 111 (2001): 61–97. © The British Academy 2001. Reprinted by permission of the British Academy.
1. Read at the Academy 12 December 2000. I quote throughout from the edition of F. Klaeber, *Beowulf and the Fight at Finnsburg*, 3rd ed. (Boston, 1950), but without reproducing Klaeber's diacritics (macrons, italics, etc.).
2. The most relevant analogues are translated by G. N. Garmonsway and J. Simpson, *Beowulf and Its Analogues*, rev. ed. (London, 1980); for general discussion, see the still indispensable compendium by R. W. Chambers, *Beowulf: An Introduction to the Study of the Poem with a Discussion of the Stories of Offa and Finn*, rev. C. L. Wrenn (Cambridge, 1959). There is an excellent conspectus of *Beowulf* scholarship in *A Beowulf Handbook*, ed. R. E. Bjork and J. D. Niles (Lincoln, NE, 1997).
3. The distinction between *l'histoire* and *discours* goes back to E. Benveniste, *Problèmes de linguistique générale* (Paris, 1966), p. 238; see discussion by J. Culler, *Structuralist Poetics: Structuralism, Linguistics and the Study of Literature* (London, 1975), pp. 197–8. Subsequent critics distinguish between story, narrative discourse and narrating: see, for example, Gérard Genette, *Narrative Discourse: An Essay in Method*, trans. J. E. Lewin (Ithaca, NY, 1980), pp. 27–32, and Shlomith Rimmon-Kenan, *Narrative Fiction, Contemporary Poetics* (London, 1983), pp. 3–4. For present purposes the binary distinction between story and discourse will suffice.

some 150 lines later (343). The story of Hygelac's last and fatal raid is alluded to on several occasions, but never sequentially recounted. The account which the narrator gives us of Beowulf's accomplishments at Heorot differs strikingly from that given by Beowulf himself when recounting his adventure to King Hygelac back in Geatland. And these are only some of the many unsettling discrepancies found throughout the poem. The narrative looks forward and back, now moving rapidly, now moving at a snail's pace. Friedrich Klaeber, one of the poem's greatest editors, rubricated one section of his Introduction with the title "lack of steady advance,"[4] and Kenneth Sisam, in one of the earliest Gollancz lectures (1933), observed that, "if *Beowulf* is a fair specimen of the longer secular poems, the Anglo-Saxons were poor story-tellers, weak in proportion and too ready to be distracted from the regular sequence of events."[5] One great critic of the poem—J. R. R. Tolkien, in another Gollancz lecture delivered to the Academy in 1936—even denied that the poem *is* a narrative.[6] The non-linearity of *Beowulf*ian narrative discourse is a feature of the poem which no reader could miss, but, as I have already said, it has been very little studied.[7] In what follows I shall argue that this non-linearity was wholly intentional, and is a reflex of the poet's concern with the mental processes of perception and understanding. But my first task is to demonstrate that the

4. Klaeber, *Beowulf*, pp. lvii–lviii: "The reader of the poem very soon perceives that the progress of the narrative is frequently impeded . . . Typical examples of the rambling, dilatory method—the forward, backward, and sideward movements—are afforded by the introduction of Grendel, by the Grendel fight, Grendel's going to Heorot, and the odd sequel of the fight with Grendel's mother. The remarkable insertion of a long speech by Wiglaf, together with comment on his family, right at a critical moment of the dragon fight (2602–60) can hardly be called felicitous. But still more trying is the circuitous route by which the events leading up to that combat are brought before the reader."
5. K. Sisam, "Cynewulf and His Poetry," *Proceedings of the British Academy* 18 (1933 for 1932): 303–31, at 312, repr. in his *Studies in the History of Old English Literature* (Oxford, 1953), p. 14.
6. J. R. R. Tolkien, "*Beowulf*: The Monsters and the Critics," *Proceedings of the British Academy* 22 (1936): 245–95, at 271–2: "We must dismiss, of course, from mind the notion that *Beowulf* is a 'narrative' poem, that it tells a tale or intends to tell a tale sequentially . . . the poem was not meant to advance, steadily or unsteadily. It is essentially a balance, an opposition of ends and beginnings."
7. For example, there is no chapter devoted to narrative in *A Beowulf Handbook*, ed. Bjork and Niles (though the article by T. A. Shippey, "Structure and Unity," pp. 149–74, contains much incidental discussion of how the story is told), and the chapter devoted to "*Beowulf* and Contemporary Critical Theory" by Seth Lerer (pp. 325–39) contains no mention of narratology. Exceptions include L. N. De Looze, "Frame Narratives and Fictionalization: Beowulf as Narrator," *Texas Studies in Language and Literature* 26 (1984): 145–56, and E. G. Stanley, "The Narrative Art of *Beowulf*," in *Medieval Narrative: A Symposium*, ed. H. Bekker-Nielsen (Odense, 1980), pp. 58–81. Stanley expresses awareness of structuralist criticism (p. 65: "I do not wish to make use of modern critical theory, such as is practised especially in France, partly because I am not sufficiently knowledgeable about the theory, partly because I have not read many of the novels on which the critics expend their subtle art"), but contents himself with quoting the definition of narrative given in the *Oxford English Dictionary* (p. 58). One of the most sensitive studies of *Beowulf*ian narrative is Clare Kinney, "The Needs of the Moment. Poetic Foregrounding as a Narrative Device in *Beowulf*," *Studies in Philology* 82 (1985): 295–314.

non-linearities are intentional and not the result of separate lays being stitched incompetently together: in short, that the form of the poem as we have it was essentially that which left the poet's pen, and that its narrative design is his.

I wish to begin this demonstration by considering a passage which occurs near the middle of the poem (1785–1802). But before coming to the passage in question, it is well to remind ourselves about certain general aspects of the poet's narrative technique. The action of *Beowulf* proceeds as it were in pulses: things go well for a while, but then disaster strikes; when the disaster has passed, things go well again, *until* the next disaster strikes, and so on.[8] The focal point of the narrating is the moment of reversal, what the poet calls an *edwenden* or *edhwyrft*. Thus Beowulf tells the coast-guard that he has come to help Hrothgar, if ever Hrothgar is to experience an *edwenden* in his misfortunes (280); Hrothgar himself later refers to the onslaught of Grendel as an *edwenden* (1774: *Hwæt, me þæs on eple edwenden cwom*, "Well, a reversal came to me in my kingdom"); and the narrator later describes Beowulf's defeat of Grendel—which proved so decisive a turning-point in the hero's career—as an *edwenden* (2188–9: *Edwenden cwom / tireadigum menn torna gehwylces*, "A reversal for every affliction came to the man favoured with glory"). The poet uses the adverbial construction *oð ðæt* ("until") to mark the point of reversal. Bruce Mitchell has helpfully discussed the use of *oð ðæt* to "mark the termination or temporal limit of the action of the main clause and a transition in the narrative."[9] It is this usage, to mark a transition in the narrative, that is especially characteristic of *Beowulf*,[1] as two examples will illustrate. Near the beginning of the poem, the poet describes the joyous life of the retainers in Heorot, *until* the monster began to wreak havoc:

> Swa ða drihtguman   dreamum lifdon
> eadiglice,   oð ðæt an ongan
> fyrene fremman   feond on helle (99–101).

8. See discussion by A. Brodeur, *The Art of Beowulf* (Berkeley, CA, 1959), p. 51, and esp. T. M. Andersson, "Tradition and Design in *Beowulf*," in *Old English Literature in Context: Ten Essays*, ed. J. D. Niles (Cambridge, 1980), pp. 90–106, esp. 96–102 (repr. in *Interpretations of Beowulf: A Critical Anthology*, ed. R. D. Fulk (Bloomington, IN, 1991), pp. 219–34, at 225–30: "The organizing principle in operation throughout the poem is mutability . . . No sooner is one mood established than it is superseded by its opposite. Hope gives way to disappointment, joy to grief, and vice versa. It is not just a question of occasional tonalities; the main lines of the poem as a whole can be analyzed according to this alternation" (p. 96).
9. B. Mitchell, "Old English *Oð þæt* Adverb," in his *On Old English* (Oxford, 1988), pp. 256–63, at 256; and cf. idem, *Old English Syntax*, 2 vols. (Oxford, 1985), §§1885, 2743–74, esp. 2751–4.
1. See E. B. Irving, *A Reading of Beowulf* (New Haven, CT, 1968; repr. Provo, UT, 1999, with preface by K. O'Brien O'Keeffe), pp. 30–41. There are also some brief but interesting observations by L. C. Gruber, "Motion, Perception and *oþþæt* in *Beowulf*," *In Geardagum* 1 (1974): 31–7.

Thus the noble retainers lived in joy, blessedly, UNTIL one began to perpetrate crimes, a fiend from hell.

Later in the poem, when Beowulf had returned to Geatland, he ruled that land as a wise king *until* a dragon began to wreak havoc on dark nights:

> —wæs ða frod cyning,
> eald eþelweard—, oð ðæt an ongan
> deorcum nihtum draca rics[i]an (2209–11).

[Beowulf] was then a wise king, an old guardian of the people, UNTIL one began to rule on dark nights,—a dragon.

The repetition of this phrase (*oð ðæt an ongan*)—a phrase which occurs only in *Beowulf*—to mark a turning point at two crucial points in the narrative, can hardly be a matter of coincidence.

We may now return to the narrative, to the point where Beowulf has arrived in Denmark, has been introduced to Hrothgar's court, has bested Unferth in a verbal flyting, and has reassured everyone that he means to deal straightway with the problem of Grendel. This statement restores confidence in the hall and calls for a round of drinks. Momentarily, happy times have been restored to Heorot:

> Þa wæs eft swa ær   inne on healle
> þryðword sprecen,   ðeod on sælum,
> sigefolca sweg,   oþ þæt semninga
> sunu Healfdenes   secean wolde
> æfenræste;   wiste þæm ahlæcan
> to þam heahsele   hilde geþinged,
> siððan hie sunnan leoht   geseon meahton,
> oþ ðe nipende   niht ofer ealle,
> scaduhelma gesceapu   scriðan cwoman
> wan under wolcnum.   Werod eall aras (642–51).

Then once more, as of old, within the hall brave words were spoken, the people joyous, [there was] sound of victorious folk, UNTIL presently the son of Healfdene [Hrothgar] wished to seek his nightly rest; he knew that the monster had determined to attack the lofty hall as soon as they could no longer see the sun's light, or night darkening over all things, shadowy outlines should come gliding forth, dark beneath the skies. The company all arose.

Even at this early point in the poem we have learned that a momentary period of happiness and calm is likely to be followed by a reversal: and on cue, as it were, the monster comes, gliding through the night like a shadow,[2] and bursts into the hall. Beowulf confronts him and tears off his arm and shoulder, inflicting thereby a mortal wound. Grendel escapes, and calm and happiness are restored (again) to Heorot: *Þær wæs sang ond sweg samod ætgædere* (1063: "Singing and music combined there together"), says the narrator, recalling the *hearpan sweg* (89: "music of a harp") that had resounded through Heorot years ago, before the monster's first assault. Here—for reasons which will become clear in due course—we must try to put ourselves in the position of the original audience, who did not know what might happen next, but who by now had internalized the poet's perception of the transitory nature of human happiness, with periods of tranquility inevitably punctuated by reversals. Predictably, on the following night, out of the darkness comes another monster to Heorot, the advance of this monster (who turns out to be Grendel's mother) marked by diction that recalls Grendel's earlier attack (1279: *com þa to Heorote*, "she then came to Heorot"; cf. 720: *com þa to recede*, "[the warrior] then came to the hall"). This one's attack is a terrifying reversal (*edhwyrft*) for the Danes who—thinking danger has passed— have returned to sleeping in the hall:

> Þa ðær sona wearð
> edhwyrft eorlum,   siþðan inne fealh
> Grendles modor   (1280–2).

> Then there was, immediately, a reversal for the men, when Grendel's mother burst in.

She kills one of the men (a thegn of Hrothgar named Æschere) and drags his body to the ghastly mere which she inhabits; the following morning Beowulf pursues her into the mere and, after a struggle, kills her. So peace and tranquility are yet again restored to Heorot. Hrothgar praises Beowulf and offers him some wise advice. Beowulf— and everyone else—is happy. Then occurs the passage to which all this preamble has been leading:

> Geat wæs glædmod,   geong sona to,
> setles neosan,   swa se snottra heht.
> Þa wæs eft swa ær   ellenrofum,
> fletsittendum   fægere gereorded
> niowan stefne.—   Nihthelm geswearc
> deorc ofer dryhtgumum.   Duguð eall aras . . . (1785–90).

2. These lines describing Grendel's advance (702–3: "Com on wanre niht / scriðan sceadugenga") are in turn an intentional repetition, or retroaction, of the diction describing the onset of night (649–51), quoted above.

The Geat [Beowulf] was happy; he went at once to take his seat, as the wise one [King Hrothgar] commanded. Then once more, as of old, a feast was splendidly spread out for the hall-retainers, one more time.—The shadow of night grew dark, black, over the men. The company all arose . . .

Let us (again) try to place ourselves in the position of the poem's original audience.[3] Such an audience could not anticipate what would happen next, but could only reflect on what had already happened. The audience is encouraged, by the poet's repetition of earlier phrases, to recall the scene in the hall on the night before Grendel's first attack: then, too, all "was as it had been before" (642: *Þa wæs eft swa ær*); there, too, the "shadow of night" crept over everything (with *nihthelm* here cf. 650: *scaduhelma gesceapu*, "shapes of covering shadows"); there, too, "the company all arose" (651: *werod eall aras*). On the eve of Grendel's assault, there was joy in the hall *until* Hrothgar got up, anticipating the monster's assault. Here Beowulf rests peacefully, *until* a black raven . . .

> Reste hine þa rumheort;   reced hliuade
> geap ond goldfah;   gæst inne swæf,
> oþ þæt hrefn blaca . . .   (1799–1801).

The magnanimous one took his rest; the building towered up, gabled and gold-bedecked; the guest slept within, UNTIL a black raven . . .

How did the first audience (or indeed: how do we) know that there is not a third monster, or an unending supply of monsters, lurking outside in the shadows of night, ready to attack the hall? That disaster might again be impending is hinted by the poet's characteristic use of *oþ þæt*, anticipating a reversal; and the appearance of the black raven—one of the traditional beasts of battle and slaughter[4]—also suggests imminent carnage.[5] The tension builds to this point, and then is swiftly dissipated by the b-verse: "until the black raven . . . happily announced the joy of heaven [i.e. bright day]." The question is: why did the poet choose the black raven to announce the joy of

---

3. The concept of the "original" audience is highly problematical (and ultimately unknowable); I use the term here and throughout as a mere shorthand to refer to any audience hearing or reading the poem for the first time, without having any knowledge of its content.
4. See M. S. Griffith, "Convention and Originality in the Old English 'Beasts of Battle' Typescene," *Anglo-Saxon England* 22 (1993): 179–99.
5. Cf. the comment in *Beowulf: A Dual-Language Edition*, ed. H. D. Chickering (New York, 1977), p. 344: "It is hard to imagine that the poet who also used the ominous *oððæt an angan* (100b, 2210b) would say *oððæt hrefn blaca* 'until the black raven' here without intending to awaken a sense of impending carnage."

the coming day?[6] Why not a meadowlark, or a cheery robin? As far as I know (from the advice of ornithologists) ravens have at best a very dubious "dawn song": *The Handbook of British Birds* describes "a sort of liquid gargle, like wine poured from a long-necked decanter, uttered with bill pointing upwards."[7] But the carefully-drawn parallel with the earlier passage suggests that the *Beowulf*-poet had in mind a narrative design irrelevant to the exactitude of ornithology: the raven was chosen because of its sinister associations with death and carnage, teasing the audience (as it were) with the anticipation of yet another slaughter-attack, and then dispelling the tension by allowing the raven, improbably, to announce the light of day. This design could only be successful if the poet could expect the audience to recall the first passage while hearing or reading the second. The narrative repetition, in other words, must be intentional.

The use of repetition to inform and encourage the reader's re-interpretation of the text is a literary technique which the structur-alist critic Michael Riffaterre has called "retroaction,"[8] namely the process by which a reader is induced to reflect on what has pre-ceded, so that the text becomes the object of progressive discovery, of a dynamic perception which is constantly changing. That is to say, the reader's understanding of a text is reflective and retroac-tive.[9] In *Beowulf* the process of retroaction works not only in micro-contexts (as Riffaterre would call them),[1] that is at the level of repeated words and phrases, but also in macrocontexts, by which I understand the repetition of episodes. Macrocontextual repetition is one of the most unusual features of *Beowulf*ian narrative dis-course. Three such repetitions require comment: the accounts of

6. This question has exercised many students of the poem. S. H. Horowitz, "The Ravens in *Beowulf*," *Journal of English and Germanic Philology* 80 (1981): 502–11, associates the present raven with that sent out from the Ark, hence understanding it as an omen of future corruption; and M. Osborn, "Domesticating the Dayraven in *Beowulf* 1801 (with some Attention to Alison's *Ston*)," in *Heroic Poetry in the Anglo-Saxon Period*, ed. H. Damico and J. Leyerle (Kalamazoo, MI, 1993), pp. 313–30, associates it with the quasi-domestic home ravens found nowadays on farms in Iceland.
7. H. F. Witherby, *The Handbook of British Birds*, ed. F. C. Ticehurst and E. G. Tucker, 5 vols. (London, 1938–41), I, 322.
8. M. Riffaterre, *Essais de stylistique structurale*, trans. D. Delas (Paris, 1971), p. 58: "*rétroaction*: le sens et la valeur de certains faits de style déjà déchiffrés sont modifiés rétrospectivement par ce que le lecteur découvre à mesure qu'il progresse dans sa lecture. Tel mot répété, par exemple, est mis en relief du fait de la répétition."
9. Riffaterre, *Essais*, trans. Delas, pp. 327–8: "le texte est l'objet d'une découverte progres-sive, d'une perception dynamique et constamment changeante, où le lecteur non seule-ment va de surprise en surprise mais voit change, à mesure qu'il avance, sa compréhension de ce qu'il vient de lire, chaque nouvel élément conférant une dimension nouvelle à des éléments antérieurs qu'il répète ou contredit ou développe. Prendre conscience d'un de ces échos, c'est donc lire deux fois telle partie du texte, la deuxième fois rétroactive-ment." Cf. also C. F. Tosi, *La repetizione lessicale nei poeti latini* (Bologna, 1983), p. 17.
1. Riffaterre, *Essais*, trans. Delas, pp. 68–9.

Beowulf's swimming match with Breca; Beowulf's own account of his experiences at the Danish court; and the several allusions in the poem to Hygelac's last raid.[2]

First, the swimming match. After Beowulf has arrived at the Danish court and been introduced to King Hrothgar, he is challenged abruptly by the court spokesman, Unferth, concerning a youthful swimming match between Beowulf and his friend Breca. In Unferth's account of the events (506–28), Breca won the contest because, after a week in the water, he was washed up among the Heatho-Ræmas (in Norway?), from where he eventually made it back home, thus apparently obtaining victory. (It is obvious that Unferth's account of the story derives, however indirectly, from Breca.) In his reply (530–606), Beowulf gives us a different version of the events: that after five days' swimming together, he and Breca did indeed become separated, and after separation Beowulf was heavily engaged in killing sea-monsters (nine of them), before being washed up in Lapland.[3] On the face of it, neither of these accounts is wholly true or demonstrably false: they simply report the incidents from differing perspectives.[4] Only after hearing Beowulf's account can we understand, in retrospect, Breca's reasons for having claimed victory.

More puzzling is the repeated narrative of events at Hrothgar's court. These events are told at length by the narrator, from the time of Beowulf's arrival in Denmark (224) until his departure from Denmark (1903) and arrival back home in Geatland (1913): some 1700 lines in all, including the account of Beowulf's struggles with the two monsters, and his leave-taking of King Hrothgar. When he is safely back home and is relaxing over a drink with his uncle, the Geatish king Hygelac, he supplies at Hygelac's request a lengthy account of his adventures at the Danish court (2000–2151). Beowulf's

---

2. There are of course other examples of narrative repetition in the poem, a feature which greatly puzzled Klaeber: "Furthermore, different parts of a story are sometimes told in different places, or substantially the same incident is related several times from different points of view. A complete, connected account of the history of the dragon's hoard is obtained only by a comparison of the passages, 3049 ff., 3069 ff., 2233 ff. The brief notice of Grendel's first visit in Heorot (122 f.) is supplemented by a later allusion containing additional detail (1580 ff.). The repeated references to the various Swedish wars, the frequent allusions to Hygelac's Frankish foray, the two versions of the Heremod legend, the review of Beowulf's great fights by means of his report to Hygelac (and to Hrothgar) and through Wiglaf's announcement to his companions (2874 ff.; cp. also 2904 ff.) are well-known cases in point" (Beowulf, ed. Klaeber, pp. lvii–lviii).

3. The discrepancies between the two accounts of the swimming match are well discussed by F. C. Robinson, "Elements of the Marvellous in the Characterization of Beowulf: A Reconsideration of the Textual Evidence," repr. in Beowulf: Basic Readings, ed. P. S. Baker (New York and London, 1995 [first printed 1974]), pp. 79–96, at 86–92.

4. It is usually assumed that Beowulf "won" the contest because he presented a truer account of the events, but there is nothing in the text to support this assumption; rather, as Peter Baker has shown ("Beowulf the Orator," Journal of English Linguistics 21 [1988]: 3–23), the palm goes to Beowulf because of the excellence of his rhetoric.

account covers much of the ground the audience has already been over, but strikingly includes many significant details which were not included in the narrator's earlier telling: the presence at Heorot of Hrothgar's daughter Freawaru, who had been promised in marriage to the Heathobard king Ingeld in order to end the enduring feud between Scyldings (Danes) and Heathobards (lines 2020–69); the fact that the Geatish warrior who was killed by Grendel on the night of the first attack was named Handscio (2076–80); and the fact that Grendel carried with him a *glof* or sack made of dragon-skin, into which he stuffed his victims (2085–90). Subsequently, in handing over to Hygelac the treasure he had been given in Denmark, Beowulf observed that this treasure included battle-gear which had belonged to Hrothgar's brother Heorogar, a striking fact—given the text's concern with military heirlooms—which was not mentioned in the narrator's previous account of Hrothgar's gifts to Beowulf (2158–9). Why such striking discrepancies? As I mentioned, earlier commentators have seen such discrepancies as a structural weakness,[5] and have taken them as evidence that the poem has been stitched together, crudely, from originally separate lays.[6] But the lines in question represent Beowulf's own perception of his experiences in Denmark,[7] and the poet clearly expected the audience retroactively to compare Beowulf's account of events with the narrator's.

5. E.g. Tolkien, "*Beowulf*: The Monsters and the Critics," p. 272: "But the only serious weakness, or apparent weakness, is the long recapitulation: the report of Beowulf to Hygelac. This recapitulation is well done. Without serious discrepancy [*sic*!] it retells rapidly the events in Heorot, and retouches the account; and it serves to illustrate, since he himself describes his own deeds, yet more vividly the character of a young man, singled out by destiny, as he steps suddenly forth in his full powers. Yet this is perhaps not quite sufficient to justify the repetition."
6. For example, L. L. Schücking (*Beowulfs Rückkehr* [Halle, 1905], pp. 9–15, with stylistic and metrical evidence set out in the following chapters, pp. 16–74) argued that the episode known as "Beowulf's Homecoming" (1888–2199) was an editorial confection created to link together two originally separate poems; and this was also the view, somewhat modified, of K. Sisam, *The Structure of Beowulf* (Oxford, 1965), pp. 44–50. But Schücking's linguistic evidence has been shown to be inconclusive, and Janet Bately has argued powerfully for the poem's linguistic consistency: "Linguistic Evidence as a Guide to the Authorship of Old English Verse: A Reappraisal, with Special Reference to *Beowulf*," in *Learning and Literature in Anglo-Saxon England: Studies Presented to Peter Clemoes*, ed. M. Lapidge and H. Gneuss (Cambridge, 1985), pp. 409–31. The oral formulaicists have seen "Beowulf's Homecoming" as evidence of the poem's oral composition: F. P. Magoun, "*Beowulf A*: A Folk-Variant," *Arv* 14 (1958): 95–101, and, more recently, J. M. Foley, "Narrativity in *Beowulf*, *The Odyssey* and the Serbo-Croatian 'Return Song'," in *Classical Models in Literature*, ed. Z. Konstantinovic, W. Anderson and W. Dietze (Innsbruck, 1981), pp. 296–301. Cf. also idem, "*Beowulf* and Traditional Narrative Song: the Potential and Limits of Comparison," in *Old English Literature in Context*, ed. Niles, pp. 117–36, at 136: "And if we find narrative inconsistencies in Homer and *Beowulf*, we should consider the possibility that they arose from an amalgamation of stories which once existed (and perhaps still did exist at the time of the composition of *Beowulf*) as individual tales."
7. Cf. Chickering, *Beowulf*, p. 353: "Beowulf's long speech to Hygelac has been important to criticism for two contrary reasons. First, it is Beowulf's own perception of events in Denmark, given out in free form without the constraints of chronological sequence.

Most puzzling of all the repetitions in the poem is the repeated reference to Hygelac's last raid. Given the facts of Beowulf's intense loyalty to Hygelac, and of the disastrous train of events which Hygelac's death precipitated, one might expect that a detailed description of the event might form the central focal point of the narrative.[8] Instead, that phase of Geatish history is passed over in a stunning ellipsis of two lines: *Eft þæt geiode ufaran dogrum / hildehlæmmum, syððan Hygelac læg* (2200–1; "It came to pass in later days / through battle-clashes, after Hygelac lay dead").[9] Hygelac's raid is never narrated directly, but is alluded to on four separate occasions. On each of these occasions a variant account is given.

(a) lines 1197–1214 (related before the event by the narrator): Hygelac was wearing a neck-torque similar to the famous *Brosinga mene* (a legendary torque) when he went to attack the Frisians; he was killed; his body fell into the hands of the Franks, as did the neck-torque.[1] Bodies of dead Geats littered the battlefield.

(b) lines 2354–66 (related after the event by the narrator): Hygelac was killed; Beowulf escaped by swimming away with the armor of thirty warriors. The Hetware had no reason to exult: few of them came home.

(c) lines 2501–8 (related after the event by Beowulf himself): Beowulf slew the Frankish champion Dæghrefn with his handgrip, apparently as Dæghrefn was getting ready to strip

---

Secondly, it feels awkward." See also R. Waugh, "Competitive Narrators in the Homecoming Scene of *Beowulf*," *The Journal of Narrative Technique* 25 (1995): 202–22, who (improbably) sees the two accounts as a poetic competition between Beowulf and the narrator.

8. On Hygelac's central role in the poem, cf. the important discussion by Brodeur, *The Art of Beowulf*, pp. 79–86.

9. Cf. Brodeur's treatment of the ellipsis, and what it omits: "Beowulf's gallant stand in Frisia, the slaying of Dæghrefn and his escape, his refusal of the crown, his protection of the boy-king Heardred, and his expedition against Onela. This is God's plenty . . . How much more, then, might he have made of the hero's deeds in those middle years, from his valiant fight in Frisia through his magnanimous service to Heardred, and his retaliation for Heardred's death! He preferred to present them in a summary of intervening action; and this must have been his deliberate choice" (*The Art of Beowulf*, pp. 72–3).

1. The neck-torque is problematical, because Beowulf subsequently presents it to Hygd, Hygelac's queen, when he returns to Geatland (2172–4). How, then, did Hygelac come to have it? We must presume that Hygd gave it to him, and that he wore it on his last raid, though the poet makes no mention of such an exchange. Klaeber thought instead that "the poet entirely forgot his earlier account (1202 ff.) when he came to tell of the presentation to Hygd" (2172 ff.) (*Beowulf*, p. 179). Klaeber adds that this explanation "is the more probable one, especially if we suppose that at an earlier stage of his work the author had not yet thought at all of queen Hygd" (ibid). As I argue, the *Beowulf*-poet did not work in so careless a manner.

the corpse of Hygelac. After killing Dæghrefn, Beowulf helped himself to Dæghrefn's sword (called Nægling).[2]

(d) lines 2913–20 (related after the event by Wiglaf): Wiglaf, reflecting on the implications of Beowulf's death, says that when it becomes known to the Franks and Frisians, there will be inevitable conflict. The conflict with the Hugas was in fact initiated on the occasion of Hygelac's raid, when the Hetware defeated Hygelac in battle. Unfortunately, Hygelac fell without paying the Merovingians, and Merovingian support has been denied to the Geats ever since.

By the end of the poem, the audience has managed to glean a relatively clear notion of what happened on Hygelac's raid: Hygelac, accompanied by Beowulf and other Geats (thirty of these?), supported by the Merovingians acting as mercenaries, confronted an alliance of Frisians, Franks, Hetware and Hugas. Hygelac was killed by the Frankish warrior Dæghrefn; when Dæghrefn tried to strip him of his armor (and the neck-torque), Beowulf killed him, took his sword and thirty suits of armor (belonging to dead Geats?) and swam home, apparently as the sole survivor of the raid. But this knowledge of the episode can only be acquired retrospectively: only after Beowulf himself has been killed, many years later, do the implications and facts of Hygelac's raid emerge (and still many questions remain unanswered).

These repetitions or retroactions are far from being the only unusual aspect of *Beowulf*ian narrative. It is often asserted that the story of *Beowulf* derives from folk tales.[3] But the narrative mode of the folktale is linear and chronological; and *Beowulf*ian narrative is anything but linear and chronological. Sometimes, it is true, a story is told straightforwardly, in correct chronological sequence, as in the case of the story of Ingeld (2024–69);[4] on other occasions, such as the account of the wars between the Swedes and the Geats, the story is narrated, confusingly, in very nearly the reverse order from that

2. A very different interpretation of these lines is given by P. Cavill, "A Note on *Beowulf* lines 2490–2509," *Neophilologus* 67 (1983): 599–604.

3. The classic study of the folktale elements in *Beowulf* (especially the so-called "Bear's Son" motif) is by F. Panzer, *Beowulf* (Munich, 1910), pp. 1–245; see also T. A. Shippey, "The Fairy-Tale Structure of *Beowulf*," *Notes & Queries* 214 (1969): 2–11; D. R. Barnes, "Folktale Morphology and the Structure of *Beowulf*," *Speculum* 45 (1970): 416–34; and B. A. Rosenberg, "Reconstructed Folktales as Literary Sources," in *Historical Studies and Literary Criticism*, ed. J. J. McGann (Madison, WI, 1985), pp. 76–89.

4. Cf. Brodeur, *The Art of Beowulf*, pp. 158–9: "The poet has adopted a direct and consecutive manner of narration quite different from that which characterizes most of the legendary episodes of Part I; the contrast with the manner in which he deals with the legend of Finn and Hengest is striking."

in which the narrated events took place.[5] Throughout the poem the narrative looks now forward, now backwards; proceeds at one moment at a snail's pace, at another so rapidly that the events of fifty years are recounted within a few lines; and is sometimes told from the point of view of the narrator, sometimes from that of the characters. The narrative order, pace and point of view vary drastically throughout the poem. In his classic study of narrative discourse, Gérard Genette elucidated these principal features of narrative discourse—order, pace and point of view—and it will be helpful to keep his descriptions (and terminology) in mind when trying to isolate the characteristic features of Beowulfian narrative.[6]

First, order, that is to say, the relationship between the temporal order of succession of the events in the story and the pseudo-temporal order of their arrangement in the narrative.[7] Genette distinguishes between what he terms analepses (roughly: flashbacks) and prolepses (or anticipations[8]); and for each of these he further distinguishes between those which refer to events external to the story (heterodiegetic or external analepses or prolepses), and those which refer to events internal to the story (homodiegetic or internal analepses or prolepses). Much of Beowulf is taken up with analepses and prolepses of one kind or another. For example, the narrative of Sigemund (874–97), or of the fight at Finnsburg, or Beowulf's account of Freawaru and Ingeld, or the two references to Heremod's

5. The events of these wars take place in the following chronological sequence: 1. Hæthcyn the Geat accidentally kills his elder brother Herebeald (2435–40); 2. King Hrethel, the father of Hæthcyn and Herebeald, dies of grief (2462–71); 3. after Hrethel's death, Ohthere and Onela, the sons of Ongentheow, king of the Swedes, attack the Geats at Hreosnaburh (2472–8); 4. Hæthcyn retaliates by attacking Ongentheow in Sweden (2925–7); 5. Hæthcyn is killed by Ongentheow at Hrefnawudu (2927–35); 6. Ongentheow surrounds the remaining Geatish warriors, but Hygelac comes to their rescue (2936–45); 7. Hygelac's retainers Wulf and Eofor then kill Ongentheow (2961–82); 8. Hygelac is killed on a raid in Frisia (2915–19); 9. Hygelac's son Heardred then becomes king with Beowulf's support (2373–9); 10. Heardred offers hospitality to the sons of Ohthere (who are also the grandsons of Ongentheow), Eanmund and Eadgils (2379–84); 11. for this reason Onela, now king of the Swedes, attacks and kills Heardred (2384–8); 12. Eadgils subsequently returns to Sweden and kills Onela (2391–6). If, following the example of Genette (Narrative Discourse, pp. 35–47, and see below, n. 7), we designate the chronological order of these twelve events with the numbers 1–12, and then designate the order in which they are narrated with capital letters A–L, the narrative anachronies immediately become clear:

A9—B10—C11—D12—E1—F2—G3—H8—I4—J5—K6—L7.

6. Genette's terminology has the merit of precision, unlike that which is found in earlier Beowulf scholarship ("main story," "subplot," "digression," "Leitmotiv," etc.).
7. Genette, Narrative Discourse, p. 35: "To study the temporal order of a narrative is to compare the order in which events or temporal sections are arranged in the narrative discourse with the order of succession these same events or temporal segments have in the story." See also the brief elucidation by Rimmon-Kenan, Narrative Fiction, pp. 46–51.
8. Prolepses or anticipations have been discussed by earlier critics—they are an obvious feature of the poem—such as A. Bonjour, "The Use of Anticipation in Beowulf," Review of English Studies 16 (1940): 290–7; Brodeur, The Art of Beowulf, pp. 220–8; and G. I. Berlin, "Grendel's Advance on Heorot: The Functions of Anticipation," Proceedings of the PMR Conference 11 (1986): 19–26.

disastrous reign, are heterodiegetic analepses. On the other hand, Beowulf's report to Hygelac of his adventures at Heorot is a homodiegetic analepsis; furthermore, because it fills in, after the event, some earlier gaps in the narrative, it is what Genette would call a "completing analepsis." The recollections by Beowulf and Wiglaf of the events of Hygelac's last raid are also, in this terminology, completing homodiegetic analepses, as are the "Lay of the Last Survivor" (2236–70), and indeed the entire narrative of the Swedish wars. By the same token, the poem contains a number of heterodiegetic prolepses (such as the anticipations of conflict between Hrothulf and Hrothgar's sons, or of the burning of Heorot), and also homodiegetic prolepses, such as the various anticipations that Beowulf will meet his death in combat with the dragon.[9] The narrative focus in *Beowulf*, in other words, is always shifting, and moves continually backwards and forward in time.[1]

Then, secondly, the question of narrative pace.[2] In theory, a narrative might proceed throughout at a steady pace, without acceleration or deceleration; such a narrative would be described by Genette as "isochronous," and is to be found (more or less) in epics of classical antiquity. In *Beowulf*, by contrast, there is wild variation in narrative pace.[3] The narrative is ponderously slow, for example, in the description of the interrogation of the newly-arrived Geats by the Danish coastguard (229–319), or the subsequent account of their arrival at Heorot and interrogation there by Wulfgar (320–404). Elsewhere it progresses steadily, as in the description of Beowulf's encounter with the dragon, where the narrated events take place within a span of twenty-four hours. The most rapid pace of all is described by Genette as ellipsis, where story time is passed over so

---

9. Beowulf's own death is foretold in 2341–4, 2397–2400; 2419–24 and 2573–5. Genette also describes the narrative technique of what he calls paralipsis (ibid. p. 52), the side-stepping or omission of a given element which is later filled in. In *Beowulf*, an example of paralipsis in the Genettian sense would be Hrothgar's recollection, after the fact of Grendel's mother's assault on Heorot, that land dwellers had seen two monsters walking the moors, of which one was in the likeness of a woman (1345–53).
1. The question of the temporal framework within which events of the poem are situated in relation to the narratorial present is immensely complex, and has been helpfully discussed by J. D. Niles, *Beowulf: The Poem and Its Tradition* (Cambridge, MA, 1983), pp. 179–96; see also J. M. Hill, "*Beowulf,* Value and the Frame of Time," *Modern Language Quarterly* 40 (1979): 3–16; Kinney, "The Needs of the Moment," pp. 299–307 (on verb tenses as part of the narrative design); H. Chickering, "Lyric Time in *Beowulf,*" *Journal of English and Germanic Philology* 91 (1992): 489–509; and R. J. Schrader, *Old English Poetry and the Genealogy of Events* (East Lansing, MI, 1993), pp. 76–9.
2. In *Narrative Discourse*, Genette referred to this feature as "duration" (pp. 86–112); after some reflection, he suggested using the term "speed" or "speeds" in his *Narrative Discourse Revisited*, trans. J. E. Lewin (Ithaca, NY, 1988), pp. 33–7. See also Rimmon-Kenan, *Narrative Fiction*, pp. 51–6.
3. Cf. the interesting remarks of A. L. Harris, "Techniques of Pacing in *Beowulf,*" *English Studies* 63 (1982): 97–108, who, however, confines her discussion to the use of variation (in the sense defined by F. C. Robinson: see below, n. 4 [on p. 261]) to retard or accelerate the narrative.

rapidly that it is in effect omitted or elided. When the period of time passed over is specified, Genette describes the ellipsis as explicit. There are several explicit ellipses in *Beowulf*: the twelve years during which Grendel ravaged Heorot and the hall stood empty (144–9); and, most striking of all, the fifty-plus years during which the kingdom of the Geats was taken over by Beowulf and ruled by him into his old age (2200–9). This is one of the most stunning ellipses in the whole of English literature.

The third of Genette's categories concerns the text's modality, or the way the narratorial point of view is expressed or "focalized."[4] Genette distinguishes between third-person narratives by an omniscient narrator, which he calls "non-focalized" narrative, and which is the characteristic form of most ancient classical narrative, and, on the other hand, narrative which is expressed through a character in the text, and which therefore may be said to express that character's point of view. Such narrative is, in Genette's terms, "focalized" through the character, and is described by him as "internal focalization." Much of the narrative in *Beowulf* is recounted through the poem's characters: mostly through Beowulf himself, but also through Unferth, Hrothgar, Hrothgar's scops, and Wiglaf. I have already referred to the episode of Hygelac's last raid, which is recounted once, proleptically, by the narrator and hence is non-focalized, but is then focalized, analeptically, through Beowulf himself (twice) and then through Wiglaf. Genette refers to this technique as "multiple internal focalization."[5] Multiple internal focalization is an extremely rare and unusual narrative technique, and is not found in the narrative literature of classical antiquity. In order to illustrate the form, Genette points to epistolary novels of the eighteenth century, and in particular to Browning's long narrative poem *The Ring and the Book* (1868), which relates a criminal case as perceived successively by the murderer, the victims, the defense, the prosecution, and others. More striking examples can be found in two novels of William Faulkner. *The Sound and the Fury* (1929) consists of three separate recollections (or: homodiegetic analepses), recorded long after the event and focalized through the male children of the Compson family (a southern white family from Jefferson, Mississippi) concerning certain dramatic events of their childhood, especially the circumstances surrounding the loss of their sister Caddy's virginity (the recollections are, in order, those of Benjy, a thirty-three-year-old idiot with the mind of a three-year-old; Quentin, whose recollection is in effect a suicide note written at Harvard on

4. On focalization, see Genette, *Narrative Discourse*, pp. 189–98 (with further reflections in his *Narrative Discourse Revisited*, pp. 72–8), and Rimmon-Kenan, *Narrative Fiction*, pp. 71–85.
5. Genette, *Narrative Discourse*, pp. 189–90.

the last day of his life; and Jason, the self-righteous but apparently sane brother). Only after reading all these recollections do the youthful events assume some clarity; but, as in the case of Hygelac's last raid, certain details concerning Caddy never emerge. There is no truth; only—in each case—independent perceptions of a searingly memorable sequence of events. By the same token, Faulkner's next novel, *As I Lay Dying* (1930), concerns the death of Addie Bundren, and the harrowing (and often comical) journey taken by her husband Anse and her various children—Cash, Darl, Jewel, Dewey Dell and Vardaman—to return her corpse in its coffin, during a hot week in July, to Jefferson, Mississippi, whence she had come. There is no extradiegetic narrative; the novel consists of a series of brief personal observations by Anse and the children, as well as by various neighbors, as the stinking coffin makes its way to its final resting place. Faulkner's interest in the perception of events led him to create a wholly new narrative vehicle, seen in slightly different experimental forms in these two novels.[6] I am suggesting that the *Beowulf*-poet's interest in perception led him to make a similar experiment in narrative form.

For the *Beowulf*-poet's deployment of these narrative devices there is no satisfactory model in antecedent western literature. One can point to individual, isolated features in the earlier narrative verse of Roman poets arguably known to the *Beowulf*-poet.[7] Consider Vergil's *Aeneid*, for example.[8] Like the Homeric epics which Vergil was imitating, the narrative of the *Aeneid* is characterized on the whole by "calm, steady development . . . in a single direction";[9] only rarely is the overall progression interrupted by analepses (such as Aeneas's account of the sack of Troy in book II, or that of Deiphobus in VI.

6. A further experiment is found in his *Absalom, Absalom!* (1936), where the murder of Charles Bon by Colonel Henry Sutpen is narrated thirty-nine times by various narrators; see S. Rimmon-Kenan, "From Reproduction to Production: The Status of Narration in Faulkner's *Absalom, Absalom!*," *Degrés* 16 (1978): 1–19. This aspect of Faulkner's narrative technique has (oddly) been very little studied; for a general discussion of the models which inspired Faulkner's experiments in narrative, see A. F. Kinney, *Faulkner's Narrative Poetics: Style as Vision* (Amherst, MA, 1978), pp. 38–67 and, for Faulkner's interest in perception, pp. 15–24.
7. On Roman narrative in general, see K. Quinn, *Texts and Contexts. The Roman Writers and Their Audience* (London, 1979), pp. 48–119 ("The Poet as Storyteller"). I omit from discussion Ovid's *Metamorphoses*, which, although they may well have been read in Anglo-Saxon England (probably by Aldhelm and Bede), consist rather of brief episodes rather than extended narrative on the scale which we encounter in *Beowulf*.
8. The question of whether the *Beowulf*-poet had read Vergil is complex, and there is no scholarly consensus on the matter. The principal discussions are F. Klaeber, "*Aeneis* und *Beowulf*," *Archiv* 126 (1911): 40–8 and 339–59; A. Brandl, "*Beowulf*-Epos und *Aeneis* in systematischer Vergleichung," *Archiv* 171 (1937): 161–73; and T. B. Haber, *A Comparative Study of 'Beowulf' and the 'Aeneid'* (Princeton, NJ, 1931).
9. R. Heinze, *Virgil's Epic Technique*, trans. H. and D. Harvey and F. Robertson (Berkeley and Los Angeles, CA, 1993 [originally publ. in German, 1915]), p. 254; cf. also pp. 251 ("Virgil intends us never to lose the feeling that the action is *moving forward*" [Heinze's italics]) and 301.

509–34)[1] or prolepses (such as Anchises's prophecy concerning the future of Rome in VI. 752–892). Vergil occasionally shattered the narrative calm by describing an abrupt reversal (known in Aristotelian criticism of the drama as a *peripeteia*):[2] thus at one moment in book IV Aeneas is seen, after the consummation of his affair with Dido, happily at work building houses in Carthage (IV. 260–1); but then Mercury appears to him and reminds him of his Roman destiny, and he suddenly "burns to be gone and to leave these sweet lands" (IV. 281: *ardet abire fuga dulcisque relinquere terras*); or again, in book V, at the height of celebration of the funeral games in Sicily, Fortuna engineers a *peripeteia* (V. 604: *hic primum Fortuna fidem mutata novavit*, "here first fortune changed and broke her faith"[3]), and the next minute the entire Trojan fleet is in flames. These Vergilian reversals might be said in some sense to correspond to the *Beowulf*ian *edwenden*. But in fundamental respects, Vergilian narrative is palpably different from that of *Beowulf*. The story of the *Aeneid* is related almost wholly throughout by an extradiegetic narrator, who is presumably identical with Vergil himself; the narrative is only focalized through one of the characters on rare occasions.[4] It is true that in recent times Vergilian scholars have begun to respond to the challenges of structuralist criticism: Gian Biagio Conte has identified in Vergilian narrative what he calls "point of view,"[5] and the late Don Fowler has described the same phenomenon as "embedded focalization."[6] For example, in the line which was quoted above, *dulcisque relinquere terras* (IV. 281), the lands of Carthage are only "sweet" because at that moment they are perceived by Aeneas to be so.[7] Examples of embedded focalization such as this

1. The narrative of Deiphobus, who was killed treacherously during the sack of Troy and who as a shade in the underworld relates his experiences to Aeneas, is a good example of what Genette calls a completing analepsis, and is comparable in this respect to the completing analepses of *Beowulf* described above.
2. Heinze, *Virgil's Epic Technique*, pp. 254–5. Elements of tragedy (as defined by Aristotle) in the *Aeneid* are well discussed by P. Hardie, "Virgil and Tragedy," in *The Cambridge Companion to Virgil*, ed. C. Martindale (Cambridge, 1997), pp. 312–26; for *peripeteia*, see p. 313.
3. Translation from H. Rushton Fairclough, ed. and trans., *Virgil: Eclogues, Georgics, Aeneid: Books 1–6*, Loeb Classical Library 63, revised by G. P. Goold (Cambridge, MA, 1999), 513 [*Editor*].
4. One such occasion occurs at the very end of the poem (XII. 908–17), where Turnus's terror as he steps forward to confront the ferocious Aeneas is described in terms of his mental perception. I have discussed this passage in the context of *Beowulf*ian narrative in "The Comparative Approach," in *Reading Old English Texts*, ed. K. O'Brien O'Keeffe (Cambridge, 1997), pp. 20–38, at 31–3.
5. G. B. Conte, *The Rhetoric of Imitation. Genre and Poetic Memory in Virgil and Other Latin Poets*, ed. C. Segal (Ithaca, NY, 1986), p. 154. As Conte quickly points out (ibid. n. 10), his use of the term "point of view" here differs from that of the narratologists such as Genette.
6. D. P. Fowler, "Deviant Focalisation in Virgil's *Aeneid*," *Proceedings of the Cambridge Philological Society* 36 (1990): 42–63, and idem, "Virgilian Narrative: Story-Telling," in *The Cambridge Companion to Virgil*, ed. Martindale, pp. 259–70.
7. This same line is discussed by Conte, *The Rhetoric of Imitation*, p. 156, and by Fowler, "Virgilian Narrative," pp. 266–7.

can be found in *Beowulf* as well;[8] but they are wholly different in scope and scale from the multiple internal focalization which is also found in *Beowulf*.

Vergilian narrative, then, cannot easily be invoked as a model for *Beowulf*ian narrative. Nor is the situation any different with respect to other epic narratives of classical antiquity which might have been known to an Anglo-Saxon poet. For example, Lucan's *Bellum civile*, an account of the civil war between Caesar and Pompey (49–48 B.C.), follows historical chronology in that it proceeds throughout in a linear direction,[9] from Caesar's crossing of the Rubicon (book I), to the first naval encounter off Marseilles (book III), to the first meeting of the armies in Spain (book IV), to the mighty battle at Pharsalus on the plains of Thessaly and the destruction of Pompey's army (book VII), to Pompey's flight and death in Egypt (book VIII), and the aftermath of Caesar's victory (books IX–X). Lucan delays and expands his narrative by means of various lengthy *ekphraseis* (the account of Thessalian witches in book VI, the catalogue of African snakes in book IX, etc.)[1] and by the occasional analepsis (the aged Roman citizen's recollection of previous civil war: II. 68–232) or prolepsis (the prophecy of Figulus: I. 638–72). Scholars have recently turned their attention to peculiarities in Lucan's narrative, especially his presentation of the poet (himself) as narrator;[2] but on the whole his narrative proceeds in chronological order, retelling (if often distorting) the events of recorded history. The same may be said of Statius's *Thebaid* which, although its story is drawn from mythology rather than history, proceeds in linear fashion.[3] It

---

8. Instances of embedded focalization (though he does not call it that) are discussed by Peter Clemoes, "Action in *Beowulf* and Our Perception of It," in *Old English Poetry: Essays on Style*, ed. D. G. Calder (Berkeley and Los Angeles, CA, 1979), pp. 147–68, esp. 155: "[the poet's] descriptive adverbs . . . have to do primarily with the doer's attitude to the action, his involvement in it, not with the impression which this action makes outside as a movement."

9. For an overview, see P. Grimal, "Le poète et l'histoire," in *Lucain*, Entretiens sur l'antiquité classique 15 (Geneva, 1970), 51–117. Lucan's account of the civil war was framed by his own fierce republican, anti-imperial sentiments, which account for many of the historical distortions in the poem; for helpful comment, see F. M. Ahl, *Lucan: An Introduction* (Ithaca, NY, 1976).

1. On Lucan's *ekphraseis*, see the methodical survey by L. Eckardt, *Exkurse und Ekphraseis bei Lucan* (Heidelberg, 1936).

2. See J. Masters, *Poetry and Civil War in Lucan's Bellum Civile* (Cambridge, 1992); P. Hardie, *The Epic Successors of Virgil* (Cambridge, 1993), pp. 107–9; and M. Leigh, *Lucan: Spectacle and Engagement* (Oxford, 1997), esp. p. 4: "The mediation of narrative through the point of view or focalization of a character involved encodes responses to the action often very different from those expressed by the primary narrator. The importance of this concept to modern evaluations of the ideology of the *Aeneid* from Heinze to Conte and on is well known. What is striking about Lucan is that, while his narrative responds to the same fundamental analysis as that of Vergil, it does so in a manner almost diametrically opposed to that found in the *Aeneid* . . . Lucan's internal audience repeatedly transforms into spectacle and seeks an admiring audience for a civil war which the primary narrator affects to abhor."

3. Cf. the remarks of D. Vessey, *Statius and the Thebaid* (Cambridge, 1973), p. 320: "His [Statius's] epic, full of variety and contrast, with frequent changes of tempo and mood,

concerns the internecine strife between the brothers Eteocles and Polyneices, sons of Oedipus. Because they have neglected him in his blind old age, Oedipus curses them and consigns them to perpetual rivalry, whereby the governance of Thebes will be shared in alternate years between the two brothers. Polyneices draws the losing lot and goes into exile at Argos; in his absence, Eteocles rejects the agreement and claims the Theban throne in perpetuity, thus precipitating war (all this in book I). The remainder of the epic concerns the exile of Polyneices in Argos with King Adrastus, the willingness of Adrastus to support his cause, and the expedition of Polyneices and Adrastus, accompanied by five further heroes and their troops (hence the 'Seven against Thebes') to confront Eteocles at Thebes and to reclaim the kingdom. With the exception of one lengthy homodiegetic analepsis (the narrative of Hysipyle, who shows up from Lemnos in book V), and several pauses in the forward movement (the funeral games at Nemea in book VI, for example), the narrative proceeds in a steady and linear fashion, with one or other of the Argive heroes being killed until finally, in book XI, Eteocles and Polyneices confront and kill each other (book XII concerns the aftermath and establishment of concord at Thebes through Athenian intervention). In short, even if it could be shown convincingly that Statius's *Thebaid* was read in Anglo-Saxon England, it could scarcely have served as a model for *Beowulf*ian narrative. And although other Latin epics have survived from classical antiquity, such as the *Argonautica* of Valerius Flaccus[4] or the *Punica* of Silius Italicus, there is no evidence that these were read or studied in Anglo-Saxon England, and so are not relevant to the present enquiry.

What was studied in Anglo-Saxon schools was the Christian-Latin "epic" verse of late antiquity.[5] Three such epics are in question. The *Evangelia* of Juvencus follow the synoptic gospels' version of the life of Christ, from His birth and childhood through to His crucifixion; all is told in one narrative voice, and there are no analepses, prolepses or internal focalizations. The *Carmen paschale* of Caelius Sedulius

---

presses onward through a series of episodes towards its final denouement . . . Each major part possesses its own self-sufficient value and unity, and all integrated into the stream of narrative by symbol, image and theme; but that stream is never dammed or obstructed in its flow"; and idem, *Statius: Thebaid*, trans. A. D. Melville, introd. D. W. T. Vessey (Oxford, 1992), p. xi: "There is a distinct and ordered progression of events, though some license for discursiveness."

4. In any event, the *Argonautica* were left incomplete at the author's death, and it is therefore perilous to interpret e.g. prolepses in light of what might or might not have been included in the finished work; see D. Hershkowitz, *Valerius Flaccus' Argonautica: Abbreviated Voyages in Silver Latin Epic* (Oxford, 1998), pp. 22–4.

5. On the way that biblical narrative was rendered in verse in these Late Latin poems, see M. Roberts, *Biblical Epic and Rhetorical Paraphrase in Late Antiquity* (Liverpool, 1985); on the way that they were studied in Anglo-Saxon England, see M. Lapidge, "The Study of Latin Texts in Late Anglo-Saxon England" in his *Anglo-Latin Literature, 600–899* (London, 1996), pp. 455–98 and 516 (addenda).

also treats the life of Christ in chronological order; and although the typological significance of each event in Christ's life is amplified through collocation with Old Testament events, the progression of the narrative is not interrupted with analepses or prolepses, and the entire poem is told in one narrative voice. Arator's poem, the *Historia apostolica*, is concerned with events in the lives of Saints Peter and Paul; and although the poet devotes his greatest energy to explaining the figural significance of these events, rather than the events themselves, the poem otherwise contains no departures from linear narrative.[6]

These, then, are the narrative poets—Vergil, Lucan, Statius, Juvencus, Caelius Sedulius, Arator—which an Anglo-Saxon poet writing no later than the mid-eighth century could reasonably be assumed to have read; and the narrative discourse of none of them bears any resemblance to *Beowulf* in anything other than minor details. Poets later than the mid-eighth century do not come into consideration because, as paleographical evidence unambiguously indicates, a written text of *Beowulf*, which was the ultimate ancestor or archetype of the sole surviving copy, existed by no later than c. 750.[7] One could even say that no medieval poem—in Latin or the vernacular—composed before c. 1100 bears any resemblance to *Beowulf* either in its structure or in its narrative discourse.[8]

That is why, in trying to illustrate the unusual nature of *Beowulf*ian narrative, I drew an analogy with the novels of William Faulkner. In fact many aspects of *Beowulf*ian narrative have closer analogues in the modern novel than in ancient epic. Mikhail Bakhtin has helpfully clarified the distinction between the narrative of the epic and of the novel (by which he refers not merely to modern "novels," but to prose narratives of classical antiquity, from Plato through Petronius and Apuleius and others).[9] There is no doubt that *Beowulf* would

6. The narrative itself is contained in prose summaries which precede sections of verse in which the figural significance is expounded. On the form, see M. Lapidge, "Bede's Metrical *Vita S. Cuthberti*" in *Anglo-Latin Literature, 600–899*, pp. 339–55, at 348–50; on the figural meaning of the poem, see Richard Hillier, *Arator on the Acts of the Apostles: A Baptismal Commentary* (Oxford, 1993).

7. See M. Lapidge, "The Archetype of *Beowulf*," *Anglo-Saxon England* 29 (2000): 5–41.

8. By c. 1100 vernacular poets were beginning to experiment with narrative structure. The *Song of Roland* with its *laisses similaires*, for example, is apparently an experimental form in which consecutive *laisses* or strophes recount the same incident in nearly identical, but significantly varying, wording: Roland sounding the oliphant (str. 133–4), Roland striking the stone with his sword Durendal (str. 172–3), etc. See G. J. Brault, *The Song of Roland: An Analytical Edition*. I. *Introduction and Commentary* (University Park, PA, 1978), pp. 78–9, as well as (briefly) E. Vinaver, *The Rise of Romance* (Oxford, 1971), p. 7 ("'Repetition with variation,' to which there is no exact parallel in our modern method of exposition"). A similar phenomenon, described here as "double narration," has been noted in the *Poema del mio Cid* by J. Gornall, "How Many Times Was the Count of Barcelona Offered His Freedom? Double Narration in the *Poema del mio Cid*," *Medium Aevum* 56 (1987): 65–77.

9. M. M. Bakhtin, *The Dialogic Imagination: Four Essays*, ed. M. Holquist, trans. C. Emerson and M. Holquist (Austin, TX, 1981), pp. 3–40 ("Epic and Novel: Toward a Methodology

be classed by Bakhtin as epic, insofar as it deals with a "national heroic past," one which is separated "from the contemporary reality, that is, from the time in which the singer (and author and his audience lives) by an absolute epic distance";[1] but there are nevertheless many features of the poem which associate it strikingly with Bakhtinian novel, especially its "radical transformation of temporal coordinates."[2] Bakhtin argued that the genesis of the novel is to be found in Plato's Socratic dialogues, where a "speaking and conversing man is the central image of the genre," and that the characteristic feature of this "speaking man" or narrator is his *apomnemoneumata* or "recollections," which serve to link the past with the narratorial present, to bridge (in effect) the "absolute epic distance" which separates the narrator of epic from his subject. (Bakhtin's "recollections" would be described by Genette as homodiegetic analepses.) I have suggested that *Beowulf* is structured by "recollections" of a similar sort: Beowulf's recollections of his swimming match with Breca, of his activities at Heorot, and of his participation in Hygelac's last raid. Interestingly, Bakhtin went on to suggest that "when the novel becomes the dominant genre, epistemology becomes the dominant discipline."[3] Bakhtin's remark is pertinent to *Beowulf* because, on my understanding of the poem, one of the poet's principal concerns was epistemological: the processes of acquisition and evaluation of knowledge, of the mental perception of an event rather than the event itself, and the arrangement of these mental perceptions in a narrative structure.

The narrative mode of *Beowulf* is retrospective rather than prospective.[4] Events and action are defined and redefined through subsequent perception, through what Riffaterre called retroaction. The process of perceptual redefinition, of movement from the vague to the definite, takes place at all levels of the poem's narrative. At the microcontextual level it is a pervasive feature of the poet's diction. A clear example is found in lines quoted earlier concerning the first ravages of Grendel: the Geats lived blessedly "until one began to perpetrate crimes, a fiend from hell" (100–1: *oð ðæt an ongan / fyrene fremman feond on helle*), where the ambiguous and unspecified *an*

for the Study of the Novel"). See also the important qualifications pertaining to Bakhtin's knowledge and understanding of medieval narrative, especially of medieval French romance, by Cesare Segre, "What Bakhtin Left Unsaid: The Case of the Medieval Romance," in *Romance: Generic Transformation from Chrétien de Troyes to Cervantes*, ed. K. and M. S. Brownlee (London, 1985), pp. 23–46.

1. Ibid. p. 13; and cf. discussion by Tzvetan Todorov, *Mikhail Bakhtin: The Dialogical Principle*, trans. W. Godzich (Manchester, 1984), pp. 88–9.
2. Bakhtin, *The Dialogic Imagination*, p. 11; Todorov, *Mikhail Bakhtin*, p. 88.
3. Bakhtin, *The Dialogic Imagination*, p. 15.
4. F. C. Robinson, *Beowulf and the Appositive Style* (Knoxville, TN, 1985), p. 7: "Few readers would deny that *Beowulf* is a profoundly retrospective narrative."

is subsequently qualified by the phrase *feond on helle*. Or consider the description of the Geats' departure for Denmark:

> Fyrst forð gewat;   flota was on yðum,
> bat under beorge (210–11).

Time passed; something was floating on the waves—a boat, beneath the cliffs.

Here a vague term (*flota*) is qualified by a precise, defining term (*bat*): a device which Fred Robinson has called "clarifying apposition."[5] On the macrocontextual level, the same movement from vagueness towards clarity of perception characterizes the poet's narrative discourse. I mention (briefly) two examples: the presentation of Grendel and that of Beowulf himself.

When first the monster is mentioned, he is described vaguely as an *ellengæst* (86)—if the text is sound here[6]—then successively as a fiend from hell (101), then a grim spirit, a notorious wanderer in marchlands (103) who was called Grendel, then a wretched man (105: *wonsæli wer*, the first indication that the monster is in human form), then a *wiht* or "creature" (120), then an *æglæca* (159), a difficult word implying at least the creature's terrifying nature, then a "dire solitary" (165: *atol angengea*); and so on. By the time this terrifying creature comes to attack the hall occupied by Beowulf and his men (702–21), the audience knows nothing precise about its appearance, save that it is in human form. Of course subsequent events allow a much clearer perception of this humanoid monster: that he was bigger than a man (1353), so big that it took four men to carry his head (1634–9), that he had fingernails like steel (985), that a terrifying light shone from his eyes (726–7), that he was invulnerable to iron weapons (802–3, 987–9), that he carried a *glof* or dragon-skin sack into which he stuffed his victims (2085), and that he bit off their heads and drank their blood like a vampire (742–5). But none of these descriptive details of the monster's nature was known to the original audience when Grendel was described as approaching Heorot. I have suggested elsewhere that it was part of the poet's narrative "design for terror" to describe the monster in intentionally vague terms, so that what approached Heorot was the unknown, and was evoked by the poet in terms

5. Ibid. p. 63; cf. also Robinson's earlier discussion of the same phenomenon, which he then described as "clarifying variation," in "Two Aspects of Variation in Old English Poetry," in *Old English Poetry: Essays on Style*, ed. Calder, pp. 127–45, esp. 130–7, where the following examples from *Beowulf* are cited: 1121–4, 1143–4, 1368–9 (the vague *hæðstapa*, "heath-stalker," is clarified as *heorot*, "hart"), 1522–4, 1745–7, and 1829–35.
6. Like many editors, I suspect that *ellengæst* here is a scribal slip for *ellorgæst*; cf. lines 807, 1349, 1617 and 1621.

suggestive of a nightmare.[7] Here I wish simply to stress that it is only in retrospect that we can form a visual perception of the monster; in prospect, the original audience could not have done so.

Similarly, it is only in retrospect that we learn who Grendel's great adversary is to be. As the fame of Grendel's depredations spread abroad, a thegn of King Hygelac learned of them:

> Þæt fram ham gefrægn   Higelaces þegn
> god mid Geatum,   Grendles dæda (194–5).

Then, from home, Hygelac's thegn, a good (man) among the Geats, learned of Grendel's deeds.

Of course we know, with the benefit of hindsight, that this thegn is Beowulf himself; but the original audience could not have known this. This audience may well have heard of Hygelac, who is attested in contemporary records such as the *Liber monstrorum* (a text composed, on my understanding of the evidence, by a colleague or disciple of Aldhelm at Malmesbury in the early eighth century);[8] but the audience cannot have known of Beowulf since, as we deduce from Scandinavian analogues, Beowulf is a fictional character created by the poet and inserted into a known legendary context. So the anonymous thegn of Hygelac sails from the land of the Geats to Denmark, where on landing he and his men encounter Hrothgar's coastguard, who asks them what sort of warriors they are (237–40). He is told that they are Hygelac's thegns, and that their leader's father was called Ecgtheow (262–3). Again, the audience is none the wiser for this information, since the name Ecgtheow does not occur in sources or analogues outside the poem. Only when the troop of Hygelac's thegns reaches the hall and they are interrogated by the hallguard (Wulfgar) does the audience learn the leader's name: *Beowulf is min nama* (343). Wulfgar reports this name to King Hrothgar, and Hrothgar is able to situate Beowulf in a genealogy and to explain who Ecgtheow was. But it has taken nearly 150 lines for the audience to discover the name and kin of the warrior who has set out to confront Grendel.

7. M. Lapidge, "*Beowulf* and the Psychology of Terror," in *Heroic Poetry in the Anglo-Saxon Period*, ed. Damico and Leyerle, pp. 373–402. The OE word for "nightmare" was *nihtgenga* (literally "night-traveller"); and although the poet does not use this word, he evokes it by describing Grendel as *nihtbealwa mæst* (193), *sceadugenga on niht* (703), and *angenga* (165, 449).

8. M. Lapidge, "*Beowulf*, Aldhelm, the *Liber monstrorum* and Wessex," *Studi medievali* 3rd ser. 23 (1982): 151–92, repr. in *Anglo-Latin Literature, 600–899*, pp. 271–312. The attribution is confirmed by links between the *Liber monstrorum* and the Canterbury glosses: see P. Lendinara, "The *Liber monstrorum* and Anglo-Saxon Glossaries," in her *Anglo-Saxon Glosses and Glossaries* (Aldershot, 1999), pp. 113–38; see also A. Orchard, *Pride and Prodigies: Studies in the Monsters of the Beowulf-Manuscript* (Cambridge, 1995), pp. 86–7.

This pattern of perception—the retrospective movement from the vague and unknown to the qualified and defined—animates the narrative structure of the poem. It is clear that the poet was fascinated by these processes of perception and understanding, and it is for this reason, I think, that he frequently describes events in the poem not from the point of view of an extradiegetic narrator but focalizes them through the characters' own perceptions of the events.[9] For example, the mental perceptions of each of Beowulf's three adversaries are described at the outset of the respective encounters. Thus when Grendel bursts into Heorot and seizes hold of Beowulf, he immediately perceives (*onfunde*)[1] that he has never previously encountered a stronger grip:

> Sona þæt onfunde   fyrena hyrde,
> þæt he ne mette   middangeardes,
> eorþan sceata   on elran men
> mundgripe maran   (750–3).

Immediately he perceived, the keeper of sins, that he had never met, in any corner of the earth, in any other man, a stronger handgrip.

Similarly, as Beowulf swims down through the ghastly mere to confront Grendel's mother, she immediately perceives (*onfunde* again) that someone is invading the abode she has inhabited for a hundred years:

> Sona þæt onfunde   se ðe floda begong
> heorogifre beheold   hund missera,
> grim ond grædig,   þæt þær gumena sum
> ælwihta eard   ufan cunnode   (1497–1500).

Immediately the one who occupied the waters' expanse, bloodthirsty, for 100 years, angry and fierce, perceived that some man was exploring the monsters' lair from above.

And when, at the outset of the chain of events which will bring the poem to its tragic conclusion, the dragon's lair was burgled, the dragon immediately perceived (*onfand*) that someone has tampered with his treasure:

9. A similar observation is made by Kinney, "The Needs of the Moment," pp. 308–9.
1. The verb *onfindan* is Class III strong, with regular preterite singular *onfand*. The form *onfunde* was created on the analogy of weak verbs; see A. Campbell, *Old English Grammar* (Oxford, 1959), §741. Campbell surmises that *onfunde* is a West Saxon form; attestations in the online Corpus of Old English tend to support Campbell's observation: the form is found in *Christ I*, *Beowulf*, Alfred's *Pastoral Care*, the OE *Orosius*, the *Boethius*, Wærferth's translation of Gregory's *Dialogues*, the OE *Bede* and other later texts, including *The Battle of Maldon*.

He þæt sona onfand,
ðæt hæfde gumena sum   goldes gefandod,
heahgestreona   (2300–2).

He immediately perceived that some man had explored his gold,
his excellent treasure.

It is clear from these examples that the *Beowulf*-poet used the
verb *onfindan* to describe the mental process of perception and
intellection: realization, in short. However, the poet carefully dis-
tinguished this mental activity from the physical process of per-
ception, for which he normally used the word *ongi(e)tan*. In
other words, from the extensive Old English vocabulary of per-
ception, the poet has privileged these two words: *onfindan* and
ongi(e)tan. Whereas the mental act of perception and intellection
was connoted by *onfindan*, the physical, mechanical process of
perception through the sense organs, especially seeing or hearing,
was connoted by *ongi(e)tan*, as some examples will illustrate. First,
when Beowulf and the Geats returned home, the boat proceeded
to the point where they could "see" (*ongitan*) the headlands of
Geatland:

fleat famigheals   forð ofer yðe,
bundenstefna   ofer brimstreamas,
þæt hie Geata clifu   ongitan meahton,
cuþe næssas   (1909–12).

The foamy-necked [ship] sailed over the waves, the bound-prowed
[boat], across the currents, until they could see the cliffs of
Geatland, the familiar headlands.

Or in describing the behavior of the sea-monsters in the ghostly mere
when they "heard" the sound of the battle-horn:

Hie on weg hruron
bitere one gebolgne;   bearhtm ongeaton,
guðhorn galan   (1430–2).

They rushed about, furious and enraged; they heard the sound,
the battle-horn wailing.

Or, again, when the Geatish warriors were surrounded in Ravens-
wood by Ongentheow, they "heard" the sound of Hygelac's battle
horn coming to their rescue:

Frofor eft gelamp
sarigmodum   somod ærdæge,

> syððan hie Hygelaces   horn ond byman,
> gealdor ongeaton,   þa se goda com   (2941–4).

Help came for the weary ones at daybreak, when they heard Hygelac's horn and battle-trumpet, when the good man arrived.

Many such examples could be quoted. In any case, the poet's distinction between the physical act of perception and the mental process of intellection is a subtle one, not easily paralleled elsewhere in an Old English text.[2]

In fact the distinction and interaction between the physical process of perception and the mental process of intellection is one which occupied the philosophical schools of antiquity, particularly the Epicureans and Sceptics, and it is worth at least posing the question of whether the *Beowulf*-poet's distinction between *ongi(e)tan* and *onfindan* could have been informed by antique philosophical thought. For practical purposes we may omit Greek philosophical texts such as Plato's *Theaetetus*, the *locus classicus* of ancient epistemology, since no one in Anglo-Saxon England—with the exception of Archbishop Theodore and his colleague Abbot Hadrian—could have read them.[3] Of Latin texts, Lucretius's poem *De natura rerum* contains at one point (IV.478–85) a brief discussion, based on Epicurus, of the validity of sense-perceptions; but the evidence that Lucretius was studied in Anglo-Saxon England is very slight, limited to the quotation of a single line by Aldhelm[4] and some "rather doubtful" parallels of diction between Aldhelm's poetry and that of Lucretius.[5] A more extensive treatment of the distinction between physical and mental processes of perception is found in Cicero's *Academica priora*, where a distinction is drawn between *visa* ("things seen, perceived by the senses") and *comprehensa* ("things understood by the intellect"): in other words, precisely the distinction between *ongi(e)-tan* and *onfindan* drawn by the *Beowulf*-poet. But there is no

---

2. A similar distinction is drawn, but using different vocabulary, in King Alfred's translation of Augustine's *Soliloquia* where, in explaining the process of learning, "Augustine" explains to *Gesceadwisnys* that learning takes place first through the eyes and then with inner thought (*ingeþanc*), since it is the eyes which communicate that which is seen to the inner thought, whence understanding results (*ac siðþan ic hyt þa ongyten hæfde*) (ed. Carnicelli, p. 61). Note that Alfred's use of *ongi(e)tan* here differs significantly from that of the *Beowulf*-poet.

3. On Theodore's philosophical training at Constantinople, see B. Bischoff and M. Lapidge, *Biblical Commentaries from the Canterbury School of Theodore and Hadrian* (Cambridge, 1994), pp. 255–9.

4. *Aldhelmi Opera*, ed. R. Ehwald, MGH, Auctores Antiquissimi (Berlin, 1919), p. 165, line 10 (quoting *De natura rerum* II. 661); note also Ehwald's observation (ibid. n. 1) that Aldhelm very possibly derived the line indirectly from a grammarian such as Nonius Marcellus.

5. A. Orchard, *The Poetic Art of Aldhelm* (Cambridge, 1994), p. 130.

evidence that Cicero's *Academica priora* were ever read in Anglo-Saxon England. By the same token, Augustine's treatise *Contra Academicos*, which is based extensively on Cicero's *Academica priora* and which reproduces much of its argument concerning sense perception, does not appear to have been known in Anglo-Saxon England: there is no surviving pre-Conquest manuscript of the work, and no certain quotation has yet been identified.

I cannot think, in short, that the poet had a literary model for the terminological distinction which he drew between physical perception and mental realization. Rather, the terminological distinction should be understood as a reflex of the poet's interest in narrative perception: the recording and subsequent interpretation of past events, as in the cases of the swimming-match with Breca, or the events at Hrothgar's court later recounted in Geatland, or the varying reports of Hygelac's disastrous last raid. As I have stressed throughout, knowledge in *Beowulf* is always a matter of retrospection and re-interpretation. Present action, heroic or otherwise, is therefore always framed in the awareness of transience, as in the poet's fundamental assertion, repeated by him three times, that Beowulf was the strongest of men "on *that* day of *this* life" (197, 790, 806: *on þæm dæge þysses lifes*)—the implication being that, at a subsequent time, on another day of another life, the situation will inevitably be very different. Events in a hero's life, or indeed in any life, pass quickly, and we are left with nothing more than present perceptions—recollections—of past events. Hence the tone of nostalgia and elegy which pervades the poem. Even our recollections are fragmentary at best, like the varying reminiscences of Hygelac's last raid. I therefore take as a statement of grim and intentional irony the poet's comment, that "understanding is always best, forethought of the mind" (1059–60: *Forþan bið andgit æghwær selest / ferhðes foreþanc*). Forethought or providence—*foreþanc*—is the property of God alone; for man, knowledge can only come, in retrospect, from the re-interpretation of events perceived.[6]

---

6. Cf. the interesting remarks on this subject by L. C. Gruber, "Forethought: The New Weapon in *Beowulf*," *In Geardagum* 12 (1991): 1–14, esp. p. 4: "*Beowulf*'s subject is that of the limitations of human knowledge, of rational and receptive mentality, of human understanding and bestial instinct." The distinction between *providentia* (God's foreknowledge of events) and *fortuna* (man's limited understanding of them) is Boethian, and scholars—in my view—are right to see Boethian influence in the poem; see, for example, W. F. Bolton, "Boethius and a Topos in *Beowulf*," in *Saints, Scholars and Heroes: Studies in Medieval Culture in Honour of Charles W. Jones*, ed. M. H. King and W. M. Stevens, 2 vols. (Collegeville, MN, 1979), I, 15–43.

My argument, in a word, is that the *Beowulf*-poet's mental orientation was philosophical and epistemological,[7] and that this orientation is the explanation for the eccentric and unprecedented nature of the poem's narrative structure. There is no doubt that the poet intended the audience of the poem to reflect, retroactively, on the narrated events and their relationships, during the course of the telling. There can be no doubt, either, that the sophisticated and unprecedented narrative structure of the poem is the work of a highly literate and meditative poet and not the product of impromptu composition by a *scop* or the result of stitching together originally separate lays.[8] For various reasons, however, it is difficult if not impossible for a modern audience to respond adequately to the intention lying behind the narrative structure. The poem's diction is difficult and allusive, and for this reason it is most accessibly taught in excerpts, in situations where the teacher has the opportunity of explaining the context of each excerpt before translation begins: with the result that apprentice-readers usually know what happens in a particular episode before they begin to read it. The only (hypothetical) modern reader who could respond adequately to the poet's intention would be one who had absolute mastery of Old English, but in the process of acquiring this mastery had somehow never heard of Beowulf and who, on beginning to read the poem, did not know who or what Grendel was, or who was the thegn of Hygelac who went to Heorot to confront him: a reader, in short, who lacked *foreþanc* of the poem's events. Of course there can no longer be such a reader. But if, as modern readers, we make the effort to keep constantly in mind the way the events of the poem are meant to be perceived, then the design behind the complex and sophisticated structure of the poet's narrative will become more easily comprehensible.

7. Cf. the interesting remarks on the poet's concern with epistemology by R. Butts, "The Analogical Mere: Landscape and Terror in *Beowulf*," *English Studies* 68 (1987): 113–21, esp. 114 and 118.
8. The distinction between oral and written composition is sharply defined by W. J. Ong, *Orality and Literacy: The Technologizing of the Word* (London and New York, 1982), p. 148: "the writer can subject the unconscious inspiration to far greater conscious control than the oral narrator"; and cf. pp. 141, 145 and 150 ("the very reflectiveness of writing—enforced by the slowness of the writing process as compared to oral delivery as well as by the isolation of the writer as compared to the oral performer—encourages growth of consciousness out of the unconscious"). It is my argument that the *Beowulf*-poet exercised *conscious* and demonstrable manipulation of the text, as illustrated by the intratextual references in lines 1785–90 (discussed above [pp. 246–47]), as well as by the overall structure of the narrative, however unusual this structure might seem by comparison with earlier narrative verse.

ANDREW SCHEIL

"Beowulf" and the Emergent Occasion[†]

The years had passed like a shadow, unnoted, uncounted, and had brought him to this point of pause, of change momentous, when he must needs look before and after.[1]

There is a difference between one and another hour of life, in their authority and subsequent effect. Our faith comes in moments; our vice is habitual. Yet there is a depth in those brief moments which constrains us to ascribe more reality to them than to all other experiences. For this reason, the argument which is always forthcoming to silence those who conceive extraordinary hopes of man, namely, the appeal to experience, is for ever invalid and vain. We give up the past to the objector, and yet we hope.[2]

Change has always been the presiding author of our lives. Whether incremental or swift, unexpected or foreseen, change demarcates our perception of time and time's ongoing narrative expression. As the narrative theorists have long told us, we live according to the narratives that give our lives sense and form, in response to the complex interplay of peripeteia and anagnorisis. Changing circumstances—especially sudden, unexpected changes—stress or rupture our expectations of reality; we respond to the force of emergent occasions, like Donne, by suturing over those breaks, using allegory, myth, metaphor, narratives of tradition and renewal, devotions and prayers of all types, in order to accommodate the "[v]ariable, and therefore miserable condition of Man."[3] It is at those moments of pause and change that human individuality is perhaps felt most keenly; the reverberations of the emergent occasion play about the border between individual lives and their enveloping contexts. *Beowulf* is the earliest text in the English tradition that takes the emergent occasion and its effect on human lives as one of its central concerns. Through its representation of unprecedented change, *Beowulf* deliberates upon the most complex of issues: the formation of human character in the exigency of the changing historical moment. Our poet sets his characters and his audience in a

† From *Literary Imagination* 11.1 (2009): 83–98. © Andrew Scheil 2008. Reprinted by permission of Oxford University Press on behalf of the Association of Literary Scholars and Critics. All rights reserved.

1. George Gissing, *The Whirlpool* (1897; repr. London: The Hogarth Press, 1984), 130.
2. Ralph Waldo Emerson, "The Over-Soul," repr. in *Essays: First Series* in *The Essential Writings of Ralph Waldo Emerson*, ed. Brooks Atkinson (New York: Modern Library, 2000), 236–251, at 236.
3. John Donne, *Devotions Upon Emergent Occasions*, ed. Anthony Raspa (Oxford: Oxford University Press, 1987), 7.

world of secure knowledge and expectations, and then he tracks the complex emotions produced when unexpected change nevertheless falls into inevitable place.[4]

My focus is on those narrative moments when an awareness of imminent change rises to a self-conscious point; when the inevitability of transition gathers itself and the rhetoric of a narrative pauses to survey past, present and future in a moment of temporal narrative simultaneity. What is important here, in other words, is that moment of pause when it is made clear that a nexus of change beckons, or is at hand, or recedes now steadily into the distance of memory. I have in mind those fascinating spaces of suspension and slow time, when the world seems to stand still for a moment before plunging on, that interval, that significant season, to use Frank Kermode's phrase.[5] Just as Macbeth, in his proleptic idiom, periodically stops to ponder his frustrated desire to know the future in the instant, so too the *Beowulf*-poet allows moments of reflection upon the wayward action of time to enter his interwoven narratives.[6] As he stands before the specter of the emergent occasion, Macbeth gives voice to the dreadful entropic energy of causality: "I am in blood / Stepped in so far that, should I wade no more, / Returning were as tedious as go o'er."[7] Our poet is drawn to similar moments of reflection. If, as Michael Lapidge has recently argued, the *Beowulf*-poet is a philosophical poet fascinated by human perception and epistemology, he is also a poet of the concatenation of historical events, a poet of the emergent occasion.[8]

This study will first show the extent of the *Beowulf*-poet's preoccupation with unprecedented change: a fascination with the turn of

---

4. Critics who have addressed the notion of change in the poem usually do so in terms of the poem's "elegiac" dimension, invoking the poet's deployment of the mutability topos. T. A. Shippey's statement that the poem is about "change and the certainty of death and how to balance pessimism with optimism" [*Beowulf* (London: Edward Arnold, 1978), 60] reflects a commonplace in the critical literature that the poem takes fate as its subject.
5. Frank Kermode, *The Sense of an Ending: Studies in the Theory of Fiction* (Oxford: Oxford University Press, 1966), 46.
6. The poet's handling of time has been noted as unusual and distinctive: "Almost no other feature of the poem's composition distinguishes it so clearly from the narrative mode of the folktale or the heroic lay as does its handling of the dimension of time" [John D. Niles, *Beowulf: The Poem and Its Tradition* (Cambridge, MA: Harvard University Press, 1983), 179; see the whole chapter, pp. 179–196]. For important analyses of the poet's use and representation of time see Stanley B. Greenfield, "The Authenticating Voice in *Beowulf*," *Anglo-Saxon England* 5 (1976): 51–72; repr. Stanley B. Greenfield, *Hero and Exile: The Art of Old English Poetry*, ed. George H. Brown (London: The Hambledon Press, 1989), 43–54; John M. Hill, "*Beowulf*, Value, and the Frame of Time," *Modern Language Quarterly* 40 (1979): 3–16; Howell Chickering, "Lyric Time in *Beowulf*," *Journal of English and Germanic Philology* 91 (1992): 489–509; Paul Dean, "*Beowulf* and the Passing of Time," *English Studies* 75 (1994): 103–209 and 293–302.
7. *Macbeth* 3.4.137–9 in *The Complete Works of Shakespeare*, ed. David Bevington, 5th ed. (New York: Longman, 2004).
8. Michael Lapidge, "*Beowulf* and Perception," Sir Israel Gollancz Memorial Lecture, 2000, *Proceedings of the British Academy* 111 (2001): 61–97 [pp. 242–68 of this volume].

events layers the narrative in rich and complex ways, beyond a simple use of the medieval mutability topos. Further, this preoccupation has a studied effect upon the audience (reader or auditor, medieval or modern): it produces a cascade of caesurae, a series of rhetorical pauses as readers and characters within the narrative contemplate the ongoing mystery of contingency and causality in human affairs. In the end I suggest that through this rhetoric of novelty the poet develops a more complex representation of human individuality in the poem than is generally seen in literature of the early Middle Ages. At moments of unprecedented change the poet attempts to give us literary characters seen not as static heroic figures, but rather as complex human lives subject to historical contingency—and even at times self-aware, in a shadowy fashion, of the powerful rhythms of causality. In an early medieval context, such a novel perspective on human individuality points to the idiosyncratic, experimental, and unexpected nature of the poem itself.

I

In the interwoven paths of its entire complex narrative, the *Beowulf*-poet delights in the errant and surprising course of events. Here we see the advantage of the poem's unusually broad temporal scale: as the poet depicts several generations of interrelated lives before and after Beowulf's foregrounded moments of heroic action, this allows him to contextualize the monster fights with a complex web of precedent and outcome, a lattice of historical events as subtle and meditative as the monster fights are bloody and garish. For example, events or characters of little initial promise turn out later to end up very important indeed. Scyld's arrival begins the poem on a note of the unexpected, as does his success as a glorious and powerful king: who would have thought that from such humble beginnings—a foundling adrift on the sea, without family ties—he would grow to such a fearsome prodigy?[9] Beowulf's success in Denmark is perhaps just as unexpected as Scyld's. Hygelac (Beowulf's king) tells us that his young retainer suddenly (*færinga*, 1988a) decided to take up his adventure to Heorot; the Geat king tried to dissuade him, thinking a positive outcome for the journey unlikely (1992b–1997a). Beowulf,

9. Thomas Hill notes the unusual nature of Scyld's success: "It is also significant that Scyld is (on a *de facto* basis) fatherless and motherless, and therefore exists outside of the kinship structure of the people over whom he will rule. This is a very anomalous situation in certain ways. In a traditional society a foundling, who exists apart from the bonds of kinship, is at the nadir of the social structure; in this instance, Scyld Scefing ascends from this humble beginning to the most exalted position within the society which adopted him" ["Scyld Scefing and the 'Stirps Regia': Pagan Myth and Christian Kingship in 'Beowulf,'" in *Magister Regis. Studies in Honor of Robert Earl Kaske*, ed. Arthur Groos with Emerson Brown, Jr., Thomas D. Hill, Giuseppe Mazzota, Joseph Wittig (New York: Fordham University Press, 1986), 37–47, at 39].

after all, is the son of Ecgtheow, a man of uncertain background and formerly on the run for his slaying of Heatholaf and only saved by the intervening, generous hand of Hrothgar. That Beowulf, son of a previously outlawed exile and also a warrior perceived as lazy and timid (*sleac, unfrom,* 2187b, 2188a), not of much account in his youth, surely such a man could not save the Danish kingdom and later even become king of the Geats?[1]

Just as the young Beowulf turns out in the end better than the promise of his youth and paternity might imply, so too does Wiglaf, the young hero left alone at the end of the poem, follow a similar path. The untried Wiglaf helps Beowulf defeat the dragon and the passing of the heroic torch from one generation to the next is nothing surprising; however, Wiglaf also is an unexpected success. Buried in the complex "digressions" of the poem's second half we learn that Wiglaf's father Weohstan was also a man of uncertain background, at least from the Geat perspective: Weohstan fought on the side of the Swedes in their war against the Geats. Weohstan stood with the Swede Onela, the murderous slayer of his own brother, King Ohthere; looking to finish the job of wiping out rivals to the throne, Onela invaded the Geat kingdom searching for the heads of his brother's sons, Eanmund and Eadgils, sheltered by Hygelac's son King Heardred. Onela kills Heardred (in other words, kills Beowulf's lord and king) and Weohstan kills Eanmund and claims his sword as a trophy. Later (in a way left opaque by the poem), Weohstan's son Wiglaf becomes a member of the Geats and is in fact the only retainer to stand by Beowulf against the dragon. Wiglaf kills the beast with Eanmund's sword, handed down as treasured battle-spoil from father to son, the all-important weapon used to pierce the dragon's hide when Beowulf's own sword failed. Who could have predicted that Wiglaf, an untried young warrior in his first rush of battle (2625b–2627), a man whose father was at one time an enemy of the Geats, would turn out to be the one loyal retainer to stand with Beowulf against the dragon and save the Geats from the fire? Apparently our poet wishes to show that heroic salvation can come from unlikely or unpredictable sources across the generations, and that the implications of events can only be seen in a broad historical context.

Conversely, our poem also tracks the unforeseen reverberation of events that are significant at their inception, but twist and turn in

---

1. Adrien Bonjour notes that "Neither [i.e., Scyld or Beowulf] showed the slightest promise of a brilliant future: Scyld was found a wretched and abandoned child (*feasceaft*), and Beowulf is conspicuous for his inglorious youth. Now the interesting point is that in both cases the striking reversal in their fortune is clearly stressed by the poet" [*The Digressions in Beowulf*, Medium Ævum Monographs 5 (Oxford: Oxford University Press, 1965), 5–6].

the years to come in utterly unpredictable ways: the consequences of sheltering exiles, for example. Hrothgar befriends an exiled outlaw named Ecgtheow, pays his *wergild* and befriends him for little apparent reason. Years later, that man's son, Beowulf, arrives to help the king in his moment of greatest need, past and present suddenly meeting. According to the world of medieval heroic narrative, offering shelter to an exile is not an insignificant act; in Hrothgar's case that moment of generosity later made all the difference. But again, in the poem's complex and enigmatic second half we see that similar events have darker outcomes. Heardred, Hygelac's ill-fated son, offers sanctuary to the exiled Swedes Eanmund and Eadgils. As we saw above, that decision does not work out as happily—Hygelac was behind their grandfather Ongentheow's death, giving Onela more than enough reason to invade Geat territory in search of his nephews. Onela kills Heardred (payback for an earlier generation's feud), and allows Beowulf to take up the throne. By sheltering exiles Heardred brings about his own death, but in the larger context his self-destructive actions also clear the way for Beowulf's long, glorious reign, and through the consequent journey of Eanmund's sword from the dead Swedish prince to Wiglaf's hand, ultimately enable the slaying of the dragon. In its interwoven plot, our poem invites us to marvel that, like the ambiguous final destination of Scyld's death ship (50b–52), the final ends of events cannot be clearly seen.

And so, as occasions follow their strange, sometimes ironic course and ripple between past and future, our poem pushes the audience to look backward and forward at the same time, moving between analepsis and prolepsis.[2] In this way the poem dramatizes the hermeneutic circle, when the onset of novelty, the unexpected experience, races back down the corridor of our formerly held perceptions, altering our preunderstanding even as that preunderstanding re-constitutes itself to perceive and understand new, subsequent events. What our poem seems to be drawn to is the immeasurable moment before the hermeneutic circle completes its circuit. The emergent occasion possesses an analeptic/proleptic simultaneity: in the shock of its advent such a moment seems completely unforeseen; it achieves a conceptual and epistemological dissonance as it erupts into the world. But then, in its wake, such an event attains

2. See Edward B. Irving, Jr., *A Reading of Beowulf* (New Haven: Yale University Press, 1968), 199–200, and Lapidge, *"Beowulf* and Perception," 73–74. According to Gerald Prince, *A Dictionary of Narratology* (Lincoln: University of Nebraska Press, 1987), *prolepsis* is an "anachrony going forward to the future with respect to the 'present' moment; an evocation of one or more events that will occur after the 'present' moment (or moment when the chronological recounting of a sequence of events is interrupted to make room for the prolepsis)"; *analepsis* is an "anachrony going back to the past with respect to the 'present' moment, an evocation of one or more events that occurred before the 'present' moment (or moment when the chronological recounting of a sequence of events is interrupted to make room for the analepsis)" (77, 5).

an air of inevitability as the workings of causality become clear and
manifest, and become part of our hermeneutic framework and our
preunderstanding.

But, as the poem delights in showing, preunderstanding and
expectations can be treacherous. *Beowulf* consistently undermines
expected outcomes, as if responding to a certain tragedy of human
epistemology. Precedents describe, if anything, only probability;
preunderstanding is only half of the hermeneutic circle, yet it is the
only half we have access to before the leading edge of experience.
Beowulf constantly dramatizes the unexpected betrayal of precedent
understanding, those startling moments when theory falls before
praxis. For example, old and proven swords such as Hrunting and
Nægling fail for the first time, not biting in their expected manner.
This is not simply mentioned in passing: the poet lingers over these
failures. For example, in a moment of pause he sets up the pedigree
and abilities of Hrunting in detail:

> Næs þæt þonne mætost   mægenfultuma
> þæt him on ðearfe lah   ðyle Hroðgares
> —wæs þæm hæftmece   Hrunting nama—
> þæt wæs an foran   ealdgestreona;
> ecg wæs iren   atertanum fah
> ahyrded heaþoswate;   næfre hi æt hilde ne swac
> manna ængum   þara þe hit mid mundum bewand
> se ðe gryresiðas   gegan dorste
> folcstede fara;   næs þæt forma sið
> þæt hit ellenweorc   æfnan scolde.[3]   (1455–1464)

Nor was that the least powerful help which Hrothgar's spokes-
man lent to him in his need—Hrunting was the name given to
the hilted sword. It was one of the foremost of ancient treasures;
its blade was iron, marked by a poison-weave, tempered in the
blood of battle. Never had it failed any men who held it in hand
during a battle, who dared to undertake dire adventures in the
meeting place of foes. It was not the first time that it would per-
form deeds of courage.

Never had it failed; it was *not* the first time it had succeeded in the
rush of battle. The poet leads his audience to have faith in Hrunt-
ing's power. These details set the imminent failure of the sword in
deeper relief; and in turn, when the sword does fail against Gren-
del's mother, what the poet dwells on is the unprecedented nature
of this failure:

3. All citations from *Beowulf* are from *Beowulf: An Edition*, ed. Bruce Mitchell and Fred C.
Robinson (Oxford: Blackwell, 1998), with macrons removed. Translations throughout
are my own unless otherwise noted.

Ða se gist onfand
þæt se beadoleoma   bitan nolde,
aldre sceþðan   ac seo ecg geswac
ðeodne æt þearfe;   ðolode ær fela
hondgemota,   helm oft gescær
fæges fyrdhrægl;   ða wæs forma sið
deorum madme   þæt his dom alæg.   (1522b–1528)

Then the stranger [i.e., Beowulf] found that the sword would
not bite, harm her life, but the edge failed the prince in his
need. It had previously endured many hand-battles, had often
cut through helm and war-gear of a man marked for death; that
was the first time for the precious treasure that its reputation
failed.

The immediate effect of the failure in context here is heightened
suspense, another turn of the screw: just when things could not get
worse, they do. The repetition of the phrase "in need / at the moment
of need" (*on ðearfe* [1456a], *æt þearfe* [1525a]) connects these two
passages and emphasizes the decisive character of this exceptional
moment. The lines the poet devotes to these moments serve as a
complex analepsis—the moment of sudden collapse gestures back
to all the past moments of triumph in the sword's history.[4]

The failure of swords is representative of a pervasive narrative pat-
tern in the poem: the unexpected and unforeseen nullification of
commonsensical, established knowledge. On one level, for example,
the poet goes to some length to show us startling exceptions to ethi-
cal conventions and assumptions. It is a truism of the poem and early
medieval heroic convention that men will be loyal to their lord if
rewarded and well-led. And so in the poem's prologue, we learn that
Beow was a model young leader, rewarding his household men; the
narrator approves and explains that a leader should be generous and
give freely so that in his old age (*on ylde*, 22a) dear companions (*wil-
gesiþas*, 23a) will stand by him and serve him whenever war comes
(*þonne wig cume*, 23b). This is the theory, and in the second half of
the poem, having been rewarded generously by their king, it is thus
to be expected that Beowulf's *wilgesiþas* should support him bravely
in his final struggle—yet, defying expectations, they do not do so,
when put to the test and the dragon's fire.[5] Further, it is a common-
sense theory that women married off to the right person should
solve the problem of potential or ongoing feud, since the ethical

4. For general discussion of the symbolic significance of Beowulf's arms and armor see
George Clark, "Beowulf's Armor," *ELH* 32 (1965): 409–441; T. A. Shippey's succinct sum-
mary on swords in *Beowulf*, 21–22; Caroline Brady, "'Weapons' in Beowulf: An Analysis
of the Nominal Compounds and an Evaluation of the Poet's Use of Them," *Anglo-Saxon
England* 8 (1979): 79–141.
5. See Wiglaf's words at 2631–2660 and 2862–2891.

prohibitions on kin-slaying ought to inhibit violence. Yet in the world of the poem, its tragic treatment of both Hildeburh and Freawaru argues that this theory, this precedent, will not work. There is another simple, natural axiom in heroic society: kin should not fight each other. And so Wealhtheow posits a future of peace and amity for the next generation of Danish royalty (1180–1191); but the poem implies otherwise: a future of destructive kin-strife (1018b–1019). It is to be expected that kings govern their people according to respected ethical conventions: our poem shows us the exception in Heremod (1709b–1723a). Likewise the customary role for queens is to weave peace and provide a source of social/ethical stability: in a narrative diptych our poet shows us the ideal in Hygd and the exception in Modthryth (1925–1957a), who defies the traditions of queenly femininity, producing terror, not peace. According to all accepted heroic conventions, a good warrior is always ready for anything and will prosper if he follows that precept. Thus although the Danish retainers asleep in Heorot after celebrations following the defeat of Grendel have little apparent reason for fear with the threat removed, nevertheless they are poised for action, as any good troop of warriors should be. The poet goes to some length to tell us that their shields, helmets, mail and spears are all ready to hand as they prepare the hall for sleep "as they always did before" (*swa hie oft ær dydon*, 1238b); it was their custom (*þeaw*, 1246b) to be ready for war anywhere, at home or on the field of battle or anywhere need befell their prince (1248–1250a); such prudence and readiness defines their character: in the narrator's consequent summary judgment, "that was a good nation" (*wæs seo þeod tilu*, 1250b). However, all this surety and admirable adherence to heroic convention is for naught: although common sense tells them they have no monster left to fear, and although they are nevertheless poised for any contingency, their frame of expectation apparently cannot include Grendel's mother—another sudden unanticipated occasion for the characters within the poem and the audience. This interaction between theory and praxis constitutes one of the poet's main concerns; it is evidence for the poem's true claim to an ambitious depth of feeling and affect.

In fact, armed retainers in the poem are often caught in that moment between expectation and unanticipated change. Beowulf's men never seem to predict accurately what will happen, even if their prediction is based on prior experience and common sense. For example, our hero himself is confident when he lays his head to rest in Heorot, waiting for Grendel; he delivers a final boast (*gylpworda sum*, 675b) in which he resolves to fight Grendel barehanded, without weapons. However, as his men join him in sleep, they are not so optimistic:

Nænig heora þohte   þæt he þanon scolde
eft eardlufan   æfre gesecean
folc oþðe freoburh   þær he afeded wæs;
ac hie hæfdon gefrunen   þæt hie ær to fela micles
in þæm winsele   wældeað fornam
Denigea leode. (691–696)

Not one of them thought that he would ever again seek from there his dear home, people or noble city where he had been nurtured; for they had heard that previously murderous death had seized far too many men, folk of the Danes, in the wine-hall.

The precedent is there: *wældeað* has carried off too many men for any reasonable person to expect that this night will be any different; they have all heard the stories. Yet, beyond expectation, this night *is* different: Beowulf triumphs and they do see their homes again.[6]

Likewise, later in the poem, when Grendel's blood wells up out of the mere, the Danes leave in defeat; the dejected Geats cannot quite bring themselves to depart, but nevertheless they do not think their leader will come back:

Gistas sætan
modes seoce   ond on mere staredon,
wiston ond ne wendon   þæt hie heora winedrihten
selfne gesawon.   (1602b–1605a; cf. 1594b–1599)

The strangers sat sick at heart and looked at the mere. They wished—and did not expect—that they would see their lord himself.

Yet they do. The triumph of Beowulf's beheading of Grendel's body below is contrasted with the pessimism and dejection of the men above. In fact, a most wondrous unexpected event is happening below at that very moment—the giant sword blade is melting away like ice. This unexpected wonder below anticipates the marvel to come above when Beowulf breaks the surface of the water and returns.

Nameless retainers are not the only characters who live to experience an elemental moment when their accustomed view of the world suddenly turns out to be hollow and wanting. Beowulf and the dragon both find things turn out very differently than they expect. The dragon has faith in something that has never failed him before; he "had trust in his barrow, in his prowess and in his wall: his expectation deceived him" (*beorges getruwode / wiges ond wealles; him seo wen geleah,* 2322b–2323). We remember this misplaced confidence when, after

6. All the men, that is, except Hondscioh, of course: *requiescat in pace.*

the battle, the Geats look upon the wreck of the creature's once-soaring body; the poet allows a characteristic moment of analeptic reflection to enter his construction of the scene, as he contrasts the freedom and confidence of the "joyous sky" with the earth-bound outcome of the grave:

> lyftwynne heold
> nihtes hwilu,   nyðer eft gewat
> dennes niosian;   wæs ða deaðe fæst,
> hæfde eorðscrafa   ende genyttod. (3043b–3046)

he [the dragon] ruled the joyous sky at night and again went down to seek his lair; then he was held fast in death, he had made his last use of earth-caves.

Similarly, Beowulf thinks an iron shield might provide better protection against the dragon's fire than a wooden one. However, this innovation does not work as well as expected, leading to an unprecedented defeat for the formerly invincible hero:

> Scyld wel gebearg
> life ond lice   læssan hwile
> mærum þeodne   þonne his myne sohte;
> ðær he þy fyrste   forman dogore
> wealdan moste   swa him wyrd ne gescraf
> hreð æt hilde.   (2570b–2575a)

The shield adequately protected the great lord in life and limb for a shorter time than his mind sought; there, on that occasion, for the first time, he had to endure without fate granting him victory in battle.

The poet goes to some lengths to tell us that defeat was not something Beowulf could predict. Beowulf, a tried and proven noble (æþeling ærgod, 2342a), does not fear the dragon because he "previously survived many perils, clashes of battle, daring many a tight place" (ær fela / nearo neðende niða gedigde / hildehlemma, 2349b–2351a).[7] The poet reemphasizes Beowulf's unbeaten previous record:

> Swa he niða gehwane   genesen hæfde
> sliðra geslyhta,   sunu Ecgðiowes,
> ellenweorca   oð ðone anne dæg
> þe he wið þam wyrme   gewegan sceolde.   (2397–2400)

---

7. Emphases added; on ær ("previously, before") and its compounds in the poem, see E. G. Stanley, "Beowulf," Continuations and Beginnings: Studies in Old English Literature, ed. E. G. Stanley (London: Thomas Nelson, 1966), 104–141, at 116.

Thus he, the son of Ecgtheow, had survived every peril, every deed of courage, until that one day in which he would fight with the dragon.

As Andy Orchard notes, "Beowulf's gloriously successful past, the poet makes clear, is no guarantee of his future."[8]

What seems to fascinate the poet are these moments of punctuated novelty, when all the precedents fail to hold ground—a strange and original perspective, in a culture that values the predictability of tradition so highly. The poet thus creates a sense of constant newness, a notion that we are meant to marvel at the sequence of new, unprecedented events unfolding before us. Although these moments certainly serve to develop narrative suspense, their ubiquity in the poem's rhetorical architecture also lends them a progressive significance as the poem moves through its narrative phases.

II

These larger movements of unprecedented change in the poem are further underwritten by a chorus of verbal patterns that emphasize the unprecedented nature of the action. Edward Irving, Jr. has noted the importance of *oðð*æ*t* ("until") as a narrative marker of turnabout in the poem.[9] Another pervasive tactic is the formulaic use of negative assertion: *næfre . . . ær* ("never before") and related expressions.[1] The narrator tells us, for example, that he has *not* heard of a ship more gloriously laden with treasure than Scyld's death ship (38–40a); he has *never* heard of a company of people gathering together in better amity and decorum than the Danes (1011–12); and he has *not* heard of a better necklace than the one Hrothgar presents to Beowulf since Hama carried away the torque of the Brosings (1197–1200a). Reacting to Beowulf's farewell, Hrothgar notes that he has *never* heard such a young man speak so wisely (1842b–1843). In his report to Hygelac, Beowulf tells the assembled Geat court that in Denmark he had *never* seen anywhere under the heavens a happier

8. Andy Orchard, *A Critical Companion to Beowulf* (Cambridge: D. S. Brewer, 2005), 260.
9. For example, lines 99–101. See Irving, *A Reading of Beowulf*, 31–42; T. A. Shippey, *Old English Verse* (London: Hutchinson and Co., 1972), 38; Lapidge, "*Beowulf* and Perception," 63–64.
1. Cf. Irving's close reading of selected passages in *A Reading of Beowulf*, 22–31, where he finds that the "emphatic negative or negative-plus-adversative is often used to express a conflict of wish, hope, or intention with actuality, a conflict, that is, where what someone expects to happen does not happen" (22). For Irving, these recurrent patterns "by their stress on intention and determination, keep before us the typical preoccupation of epic poetry with the will. Usually they offer a perspective on 'fate' as being fundamentally a will-blocking force indifferent to the wishes of the characters, and often they bring out the complex role of the hero in cooperating with fate or serving as fate's agent" (31). My emphasis here is not on the expression of the heroic will, but on this pattern as an example of a broader dynamic: the poem's complex exploration of change and causality.

people (2014b–2016a). When he challenges Beowulf and his men, the Danish coast-guard says that an armed company has *never* approached Hrothgar's realm so brashly, and *never* has he seen a more impressive sight than their leader (244–248); Wulfgar, the hall-guard of Heorot, echoes the trope, declaring that he has *never* seen so many strangers arrive in such a bold fashion (336b–337); and on the eve of the great battle, Hrothgar tells his court that he has *never* handed keeping of Heorot over to any other man. Deeding such responsibility to a stranger—or anyone—is an unprecedented act, as Hrothgar himself makes clear:

> Næfre ic ænegum men   ær alyfde,
> siþðan ic hond ond rond   hebban mihte,
> ðryþærn Dena   buton þe nu ða. (655–657)

Never before, since I could lift hand and shield, have I entrusted to any man the mighty hall of the Danes, except now to you.

These repeated uses of "næfre" have a cumulative effect—they embellish the poem's narrative patterns of defeated expectations detailed above and together generate an unusual pervasive atmosphere of uncertainty.

The narrator expresses the monsters' experience in the same way. For example, as Grendel approaches Heorot to meet his doom, the poet tells us that it was not the first time the monster had sought the hall; thus he has the expectation of an extensive feast (*wistfylle wen*, 734a), and why should his expectation be any different this time?

> Ne wæs þæt forma sið
> þæt he Hroðgares   ham gesohte;
> næfre he on aldordagum   ær ne siþðan
> heardran hæle   healðegnas fand.   (716b–719)

Nor was that the first time that he sought the home of Hrothgar; never before or after, in all the days of his life, did he find hall-thanes with harder luck.

When he reaches for his next victim and instead finds Beowulf, this celebrated moment delights in its unprecedented reversal:

> Sona þæt onfunde   fyrena hyrde
> þæt he ne mette   middangeardes
> eorþan sceata   on elran men
> mundgripe maran,   he on mode wearð
> forhte on ferhðe. . . .   (750–753a)

As soon as the keeper of crimes found that he had never met a greater handgrip in another man in middle-earth, anywhere in the world, he became terrified in his mind and spirit. . . .

The poet summarizes, dwelling further upon the moment: "Nor was his predicament there like any he had ever before met in the days of his life" (*ne wæs his drohtoð þær / swylce he on ealderdagum ær gemette*, 756b–757).

The poet also tells us that the Danes marveled that the hall withstood the violent forces inside it, and that he has heard that many mead benches were overturned in the fight. He has told us that it was a great wonder that the hall held together in the first place, and that was only due to the skill of the smiths who had bound it in iron. Yet the Danes nevertheless marvel at the unprecedented damage:

> Þær fram sylle abeag
> medubenc monig   mine gefræge
> golde geregnad   þær þa graman wunnon.
> Þæs ne wendon ær   witan Scyldinga,
> þæt hit a mid gemete   manna ænig
> betlic ond banfag   tobrecan meahte,
> listum tolucan   nymþe liges fæþm
> swulge on swaþule.   (775b–782a)

I have heard tell that many a mead-bench there adorned with gold was overturned on the floor where the angry ones fought. Concerning that the wise men of the Scyldings never before thought that any man ever, in any way, could break it, magnificent and horn-adorned, destroy it by cunning, unless the embrace of flames should swallow it in fire.

The emphasis on contingency generated by these phrasal patterns help intensify and unite the other disparate unexpected/unprecedented events that occur at different points in the narrative. As the experience of the poem unfolds in time for reader or auditor, the constant interplay of contingency and causality conditions the meaning of the poem's narrative for the human lives caught up in the events. From this perspective human decisions seem both more and less important at the same time as the broader defining context of historical change inflects the characters' lives and circumstances.

As if to punctuate this pervasive rhetoric of novelty, the rare nouns *edwenden* and *edhwyrft* (both meaning "turnabout or change in fortune") occur at important narrative moments, as is well known.[2] Beowulf explains to the coast-guard that Hrothgar must accept Beowulf's help if the king is ever to find *edwenden* (277b–285, at 280a).

---

2. * * * For discussion of *edwenden* and *edhwyrft* see Shippey, *Old English Verse*, 38–41; Phyllis R. Brown, "Cycles and Change in *Beowulf*," *Manuscript, Narrative, Lexicon: Essays on Literary and Cultural Transmission in Honor of Whitney F. Bolton*, ed. Robert Boenig and Kathleen Davis (Lewisburg: Bucknell University Press, 2000), 171–192, at 183–186.

The narrator describes the sudden attack of Grendel's mother upon the sleeping Danes as an *edhwyrft* (1280b–1282a, at 1281a). In his central speech upon contemplation of the giant sword-hilt from Grendel's lair, Hrothgar explains how he ruled the Danes joyfully for fifty years, until Grendel brought *edwenden* upon him in his hall (1774–1778a, at 1774b).

Finally, Beowulf returns home and the narrator tells us, in a lingering framed moment of pause and transition, that his great deeds have brought him *edwenden* in his life:

> Swa bealdode   bearn Ecgðeowes
> guma guðum cuð   godum dædum,
> dreah æfter dome,   nealles druncne slog
> heorðgeneatas;   næs him hreoh sefa
> ac he mancynnes   mæste cræfte
> ginfæstan gife   þe him god sealde,
> heold hildedeor.   Hean wæs lange
> swa hyne Geata bearn   godne ne tealdon
> ny hyne on medobence   micles wyrðne
> drihten wereda   gedon wolde;
> swyðe wendon   þæt he sleac wære,
> æðeling unfrom.   Edwenden cwom
> tireadigum menn   torna gehwylces.   (2177–2189)

And so the son of Ecgtheow showed himself brave, a man renowned for his good deeds in battle, one who strove for glory. He slew no drunken hearth-companions, nor was his spirit wild, but instead he, a man brave in the fight, held fast the great gift God had given him, by means of the greatest strength among mankind. He had been long despised, so that the children of the Geats considered him no good, nor would the lord of hosts do him much honor on the mead-bench. They very much thought that he was lazy, a timid noble. Change came to the glorious man for each of his troubles.

A few lines later the scene will suddenly shift to Beowulf years hence, an old man ready for his last battle, while the word *edwenden* is still echoing in our minds. At this point, the transition from the first part of the poem to the second part (2200–2214a), which leaves out all the tumultuous events that led to Beowulf's assumption of the throne, is itself sudden and unexpected.[3] We later learn, through

3. Stanley Greenfield observes: "The poet ignores his long reign as king, quickly switching from youthful achievements in Denmark to his last exploit in his native land—a technical movement whose very swiftness and suddenness suggests the brevity of life" ["*Beowulf* and Epic Tragedy," *Comparative Literature* 14 (1962): 91–105; repr. Stanley B. Greenfield, *Hero and Exile: The Art of Old English Poetry*, ed. George H. Brown (London: The Hambledon Press, 1989), 3–17 at 14].

flashback, the detailed events that led to Beowulf's (unexpected) kingship, but the transition here highlights the crossroads, when Beowulf's life went one way, and not another.

However, it is not simply that "unexpected things" happen in the poem—that could be an element of any narrative with any sort of plot or suspense. Rather, part of our poet's narrative sensibility in the way he tracks events as they unfold is to frame these unprecedented changes in various ways, dwelling upon the pause of events as they heave to and change direction. In these large and small caesurae, the poem enables a subtle and complex view of human character. For example, when Hrothgar learns of the new attack from Grendel's mother, Beowulf is summoned and the poem gives us a studied and moving turning-point passage, a moment of paused transition:

> Þa wæs frod cyning
> har hilderinc   on hreon mode
> syðþan he aldorþegn   unlyfigendne
> þone deorestan   deadne wisse.
> Hraþe wæs to bure   Beowulf fetod
> sigoreadig secg.   Samod ærdæge
> code eorla sum   æþele cempa
> self mid gesiðum   þær se snotera bad
> hwæþer him alwalda   æfre wille
> æfter weaspelle   wyrpe gefremman.   (1306b–1315)

Then the old king, the grey warrior, was tormented in mind after he knew that his chief thane was without life, his dearest man dead. Quickly Beowulf was brought to the chamber, the warrior happy in victory. At daybreak the noble champion himself went, one man with his companions, to where the wise one waited to know whether the all-ruler would ever bring him change after tales of woe.

Using simultaneous points of view, the poet highlights the contrast between Beowulf and Hrothgar at this moment of pause: as he strides to the summons, Beowulf is content in his victory belonging to the world before the advent of Grendel's mother; but waiting on the other side of that divide Hrothgar is tormented in mind, knowing that a new threat has appeared.[4] By juxtaposing the inner mental

4. Cf. Louis Mink: "Anticipation and retrospection are not simply different attitudes or vantage points which may be taken (or must be taken) toward the same event or course of events. . . . at least in the case of human actions and changes, to know an event by retrospection is categorically, not incidentally, different from knowing it by prediction or anticipation. It cannot even, in any strict sense, be called the 'same' event. . . ." ("History and Fiction as Modes of Comprehension," *New Literary History* 1 (1970): 541–558; repr Louis Mink, *Historical Understanding*, ed. Brian Fay, Eugene O. Golob, and Richard T. Vann (Ithaca: Cornell University Press, 1987): 42–60, at 48.

states of two characters linked in a moment of pregnant pause, the poet dramatizes the effect of sudden change in the world at the level of human lives.

In some ways these moments of pause are related to what Howell Chickering defines as the "lyric sonorities" of the poem.[5] In these moments of dilation (to borrow Chickering's phrase for a different use), the poet pauses to show his characters brooding upon the sudden changes in the world around them; in this way he makes concrete and particular the more abstract movements, puzzles, ironies, and enigmas of history and causality.[6] As a way to make experience concrete, the poet is interested in individuals and how they react to unprecedented historical change.[7] Hrothgar ponders his lot with heavy emotion during Grendel's reign, again when he gazes upon Grendel's arm fixed on high, and most famously, after he looks upon the giant sword hilt. Hygelac feels the surge of emotion about his heart when Beowulf suddenly departs for Denmark, fearing the outcome (1992b–1998). Hengest and the Last Survivor both meditate upon the world and its random ways (1127b–1145, 2236b–2270a). Beowulf experiences this same emotion surging up upon the sudden attack of the dragon and the news of his home's destruction (2327b–2332).

We find this sad evocation of the individual life placed against the forces of history in one of the narrator's summary comments upon Beowulf's death:

> Wundur hwar þonne
> eorl ellenrof   ende gefere
> lifgesceafta   þonne leng ne mæg
> mon mid his magum   meduseld buan.

---

5. Chickering, "Lyric Time," *passim*. He also calls these "moments of dilation" (500); they are the "very sharpest kind of poetic *aperçu*, a sort of lyric shock in which the mental music of pattern and significance reaches beyond the sound of words into silent wondering contemplation" (501). Cf. also Clare Kinney's narrative analysis of moments of foregrounding in the poem: "The Needs of the Moment: Poetic Foregrounding as a Narrative Device in *Beowulf*," *Studies in Philology* 82 (1985): 295–314. Where I differ from Chickering's study is that he sees this effect as essentially an Augustinian cultural construct; I do not see such an explicit theological connection.

6. Cf. Peter Clemoes, "Action in *Beowulf* and Our Perception of It," *Old English Poetry: Essays on Style*, ed. Daniel G. Calder (Berkeley: University of California Press, 1979), 147–168, at 160: "The poet's predominant interest is how a person's actions successively characterize him and how these actions relate to the forces within him, to the forces that act through or on him, and to the forces that he acts on." Robert Hanning also sees the poem as "pondering the place of individual achievement within the dynamic process of history" ("*Beowulf* and Heroic History," 79). I have treated the subject of the poem's fundamental affiliation with historiography in "The Historiographic Dimensions of *Beowulf*," *Journal of English and Germanic Philology* 107.3 (2008): 281–302.

7. Orchard, *Companion*, 173: "In many ways, the *Beowulf*-poet reveals himself to be less concerned with the actions of his characters than with their reactions to what is being done both to them and around them." For a similar point see Håkan Ringbom, *Studies in the Narrative Technique of Beowulf and Lawman's Brut* (Åbo: Åbo Akademi, 1968): "It is a general trend for the *Beowulf* poet to elaborate on one particular situation: he adds depth to his narrative by revealing the characters' motives, their states of mind and emotion" (32).

Swa wæs Biowulfe   þa he biorges weard
sohte searoniðas,   seolfa ne cuðe
þurh hwæt his worulde gedal   weorðan sceolde.
(3062b–3068)

It is, then, a mystery where a brave man may reach the destined
end of his life, when a man can no longer dwell in the mead-
hall with his kin. So it was with Beowulf when he sought out
the guardian of the mound, devious hostilities—he himself
did not know in what way his parting from the world would
come.

In all of these cases, events take a changing path few might have
expected or predicted; the poet presents the human significance of
these actions. Moreover, as it constructs these narrative reflections,
the narrator's voice is not always clearly consistent in intent; these
moments of narrative pause are not simply or uniformly expressed
as "transience" or "mutability," or consistently presented through-
out the poem in accordance with any obvious dogma. What we can
say is this: the poet finds his depth in the moments of pause, when the
past feeds the present and opens up to the future. Something in
the way the narrator presents these scenes, shuttling back and forth
between enigmatic objectivity and hortatory comment, creates a
complex narrative effect, a rich and subtle emotional response that
we do not serve justly when we simply term it "fatalistic" or "elegiac"
or an expression of the *lif biþ læne* ("life is transitory") theme.[8] The
poet is peculiarly interested in consigning the reader to the complex
dialectic movement of peripeteia and anagnorisis; that is, he places
the reader/auditor in a state in which "a disconfirmation [is] followed

8. Almost every thematic or interpretive study of *Beowulf* seems to discuss mutability at
some point. For a representative account see Theodore M. Andersson, "Tradition and
Design in *Beowulf*," *Old English Literature in Context: Ten Essays*, ed. John D. Niles
(Cambridge: D. S. Brewer, 1980), 90–106 and 171–172; reprinted in *Interpretations of
Beowulf: A Critical Anthology*, ed. R. D. Fulk (Bloomington: Indiana University Press,
1991), 219–234; he concludes that "*Beowulf* is a kind of *memento mori* dwelling insis-
tently on the transitoriness of earthly things" (232). For a wide-ranging discussion of
this theme in *Beowulf* and other texts see John C. Pope, "The Existential Mysteries as
Treated in Certain Passages of Our Older Poets," *Acts of Interpretation: The Text in its
Contexts, 700–1600: Essays on Medieval and Renaissance Literature in Honor of E. Talbot
Donaldson*, ed. Mary J. Carruthers and Elizabeth D. Kirk (Norman, OK: Pilgrim Books,
1982), 345–362. In addition, many critics see a specifically Christian understanding of
mutability underwriting the cycle of rise and fall in the poem: see Martin Green, "Man,
Time, and Apocalypse in *The Wanderer, The Seafarer*, and *Beowulf*," *Journal of English
and Germanic Philology* 74 (1975): 502–518; reprinted in *Old English Shorter Poems: Basic
Readings*, ed. Katherine O'Brien O'Keeffe (NY: Garland Press, 1994), 281–302; Richard J.
Schrader, *Old English Poetry and the Genealogy of Events* (East Lansing, MI: Michigan
State University Press, 1993); Dean, "*Beowulf* and the Passing of Time"; Chickering,
"Lyric Time in *Beowulf*"; Brown, "Cycles and Change in *Beowulf*"; and so forth. In con-
trast, see Edward B. Irving, Jr.'s careful assessment of arguments about the poem's
Christianity that lean too heavily upon conjectural contexts exterior to the poem: "The
Nature of Christianity in *Beowulf*," *Anglo Saxon England* 13 (1984): 7–21, esp. his
conclusion 20–21.

by a consonance."[9] As Kermode further explains, the "end comes as expected, but not in the manner expected."[1] This dialectic makes *Beowulf* an intellectually demanding, "participatory" poem, requiring much from its readers, as others have noted.[2]

The poem does not provide us with definitive answers to these and similar dilemmas; that is, in fact, part of the poem's intent—to elaborate a sharp view of human lives in history, a view that in the end resists full assimilation to sentiment or dogma of any sort.[3] The poet's construction of human character through these artful ambiguities destabilizes any systematic apprehension of humanity's place in the world; instead, the poet creates an "abiding mystery" set between contingency and causality, an innovative *narrative* construction and apprehension of character.[4] In its meditations upon the emergent occasion, "unprevented for all our diligence, unsuspected for all our curiosity,"[5] *Beowulf* dramatizes the changing shape of human lives in response to fortune and fluctuating circumstances. The poet shows us man in time, *homo historicus*, man the political animal caught in the entropy of time and change. In the end, when the complex voices in *Beowulf* are weighed one against the other, the varied pronouncements of our narrator against the overall action and its final ambiguities, we find that this most puzzling and unexpected of poems offers no easy answers—only a stark, enigmatic view of time, history, and change.

9. Kermode, *Sense of an Ending*, 18.
1. Kermode, *Sense of an Ending*, 53.
2. As Alvin Lee explains: "It is a poem whose imagining remains incomplete, both for those early people and for us. As in a kenning or a riddle, the audience and we are told all we need to be, but we are not told everything" [*Gold-Hall and Earth-Dragon: Beowulf as Metaphor* (Toronto: University of Toronto Press, 1998), 116].
3. Cf. Helen Vendler's meditation upon the never-tidy closure of the philosophical reflections a poet engages in when ideas are committed to poetic form: "It is probably true to say that no great poem leaves us without a lasting sense of its conflicting passions, even if it tends to end in 'perfection,' or announces—to cite Milton's most violent work—that 'nothing is here for tears.' Poetic thinking cannot, and does not, obliterate or disavow the reflections it engages in en route to its arrival at a 'solution'" [*Poets Thinking: Pope, Whitman, Dickinson, Yeats* (Cambridge, MA: Harvard University Press, 2004), 108].
4. The quoted phrase is borrowed from Robert Alter's analysis of the techniques of biblical narrative: "We are compelled [in biblical narrative] to get at character and motive, as in Impressionist writers like Conrad and Ford Madox Ford, through a process of inference from fragmentary data, often with crucial pieces of narrative exposition strategically withheld, and this leads to multiple or sometimes even wavering perspectives on the characters. There is, in other words, an abiding mystery in character as the biblical writers conceive it, which they embody in their typical methods of presentation" [*The Art of Biblical Narrative* (New York: Basic Books, 1981), 126]. Cf. Erich Auerbach, *Mimesis: The Representation of Reality in Western Literature*, trans. Willard Trask (Princeton: Princeton University Press, 1953), 12.
5. Donne, *Devotions Upon Emergent Occasions*, 7.

Glossary of Personal Names

Many Old English names are compounds in which the meaning of each element would be obvious to native speakers. In the case of "Dæg-hrefn," for example, Heaney translates each part into "Day-raven," which gives an idea how the Anglo-Saxons would understand it. But the regular practice in this translation is to leave the Old English names in much the same form as they are in the original poem. The glossary given here does not translate the names either, but it divides the compounds into their component parts. For Beowulf's name, see pp. 105–07.

Hints for pronunciation: the letter combinations <ae> and <sc> are both illustrated in the name Aesc-here, pronounced "ASH-hair-eh." The pronunciation of <cg> as found in Ecg-laf is "EDGE-lahf." Initial <h> as in Hreth-ric is always pronounced, and final <c> has the value illustrated in "HRETH-rich." For every name the strongest accent falls on the first syllable, and final-*e* is never silent. For the finer points of pronunciation, consult any Old English grammar.

For names of the tribes and geographical regions, consult pp. 103–05.

Abel   brother of Cain; for the story see Genesis 4.1–16 (pp. 90–91)
Aelf-here   kinsman of Wiglaf
Aesc-here   beloved adviser to Hrothgar
Beow   an early Danish king, son of Shield
Beowulf   son of Ecgtheow, later king of the Geats
Breca   Bronding leader, competed with Beowulf in a swimming match
Cain   brother of Abel, progenitor of Grendel and his mother
Day-raven   a warrior killed by Beowulf in Hygelac's raid into Frisia
Ead-gils   a Swedish prince, son of Ohthere, befriended by Beowulf
Ean-mund   another son of Ohthere, killed by Weohstan
Ecg-laf   a Dane, father of Unferth
Ecg-theow   father of Beowulf
Ecg-wela   an early, unknown Danish king
Eofor   a Geat who killed the Swedish king Ongentheow
Eo-mer   a son of Offa, king of the Angles
Eormen-ric   king of the East Goths
Finn   king of the Frisians, married to Hnaef's sister Hildeburh
Fitela   nephew *and* son of Sigemund
Folc-wald   father of Finn

Frea-waru   daughter of Hrothgar
Gar-mund   father of Offa
Grendel   monstrous cannibal killed by Beowulf
Guth-laf   a Danish warrior
Haereth   father of Hygd
Haeth-cyn   second son of the Geatish king Hrethel
Half-dane   father of the Danish king Hrothgar
Halga   younger brother of the Danish king Hrothgar
Heard-red   son of King Hygelac, later king of the Geats
Heatho-laf   a warrior of the Wulfing tribe
Hemming   a relative of Offa and Eomer
Hengest   the leader of the Danish party after Hnaef is killed by Finn's
   men
Heoro-gar   older brother of Hrothgar, a Danish king
Heoro-weard   son of Heorogar
Here-beald   oldest son of the Geatish king Hrethel
Here-mod   a king of the Danes
Hilde-burh   wife of the Frisian king Finn, sister of the Dane Hnaef
Hnaef   leader of the Danes visiting Finn, brother of Hildeburh
Hoc   father of Hildeburh and Hnaef
Hond-scio   one of Beowulf's companions, killed by Grendel
Hrethel   king of the Geats, Hygelac's father, grandfather of Beowulf
Hreth-ric   son of Hrothgar
Hroth-gar   king of the Danes, husband of Wealhtheow
Hroth-mund   son of Hrothgar
Hroth-ulf   son of Halga, nephew of Hrothgar
Hrunting   Unferth's sword
Hun-lafing   a Danish warrior in Hengest's party
Hygd   wife of Hygelac, daughter of Haereth
Hyge-lac   king of the Geats, husband of Hygd, uncle of Beowulf
Ing   a mythical ancestor of the Danes
In-geld   a prince of the Heatho-Bards
Mod-thryth   queen of the Angles, wife of Offa
Naegling   Beowulf's sword
Offa   king of the Angles, husband of Modthryth
Oht-here   son of the Swedish king Ongentheow
Onela   king of the Swedes, son of Ongentheow
Ongen-theow   king of the Swedes
Os-laf   a Danish warrior
Shield   a legendary king, founder of the Danish royal family
Sige-mund   a legendary Germanic hero
Swerting   grandfather of Hygelac
Un-ferth   a member of Hrothgar's court
Wael   father of Sigemund
Wealh-theow   queen of the Danes, wife of Hrothgar
Weland   a mythical Germanic smith, famous for weapons
Weoh-stan   father of Wiglaf, killer of Eanmund
Wig-laf   a relative and follower of Beowulf

Wither-geld   a Heatho-Bard warrior
Won-red   a Geat, father of Wulf and Eofor
Wulf   a Geatish warrior
Wulf-gar   a Wendel chief attached to Hrothgar's court
Yrmen-laf   a Dane, brother of Aeschere

Selected Bibliography

The items have been chosen primarily for students approaching *Beowulf* for the first time using Heaney's translation. The number of books and articles published on *Beowulf* is vast and growing, most of it presupposing a detailed knowledge of the Old English language, but the selection here privileges those studies that can be profitably used by nonspecialists, and it includes reference works and general histories of pre-Conquest England. The bibliographies given here offer a comprehensive listing for those who wish to pursue further study. Students interested in studying the original poem are encouraged to enroll in an Old English course, because even with the high quality of the grammars, editions, and reference works given here, the language of *Beowulf* is old enough that it needs to be learned as a foreign language. A final selection of writings by Seamus Heaney helps put his translation of *Beowulf* in the context of his career as a poet.

EDITIONS AND TRANSLATIONS

Chickering, Howell D., trans. and ed. *Beowulf: A Dual-Language Edition.* Garden City, NY: Anchor Books, 1977.

Clark Hall, John R., trans. and C. L. Wrenn, ed. *Beowulf and the Finnesburg Fragment: A Translation into Modern English Prose.* Rev. ed. London: Allen & Unwin, 1950.

Donaldson, E. Talbot, trans. *Beowulf: A Norton Critical Edition.* 2nd ed. Ed. Nicholas Howe. New York: Norton, 1998. [Donaldson/Howe]

Fulk, R. D., ed. *The Beowulf Manuscript: Complete Texts and the Fight at Finnsburg,* Dumbarton Oaks Medieval Library 3. Cambridge: Harvard University Press, 2010. [*Klaeber's Beowulf*]

Fulk, R. D., Robert E. Bjork, and John D. Niles, eds. *Klaeber's Beowulf and the Fight at Finnsburg.* Toronto Old English Series 21. 4th ed. Toronto: U of Toronto P, 2008. [The standard critical edition.]

Heaney, Seamus, trans., and John D. Niles, ed. *Beowulf: An Illustrated Edition.* New York: Norton, 2007.

Jack, George, ed. *Beowulf: A Student Edition.* Oxford: Oxford University Press, 1994.

Kiernan, Kevin, ed., and Ionut Emil Iacob, programmer. *Electronic Beowulf 4.0.* http://ebeowulf.uky.edu/ebeo4.0/start.html.

Liuzza, Roy Michael, trans. *Beowulf: A New Verse Translation.* 2nd ed. Peterborough, Ont.: Broadview, 2012.

Mitchell, Bruce and Fred C. Robinson, eds. *Beowulf: An Edition.* Oxford: Blackwell, 1998.

Morgan, Edwin, trans. *Beowulf: A Verse Translation into Modern English*. Manchester, UK: Carcanet, 2002.

Tolkien, J. R. R., and Alan J. Bliss, eds. *Finn and Hengest: The Fragment and the Episode*. London: Allen & Unwin, 1982.

Tolkien, J. R. R., ed. and trans., and Christopher Tolkien, ed. *Beowulf: A Translation and Commentary Together with Sellic Spell*. Boston: Houghton Mifflin Harcourt, 2014. [See especially the "Commentary," pp. 137–353, which includes excerpts from Tolkien's lectures.]

BIBLIOGRAPHIES

Annual bibliographies are compiled by two journals: *Anglo-Saxon England* and *The Old English Newsletter*.

Greenfield, Stanley B., and Fred C. Robinson. *A Bibliography of Publications on Old English Literature to the End of 1972*. Toronto: University of Toronto Press, 1980.

Hasenfratz, Robert J. *Beowulf Scholarship: An Annotated Bibliography, 1979–1990*. New York: Garland, 1993. [Supplements Short's bibliography.]

Sauer, Hans, and Julia Hartmann. *205 Years of Beowulf Translations and Adaptations (1805–2010): A Bibliography*. Trier, Germany: Wissenschaftlicher Verlag Trier, 2011.

Short, Douglas D. *Beowulf Scholarship: An Annotated Bibliography*. New York: Garland, 1980. [Supplemented by Hasenfratz up to 1990.]

REFERENCE WORKS AND GRAMMARS

Cassidy, Frederic G., and Richard N. Ringler. *Bright's Old English Grammar and Reader*. 3rd ed. Fort Worth: Harcourt Brace Jovanovich, 1971.

Dolan, T. P. *A Dictionary of Hiberno-English*. Dublin: Gill & Macmillan, 1998.

Fulk, R. D., ed. *An Introductory Grammar of Old English with an Anthology of Readings*. Tempe: Arizona Center for Medieval and Renaissance Studies, 2014.

Fulk, R. D., and Christopher M. Cain. *A History of Old English Literature*. 2nd ed. Chichester: Wiley-Blackwell, 2013.

Garmonsway, G. N., Jacqueline Simpson, and H. E. Davidson, eds. *Beowulf and Its Analogues*. London: Dent, 1980.

Hall, J. R. Clark, and Herbert Dean Meritt. *A Concise Anglo-Saxon Dictionary*. 4th ed. Toronto: U of Toronto P in association with the Medieval Academy of America, 1984.

Hill, David. *An Atlas of Anglo-Saxon England*. Toronto: U of Toronto P, 1981.

Lapidge, Michael; with John Blair, Simon Keynes, and Donald Scragg. *The Blackwell Encyclopedia of Anglo-Saxon England*. Oxford: Blackwell, 1999.

Mitchell, Bruce, and Fred C. Robinson. *A Guide to Old English*. 8th ed. Oxford: Wiley-Blackwell, 2012.

Quirk, Randolph, C. L. Wrenn, and Susan E. Deskis. *An Old English Grammar*. DeKalb: Northern Illinois U P, 1994.

Strayer, Joseph R., et al. *Dictionary of the Middle Ages*. New York: Scribner, 1982.

Szarmach, Paul E., M. Teresa Tavormina, and Joel Thomas Rosenthal, eds. *Medieval England: An Encyclopedia*. Garland Reference Library of the Humanities. New York: Garland, 1998.

Whitelock, Dorothy, ed. *English Historical Documents*. Vol. I: *c. 500–1042*. 2nd ed. London: Routledge, 1979.

COLLECTIONS OF CRITICAL ESSAYS

Baker, Peter S., ed. *Beowulf: Basic Readings*. New York: Garland, 1995. [Baker, *Basic Readings*]

Benson, Larry Dean. *Contradictions: From Beowulf to Chaucer: Selected Studies of Larry D. Benson*. Ed. T. M. Andersson and Stephen A. Barney. Aldershot, UK: Scolar Press, 1995. [Benson, *Contradictions*]

Bjork, Robert E., and John D. Niles, ed. *A Beowulf Handbook*. Lincoln: U of Nebraska P, 1997. [Bjork, *Handbook*]

Bloom, Harold. *Beowulf*. Bloom's Modern Critical Interpretations. Updated ed. New York: Chelsea House, 2007.

Chase, Colin, ed. *The Dating of Beowulf*. Repr. with a new Afterword. Toronto: U of Toronto P, 1997.

Chickering, Howell D., Allen J. Frantzen, and Robert F. Yeager, eds. *Teaching Beowulf in the Twenty-First Century*, Medieval and Renaissance Texts and Studies 449. Tempe: Arizona Center for Medieval and Renaissance Studies, 2014. [Chickering, *Teaching Beowulf*]

Creed, Robert P., ed. *Old English Poetry: Fifteen Essays*. Providence, RI: Brown U P, 1967. [Creed, *Fifteen Essays*]

Damico, Helen, and Alexandra Hennessey Olsen, eds. *New Readings on Women in Old English Literature*. Bloomington: Indiana U P, 1990. [Damico/Olsen]

Damico, Helen, and John Leyerle, eds. *Heroic Poetry in the Anglo-Saxon Period: Studies in Honor of Jess B. Bessinger, Jr.* Kalamazoo, MI: Medieval Institute Publications, 1993. [Damico/Leyerle]

Fry, Donald K. *The Beowulf Poet: A Collection of Critical Essays*. Twentieth Century Views. Englewood Cliffs, NJ: Prentice-Hall, 1968. [Fry, *Collection*]

Fulk, R. D. *Interpretations of Beowulf: A Critical Anthology*. Bloomington: Indiana U P, 1991. [Fulk, *Interpretations*]

Godden, Malcolm, and Michael Lapidge. *The Cambridge Companion to Old English Literature*. 2nd ed. Cambridge: Cambridge U P, 2013. [Godden, *Companion*]

Hill, John M., ed. *On the Aesthetics of Beowulf and Other Old English Poems*, Toronto Anglo-Saxon Series 6. Toronto: U of Toronto P, 2010. [Hill, *Aesthetics*]

Joy, Eileen A., Mary K. Ramsey, and Bruce D. Gilchrist. *The Postmodern Beowulf: A Critical Casebook*. Morgantown: West Virginia U P, 2006.

Neidorf, Leonard, ed. *The Dating of Beowulf: A Reassessment*, Anglo-Saxon Studies 24. Cambridge: Brewer, 2014.

Nicholson, Lewis E., ed. *An Anthology of Beowulf Criticism*. Notre Dame, IN: U of Notre Dame P, 1963. [Nicholson, *Anthology*]

Robinson, Fred C. *The Tomb of Beowulf and Other Essays on Old English*. Oxford: Blackwell, 1993. [Robinson, *Tomb*]

Schulman, Jana K., and Paul E. Szarmach. *Beowulf at Kalamazoo: Essays on Translation and Performance*. Studies in Medieval Culture. Kalamazoo, MI: Medieval Institute Publications, Western Michigan University, 2012. [Schulman, *Kalamazoo*]

Shippey, T. A., and Andreas Haarder. *Beowulf: The Critical Heritage*. The Critical Heritage Series. London: Routledge, 1998.

CRITICAL STUDIES

Studies reprinted in one of the collections listed earlier are cross-referenced, with the exception of those appearing in this volume.

- indicates works included or excerpted in this volume

Acker, Paul. "Horror and the Maternal in *Beowulf*." *PMLA* 121 (2006): 702–16.

Andersson, Theodore M. "Tradition and Design in *Beowulf*." In *Old English Literature in Context: Ten Essays*. Ed. John. D. Niles. Cambridge: Brewer, 1980. 90–106. Repr. in Fulk, *Interpretations*, 219–34.

Anlezark, Daniel. "Old English Epic Poetry: *Beowulf*." In *A Companion to Medieval Poetry*. Ed. Corinne Saunders. Blackwell Companions to Literature and Culture 67, 141–60. Chichester, UK: Wiley-Blackwell, 2010.

Baker, Peter S. *Honour, Exchange and Violence in Beowulf.* Anglo-Saxon Studies 20. Cambridge, UK: Brewer, 2013.

Bartlett, Adeline Courtney. *The Larger Rhetorical Patterns in Anglo-Saxon Poetry.* New York: Columbia U P, 1935.

Bennett, Helen. "The Female Mourner at Beowulf's Funeral: Filling in the Blanks/Hearing the Spaces." *Exemplaria: A Journal of Theory in Medieval and Renaissance Studies* 4 (1992): 35–50. Repr. in Donaldson/Howe.

Benson, Larry D. "The Literary Character of Anglo-Saxon Formulaic Poetry." *PMLA* 81 (1966): 334–41. Repr. in Benson, *Contradictions,* 1–14.

———. "The Pagan Coloring of *Beowulf.*" In *Old English Poetry: Fifteen Essays.* Ed. Robert P. Creed. Providence, RI: Brown University Press, 1967. 193–213. Repr. in Baker, *Basic Readings,* 35–50; Benson, *Contradictions,* 15–31.

———. "The Originality of *Beowulf.*" In *The Interpretation of Narrative: Theory and Practice.* Ed. Morton W. Bloomfield. Cambridge: Harvard University Press, 1970. 1–43. Repr. in Benson, *Contradictions,* 32–70.

Biggs, Frederick M. "Beowulf's Fight with the Nine Nicors." *Review of English Studies,* 53 (2002): 311–28.

Bjork, Robert E. "Speech as Gift in *Beowulf.*" *Speculum* 69 (1994): 993–1022.

Bliss, A. J. "The Appreciation of Old English Metre." In *English and Medieval Studies Presented to J. R. R. Tolkien.* Ed. Norman Davis and C. L. Wrenn. London: Allen & Unwin, 1962. 27–40.

Bonjour, Adrien. *The Digressions in Beowulf.* Oxford: Blackwell, 1950.

Brodeur, Arthur Gilchrist. *The Art of Beowulf.* Berkeley: U of California P, 1959. Ch. 2 repr. in Fulk, *Interpretations,* 66–87.

• Bullough, Donald A. "What Has Ingeld to Do with Lindisfarne?" *Anglo-Saxon England* 22 (1993): 93–125.

Cable, Thomas. *The English Alliterative Tradition.* Middle Ages Series. Philadelphia: U of Pennsylvania P, 1991.

Campbell, Alistair. "The Old English Epic Style." In *English and Medieval Studies Presented to J. R. R. Tolkien.* Ed. Norman Davis and C. L. Wrenn. London: Allen & Unwin, 1962. 13–26.

Campbell, James, gen. ed. *The Anglo-Saxons.* London: Penguin, 1991. [General history.]

Carver, M. O. H. *The Sutton Hoo Story: Encounters with Early England.* Woodbridge, UK: Boydell & Brewer, 2017.

Cavill, Paul, ed. *The Christian Tradition in Anglo-Saxon England: Approaches to Current Scholarship and Teaching,* Christianity and Culture. Woodbridge, UK: Brewer, 2004.

———. "Christianity and Theology in *Beowulf.*" In *The Christian Tradition in Anglo-Saxon England: Approaches to Current Scholarship and Teaching.* Ed. Paul Cavill. Christianity and Culture 1, 15–39. Woodbridge, UK: Brewer, 2004.

Chambers, R. W. *Beowulf; An Introduction to the Study of the Poem with a Discussion of the Stories of Offa and Finn.* 3rd ed. Cambridge: Cambridge U P, 1959.

• Chance, Jane. "The Structural Unity of *Beowulf*: The Problem of Grendel's Mother." *Texas Studies in Literature and Language* 22 (1980): 287–303.

———. *Woman as Hero in Old English Literature.* Syracuse, NY: Syracuse U P, 1986. Ch. 7 repr. in Fulk, *Interpretations,* 251–63.

Christie, E. J. "'An Unfollowable World': *Beowulf,* English Poetry, and the Phenomenalism of Language." *Literature Compass* 10.7 (2013): 519–34.

Clark, George. *Beowulf.* Twayne's English Authors Series 477. Boston: Twayne, 1990.

Clover, Carol J. "The Germanic Context of the Unferth Episode." *Speculum* 55 (1980): 444–68. Repr. in Baker, *Basic Readings,* 127–54.

———. "Regardless of Sex: Men, Women, and Power in Early Northern Europe." *Speculum* 68 (1993): 363–87.

Cramp, Rosemary J. "*Beowulf* and Archaeology." *Medieval Archaeology* 1 (1957): 57–77. Repr. in Fry, *Collection*.

———. "The Hall in *Beowulf* and in Archaeology." Damico/Leyerle, 331–46.

Damico, Helen. *Beowulf's Wealhtheow and the Valkyrie Tradition*. Madison: U of Wisconsin P, 1984.

Davis, Craig R. *Beowulf and the Demise of Germanic Legend in England*. New York: Garland, 1996.

———. "Cultural Assimilation in the Anglo-Saxon Royal Genealogies." *Anglo-Saxon England* 21 (1992): 23–39.

de Looze, Laurence N. "Frame Narratives and Fictionalization: Beowulf as Narrator." *Texas Studies in Literature & Language* 26 (1984): 145–56. Repr. in Fulk, *Interpretations*, 242–50.

Deskis, Susan E. *Beowulf and the Medieval Proverb Tradition*. Tempe: Arizona State U, 1996.

Dockray-Miller, Mary. *Motherhood and Mothering in Anglo-Saxon England*. New York: St. Martin's, 2000.

Donahue, Charles. "*Beowulf* and Christian Tradition: A Reconsideration from a Celtic Stance." *Traditio* 21 (1965): 55–116.

———. "Beowulf, Ireland and the Natural Good." *Traditio* 7 (1949–51): 263–77.

———. "Grendel and the Clanna Cain." *Journal of Celtic Studies* 1 (1950): 167–75.

Donoghue, Daniel. "The Languages of *Beowulf* between Klaeber and Heaney." In Schulman, *Kalamazoo*, 15–30.

• ———. "The Philologer Poet: Seamus Heaney and the Translation of *Beowulf*." *Harvard Review* 19 (2000): 12–21.

———. "Using Heaney's Translation to Teach *Beowulf*." In Chickering, *Teaching Beowulf*, 75–82.

Dumville, David N. "Kingship, Genealogies and Regnal Lists." In *Early Medieval Kingship*. Ed. P. H. Sawyer and I. N. Wood. Leeds, UK: Leeds U P, 1977. 72–104.

Earl, James Whitby. *Thinking about Beowulf*. Stanford, CA: Stanford U P, 1994.

———. "The Forbidden *Beowulf*: Haunted by Incest." *PMLA* 125.2 (2010): 289–305.

Eliason, Norman E. "The Burning of Heorot." *Speculum* 55 (1980): 75–83.

Fell, Christine. *Women in Anglo-Saxon England*. Oxford: Blackwell, 1984.

Finlay, Alison. "Putting a Bawn into *Beowulf*." In *Seamus Heaney: Poet, Critic, Translator*. Ed. Ashby Bland Crowder and Jason David Hall. London: Palgrave Macmillan UK, 2007. 136–54.

Foley, John Miles. *Traditional Oral Epic: The Odyssey, Beowulf, and the Serbo-Croatian Return Song*. Berkeley: U of California P, 1990.

Frank, Roberta. "*Beowulf* and Sutton Hoo: The Odd Couple." In *Voyage to the Other World: The Legacy of Sutton Hoo*. Ed. Calvin B. Kendall and Peter S. Wells. Minneapolis: U of Minnesota P, 1992. 47–64.

• ———. "The *Beowulf* Poet's Sense of History." In *The Wisdom of Poetry: Essays in Early English Literature in Honor of Morton W. Bloomfield*. Ed. Larry Dean Benson and Siegfried Wenzel. Kalamazoo, MI: Medieval Institute, 1982. 53–65.

———. "Skaldic Verse and the Date of *Beowulf*." In *The Dating of Beowulf*. Ed. Colin Chase. Toronto: Centre for Medieval Studies by U of Toronto P, 1997. 123–139. Repr. in Baker, *Basic Readings*: 155–80.

Frantzen, Allen J. *Desire for Origins: New Language, Old English, and Teaching the Tradition*. New Brunswick, NJ: Rutgers U P, 1990.

Fulk, R. D. "The Etymology and Significance of Beowulf's Name." *Anglo-Saxon* 1 (2007): 109–36. http://mypage.iu.edu/~fulk/Name.pdf.

———. *A History of Old English Meter*. Middle Ages Series. Philadelphia: U of Pennsylvania P, 1992.

———. "Unferth and His Name." *Modern Philology* 85 (1987): 113–27.

Gahrn, Lars. "The Geatas of *Beowulf.*" *Scandinavian Journal of History* 11 (1986): 95–113.

Galloway, Andrew. "*Beowulf* and the Varieties of Choice." *PMLA* 105 (1990): 197–208.

Garner, Lori Ann. "Returning to Heorot: *Beowulf*'s Famed Hall and Its Modern Incarnations." *Parergon* 27.2 (2010): 157–81.

Georgianna, Linda. "King Hrethel's Sorrow and the Limits of Heroic Action in *Beowulf.*" *Speculum* 62 (1987): 829–50.

Goldsmith, Margaret E. "The Christian Perspective in *Beowulf.*" *Comparative Literature* 14 (1962): 71–90. Repr. in Fulk, *Interpretations,* 103–119; Nicholson, *Anthology,* 373–86.

Greenfield, Stanley B. "The Authenticating Voice in *Beowulf.*" *Anglo Saxon England* 5 (1976): 51–62. Repr. in Baker, *Basic Readings,* 97–110.

———. "Grendel's Approach to Heorot: Syntax and Poetry." Creed, *Fifteen Essays,* 275–284.

Grimm, Jacob. *Deutsche Mythologie.* 3 vols. 4th ed. Repr. Frankfurt/Main: Keip, 1985. (First ed. 1835).

Gwara, Scott. *Heroic Identity in the World of Beowulf.* Medieval and Renaissance Authors and Texts 2. Leiden: Brill, 2008.

Harris, Joseph. "*Beowulf* in Literary History." *Pacific Coast Philology* 17 (1982): 16–23. Repr. in Fulk, *Interpretations,* 235–42.

———. "*Beowulf*'s Last Words." *Speculum* 67 (1992): 1–32.

———. "A Nativist Approach to *Beowulf*: The Case of Germanic Elegy." *Companion to Old English Poetry.* Ed. Henk Aertsen and Rolf H. Bremmer Jr. Amsterdam: Uitgeverij Vesuvius U P, 1994. 45–62.

Higley, Sarah L. "Thought in *Beowulf* and Our Perception of It: Interiority, Power, and the Problem of the Revealed Mind." In *The Hero Recovered: Essays on Medieval Heroism in Honor of George Clark.* Ed. Robin Waugh and James Weldon. Kalamazoo, MI: Medieval Institute, Western Michigan University, 2010. 23–46.

Hill, John M. *The Cultural World in Beowulf.* Anthropological Horizons 6. Toronto: U of Toronto P, 1995.

———. *The Narrative Pulse of* Beowulf: *Arrivals and Departures.* Toronto Old English Series. Toronto: U of Toronto P, 2008.

Hill, Joyce M. "'Þæt wæs geomuru ides!': A Female Stereotype Examined." Damico/Olsen. 235–47. Repr. in Donaldson/Howe.

Hill, Thomas D. "The Christian Language and Theme of *Beowulf.*" *Companion to Old English Poetry.* Ed. Henk Aertsen and Rolf H. Bremmer Jr. Amsterdam: Uitgeverij Vesuvius U P, 1994. 63–77.

Hills, C. M. "*Beowulf* and Archaeology." In Bjork, *Handbook,* 291–310.

Howe, Nicholas. "The Afterlife of Anglo-Saxon Poetry: Auden, Hill and Gunn." In *Words and Works: Studies in Medieval English Language and Literature in Honour of Fred C. Robinson.* Ed. Nicholas Howe and Peter S. Baker. Toronto: U of Toronto P, 1997.

Irving, Edward B. Jr. *A Reading of Beowulf.* New Haven, CT: Yale U P, 1968. Ch. 1 repr. in Fulk, *Interpretations,* 168–93.

———. *Rereading Beowulf.* Middle Ages Series. Philadelphia: U of Pennsylvania P, 1989.

Jager, Eric. "Speech and the Chest in Old English Poetry: Orality or Pectorality?" *Speculum* 65 (1990): 845–59.

Jones, Chris. *Strange Likeness: The Use of Old English in Twentieth-Century Poetry.* Oxford: Oxford U P, 2006. [See especially ch. 4, "Old English Escape Routes: Seamus Heaney—the Cædmon of The North."]

———. "Where Now the Harp? Listening for the Sounds of Old English Verse, from *Beowulf* to the Twentieth Century." *Oral Tradition* 24.2 (2009): 485–502.

Kaske, Robert E. "*Sapientia et Fortitudo* as the Controlling Theme of *Beowulf.*" *Studies in Philology* 55 (1958): 423–56. Repr. in Nicholson, *Anthology,* 269–310.

Kendall, Calvin B., and Peter S. Wells. *Voyage to the Other World: The Legacy of Sutton Hoo*. Medieval Studies at Minnesota 5. Minneapolis: U of Minnesota P, 1992.
Kennedy, Adrienne. "Grendel and Grendel's Mother." In *The Adrienne Kennedy Reader*. Minneapolis: U of Minnesota P, 2001. 300–05.
Ker, W. P. *Epic and Romance: Essays on Medieval Literature*. London: Macmillan, 1897.
Kiernan, Kevin S. *Beowulf and the Beowulf Manuscript*. New Brunswick, NJ: Rutgers U P, 1981.
Kisor, Yvette. "The Aesthetics of *Beowulf*: Structure, Perception, and Desire." In Hill, *Aesthetics*, 227–46.
Knapp, Peggy A. "*Beowulf* and the Strange Necessity of Beauty." In Hill, *Aesthetics*, 81–100.
• Lapidge, Michael. "*Beowulf* and Perception." *Proceedings of the British Academy* 111 (2001): 61–97.
———. "*Beowulf* and the Psychology of Terror." In Damico/Leyerle, 373–402. Repr. in Donaldson/Howe.
Lee, Alvin A. *The Guest-Hall of Eden: Four Essays on the Design of Old English Poetry*. New Haven, CT: Yale U P, 1972.
Lerer, Seth. "Grendel's Glove." *ELH* 61 (1994): 721–51.
———. *Literacy and Power in Anglo-Saxon Literature*. Lincoln: U of Nebraska P, 1991.
———. "'On Fagne Flor': The Postcolonial *Beowulf*, from Heorot to Heaney." In *Postcolonial Approaches to the European Middle Ages: Translating Cultures*. Ed. Ananya Jahanara Kabir and Deanne Williams. Cambridge Studies in Medieval Literature 54. Cambridge: Cambridge U P, 2005. 77–102.
Leyerle, John. "The Interlace Structure of *Beowulf*." *University of Toronto Quarterly* 37 (1967): 1–17. Repr. in Fulk, *Interpretations*, 146–67.
Lionarons, Joyce Tally. "*Beowulf*: Myth and Monsters." *English Studies* 77 (1996): 1–14.
Liuzza, Roy M. "*Beowulf*: Monuments, Memory, History." *Readings in Medieval Texts: Interpreting Old and Middle English Literature*. Ed. David F. Johnson and Elaine Treharne. Oxford: Oxford U P, 2005. 91–108.
Lord, Albert Bates. "*Beowulf* and Oral Epic Tradition." In *The Singer Resumes the Tale*. Ed. Mary Louise Lord. Ithaca, NY: Cornell U P, 1995. 96–116.
Magennis, Hugh. *Translating Beowulf: Modern Versions in English Verse*. Woodbridge, UK: Brewer, 2011.
Magoun, Francis P. Jr. "The Oral-Formulaic Character of Anglo-Saxon Narrative Poetry." *Speculum* 28 (1953): 446–67. Repr. in Fry, *Collection*; Fulk, *Interpretations*, 45–65; Nicholson, *Anthology*, 189–221.
McCarthy, Conor. *Seamus Heaney and Medieval Poetry*. Woodbridge, UK, and Rochester, NY: Boydell & Brewer, 2008.
McGowan, Joseph. "Heaney, Cædmon, *Beowulf*." *New Hibernia Review / Iris Éireannach Nua: A Quarterly Record of Irish Studies* 6 (2002): 25–42.
Milfull, Inge B., and Hans Sauer. "Seamus Heaney: Ulster, Old English, and *Beowulf*." In *Bookmarks from the Past: Studies in Early English Language and Literature in Honour of Helmut Gneuss*. Ed. Lucia Kornexl and Ursula Lenker. Münchner Universitätsschriften. Texte und Untersuchungen zur Englischen Philologie 30. Frankfurt am Main: Peter Lang, 2003. 81–141.
Mitchell, Bruce. "1987: Postscript on *Beowulf*." In *On Old English: Selected Papers*. Oxford: Blackwell, 1988.
Newton, Sam. *The Origins of Beowulf and the Pre-Viking Kingdom of East Anglia*. Cambridge, UK: Brewer, 1993.
Niles, John D. "Afterword: Visualizing *Beowulf*." In *Beowulf, Translated by Seamus Heaney: An Illustrated Edition*. Ed. John D. Niles. New York: Norton, 2007. 213–48.
———. *Beowulf: The Poem and Its Tradition*. Cambridge: Harvard U P, 1983.

————. "*Beowulf*: Poetry as Social Praxis." *College English* 61 (1998): 143–66. Repr. in Donaldson/Howe.

————. "Heaney's *Beowulf* Six Years Later." In *Old English Heroic Poems and the Social Life of Texts*. Ed. John D. Niles. Studies in the Early Middle Ages 20. Turnhout, Belgium: Brepols, 2007. 325–53.

Niles, John D., Tom Christensen, and Marijane Osborn. *Beowulf and Lejre*. Medieval and Renaissance Texts and Studies 323. Tempe: Arizona Center for Medieval and Renaissance Studies, 2007.

Norris, Robin. "Mourning Rights: *Beowulf*, the *Iliad*, and the War in Iraq." *Journal of Narrative Theory* 37.2 (2007): 276–95.

O'Brien O'Keeffe, Katherine. "Diction, Variation, the Formula." In Bjork, *Handbook*, 85–104.

O'Donoghue, Heather. "Heaney, *Beowulf* and the Medieval Literature of the North." In *The Cambridge Companion to Seamus Heaney*. Ed. Bernard O'Donoghue. Cambridge Companions to Literature. Cambridge: Cambridge U P, 2008. 192–205.

Opland, Jeff. *Anglo-Saxon Oral Poetry: A Study of the Traditions*. New Haven, CT: Yale U P, 1980.

Orchard, Andy. "*Beowulf*." In *The Cambridge Companion to Old English Literature*. Ed. Malcolm Godden and Michael Lapidge. Cambridge Companions to Literature. Cambridge: Cambridge U P, 2013. 137–58.

————. *A Critical Companion to Beowulf*. Woodbridge, UK: Boydell & Brewer, 2003.

————. *Pride and Prodigies: Studies in the Monsters of the* Beowulf *Manuscript*. Cambridge UK: Brewer, 1995.

• Osborn, Marijane. "The Great Feud: Scriptural History and Strife in *Beowulf*." *PMLA* 93 (1978): 973–81. Repr. in Baker, *Basic Readings*, 111–25.

Overing, Gillian R. *Language, Sign, and Gender in* Beowulf. Carbondale: Southern Illinois U P, 1990. Ch. 4 appears rev. in Baker, *Basic Readings*, 219–60.

Owen-Crocker, Gale R. *The Four Funerals in* Beowulf: *And the Structure of the Poem*. Manchester and New York: Manchester U P, 2000.

Pope, John C. "Beowulf's Old Age." In *Philological Essays: Studies in Old and Middle English Language and Literature in Honour of Herbert Dean Meritt*. Ed. James L. Rosier. The Hague: Mouton, 1970. 55–64.

Puhvel, Martin. *Beowulf and Celtic Tradition*. Waterloo, Ont.: Wilfrid Laurier U P, 1979.

Raw, Barbara. "Royal Power and Royal Symbols in *Beowulf*." In *The Age of Sutton Hoo: The Seventh Century in North-Western Europe*. Ed. M. O. H. Carver. Woodbridge, UK: Boydell, 1992. 167–74

Renoir, Alain. "Point of View and Design for Terror in *Beowulf*." *Neuphilologische Mitteilungen* 63 (1962): 91–105. Repr. in Fry, *Collection*.

Ringler, Richard N. "*Him seo wen geleah*: The Design for Irony in Grendel's Last Visit to Heorot." *Speculum* 41 (1966): 49–67.

Robinson, Fred C. *Beowulf and the Appositive Style*. The Hodges Lectures. Knoxville: U of Tennessee P, 1985. Ch. 1 repr. in Donaldson/Howe.

————. "Elements of the Marvellous in the Characterization of *Beowulf*: A Reconsideration of the Textual Evidence." In *Old English Studies in Honour of John C. Pope*. Ed. Robert B. Burlin and Edward B. Irving Jr. Toronto: U of Toronto P, 1974. 119–37. Repr. in Baker, *Basic Readings*; Robinson, *Tomb*.

• ————. "The Tomb of Beowulf." In Robinson, *Tomb*, 3–19

Rogers, H. L. "Beowulf's Three Great Fights." *Review of English Studies* n.s. 6 (1955): 339–55. Repr. in Nicholson, *Anthology*, 233–56.

Saltzmann, Ben. "Secrecy and the Hermeneutic Potential in *Beowulf*." *PMLA* 133.1 (2018): 36–55.

Savage, Anne. "The Grave, the Sword, and the Lament: Mourning for the Future in *Beowulf*." In *Laments for the Lost in Medieval Literature*. Ed. Jane Tolmie, M. J. Toswell, and Derek Pearsall. Medieval Texts and Cultures of Northern Europe 19, 67–80. Turnhout, Belgium: Brepols, 2010.

Sawyer, P. H. *From Roman Britain to Norman England.* 2nd ed. New York: Rout-
ledge, 1998. [General history.]
• Scheil, Andrew. "'Beowulf' and the Emergent Occasion." *Literary Imagination*
11.1 (2008): 83–98.
Scowcroft, R. Mark. "The Irish Analogues to Beowulf." *Speculum* 74 (1999):
22–64.
Shippey, T. A. *Beowulf.* Studies in English Literature 70. London: Edward
Arnold, 1978.
———. "The Case of *Beowulf.*" In *Editing the Nation's Memory: Textual Schol-
arship and Nation-Building in Nineteenth-Century Europe.* Ed. Dirk Van Hulle
and Joep Leerssen. European Studies: An Interdisciplinary Series in Euro-
pean Culture, History, and Politics 26. Amsterdam: Rodopi, 2008. 223–39.
Sisam, Kenneth. "Anglo-Saxon Royal Genealogies." *Proceedings of the British
Academy* 39 (1953): 287–348.
———. *The Structure of Beowulf.* Oxford: Clarendon, 1965.
Stanley, Eric G. "*Beowulf.*" In *Continuations and Beginnings.* London: Thomas
Nelson, 1966. 104–40. Repr. in Baker, *Basic Readings:* 3–34.
• Tolkien, J. R. R. "*Beowulf:* The Monsters and the Critics." *Proceedings of the
British Academy* 22 (1936): 245–95.
———. "Prefatory Remarks on Prose Translations of 'Beowulf'." In J. R. Clark
Hall, *Beowulf and the Finnesburg Fragment.* ix–xliii.
Tolkien, J. R. R., ed. and trans., and Christopher Tolkien, ed. *Beowulf: A Trans-
lation and Commentary Together with Sellic Spell.* Boston: Houghton Mifflin
Harcourt, 2014. [See especially the "Commentary," pp. 137–353, which includes
excerpts from Tolkien's lectures.]
Vendler, Helen H. *Seamus Heaney.* London: HarperCollins, 1998.
• Webster, Leslie. "Archaeology and *Beowulf.*" In Mitchell and Robinson, *Beowulf:
An Edition.* 183–94. [A revised and updated version is included in this NCE.]
Wentersdorf, Karl P. "The *Beowulf*-Poet's Vision of Heorot." *Studies in Philology*
104.4 (2007): 409–26.
Whitelock, Dorothy. *The Audience of Beowulf.* Oxford: Clarendon, 1951.
———. *The Beginnings of English Society.* Rev. ed. Harmondsworth: Penguin,
1974. [General history.]
Wormald, Patrick. "Bede, *Beowulf* and the Conversion of the Anglo-Saxon Aris-
tocracy." In *Bede and Anglo-Saxon England.* Ed. Robert T. Farrell. Oxford:
British Archaeological Reports, 1978. 32–95.
———. *The Making of English Law: King Alfred to the Twelfth Century.* Oxford:
Blackwell, 1999. [Legal history.]

SELECTED WRITINGS OF SEAMUS HEANEY

Preoccupations: Selected Prose, 1968–1978. New York: Farrar Straus & Giroux,
1980.
Poems, 1965–1975. New York: Farrar Straus & Giroux, 1980.
The Government of the Tongue: Selected Prose, 1978–1987. New York: Farrar
Straus & Giroux, 1989.
The Redress of Poetry. New York: Farrar Straus & Giroux, 1995.
Opened Ground: Poems, 1966–1996. New York: Farrar Straus & Giroux, 1998.
Electric Light. New York: Farrar Straus & Giroux, 2001.
Finders Keepers: Selected Prose, 1971–2001. New York: Farrar Straus & Giroux,
2002.
District and Circle. New York: Farrar Straus & Giroux, 2006.
Human Chain. New York: Farrar Straus & Giroux, 2010.